Pat

april
2017

Honored and Dishonored Guests

HARVARD EAST ASIAN MONOGR

Honored and Dishonored Guests

Westerners in Wartime Japan

W. Puck Brecher

Published by the Harvard University Asia Center
Distributed by Harvard University Press
Cambridge (Massachusetts) and London 2017

The Harvard University Asia Center publishes a monograph series and, in coordination with the Fairbank Center for Chinese Studies, the Korea Institute, the Reischauer Institute of Japanese Studies, and other facilities and institutes, administers research projects designed to further scholarly understanding of China, Japan, Vietnam, Korea, and other Asian countries. The Center also sponsors projects addressing multidisciplinary and regional issues in Asia.

Library of Congress Cataloging-in-Publication Data

Names: Brecher, W. Puck, author.
Title: Honored and dishonored guests : Westerners in wartime Japan / W. Puck Brecher.
Other titles: Harvard East Asian monographs ; 399.
Description: Cambridge, Massachusetts : Published by the Harvard University Asia Center, 2017. | Series: Harvard East Asian monographs ; 399 | Includes bibliographical references and index.
Identifiers: LCCN 2016028795 | ISBN 9780674975149 (hardcover : alk. paper)
Subjects: LCSH: Japan—Race relations—Political aspects. | Japan—Race relations—History. | World War, 1939–1945—Japan. | Racism—Japan—History.
Classification: LCC DS832.7.A1 B65 2017 | DDC 940.53/5208909—dc23
LC record available at https://lccn.loc.gov/2016028795

Index by Stephen Ullstrom

♾ Printed on acid-free paper

Last figure below indicates year of this printing
26 25 24 23 22 21 20 19 18 17

For my family

Contents

Tables and Figures

Tables

Figures

Acknowledgments

Members of the Frank family generously provided me with many of the materials that would become the lifeblood of this book. Nicholas Frank was the first to introduce me to his family history. Patrick and Michael Frank then entrusted me with the family's collection of journals, letters, memoirs, interviews, and photos from the war years and earlier. They also put me in touch with their cousin Barbara Weldon, who graciously shared with me her own trove of historical documents. I am indebted to Patrick and Michael for reading and commenting on an early draft of this book. Patrick in particular spent many hours researching and vigorously critiquing some of my assertions; the book has benefited enormously from his input.

Many others with personal ties to wartime Japan were also kind enough to furnish me with their own unpublished or otherwise proprietary materials. I am grateful to Thomas Haar for sharing Syd Duer's unpublished manuscript and for allowing me to use photos taken by his father, Francis, during the war. I would like to thank Dr. Maureen Donovan at The Ohio State University for her assistance in accessing OSU library holdings. I also gratefully acknowledge the Tauber Holocaust Library of the Jewish Family and Children's Services Holocaust Center for allowing me to use its transcript of an interview with Margaret Bendahan, and The Ohio State University Billy Ireland Cartoon Library and Museum for allowing me to use images from its holdings. The U.S. Holocaust Memorial Museum generously provided me with documents from its collections, and Dr. Meron Medzini kindly shared a draft of his forthcoming *Under the Shadow of the Rising Sun: Japan and the Jews during the Holocaust Era* (Brighton, MA: Academic Studies Press). My thanks also to Rod Miller for sending his manuscript *Lost Women of Rabaul* along with his other research on the Japanese invasion of Australian territory. Cecil Uyehara and Ehrhardt I. Lang also shared with me unpublished memoirs of their wartime experiences in Japan. The American Heritage Center at the University of Wyoming, Grant McLachlan, Wes Injerd, and Mimi Malayan all provided me with assistance in locating, procuring, and receiving reproduction permissions for photos. I am grateful for Ishii Kana's assistance in deciphering handwritten documents. I also wish to thank the anonymous readers and Robert Graham at the Harvard University Asia Center for their valuable suggestions. Finally, I wish to thank Midge, Thistle, Kayo, Zoe, and Rio for their love and support.

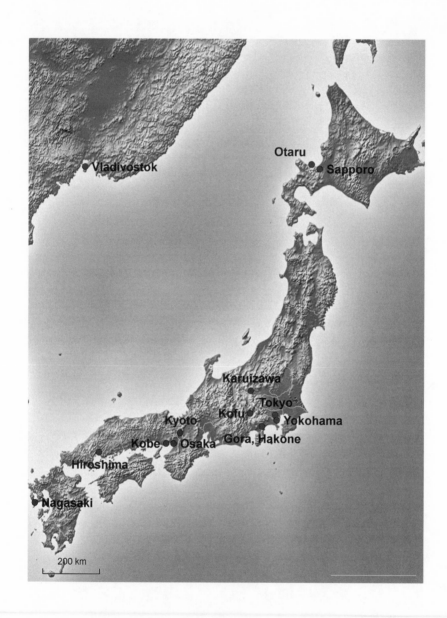

200 km

INTRODUCTION

[handwritten annotations: JANUARY 1945 Yokohama · visited by mother · Ludy]

Hugo Frank's prison was enclosed by a gray twenty-five-foot wall. The visitation, his brother Ludy wrote later, took place in a cell divided by a glass panel, with an opening on one end from which a guard could listen to both sides. Tables and chairs were pushed against either side of the glass. Ludy entered and sat.

> On the other side of the glass stood the figure of a tall, bent man, his face covered by a cone-shaped straw hood. The guard commanded the prisoner to take off his hood. With a deep, cringing obeisance to the guard, the prisoner uncovered his face—it was my brother. Hair cropped, shoulders bent, cheeks sunken in, in his eyes a look of wild fright, the large eyes of an emaciated, hunted animal. He asked the guard whether he might speak to me, who nodded permission.
> The conversation had to be in Japanese. "Ludy, thank you so much for coming all this way to see me; it is terribly nice of you. I am perfectly alright. Nothing is wrong with my body, it is in perfect condition, give me medicine, any kind of medicine, I am hungry, send food in please, I am so hungry, my body is perfectly alright, send me medicine!" While he was talking to me he bowed and pleaded, cast furtive glances at the warden listening in. I couldn't talk at first. I felt as if my chest would burst.[1]

So reads Ludy (Ludwig) Frank's account of that visitation with his older brother in January 1945, written in a memoir a year later. Ludy had not been permitted to ask about the charges against Hugo nor about Hugo's treatment at the prison. No need to; his brother's desperation was plain enough. The signs of torture were obvious, and the charge would be espionage, as it was for the other anti-Nazi Germans being held.

This was Ludy's first visit to Gumyōji Prison in Yokohama. His next would be on February 14, 1945, the day before Hugo's sentencing. On that occasion Hugo was equally distraught. "I had the audacity of asking him whether all the charges brought against him were true," Ludy wrote. "The guard interfered loudly, threatening to throw me out if I asked such a question again. Nevertheless, I asked it again, upon which my brother answers, 'No—yes, yes, yes, it is all true, every word of it!' This cost me the interview, my last one with my brother, and a fine of 200 yen for breaking prison regulations. The next day I saw him receiving his sentence in the courthouse."[2] The sentence was five years for violation of the National Defense Security Law (*Kokubō hoan-hō*). This was the last time Ludy would see his brother alive.

The Frank brothers were among the thousands of Western civilians stranded in Japan during the Asia-Pacific War. Hugo was one of over one hundred arrested for suspicion of espionage, and Ludy was among the roughly one thousand forced to evacuate coastal cities for safety in the mountains.[3] Japanese authorities interned about one thousand others as enemy aliens.[4] The existence of these expats remains largely unknown, their stories neglected by the shelves of books on ideological and military aspects of the war. The oversight is understandable, for as a mixture of nationalities and ethnicities this diffuse cohort of business professionals, missionaries, teachers, diplomats, and miscellaneous others shared no common association or legacy other than residency in wartime Japan. As such, there has been little political incentive to recover them. Their diversity of containment experiences also defies easy summation. From the Japanese perspective, Germans and Italians were allies; Swiss and French were neutral; Americans, British, and Dutch were enemy nationals; Jewish refugees, White Russians, and other stateless individuals held a separate status; and diplomats and missionaries called for yet different treatment. Moreover, as Christina Twomey suggests, some Western researchers have been disinclined to acknowledge this diverse assemblage because its mere existence stirs vestiges of Western guilt over atrocities committed in the name of colonial ambition in Asia.[5] Consequently, these individuals remain collectively unclaimed by postwar researchers, and their omission from history has impoverished our knowledge of how Japanese authorities and citizens contended with "the other within."

A dearth of historical materials also explains the virtual nonexistence of Anglophone scholarship on foreign civilians in wartime Japan. Records on domestic POW camps, evacuation communities, court hearings, and police surveillance were destroyed either in the air raids or by Japanese authorities following the surrender. An inert civil society and the virtual elimination of independent publishing, broadcasting, and photography have also left few documentary traces of this demographic. The unfortunate paucity of firsthand accounts is further explained by a pervasive reluctance to relive wartime hardships through writing. Many Japanese, Miyabara Yasuharu asserts, desired to forget those years of suffering.[6] Consequently, much remains unknown. "People's histories" like Yoshimi Yoshiaki's *Grassroots Fascism: The War Experience of the Japanese People*, Samuel Hideo Yamashita's *Leaves from an Autumn of Emergencies: Selections from the Wartime Diaries of Ordinary Japanese*, and Thomas R. H. Havens's *Valley of Darkness: The Japanese People and World War Two* offer great interest and historical value by recovering wartime experience through the voices of civilian Japanese, but omit the voices of foreign residents trapped in the country during those years, as well as Japanese testimonies about them.

For these reasons, the Western experience of wartime Japan currently enjoys no coherent narrative. Published accounts authored by interned individuals are rare; firsthand accounts of incarceration and torture are rarer. The Western experience survives mainly within private letters, journals, and testimonies given to Occupation forces. It is also transmitted through a disparate assortment of thinly contextualized memoirs, most self-published and written decades later, that recount their authors' daily struggles with privation, air raids, and police harassment. Not only do these memoirs, many vivid and rich in detail, collectively resurrect daily life in wartime Japan, they illuminate "on the street" wartime race relations.

Interpretations of "Race Hate" in a "Race War"

Within this diverse body of testimonies, race consciousness (as distinguished from racial hatred) emerges as a salient feature of human relations during Japan's imperial era (1895–1945). For resident foreigners, certainly, race was the singular defining feature of life in Japan. Memoirs written during and immediately following the war best preserve the racial hostility typical of that era, though later works also reveal lingering prejudices. For some of these memoirists, life in wartime Japan was a simple script of heroes, traitors, and brutes. James Thomas, a civilian POW, characterizes Japan and its people as "a strange and ruthless enemy" and its view of the conflict as a "holy war to smite the lowly Caucasian infidels."[7] One cannot fault Thomas for finding his guards strange and ruthless, and he is correct that his captors likely found racial antipathy useful, as Thomas himself does, for explaining their nation's military overtures. His view of "the Japanese" as crazed fanatics "with no respect for human life and an eagerness to die in *Banzai* charges for their Emperor" reflects the sort of visceral racial bitterness typical of these biographies.[8] George Lavrov asserts that, "all gaijins [*sic*] . . . were generally viewed as enemy spies and collaborators. . . . Toward the end of the war, life in Japan deteriorated so much that people were literally starving, especially the gaijins."[9] He also describes the conditions endured by Japan's foreign residents as more torturous than those faced by Japanese Americans confined to internment camps in the United States. These statements may pertain to Lavrov's own family but are reductive and generally inaccurate. They encapsulate wartime life as an "us" versus "them" racial confrontation that assumes all Japanese shared a single mind and all resident foreigners suffered a singular wartime experience. And, whereas Japanese brutality was real, many authors attribute it to a racial predisposition rather than considering its historical context or its possible strategic and practical functions.

Nonetheless, the centrality of race in these narratives does accurately reflect a distinctly emotional dimension of the war for all involved. For the past three decades, John Dower's pioneering and voluminous scholarship has grounded research on race relations in the Pacific. This book will repeatedly engage with and cite from Dower, for there is much to learn from his writings. It also reworks some of Dower's findings, but takes particular issue with how others have interpreted him. Of particular concern is the legacy of Dower's scholarship on the mutual racial hatred permeating the Pacific War, his characterization of the conflict as a "race war" permeated by "race hate."[10] In the United States, Dower writes, war against Japan "stirred the deepest recesses of white supremacism and provoked a response bordering on the apocalyptic. . . . This was true of both sides. The Japanese were racist too—toward the white enemy and in conspicuously different ways toward the other Asians who fell within their 'Co-Prosperity Sphere.' "[11] Given that these assertions echo rhetoric issued by Japan's wartime authorities, one can assume that the terms "Japan" and "the Japanese" refer to governmental and military elites, policy makers and journalists, academics and social theorists, and scientists and ideologues—those who tell the rest what to think and believe. They are not meant to include the Japanese public. What the public actually thought and believed has been omitted from the conversation, and largely omitted from consideration altogether. State propaganda and militarist ideologues spoke for the Japanese people during the war, and, in its omission of public opinion, postwar academic discourse has allowed them to continue doing so. Postwar Japanese themselves have also been content with the facile assumption that racial propaganda issued by a military autocracy accurately represented their own wartime relationships with local foreigners. This most certainly was not Dower's intention, for he went on to publish a cogent study of wartime resistance, demonstrating that many Japanese were not duped by state ideology, racial or otherwise.[12]

Nonetheless, assumptions of fierce racial enmity have come to orient our understanding of both military and civilian wartime experience, and Dower's work continues to inform an expanding body of scholarship that adds needed complexity to the notion of Japan and Anglo-America as symmetrical racialized regimes. Douglas Ford, for example, has argued that both sides instilled their militaries with hatred, fear, and paranoia about their enemy's own racial objectives. Each side, the argument continues, understood the enemy to be carrying out a racial crusade in order to upset and even invert the world's standing racial order. For each, the threat of being vanquished racially was even more personally and emotionally intolerable than that of being defeated militarily. Yet, Ford continues, racial hatred did not engender an enduring incentive to fight.

On the Japanese side, indoctrination was only partially successful in instilling Japanese troops with a "fighting spirit" that would endure throughout the conflict. In fact, enthusiasm faded. Many Japanese soldiers were
reluctant to sacrifice themselves for the state and served in the military
only out of legal obligation. Enthusiasm further waned as troops confronted hunger, disease, and the hardships of battle in foreign environ-
ments. And, from 1943, when the war's momentum turned in favor of the
Allies, more Japanese troops became less willing to submit to meaningless self-sacrifice. Focusing on how military officials conducted military
planning of the war, Ford also concludes that U.S. strategy was shaped
less by racial hatred than by a good, rational understanding of the enemy
and its vulnerabilities.[13]

Gerald Horne has also described the prewar colonial world as a neu-
rotic international pecking order that organized peoples as whites, yellows, and browns. Japan, he asserts, did not oppose the notion of ethnic
taxonomies, which fit so neatly within the hierarchical nature of its own
society. It opposed only its own relegation to a middling rank within that
taxonomy. In a clear expression of pushback against the racial arrogance
endemic to Western imperialism, Horne continues, Japan's POW camps
attempted to invert the standing racial order by formulating a system of
POW treatments based on ethnic characteristics. It treated individuals
bearing Caucasian features more harshly—generally interning them—
than natives of conquered territories or those bearing Asian features.[14] This
agenda also explains the numerous stories of reverse discrimination toward
African Americans in prewar Japan, and of Japanese prison camps giving black POWs preferential treatment over whites.[15]

Other researchers have issued qualified challenges to characterizations
of the war's combatants as parallel racialized regimes fueled by roughly
congruent forms of racial hostility. Takashi Fujitani and Yukiko Koshiro
have taken important steps in this direction. Fujitani takes issue with
Dower for not fully rejecting essentialistic perceptions of the "national
character" of "the Japanese," including the totalizing cultural traits associated with them. He also rejects the dominant presumption that Japanese racist propaganda remained essentially unchanged throughout the
war, namely that it continued to adhere to earlier narratives about racial
purity and divinity. Later in the war, Fujitani shows, Japanese authorities
retreated from such positions, recognizing them to be injurious to race

relations throughout the empire. Doing so became particularly necessary as the state conscripted large numbers of Koreans and Taiwanese into military service and deployed them alongside Japanese soldiers in integrated units.[16]

Like Dower, Fujitani finds parallels in the ways that Japan and the United States functioned as war regimes. Their treatment and mobilization of colonial soldiers ("soldiers of color") illuminate congruencies in how both nations exploited race. But he also argues for a shift in wartime racism away from exclusionary or "vulgar" racism and toward a more inclusive or "polite" racism.[17] Nazi rhetoric had sensitized the international community to racist ideology, making it wary of colonialist policies that could be equated with Nazism. Japan touted its own benevolence and sought to honor the principles of freedom and racial equality by co-opting Koreans and Taiwanese as Japanese nationals and publicizing the alleged autonomy of its colonies.[18] In the United States, as early as 1942 the Joint Psychological Warfare Committee cautioned against allowing the conflict to become a Pan-Asian (racial) war and recommended defusing the racial prejudice so pervasive in the United States. While this advice did not erase the racist content of public propaganda, political authorities in both America and Britain grew more careful to avoid racial references in their public rhetoric.[19] Such measures allowed both regimes to assume a moral high ground vis-à-vis the Nazi regime, which dealt with its racial outsiders with extermination rather than inclusion. Fujitani thus finds that denunciations of racism by the United States and Japan during the war resulted in an "uneasy compatibility of racism and its disavowal" in both regimes.[20] "As powerful as the discourse on the pure Yamato race may have been in the minds of many within the elite (and outside it)," he writes, "the exigencies of war made it increasingly necessary to disavow racist discrimination and to demonstrate the sincerity of this denunciation through concrete policies."[21]

Koshiro provides two more crucial corrections to our understanding of Japanese colonialism and wartime racial attitudes. First, since initiating imperialist overtures on the mainland during the Meiji period, Japan had viewed Russia as a competitor for territory and resources. Recognizing the advantages of mitigating those tensions, ideologues determined to identify Russians as Asian, not "white" (Western), and to include rather than exclude Russia from Japan's Pan-Asian vision.[22] This accord was played up in the media as evidence that Japanese Pan-Asianism was morally superior to Nazi and American racism. The cooperation, and in some cases collaboration, between Russian residents and Japanese authorities lent credibility, complexity, and depth to Japan's colonial designs. This would be especially visible in Manchukuo, where ideologues openly welcomed a spectrum of Russian émigrés with hopes that the coexistence of multiple Asian ethnicities would be enriched by residents without typically Asian features.[23]

Second, Koshiro continues, it is simplistic and thus inaccurate to call the Pacific War a race war between whites and yellows. Japan did not unilaterally identify Western nations as simply white, nor did it view citizens of those nations equally. Japanese harbored particular ire toward British and Americans, not toward Caucasians per se, and retaliated against what they perceived as a concerted Anglo-American cultural and racial attack on Japan. In spite of its various campaigns to erase American cultural and linguistic imports from public view, Japan did not abhor all forms of Western culture.[24] Throughout the war era, the state continued to embrace select Western cultural forms that did not directly invoke the United States and Britain.

Fujitani and Koshiro have begun to dismantle the parallel racial regimes thesis by adding critical qualifications to views of the war's combatants as xenophobic nations whose racisms remained static and uniform throughout the conflict. Testimonies from resident Westerners add a neglected dimension to this discourse, their varied accounts of wartime living conditions calling for further reconsideration of the conflict as a race war driven by race hate. Did civilian Japanese subscribe to exhortations about racial purity and spiritual supremacy as evidence of their own racial preeminence? Did they extend their reverence for Japan's emperor to credence in their own moral superiority? Even if so, did they manifest such beliefs in their interactions with Westerners in the form of overt racial hostility? A preponderance of evidence indicates that whereas propaganda was variously effective in inciting nationalism and instilling fear, particularly among the young, in many cases it contradicted the life experiences of Japanese adults and was thus unsuccessful in infusing them with a hatred of Caucasians. It suggests, rather, that a clear ideological divide separated most civilians from their military and political leaders, whose rhetoric neither represented nor reflected the interests of the citi-

zenry at large. For much of the adult population, interactions with resident foreigners were guided by more practical concerns. And while it is true that neither Japan's populace nor its intelligentsia mustered any meaningful resistance to the war, a fact that some interpret as evidence of near-universal support for the state's wartime racial narratives, neither could they accept the war. Evidence demonstrates, rather, that race hate was generally limited to military and government elites (and perhaps not even to those) and reveals minimal racial abuse consistent with Beverly Daniel Tatum's definition of racism as "a personal ideology based on racial prejudice."[25] Though isolated acts of race hate occurred, they appear atypical of general racial attitudes toward Westerners.

In June 1942, 7,448 non-Asian foreigners were residing in Japan, including 2,838 (38.1 percent) myriad neutral and enemy nationals, 2,728 (36.6 percent) Axis nationals (Germans and Italians), and 1,882 (25.3 percent) stateless.[26] This contingent was numerically overshadowed by and shared little experiential common ground with other foreign demographics. The 17,277 Chinese residents, for example, were surveilled but otherwise left undisturbed. (As Japan's ongoing war against the Chinese Nationalists was undeclared and thus unofficial, resident Chinese, who were not judged to pose any destabilizing influence in any case, could not be labeled as enemy nationals. As British resident Syd Duer described the status of Chinese, "Apparently, no war, no spies, no internment!"[27])

Westerners also received treatment that was fundamentally different from that received by the twenty thousand second-generation Japanese Americans (Nisei) living in Japan, most of whom had been sent to Japan to study. The Japanese government, which subscribed to the jus sanguinis principle of Japanese citizenship as a natural extension of Japanese descent, revoked Nisei's U.S. citizenship but otherwise took no formal putative action against them.[28] Officially recognized as Japanese citizens, some male Nisei were conscripted into the Imperial Army and forced to fight for Japan. At the same time, Nisei continued to be incriminated as former Americans. Many were watched and harassed by police. At work, at school, and within their local communities, they suffered ostracism and discrimination. Nor were they eligible for repatriation via exchange ship, for while the United States acknowledged their U.S. citizenship, it viewed

that citizenship as somehow marginal or unequal. Only whites were repatriated during the war.[29]

The several thousand enemy nationals—mostly diplomats; business
professionals who had dismissed their governments' advisories to repatriate; and journalists, teachers, and missionaries who had been reluctant
to abandon their professional responsibilities—were interned or repatriated at various intervals during the war, but their collective containment under the Interior Ministry's civilian jurisdiction cannot be considered analogous to that of their 130,000 counterparts interned under
military jurisdiction throughout Japan's colonial territories in China
and Southeast Asia. These two demographics were subjected to disparate handling policies that resulted in dramatically different treatments
and mortality rates.[30] Though a numerical minority, therefore, Japan's
Western residents experienced the war altogether differently than other
foreign populations trapped under Japanese control. Their myriad nationalities and official standings also belie any possibility of collectiv-
izing their experience.

Officially, nationality was indeed the criterion used to define and
categorize foreign civilians as allied, neutral, stateless, or enemy nationals. This cohort's breadth of wartime experiences supersedes the narrow
parameters of nationality, however. To the extent that Japanese rhetoric
failed to distinguish between "the West" and whiteness, its apprehension
of the war as a struggle against Western hegemony encouraged perceptions of the conflict as fundamentally racial in nature. Not only did
characterizations of whiteness as a threat to the national polity fail to acknowledge Japan's European allies, *unofficially* (for the general public) it
rendered skin color more incriminating than nationality, which for many
Japanese was not readily discernible in any case. Focus on race thus illuminates the extent to which racial invectives came to inform unofficial
attitudes. Westerners were rarely uncritically adored, but neither was the
racial capital they had accrued since the 1850s easily erased or reversed.
For a general public that understood and cared little for distinctions between Western nationalities, race was the singular marker of otherness,
the singular determinant of how an individual was to be grouped. As an
interpretive lens, therefore, skin color was a greater factor than nationality in determining the tenor of "on the street" interactions between Japanese and foreign civilians.

For these reasons, our attention falls on Western, predominantly Caucasian, experience. In this context the term "Caucasian" is deployed to align with how the term *hakujin* was used in wartime Japan: as a catchall reference to "Caucasoid" North Americans, Europeans, and the various foreign nationals who appeared "whiter" than Japanese themselves.[31] *Hakujin* was an imprecise amalgamation of nationality and race in the sense that it considered being fair skinned and carrying the right passport to be sufficient evidence of "whiteness." An individual's actual racial background was beside the point. In other words, my use of "Caucasian" includes not just Germans, Japan's principal allies, and Caucasoid Anglo-Americans, its principal antagonists, but also, from Jews to Greeks to Russians, fairer-skinned foreigners generally. Accounts of treatment extended to African Americans visiting Japan are scarce and conflicting, and the scarcity of dark-skinned nationals of "white nations" in Japan at this time precluded the term *hakujin* from any sense of inadequacy.[32]

From the perspective of Japanese authorities, coexistence with resident Asians, whether resident Chinese or colonial subjects like Koreans and Taiwanese, represented an altogether different set of challenges and called for different strategic measures than did coexistence with Westerners. Not only did imperial Japan's professed agenda of returning Asia to Asians require this double standard, Asian immigrants were too numerous to evacuate and their labor too precious to lose.[33] The altogether separate standing of Westerners and Asians thus precludes any easy expansion of our project to include both groups or any possibility of discussing a singular, integrated "foreign experience" in wartime Japan.[34]

Beyond nationality and race, in some contexts gender also factored into Japan's handling of resident Westerners. The Interior Ministry's initial containment protocols for enemy nationals called for the immediate internment of adult men but not women, though subsequent amendments to those directives culminated in the eventual arrests of most American and British women. Some accounts suggest that Japanese police also considered women less threatening. Van Waterford claims that some camp guards were unsure how to treat female inmates and treated them more leniently as a result.[35] And, when Iva Toguri (1916–2006, aka Tokyo Rose), a Japanese American, asked to be interned with the other American citizens, police denied her request in part because she was a woman.[36] We also find evidence to the contrary. Some Japanese police and camp guards took offense at the uninhibited speech and behavior of Western women, and the torture inflicted on espionage suspect Margaret Liebeskind (1908–2009) was more perverse than that exacted on male suspects being interrogated for similar crimes. Gender bias may also have factored into the treatment of eighteen Australian nurses captured in Rabaul, Papua New Guinea, and transferred to an internment camp in Kanagawa. Mysteriously, after December 1942 the prisoners were denied visitations from the International Red Cross and their existence was not acknowledged by Japanese authorities until June 1945.

This study will not engage with long-standing historiographical discussions over the nature of Japanese "fascism." It will not deliberate on whether Japan's militarist turn in the 1930s is best understood as the predestined result of feudal structures undermining the state's efforts to modernize, or as a deviation from the nation's otherwise glorious process of modernization. Nor will it provide a comprehensive discussion of Japan's military activities, wartime politics, or imperial state (*tennōsei*) ideology. All such matters are well studied. Rather, it seeks to overturn facile myths about "the Japanese" by illuminating sharp contrasts between civilian and military experience. The project uses the living conditions and experiences of resident Westerners to reconsider the Pacific War as a race war and Japan as a nation permeated by race hate. Through this lens its seeks evidence of racial profiling and compares official containment policies with the range of handling practices actually administered by Japanese authorities and attitudes exhibited by the general public. This perspective will enable us to determine the existence of systemic racism (racist structures) in Japanese society, and the extent to which wartime authorities observed or violated international law in their handling of civilian internees. We will be taking special note of instances of race hate and race ambivalence, data that will help illuminate congruencies in racial attitudes between authorities and the public, and the extent to which racist ideology was put into practice.

The book's two overarching objectives, therefore, are to recover and chronicle the diversity of Western experiences in wartime Japan, and to use that body of experiences to reconsider race relations. Though internment of enemy nationals will be the subject of chapters 7 and 8, this study's investigation of Western civilians focuses on that cohort's breadth of wartime activities rather than the internment experience exclusively. Moreover, its focus on civilians neither denies nor apologizes for Japan's wartime brutalization of POWs, Chinese and Korean soldiers and laborers, comfort women (*ianfu*), and countless indigenous civilians throughout the Asia-Pacific region. Rather, its focus on racial ambivalence among the Japanese public helps to contextualize and affirm the brutality and racial arrogance endemic to Japan's military.

The study's centerpiece will be the Frank and Balk families, German "Jews" who immigrated to Japan seeking opportunity and adventure. (Louis Frank [1886–1973] was Jewish but his wife, Amy [1884–1979], was Anglican; Estelle Balk [ca. 1898–1966] was Jewish but her husband, Arvid [1889–1955], was not.) Aside from their nationalities and mixed Jewishness, the two families shared little. The Franks were long-term residents of Japan, whereas the Balks arrived in 1934. Louis Frank was a celebrated educator and considered a national asset, whereas Arvid Balk was a freelance journalist, a profession that, though respected, incurred state suspicion; and during the war, most of the Franks evacuated to Karuizawa while the Balks evacuated to Gora, Hakone. Their children met and married, and under various wartime circumstances endured police harassment, suspicion, relocation, starvation, denaturalization, internment, and torture, as well as extraordinary acts of charity. Although this extended family's disparate backgrounds are indicative of the multiplicity characterizing the greater Western community, its wartime experiences are noteworthy in two important respects. As mixed German Jews, their ethnic pedigree invites examination of Japan's political and racial engagement with Nazi anti-Semitism, that is, how Japan as an Axis power handled resident nonparty Germans and Jews. Second, the arrests of Hugo Frank and Arvid Balk in the summer of 1944 on suspicion of espionage afford rare insight into how Japanese authorities treated and prosecuted foreign suspects. The Franks and Balks will also serve to contextualize a broader mosaic of stories from dozens of other families and individuals stranded in Japan. This montage of experiences covers prewar life and wartime containment; extends from Tokyo, Yokohama, and Kobe to the mountain resorts of Karuizawa and Hakone; and invites extended discussion of the four general types of detention faced by Western civilians: temporary internment or house arrest prior to repatriation; evacuation; long-term internment; and arrest for suspicion of war-related crimes like espionage.

The first chapter discusses the reciprocal and bifurcated nature of Japanese race consciousness and how it shaped relations with resident Westerners throughout the imperial era. It then contextualizes our topic by reviewing how this "race war" has been analyzed by recent scholarship. Chapter 2 examines the formation of Western communities in Japan with particular focus on the insularity that was, by mutual agreement, sustained throughout the prewar period. It interprets this mutual insularity as a defensive reaction against perceived threats to national identity. The next chapter analyzes spiritual mobilization, policy making, and other strategies for containing Westerners. It uses the mixture of intolerance and leniency extended to Kobe's Jewish community and Japan's crackdown on Christianity as case studies to illustrate the situationism informing Japanese policy making. Chapter 4 begins a three-chapter discussion of the lives of nonenemy civilians during the war by investigating the destabilizing effects of the Pearl Harbor attack on the solidarity of Western communities. This is followed, in chapter 5, with discussion of the daily lives of Westerners in Tokyo, Yokohama, and Kobe following Pearl Harbor. In particular, it investigates the enemy diplomats and journalists who were apprehended and held until their repatriation via exchange ship. Chapter 6 details the evacuation order issued to urban areas in 1943 and the subsequent exodus of noninterned Westerners to several mountain resorts. Chapters 7 and 8 discuss wartime Japan's treatment of enemy civilians. The former focuses on civilian internment camps, particularly those in the Kanto region, and considers whether Japanese authorities made adequate attempts to observe international law in their treatment of civilian prisoners. The latter highlights the misfortunes of Hugo Frank and Arvid Balk, both of whom were arrested for suspicion of espionage in July 1944 and then tortured, tried, and imprisoned for the remainder of the war. The final chapter returns to the question of race, finding stark contrasts in racial attitudes between elites and the Japanese public at large.

Widespread ambivalence toward whites, along with the extreme rarity of one-on-one "on the street" racism against them, indicates that Japanese authorities failed to imbue many Japanese with anti-Caucasian sentiment. It suggests, rather, that the diversity of resident Westerners necessitated a diversity of official containment strategies and elicited an equally diffuse range of reactions from the Japanese public. The book posits that few Japanese ever internalized racial hatred for Westerners or placed much stock in racialized characterizations of the conflict; that public attitudes hinged more on practical concerns than ideological platitudes; and that amid the dehumanizing hardships of war, race consciousness was replaced by a survival consciousness that ultimately brought people together. As such, the book's excavation of Western experiences inside wartime Japan advances a complexity that corrects essentializing assertions about Japanese race consciousness.

PART I

Caucasians and Race in Imperial Japan

Part I Introduction

Narratives about racial hatred in the Pacific War are predicated on the assumption that propaganda issued by the various combatants was effective in fostering roughly analogous forms of racial hostility. Given the inseparability of war and hatred generally, fighting between disparate ethnicities can be predicted to foment racial prejudices. In the context of the Pacific War, therefore, one would be surprised if widespread racial enmity did *not* crystalize between Japan and the Allied powers, as well as between their respective citizenries.

Such narratives also support positions that underscore the ruptures wrought by war—in this case the presumption that existing (prewar) race relations at the grassroots level collapsed under mounting ethnocentrism and xenophobia. Challenging the theory that resident Westerners suffered worsening treatment and a marked decline in socioeconomic prestige during the war—that changes in race relations outweighed continuities—calls for extended discussion of how resident Westerners lived and interacted with Japanese during the prewar years. The three chapters that follow provide this context along with analysis of the various changing landscapes occupied by Westerners during Japan's imperial era. They explore prewar Japan's epistemological backdrop, including Japanese race consciousness (as distinguished from racism per se) and its concomitant inconsistencies. They also consider the generally amicable but exclusionary race relations that formed in the mid-nineteenth century and that were preserved by mutual agreement and to mutual benefit throughout the prewar era. In the 1930s, Japan's defiant withdrawal from the League of Nations and incursions into the Asian mainland punctuated a tightening ideological landscape that would create increasingly austere domestic conditions, including legislation aimed at containing Westerners and their activities. Part I engages with these developments through a broad set of case studies—individuals, families, organizations, and communities—with a view toward contextualizing and then assessing the continuities and changes that wartime experience brought to domestic race relations.

CHAPTER I

Racism, Race Consciousness, and Imperial Japan

Prussian engineer Julius Helm (1840–1922) first arrived in Yokohama in 1869.[1] After serving as a military adviser in Wakayama he married Komiya Hiro, entering into one of Japan's first Western-Japanese unions, which by law required government approval.[2] For his children and each subsequent generation of Helms, the family's mixed blood would prove a source of anxiety. Finding spouses posed particular difficulties. Julius's two daughters never married, though they were courted by half-Japanese suitors. Julius saw it as natural for his son Jules (1887–1956), whose darker features afforded him fewer options, to marry a half Japanese, half German like Jules himself. Julius's other sons, Jim, Karl, and Willie, fared somewhat more to his liking. Jim, who bore more Caucasian features than his siblings, was able to marry a Caucasian woman of high birth; Karl's wife, a Caucasian first cousin, and Willie's wife, a Caucasian widow with children, were deemed rather less satisfactory. The next generation was equally beset by racial self-consciousness. When one of Jim's daughters, the darkest of his children, married a Portuguese man, Jim did not attend the wedding, and he reduced her inheritance. And, because self-respecting Japanese did not see part Japanese as suitable partners either, Karl's quarter-Japanese daughter could do no better than marry a half-Japanese man.[3]

The Helms "believed they were better than the Japanese," reflects Leslie Helm, "yet, of mixed blood and unable to read or write Japanese, they often felt insecure in the country of their birth."[4] Though they did not deny their racial pedigree, neither did they voluntarily disclose or discuss it. Some looked fully Caucasian; others bore Japanese or Latin American features. Besides enjoying superior marital prospects, those with lighter coloring were held in higher regard within Yokohama's and Kobe's foreign communities, as well as within their own families. Though the Helm siblings became prominent members within their respective foreign circles, they were refused full membership because of their mixed blood.[5] Jim, the taller and lighter brother who ran the Helm Brothers branch in Kobe and had worked in Russia and the United States, was active and popular within the Kobe community, but his pedigree denied him full racial equality:

> He [Jim] and his charming wife moved in high circles. Jim raced in regattas, joined a water polo team, and contributed large sums of Helm Brothers' money to various charitable causes. His wife, Elizabeth, a brunette with a commanding presence and a beautiful voice, served two terms as president of the Kobe Women's Club and often sang at special occasions. Still, it was hard to escape the issue of race. Jim would never forget overhearing his friends talk about him in the locker room at his sports club. "Jim's a good sort," one man said. "Yes," said the other. "He knows his place."[6]

Discrimination based on skin color and mixed blood thus informed a racial pecking order within the Western communities, as it did in the Western world. Were these patterns of racial consciousness reciprocated by the Japanese? Colonial racism, Frantz Fanon has argued, entails the creation and then internalization of superiority and inferiority complexes based on criteria like technological advancement, military supremacy, and economic strength. Validation by their oppressors causes victims of racism to accept those oppressors' views of the world and thereby acquire a psychological dependency on them. This psychological enslavement is then reaffirmed through economic and other forms of dependence, Fanon continues, a relationship that relieves the threat of economic competition that necessitated racism in the first place.[7] Japan had developed a keen sensitivity to the racial prejudices connected with its inequitable standing in the global order. Did it also internalize racial superiority and inferiority complexes and become psychologically dependent on Westerners as Fanon's theory suggests? Western residents like the Helms projected their preference for Caucasian features onto those around them. How did Japanese respond to such preferences, and did they adhere to Western racial taxonomies or develop their own?

With a view toward discussing these and related issues of race confronted by resident Westerners, this chapter discusses Japanese race consciousness during the nation's imperial era. It forgoes a full discussion of the multiple dynamics guiding imperial Japan's formulation of a racial identity, a process already well studied by others.[8] Rather, it highlights certain prominent factors that informed Japan's discourse about its racial position vis-à-vis Western and Asian nations. We begin by recounting how a succession of racial insults by "white" imperial nations helped Japan learn racial diplomacy and formulate racial justifications for its own colonial overtures in Asia. The emergence of imperial Japan as a racial antagonist to Western imperialism has led some to argue that it and its citizenry saw the Pacific War as a fundamentally racial conflict. This book's intention to challenge such perceptions calls for discussion of the salient features of race consciousness during this era. In this context I shall discuss Japan's cultural affinities for distinction making, positionality, and pragmatism, as well as how racial propaganda, racial science, and "proper place" contextualized relations between Western expats and their Japanese hosts. I will then proceed to examine the cognitive dissonance generated by several ruptures in Japan's official deployment of racial rhetoric. Finally, I consider recent challenges to characterizations of the Pacific War as a "race war" permeated by "race hate."

A Normative Racism

Throughout the prewar era, Japanese citizens received an array of mixed messages about race that variously aligned or conflicted with what they knew to be true from personal experience. They, along with their parents and grandparents, had lived in a state that had continually extolled the virtues of Western learning and articulated national advancement as indistinguishable from Westernization. They had responded to these messages with occasional ambivalence but general hospitality toward the Westerners with whom they coexisted harmoniously to mutual benefit.

Never during this period had Western communities, or Westerners generally, become the targets of extended public suspicion, either for racial reasons or otherwise. Throughout this process, however, Japanese had adopted the West's deprecatory views of nonwhites, or, in John Dower's words, "an attitude toward weaker peoples and nations that was as arrogant and contemptuous as the racism of the Westerners."[9] In their acceptance of racial hierarchies, therefore, Western and Japanese views were roughly aligned.

Successive racist provocations added further complexity to imperial Japan's crystallizing ethnic identity. Hurt by unequal treaties (1858–99) denying it tariff autonomy and jurisdiction over Western residents, and incensed by Western essentialistic discriminations between "whites" and "yellows," Meiji-era (1868–1912) Japan had struggled to find its place within an exclusively Caucasian imperialist order. One way of doing this was by assuming a colonialist (racist) position vis-à-vis China, a strategy that ultimately failed to overcome standing perceptions of race as rooted in skin color. Despite military victories over China in 1895 and then Russia a decade later, Japan failed to receive the international respect it felt these victories deserved. In fact, its emergence as an imperial power caused many in the West to begin viewing Japan as a political threat and racial competitor. As Japan's visibility on the world stage grew, anti-Japanese and anti-Asian racial hostility in the West expanded accordingly.[10] In 1905 and 1906, California promulgated legislation that barred Asian children from attending white schools. In 1907, Japan consented to a "gentlemen's agreement" with the United States that restricted working-class (deemed genetically inferior) Japanese from immigrating to the United States. In 1913, the Alien Land Law in California prohibited Japanese from owning land while permitting land ownership to foreigners of other nationalities. Japan was again humiliated in 1919 when, after being awarded permanent membership on the League of Nations Council, other member states rejected its proposal to insert a Racial Equality Clause into the league's covenant. The Washington Naval Conference of 1921 limited the number of Japanese naval vessels to three-fifths the number allotted to the United States and Britain. In 1922, the U.S. Supreme Court's decision in *Ozawa v. United States* denied first-generation Japanese immigrants the right of naturalization.[11] This decision anticipated the Immigration Act of 1924, legislation that severely restricted Japanese immigration and signaled unambiguously America's unwillingness to embrace human rights and racial equality as national policies. This law was interpreted by Japan, certainly correctly, as clear evidence that America viewed it as a racial inferior, precipitating "extremely emotional and near mass-hysteric situations," including waves of suicides.[12] The U.S. government then dismissed letters from Japan's ambassador and Foreign Ministry communicating their outrage at the immigration law.[13] Such measures were not specific to the United States. Australia and Canada imposed similar immigration restrictions. British Columbia denied voting rights to Canadian citizens of Asian ancestry. Various reasons were supplied, including the view that Asians "were not assimilable" and not "citizens in the proper sense of the term."[14]

This succession of racial affronts catalyzed the disintegration of Japanese-U.S. relations and a hardening of Japanese public opinion toward the United States. By convincing Japan that its objective of securing equality within the international order would never be permitted and that it should adopt a new objective of assuming the role of "moderator" in harmonizing East and West, the Immigration Act magnified Japan's disassociation with the West and hastened its "return" to Asia.[15] Japan's withdrawal from the League of Nations in 1933 marked a large step in this direction. By this point Japan and the United States were committed to irreconcilable trajectories. Their mutual disgust intensified and was increasingly expressed in racial terms. Japanese propaganda depicted Caucasians, and Western culture generally, as brutish and morally degenerate, while the U.S. census of 1940 counted Japanese differently than it did individuals of other races. The census considered U.S.-born Europeans to be American but individuals of Japanese ancestry to be "Japanese," regardless of their citizenship and country of birth. Namely, although the United States recognized white individuals of Axis ancestry—German Americans and Italian Americans—as American, it did not count Japanese Americans as such.[16] The U.S. internment of 120,000 Japanese and Japanese Americans in 1942, an act that the American Civil Liberties Union claimed to be "the greatest civil rights violation in American history," only validated what Japanese propaganda had claimed for years: that Asian nations would remain the victims of Western hatred and racial discrimination until they liberated themselves by force.[17]

Japan emerged from this succession of affronts with conflicting perceptions of superiority over Asia and inferiority to the West.[18] It had also learned a great deal. By the start of the Fifteen Years' War in 1931, Japan had become well versed in colonial rhetoric, which it used to frame its own imperialist agenda in Asia. Not only did the Imperial Army justify its expansionism with racial rhetoric reminiscent of that deployed in the West, its professed objective of assuming leadership over the Asian peoples in order to liberate them from Western oppression was patterned after Western precedents. Japan also adopted Western empiricism to assert racial dominance in Asia. Just as it had been subjected to empirical "evidence" of its own racial inferiority, Japan combined nativist claims of proximity to the divine with social Darwinist assertions of civilizational superiority to assert its cultural and spiritual preeminence in Asia. Japan also found Nazi Germany an apt model for articulating national policy in racial terms. Its domestic calls for a racially homogenous and organic citizenry, for instance, borrowed directly from "Nazi sloganeering."[19] Adopting such notions was natural, even predictable, given the affinities for social hierarchies that Japan shared with Western nations. Finally, Japan had come to apprehend a Western view of the global order as a competitive arena wherein imperial expansion served as a viable self-defensive strategy. Its Greater East Asia Co-prosperity Sphere (Daitōa kyōeiken) doctrine, which asserted Japan's desire to liberate Asian peoples from Western colonization along with its right and responsibility as Asia's strongest race to lead that charge, transposed the Roosevelt Corollary (1904) to the Monroe Doctrine onto the Asian continent. This venture, Japan's own version of Manifest Destiny, even followed Western models in articulating hostilities as struggles between the yellow and white races. As disingenuous as this rhetoric sounds given its imperialist designs, Japan's expansion in Southeast Asia indeed avoided indiscriminant land grabbing. Its military duly limited its incursions to those areas under Western colonial control (the Mariana Islands, Philippines, Dutch East Indies, Burma, Hong Kong, Singapore, and British Malaya).

Given how racial inequality had framed diplomatic relations between Japan and the Allied powers for the preceding century, it is not surprising that race would be central to how both sides approached the war ideologically. (The Showa emperor himself indicated in 1946 that Western racist structures were interpreted by Japanese as national insults and that

the Immigration Act had been "a remote cause of the Pacific War."[20])
Confrontation in the European Theater, though underscored by Nazi racism, was waged between nations rather than races. The Pacific War, in contrast, has been characterized widely as a race war between East and West, yellow and white. Dower's scholarship has been intent on demonstrating parallels between Japanese and Anglo-American racism and racial hatred. Specifically, it has revealed how both sides constructed racial justifications for military aggression; deployed notions of "proper place" (*taigi mibun*), racial purity, and paternalism to advance claims of racial superiority; and interpreted their enemy's aggression through analogous colonial optics.

Both before and after Pearl Harbor, Dower has shown, Americans and British hated the Japanese more than they did the Germans. In contrast to their war against the Nazis, a political regime presiding over both "good" and "bad" Germans, the war against Japan was wholly racial.[21] Visceral hatred guided not only how the two sides engaged each other emotionally, but also how they conceptualized and justified that engagement. Western racial slurs, for example, were directed toward the Japanese race rather than the nation's leaders, expressing open repugnance toward them as subhuman racial inferiors. "Racism," Dower states, "lay at the root of American atrocities against the Japanese, for white Americans were simply incapable of accepting colored peoples as humans."[22]

In the West, xenophobia was often normative. Prejudice guided internal discourse and in many cases defined mainstream thinking about nonwhite regions. In the late 1930s, U.S. public opinion largely opposed intervention in the European Theater due to widespread identification with certain principles of the Nazi mission. Racial epithets reminiscent of the rhetoric deployed by the Nazi Party were common within U.S. public discourse, deployed even by Presidents Franklin D. Roosevelt and Harry S. Truman. Public celebrities like Charles Lindbergh openly and publicly endorsed white supremacy and the need for a nation to preserve the racial purity of its citizenry.[23] "In the sense the word has now, most people were racist in 1939–43," wrote Colonel Hugh Toye. "We were still certain of the utter superiority of Western civilization."[24] Ronald Takaki has shown that African Americans, Native Americans, Hispanic and Asian Americans, and nonwhite immigrants all suffered from institutionalized segregation and racial discrimination in the United States, obstacles that inhibited their ability to join the war effort by fighting or working for freedom and democracy.[25] Prejudices in the United States were facilitated by a pervasive ignorance about Asia and Asians. Many Americans were unable to distinguish between the Asian races. A survey conducted in 1942, when hostilities in China and India were making headlines, found that a majority of Americans held negative views of those countries, but also that 60 percent of them were unable to locate either of those two countries on a map.[26] Ignorance made racial discourse receptive to claims about biological differences—skull physiology, blood types, and skin pigmentations—as well as propagandistic assertions about Japanese cultural and moral inferiority, all of which fueled widespread disgust at the thought of Japan's slogan "Asia for Asians" and of Japan assuming leadership over Asia. In Britain, as well, Christopher Thorne asserts, it was quite normal for Caucasians to decry Nazi racism while openly harboring prejudicial views of nonwhites. Double standards of this sort became part of wartime rhetoric issued by both Western and Japanese authorities, who, depending on their audience, variously attacked and defended racist positions.[27] As Takaki's thesis suggests, however, for some Anglo-Americans the war's racial overtones became epiphanic. As they reflected on their own support or revulsion for Nazi and Japanese claims of racial supremacy, they discovered the hypocrisy of their own pretensions.

Aspects of Race Consciousness in Imperial Japan

Racial classification schemes establish a people's power position vis-à-vis racial others. Though classifications may include deprecatory value judgments and elicit racial hostility, one can note and be conscious of difference without hating it. In Japan, noting and acting on differences in age, gender, and status is expected and necessary as a matter of etiquette. Speech and behavior are strongly determined by one's relative subject position, rendering discrimination (marking difference) a cultural necessity. Ignoring, excluding, or failing to recognize difference denies individuals membership within the classifications that identify them as social actors. From ostracism (*murahachibu*) to banishment, traditional forms of punishment utilized this premise to strip offenders of their subject (power) positions. The early modern state institutionalized a hierarchical status system (*mibunsei*), and though individuals may have chafed at the injustice of their own positions within this taxonomy, they generally accepted the need for taxonomies in principle. Additionally, since the early nineteenth century, Japan's changing geopolitical relationships and national borders necessitated multiple reevaluations of both its national identity and the ethnic communities to be counted as Japanese. This ongoing self-reinvention employed assertions of imperial subjecthood to variously exclude and include peripheral peoples like Ainu, Burakumin, Okinawans, and resident Koreans. For Japanese to call attention to racial difference, to discriminate, therefore, was to acknowledge difference and thereby assign an appropriate subject position. Fundamentally, this cultural affinity aligned Japan with the Western colonial practice of positioning individuals and groups within hierarchical taxonomies.

In part, Japanese race consciousness is thus an extension of position consciousness and neither intimates nor precludes a priori racial hatred. Though race consciousness is culturally justified in this sense, prejudice arises from the value judgments that accompany discriminations. In the Japanese context, a racial affront derives not from the fact that a discrimination is made, that difference is noted, but rather from a sense that one's own perceived subject position is not recognized or, worse, that it is viewed as inferior. Judgments that invert one's perceived subject position within a hierarchy are particularly galling. The diversity and inconsistency of such discriminations directed toward Japan explains why Japanese variously viewed Westerners with curiosity, admiration, fear, and contempt, and also why so many Western expats developed ambivalent views of Japan. Racial positioning relies on assumptions of reciprocity, therefore, a bilateral agreement of parties' respective subject positions. Failure to reach an accord on this point can destabilize race relations. In the Meiji era, cultural affinities for discrimination (distinction making) and hierarchies were initially shared by Japanese and resident Westerners. Hierarchies, however, connoted a power consciousness that was naturally transposed as race consciousness. As power positions were institutionalized through mechanisms like the unequal treaties, race consciousness rose to the surface of Japanese-Western relations.

Meiji elites developed strong but conflicting emotions over racial issues, therefore, finding physiological differences like skin and hair color
to be insurmountable obstacles to assimilation in colonial contexts. While
detesting imperialist nations for the arrogance they so openly directed
toward the "yellow" Japanese, many desperately desired Japan to become
more like them. Western disdain for the yellow races, which were widely
considered indistinguishable, incensed Japanese but also caused many to
develop disdain for themselves as Asians. The movement to "escape Asia"
(*datsu-a*) in the 1880s and 1890s was, Ayu Majima contends, largely a
search for relief from self-loathing derived specifically from physical characteristics like skin color. In the early twentieth century, even as some
Japanese challenged the nation's racial inferiority complex, the stigma of
skin color remained. Japanese illustrations from the Sino- and Russo-
Japanese Wars depicted Japanese with distinctly white features but Chinese as stereotypically Asian.[28] In 1901, eminent novelist Natsume Soseki
(1867–1916) typified Japanese racial self-consciousness when, upon glimps-
ing his own reflection in a London shop window, self-described as "a
pigmy with a peculiar weird skin color." Given the unattractiveness of
Japanese features, he continued, "it is understandable that the Westerners deride us."[29] Other elites concurred. When surrealist poet Haruyama
Yukio (1902–94) created a minor sensation in the late 1920s with a poem
consisting solely of the two words *shiroi shōjo* (white girl) repeated 112
times, fellow poet Anzai Fuyue (1898–1965) commented that the poem
would have lost its poetic value if it had read "yellow boy" instead of "white
girl."[30] Regardless of whether Haruyama's poem referred to Caucasians
explicitly or simply to lighter skin tones, both it and Anzai's remark speak
to the prestige of lighter skin color in imperial Japan. Even patriotic novelist Tanizaki Jun'ichirō (1886–1965), whose *In'ei raisan* (*In Praise of Shad-
ows*, 1933) famously extolled the aesthetic and cultural virtues of shadow
and dimness, was unable to find aesthetic appreciation for the darker skin
of Japanese women. Clearly, the biological features that so deeply concerned the Helms and other Westerners were equally central to Japanese
perceptions of racial identity and racial capital.

Caucasians in imperial Japan rarely became targets of racial contempt, therefore. Though many enjoyed privileges and exhibited forms
of arrogance that piqued Japanese indignation, from their arrival in the
1850s resident Westerners were foils by which Japanese apprehended their

Japaneseness. Embodying the very civilizational ideals that Japan sought for itself, collectively they were inappropriate targets of racial discrimination. Instead, groups like Japanese Christians whose foreign worldviews contradicted those of the native family state served as "metaphorical foreigners" against whom nationalists could direct their patriotic misgivings. With the outbreak of the first Sino-Japanese War (1894–95), nationalistic forms of racial prejudice swung away from Japanese Christians and toward resident Chinese, who, in addition to being actual foreigners, were more easily portrayed as uncivilized and racially inferior.[31]

Though Japanese and Westerners share ontological predispositions to racial discrimination, theirs was not a symmetrical race consciousness. Nor is it the case that, as Dower asserts, their "patterns of supremacism are analogous."[32] Western expats tended to express racial views toward nonwhites—the Helms, for example—more openly. As prisoners and detainees, they also exhibited raw outrage when Japanese guards assumed airs of racial superiority. Japanese race consciousness, in contrast, was rarely expressed explicitly. It tended to float "oblique and submerged" beneath public discourse.[33] Yukiko Koshiro admits that racism in Japan is "hidden though tacitly practiced"; Kyle Cleveland calls it "passive" racism, "expressed in such indirect and symbolic ways that their true intention is indecipherable."[34] David Howell argues that individual passivity toward race emerges from an understanding that such issues reside beyond the individual. "Discrimination is not a problem for individual Japanese to address . . . ," he writes, "so much as a process to be brokered by the state."[35] Indeed, the scarcity of overt expressions of public racism toward Westerners in Japan is matched by the near-absence of public antiracism. In imperial Japan, similarly, few Japanese openly opposed the privileges afforded Western residents. They also generally avoided challenging systemic and ideologically validated forms of racial segregation and differentiation. Interestingly, Japanese "oblique and submerged" racism was generally reserved for races holding comparatively greater racial capital. Prejudice against Asians, even individuals of Japanese ancestry born abroad, was more explicit.[36]

Japanese race consciousness must also be recognized as highly variable, however. The state's racial rhetoric was beset by inconsistencies that challenge our ability to discern what Japanese actually believed. Japan declared racial superiority over other Asians, but neither its rhetoric nor its policies articulated a consistent vision of how it would assume the responsibilities connected to this position. Propaganda released internationally tended to assure Japanese benevolence and promise assimilation in Asia, whereas domestic discourse more often asserted Japanese racial supremacy in the region. This inconsistency was also evident in disagreements over colonial administration, with lawmakers in the colonies debating with those at home over how best to handle race relations. Beyond epistemological bifurcations between the narratives elites imposed on the masses and what they knew to be true, the inconsistency of Japanese propaganda must have compromised its effectiveness.

For all the wrangling, Japan's rhetorical (and actual) treatment of Caucasians differed from its treatment of Asians. Anxious to avoid racist assertions that would offend its Axis allies or that would echo the white supremacism endemic to Western colonialism, Japan focused more on asserting its own spiritual and moral supremacy. Its propaganda was predicated more on its enemies' historical behavior (imperialism) and cultural degeneracy (racism) than on racial grounds. Contradictions and inconsistencies of this sort suggest that race ambivalence rather than race hate predominated among the wartime public whose perceptions of Westerners were shaped primarily by practical rather than ideological or moral concerns. Race consciousness conformed to needs as dictated by changing circumstances.

Koshiro has affirmed this point by showing that Japanese authorities never rejected the West or the white races. Citing Japan's open acceptance of white immigrants in the north and its assimilationist efforts within its colonies on the mainland and in the Pacific, she asserts that the Japanese empire in the 1920s and 1930s was "multiethnic and multiracial."[37] With its eighty-five thousand Westerners, Manchukuo was a veritable melting pot, its cosmopolitanism proudly embraced by Japanese officials and residents alike. Japan was particularly hospitable to Russian migrants, advancing the notion that Russia was an Asian state and as such should join Japan's Pan-Asian mission. In the 1920s, as the United States was prohibiting Japanese immigration, Japan was accepting thousands of White Russian refugees into its colonial territories, as well as into Japan proper, where economic circumstances led them to assimilate more easily than the elite expats of other Western nations. By 1933, about forty-three thousand had settled in Manchukuo alone, and some two thousand had immigrated to Japan. Russians did not face racial discrimination, Koshiro argues.[38] They settled freely, integrated into the Japanese workforce as merchants and laborers, intermarried with Japanese, and sent their children to Japanese schools.[39]

Japan's colonial governance, however, included a mixed array of policies that promoted both racial integration and Japanese privilege. At home, the government backed promises of racial equality for colonial subjects by selectively implementing more inclusive suffrage laws for resident Asians, including a universal male suffrage law in 1925 that enabled resident Koreans to vote and run for public office. From 1930, ballots in Hangul were accepted, and in 1934 residency requirements were shortened, enabling more temporary workers to vote. Though touted as altruistic, assimilation initiatives of this sort were ultimately self-serving. The decision to extend Japanese citizenship to colonial subjects during the war, for example, also extended a legal obligation to serve in the military. As a result, between 1938 and 1945, 360,000 Koreans were either conscripted or forced to work for Japan's military.[40] Demonstrating a brazen disregard for assertions of Japanese benevolence, promises to liberate Asian peoples from the Western imperialists, and slogans touting the "cooperation of the five races" (*gozoku kyōwa*) and "the eight corners of the world under one roof" (*hakkō ichiu*), however, Japan implemented a racial caste system within its territories that subjugated natives and extended privileges to Japanese. Colonial subjects were compelled to take Japanese names, adopt Japanese as their official language, and attend Shinto services. Discriminatory structures also denied natives political freedom and established forms of economic exploitation that included inferior wages and living conditions.[41]

Though never equitable, Japanese-native coexistence in the territories adhered to somewhat more porous racial boundaries than was customary in Western colonies. After 1899, Japan not only legalized and facilitated ethnic assimilation within its colonies, it actively promoted and rewarded colonial marriages between Japanese and native colonial subjects. Then, after receiving Germany's former territories in Micronesia following World War I, Japan sought to avoid more traditional colonial relations there by encouraging integration. Its establishment of new industrial projects was aided by mass Japanese immigration to these islands.

Japanese migrants worked and lived alongside natives, in many cases as partners rather than colonizers. In Taiwan, one-third of the laborers in the sugar industry were Japanese.[42] Miscegenation laws, labor practices, and living spaces did not follow the rigid divisions between colonizer and colonized that typified Western colonial contexts. Though Japan's domestic wartime propaganda opposing intermarriage and advancing claims of Japanese racial purity and supremacy contradicted the cosmopolitanism of its own colonies, in practice Japan rarely overturned existing policies permitting integrated living spaces, labor, and intermarriage.[43]

Japanese race relations were highly contextual, therefore. The nation's alliance with Germany and Italy and its neutrality pact with Russia reveal it as a willing ally with Western nations. Moreover, its Co-prosperity Sphere doctrine included no outright rejection of Western civilization in principle, and even mirrored the West's racial taxonomies. For Japanese "to deny the validity of white supremacy," Koshiro notes, "would be to deny their own leadership. Japan's colonial empire never intended to exclude the white race."[44] Rather, it wished to demonstrate that its empire could unify East and West. Its wartime enemies were to be Anglo-Americans specifically, not Westerners or Caucasians collectively.

Sources of Cognitive Dissonance

Race relations during Japan's imperial era were also characterized by several ideological ruptures. One was a set of contradictions between what educated elites believed to be true and the platitudes they disseminated to the rest. Louis Althusser has explained this classic schism as competing self-defensive reactions to various tensions. Ruling elites (the "superstructure") assume custodianship over public knowledge while the masses ("base structure") react to economic, social, and political conditions in ways that address their own material necessities.[45] Historian Tsurumi Shunsuke has identified this bifurcation in imperial Japan, demonstrating how it became systematized through dissemination of disparate bodies of knowledge. Ruling elites ensured that what Tsurumi calls "an exoteric national cult of the family state" that included the myths of Japanese racial purity and superiority was disseminated in primary and military schools with the intention of uniting the underclasses through uncritical worship of the emperor.[46] Educated elites based their own "esoteric cult" on the Western learning taught at higher schools and universities, curricular content that they needed in order to assume responsible leadership positions. Showa statist ideology, therefore, contained an inbuilt contradiction: its architects knew it to be false. Worse, they understood that the continued success of their ruse hinged on their own adherence to this false ideology. Inconsistencies between esoteric and public knowledge thus led to internal rupture, the period's apparent fanaticism and paranoia deriving in part from the leadership's fear that this bifurcation, and the lies used to create it, would be discovered.[47] Imperial Japan's xenophobic and racial invectives, therefore, were imposed from above and did not necessarily represent popular sentiment.

Ideological content was also handed down through the establishment of neighborhood associations (*tonarigumi*). An organizational scheme originating in the medieval period, these groups consisted of five to fifteen adjacent households assigned with collective responsibilities. Association leadership rotated among member households, but all families were responsible for seeing to their neighbors' active participation. As a system of mutual support and mutual surveillance, it ensured that transgressions by any *tonarigumi* member incurred repercussions for the entire association, a threat that fostered both interdependence and distrust. *Tonarigumi* were also used to secure compliance with state directives and eradicate foreign influences and sympathies. In doing so they obstructed people's ability to form individual judgments, engendering an enforced uniformity of knowledge and opinion. Tokyo implemented the system in 1938 for the purpose of coordinating air-raid and firefighting drills, watching for spies, fighting crime, selling savings bonds, implementing government instructions, and distributing rationed food. Agendas for monthly meetings were synchronized with and directed by NHK (Nippon hōsō kyōkai) radio broadcasts, a one-way transmission of information that assured procedural uniformity among all associations. The Interior Ministry expanded on this model in September 1940, and during the war its food rationing function would prove particularly important in ensuring the system's success.[48] As food was unavailable in stores for most of the war and households refusing to participate in *tonari-gumi* were denied rations, citizens had little choice but to become willing participants in association operations.

State control over public knowledge distanced most Japanese from the state's antagonisms with its Western enemies. Mass depoliticization rendered the war an abstraction and threatened to neutralize the desired sense of alarm. In this regard, officials found the presence of resident Westerners useful in demonstrating to their constituents that foreign threats were immediate and real. The mere existence of Westerners, regardless of their nationality, lent urgency to calls for counterespionage. Using magazines like *Shūhō* (Weekly report) and *Shashin shūhō* (Photographic weekly report) as mouthpieces for counterespionage propaganda, the Cabinet Information Committee (Naikaku jōhō iinkai) fed readers a diet of intrigue that implicated all Caucasians as spies and even cast suspicion on Japanese who had traveled to the West. Such publications issued weekly warnings of how foreigners acquired secret information and relayed it to enemy nations, and recounted stories of how unsuspecting Japanese had been duped by the deceptive charms of sinister Caucasian spies.[49] Antiespionage (*bōchō*) campaigns were another means of institutionalizing national solidarity and instilling paranoia. Beginning in 1941, antispy weeks were scheduled annually in July. Posters, notices, and other forms of media cautioned people against discussing the war, instructed them to be wary of foreign spies in their midst, and encouraged them to inform police of the movements and activities of local foreigners.

Authorities also employed pseudoempirical arguments—racial science and the "proper place" doctrine, for example—to further shape public knowledge. While ethnic integration was being touted in the territories, at home racial science was variously deployed to lend empirical validity to colonial notions of the ethnic supremacy of colonizers and the dangers of racial mixing. Supporters of such claims drew on nineteenth-century discussions about skull sizes, blood types, skin color, and their concomitant racial attributes to validate discriminatory policies toward Japan's colonial subjects.[50] Some of these ideas were eventually codified in policy. Nazi-influenced ideologues, for example, formed the Japan Association of Racial Hygiene (Nippon minzoku eisei kyōkai) in 1930, which helped shape the content of propaganda. Academic turned bureaucrat Koyama Eizō (1899–1983) rearticulated scientific research on racial purity and the ill effects of intermarriage in the Ministry of Health and Welfare's six-volume report *An Investigation of Global Policy with the Yamato Race as Nucleus* (*Yamato minzoku wo chūkaku to suru sekai seisaku no kentō*, 1943).[51] While some contested scientific assertions of Japanese racial purity, they were unable to dismiss racial explanations for Japan's clear military superiority and cultural advancement over other Asian peoples. Ultimately, wartime ideologues espoused race science to advance multiple interpretations of Japanese purity, each bearing its own implications for Japanese empire building and relationship building with other Asians.[52]

"Proper place" was also invoked early and often, and attempts to avoid references to the war as a dispute between differently colored races inevitably fell back on this doctrine, itself a paradigm built on racial prejudice. The *Cardinal Principles of the National Polity* (*Kokutai no Hongi*, 1937), which sold two million copies and became required reading in schools, asserted the benefits of observing positionality within social hierarchies: "Those above receive help from inferiors, and inferiors are loved by superiors," it stated, "and in working together harmoniously is beautiful concord manifested and creative work carried out."[53] Throughout the war, government resources were diverted to create rationales for establishing proper place as a pillar of Japanese foreign policy. Rhetoric typically framed the conflict as a moral mandate for Japan to combat white supremacy so that all races could enjoy their rightful places within a new world order. As Asia's leading race, Japanese bore a moral responsibility for executing a humanitarian campaign that would bring coprosperity to the region.

Even the shrillest proponents of Japanese racial supremacy took care to frame their rhetoric with logical arguments rather than fanatical rants. In his article "Make This Mankind's Last War," ultranationalist Shiratori Toshio (1887–1949), a former ambassador to Italy who had supported the Tripartite Pact (September 27, 1940) and was later convicted as a class A war criminal, defended Japanese militarism in rational rather than emotional terms. Published June 1, 1942, in *Gendai* (Today magazine), the article predicted that Japan's victory in Asia and an Axis victory in Europe would institute a new world order based on totalitarianism rather than Anglo-American individualism. The article closed with the following racist pronouncement: "I have found Japanese to be superior to all foreigners. . . . The Japanese people have admirably proven they are a superior race unequalled in this world. If the Japanese conform to their inherent nature, they inevitably will be endowed with the divine blessing of Providence."[54] The document rejects racial hatred, however, and instead advances the principle that "each nation shall have its place in the sun and all human beings shall live in peace," a statement from the Imperial Rescript issued at the signing of the Tripartite Pact. Shiratori continues by explaining this "[proper] place in the sun" ideal in terms of Japan's national creation myth, thereby positing the campaign as a holy war rather than a race war. The current state of global turmoil he equates with an allegory from the *Kojiki* (*Records of Ancient Matters*, 712) in which the sun goddess Amaterasu is insulted by her brother and retreats into a cave, casting the world into darkness. "The modern analogy is that the world is once again in darkness," Shiratori explains, "and Japan's mission is to bring light once more to a world overcome with evil." The treatise thus provides a rationale for the war, invoking the Imperial Rescript and couching the conflict as a philanthropic endeavor whose objective is a permanent peace wherein "each nation shall have its place in the sun."[55]

The ideological edifice described here is formidable indeed, but its mere existence reveals little about its impact on public epistemology. To what extent was exoteric rhetoric internalized? The Imperial Rule Assistance Association (Taisei yokusankai) was active in disseminating propaganda, but also in conducting public opinion polls to determine the effectiveness of its efforts. Polls revealed that citizens were quite aware of being manipulated, but also that they did not resent it. Not only did many respondents feel thought control was warranted during war, in one study two-thirds indicated that the government should implement *more* such measures to rally greater public support.[56] Opinion polls also indicated what sorts of propaganda were effective. They revealed, for instance, that many did not understand explanations about why Japan was at war with China or why it had been isolated internationally. Nor were respondents particularly responsive to slogans like "All the world under one roof" and "One hundred million souls with one mind" (*ichioku isshin*), which called on them to support distant military campaigns they knew little about. Some recommended that propaganda be less informative and more emotional and entertaining.[57] Citizens' acceptance and even support for thought control indicates a general understanding that no recourse existed beyond compliance; omnipresent surveillance by police and neighbors ensured the futility of popular resistance. While these polls yield interesting data, therefore, they are unusable as metrics of actual public opinion. Respondents, well aware that polls were administered by government authorities, were certainly fearful of repercussions for responding incorrectly. Furthermore, the polls themselves were based on essentialistic presumptions of a unified "national character" or "spirit" that denied respondents any diversity of opinion.[58]

In the end, the elite's recognition that Japan could not realistically exist independently from the West while simultaneously insisting that it do just that became a source of cognitive dissonance. Many did not believe in the myths they had generated about spiritual superiority and racial purity, or about Japan's certain rise to regional supremacy. Throughout the 1930s and early 1940s, factions within the government opposed the war in China and warned against further antagonizing Western nations. Longtime resident A. Morgan Young wrote in 1938 that Western-educated elites paid public lip service to narratives about the divinity of the emperor but did not believe them.[59] Tsurumi avers that when the Imperial Army and Navy asked their officers in charge of assessing the relative strengths of the American and British militaries whether Japan had any possibility of emerging victorious from war with those countries, both had answered no.[60] Fearing that their own disbelief would be publicly exposed, the architects of Japan's statist regime grew ever more insistent, fostering a culture of compliance intolerant to any glimmer of public dissent.

For all the conflicting racial messages swirling domestically, Japan was cautious not to let questions of race define its image internationally or govern the tenor of its foreign policy. The New Order in East Asia (Tōa shinchitsujo) declared by Prime Minister Konoe Fumimaro (1891–1945) in 1938 promised to unite Japan, Manchukuo, and China as an Asian stronghold against the West. The Co-prosperity Sphere articulated by Foreign Minister Matsuoka Yōsuke (1880–1946) in 1940 extended this vision into Southeast Asia. Konoe, Matsuoka, and the other architects of Japan's Pan-Asian mission recognized that the state's ability to articulate and carry out unification in Asia without further compromising its international standing would hinge on its ability to replace the earlier, racially conceived paradigm of Asian regionalism with a more inclusive

one of ethnic comradeship.[61] Toward this end, ideologues touted assimilation by replacing the principles of racial identity (*jinshu*) and racial science debated during the Meiji era with ethnic nationality (*minzoku*), a
more inclusive paradigm that allowed for claims of Asian unity vis-à-
vis Western peoples. Extremists like Shiratori notwithstanding, wartime
ideology courted non-Japanese Asians inside and outside Japan by claiming ethnic kinship to help validate Japan's mission to liberate Asia from
the West.[62] Establishing stable diplomatic relations with Asian nations
would then require Japan to assert respect for diversity as an official policy. It was with this in mind that Japanese leadership sought to eliminate
issues of race from its rhetorical New Order.[63] The contradictions in doing
so arose not only from the fact that domestically Japan had explained
the war in racial terms. (Characterizations of Japanese racial homogeneity
released for domestic consumption contradicted assertions released internationally, namely of Japan as an immigrant society and the Japanese
as a mixed race.)[64] Japan had consistently followed up antiracist rhetoric
deployed internationally by co-opting Korean and Taiwanese natives as
Japanese subjects and denying them the privileges, living standards, and
opportunities enjoyed by Japanese.[65] The glaring disparity in rhetoric
crafted for domestic and foreign consumption thus emerged as a second
rupture and source of cognitive dissonance.

Factionalism also hampered Japan's leadership from reaching a consensus on how to address racial discrimination in Asia. Nationalist slogans like "All the world under one roof" seemed to promise benevolence
and coprosperity, and some wanted them interpreted as such. House of
Representatives member and *buraku* liberation proponent Matsumoto
Jiichirō (1887–1966) was one such advocate. Education, he argued, must
eradicate discrimination against non-Japanese ethnicities under the "roof"
of Japanese colonialism. Matsumoto called for people to forge an egali-
tarian society by opposing discriminatory policies and practices. Doing
so, he felt, would bring the empire's peoples in line with *tennōsei* ideology
and the state's mission of benevolent leadership in Asia.[66] Although a minority position at home, this sentiment did align with the designs of many
Japanese officials in Korea, Manchukuo, and China who advocated (and
variously implemented) assimilationist policies aimed at pacifying tensions between Japanese and natives.

Race was predominantly a Pan-Asian discourse, however, and rarely factored prominently into propaganda directed toward Japan's Caucasian enemies.[67] The state's differing rhetorical strategies toward Asians and Westerners thus constitutes a third rupture in its wartime racial discourse. Unable to claim superiority in civilizational terms, Japan found it difficult to assert racial superiority over its Western rivals. Its propaganda thus tended to avoid questions of race and instead focused on Japanese moral superiority. As Dower observes, whereas Western racism typically sought to denigrate others, Japanese pursued the same ends by extolling themselves.[68] A series of proposals advanced by the Educational Study Group (Kyōiku kenkyūkai) in 1936, for example, reflected prevailing assumptions about the declining nature of public morals and the need for moral retrenchment. Western education, it noted, "had brought about a dismal decline of the spirit of service, cooperativeness, and national and collective morality," a trend that warranted restorative educational reform.[69] The *Cardinal Principles of the National Polity*, published by the Ministry of Education in 1937, similarly expressed fears that Japan's appetite for foreign learning threatened national prosperity.[70]

Japan's Anti-Comintern Pact (1936) with Germany, which Italy joined in 1937, also rendered antiwhite rhetoric highly problematic.[71] Neither side was comfortable with the alliance, both viewing it as a distasteful and temporary expediency. The Nazi Party continued to view Japanese as racial inferiors, and Japan's military felt equally indignant about having to claim amity with the most stridently racist of the Western states. The alliance obliged Japan to exercise caution in how it publicized racial issues, but also permitted it to represent its expansion into Asia as a moral calling rather than as a crusade against the white races. Japan had repeatedly evoked U.S. oppression of minorities as evidence of American moral corruption and had no wish to place itself in the same camp. Although rhetorical characterizations of the war as a struggle between whites and yellows did pervade Japan's propaganda both at home and in its territories around the Pacific, the nature of those racial depictions sought to instigate contempt for Anglo-American foes specifically rather than Caucasians per se.

To some degree, distinguishing between "the white races" was facilitated by the fact that those various nationalities had incurred different reputations in Japan. As noted, the lifestyles adopted by Russian immigrants shared more with other Asians than with the more insular Western communities. (Russians owned only three of the 1,096 foreign-owned summer villas in the mountain resort of Karuizawa.) Their efforts to assimilate were rewarded with greater leniency. During the war, the fifty-seven registered Russians in Tokyo continued performing their blue-collar occupations under less surveillance and suspicion than neutral Europeans.[72] In contrast, American expats, the contingent that isolated itself more and assimilated less than any other foreign group, suffered in comparison. "With a self-important sense of mission and superior wealth," Koshiro asserts, "American residents kept themselves apart from ordinary Japanese as no other Westerners did."[73] In part, this isolation was professionally motivated. Americans constituted by far the greatest portion of foreign missionaries and teachers in Japan, meaning that more Americans considered themselves engaged in work involving a one-way transmission of learning and technology. (In 1932, 33.5 percent of American residents were missionaries and 34.7 percent were teachers.) Viewing themselves as civilizational benefactors, they endeavored to elevate Japan and its citizens by recasting them in their own image as Americans. As more of these individuals traveled to Japan together with their families than expats from other Western nations, fewer intermarried and interacted with Japanese. Census data from 1935 in Hyogo Prefecture reveals that only 3.4 percent of American residents had married Japanese, compared to 16.5 percent of French, 13.3 percent of Swiss, 11.6 percent of British, and 8.1 percent of Germans. But the significantly lower rates of intermarriage between Americans and Japanese are also attributable to race consciousness. In a 1927 survey of four hundred Western missionaries, 20 percent of Americans responded that "categorically the white race is superior to all others," and many others stated their opposition to miscegenation due to its degenerative effects on the Caucasian race. Some Americans did cultivate relationships with the more westernized, wealthy, and politically influential Japanese, who were equally eager to insert themselves into the Western communities at American-dominated resorts like Karuizawa. In 1932, 56.1 percent of missionaries and 54.5 percent of educators in Karuizawa were American. Americans also owned about half the 1,096 foreign-owned vacation villas and half the 217 foreign-owned winterized houses in town.[74] More than any other Western contingent, Koshiro concludes, the American mission sought to re-create America in Japan and to attract to this venture as many Japanese followers as possible.[75]

Imperial Japan's ambivalence toward itself as an Asian race intoned a profound ambivalence toward race generally that was ultimately reflected in both its rhetoric and its colonial policies. Neither rhetoric nor policy can speak to what the Japanese people actually believed, however. In order to further and more conclusively test the perception of wartime Japan as a nation beset by race hate and determine how Japanese civilians engaged with questions of race—whether they exhibited racial arrogance, and whether they internalized or rejected claims of their own racial superiority—we shall need to examine their engagement with racial others living in their midst. What can be unequivocally asserted at the outset is that consciousness of race was omnipresent and insurmountable, and that it framed daily interactions between Westerners and Japanese. It defined the entire expat experience in prewar Japan, the topic of chapter 2.

CHAPTER 2

Privilege and Prejudice

Being a Westerner in Imperial Japan

For whatever reasons, there exists—like a great wall of glass—an impenetrable but almost invisible psychological barrier between Japan and the rest of the world.

—John W. Dower[1]

Westerners in imperial Japan were happily and unhappily separated from mainstream life. Diaries and memoirs from the prewar and wartime years consistently identify insularity as both the salvation and the emotional bane of the expat experience. Bearing titles like "An Outsider: The Story of a European Refugee in Japan"; *Yokohama Yankee: My Family's Five Generations as Outsiders in Japan*; *Yokohama Gaijin* (foreigner); *Somehow, We'll Survive: Life in Japan during World War II through the Eyes of a Young Caucasian Boy*; and *Edokko: Growing Up a Foreigner in Wartime Japan*, these works highlight foreignness, outsider status, and isolation as fundamental to their authors' identities in Japan. In each case, racial exclusion emerges as the defining feature of daily life.

We have already noted how status consciousness and historical precedent called for qualified segregation of outsiders, and how various narratives about race were invoked toward this end. Ironically, these archetypes of exclusion were actualized by the Western community's own designs. Segregation was an arrangement agreed to in 1858 and unofficially preserved as a matter of course ever since, and as foreigners and Japanese alike viewed separation as a mutually beneficial arrangement, few on either side sought to mitigate it. For most Westerners, interaction with Japanese was limited to minimal exchanges with their Japanese maids, servants, and office staff. The establishment of colonial power structures within domestic and professional spheres was a time-honored practice that most took for granted. There were also practical reasons why, as Ludy Frank put it, "no foreign household was complete without [servants]."[2] Except for missionaries whose work demanded close interaction with locals, few who arrived in Japan as adults attempted to master more than a few words of the native language and thus lacked the skills to function independently. This was the case even for long-term residents like the Franks.[3] Children born in Japan and raised to varying degrees by Japanese nursemaids acquired some spoken proficiency but rarely developed lasting friendships with Japanese.

As geopolitical tensions worsened and war loomed, insularity intensified in two ways. First, the West's succession of racial rebukes against Japan disposed some Japanese to reciprocate by treating foreigners as they themselves were being treated. In this regard, the West established the rules of engagement that Japanese then used to frame their own handling of resident Westerners. Second, despite the apparent cosmopolitanism and solidarity of Western communities, intercommunity relations were fraught with occasional prejudices that were then aggravated by the outbreak of racial hostilities in Europe. Foreign civilians compounded their own hardships by duplicating the xenophobic nationalism concurrently rending the fabric of European society.

The diversity of individuals and living conditions within imperial-era Japan precludes any discussion of a typical Western community. As the largest and most established international center, Yokohama claimed the greatest breadth of Western enclaves. Some Westerners, like the Franks, resided in more isolated locales. In the 1930s, the growing virulence of Nazism in Europe generated greater numbers of ethnic refugees, like the Balks, that further diversified the demographics of Japan's immigrant population. This chapter gives broad coverage of the Western experience in prewar Japan by discussing each of these cases. It examines how Western families and communities manufactured their own disconnection from the Japanese mainstream and how this divide informed race relations during the prewar years. Insularity is explored, first, within the foreign settlements that formed following Japan's opening to international trade in the 1850s. Memoirs from various members of the Yokohama community then inform a discussion of that enclave's daily life and racial attitudes during the 1930s. We then look more closely at two case studies—the Frank and Balk families—to discern how their status as German Jews positioned them sociopolitically and impacted their associations with Japanese and other Westerners. Finally, we consider the development of Karuizawa as a Western summer resort, chronicling how it transformed its identity as a racially insular community to one based on socioeconomic privilege. In each of these various contexts we find Western residents crafting and retaining semiautonomous, semiexclusive societies. Japanese, while recognizing the benefits of continued associations with Westerners, tended to honor this segregation as natural and necessary. Insularity was thus formed and maintained by tacit agreement on both sides. Despite the racial tensions growing internationally, therefore, domestically practical concerns and historical precedents imbued Japanese-Western race relations with strong continuities.

Early Foreign Settlements

The "unequal treaties" that Japan negotiated with the United States, Britain, Russia, Holland, and France in 1858 set the parameters for foreign residency. Terms allowed for an ambassador to reside in Edo and for the establishment of consulates at the seven treaty ports of Yokohama, Kobe, Nagasaki, Osaka, Hakodate, Shimoda, and Niigata, each of which would accommodate segregated foreign communities. Yokohama, a small fishing village at the time, had been associated with foreigners ever since Commodore Matthew Perry (1794–1858) negotiated the Treaty of Kanagawa (*Nichibei washin jōyaku*) and buried one of his crew there in 1854. The Tokugawa government found the village's natural harbor, isolation, and relative proximity to Edo favorable criteria for a foreign settlement. Functionally, Yokohama and the other early settlements were direct descendants of Dejima, the artificial island in Nagasaki that between 1641 and 1853 had functioned as a Dutch trading outpost and the sole locus of Japanese-Western interaction. Dejima had served an exclusively mercantilist function, and the new settlements likewise emerged as highly regulated, sheltered enclaves operating largely for commercial purposes.

Foreign nationals were permitted to reside, lease property, and purchase buildings within the ports. They were permitted to travel within a

twenty-five-mile radius of the ports but required approval to venture far-
ther afield. Extraterritoriality was stipulated, in this case for British citizens, as follows: "Questions in regards to rights . . . shall be subject to the
jurisdiction of the British authorities," and crimes shall be "tried and punished by the consul . . . according to the law of Great Britain."[4] The treaties thus established a basic framework for segregated settlements wherein
foreigners would assume a measure of administrative control, including
qualified policing responsibilities. In 1867, for example, the Kanagawa
governor appointed an American director to oversee administrative
operations within Yokohama's foreign settlement. Special provisions in
Tokyo established a foreigner police force composed of Westerners from
several nationalities. Japanese authorities were allowed some measures of
control, such as enforcement of prohibitions against the cohabitation of
Japanese and foreigners, and against unapproved foreigner travel beyond
the twenty-five-mile radius. Japanese administration over travel and work
licenses also helped authorities monitor foreigners' recreational and occupational activities.[5]

Settlement residents enjoyed considerable autonomy, however, including independent and exclusive use of residential spaces. As Harold Williams describes Yokohama, these sites quickly crystallized into centers of
commercial activity teeming with ethnic diversity.

> The residents and transients in the Foreign Concession represented a var-
> ied bloc of humanity. Well-dressed merchants and bankers in suits . . . Brit-
> ish soldiers in red, and French in blue, French Catholic priests, Russian
> and Greek priests, Japanese itinerant priests, Jews orthodox and otherwise
> from every nation, nuns, Yankees with carpetbags, drunken sailors of many
> countries, whaling captains, blustering Russians and epaulet wearers of all
> sorts, well dressed compradores, English butchers, French bakers, German
> sausage-makers and Chinese shroffs, a few sun-tanned Australians from
> the goldfields, missionaries, ladies of fashion, little girls in pantaloons,
> Chinese amahs, Japanese porters, money-changers, beachcombers, and
> bums.[6]

Initially the Yokohama settlement exhibited the stench and semi-
lawlessness of a Wild West town, but after a fire razed portions of the
city in 1866, resident foreigners helped negotiate the urban planning and

reconstruction protocols that would reestablish order. Wealthier, more permanent residents rebuilt in ways that insulated themselves from itinerants and others they deemed of lower standing. Bankers and businessmen built fine Western homes on the Bluff in Yamate-chō, a two-mile swath of highlands overlooking the Japanese, Chinese, and other populations occupying the cluttered neighborhoods below (fig. 2.1). Within two decades this prosperous residential site had constructed Bluff Gardens, Japan's first Western-style park; the Gaiety Theater; the Yokohama Cricket Club (later the Yokohama Country and Athletic Club); the Ladies Lawn Tennis and Croquet Club; and the Yokohama Foreign General Cemetery, along with several hospitals, missions, churches, schools, and a fire station, many for the exclusive use of Western residents.

The Kobe community, though smaller, was as active as its counterpart in Yokohama. In 1869 it established the Hyogo Race Club for horse racing and the following year founded the Kobe Regatta and Athletic Club. The Kobe Cricket Club (Hyogo Cricket Club), also established in 1870, held regular sports competitions with the Yokohama club. From the formation of such communities, writes Williams, "a caste system in the Foreign Settlements developed."[7]

The prejudices of this colonial caste system were not always borne gracefully. For Westerners, the treaty ports were colonial spaces that promised opportunities for socioeconomic advancement. And so although many of the expats living in the colonies were "duds" and "third rate men" to their compatriots, abroad they recast themselves as colonizers (racial elites).[8] For some among the eight thousand Westerners residing in settlements during the mid-Meiji years, privileges codified by the treaties, inflated salaries, and other forms of racialized preferential treatment fostered perceptions of untouchability. Periodic displays of arrogance by some became a source of chagrin for those who were more cognizant of the responsibilities that accompanied their status and prestige as colonizers. Some decried that their own "third rate men" were, on the basis of race alone, being given positions of authority over Japanese of greater intelligence and ability.[9] Tokyo Imperial University professor Basil Hall Chamberlain (1850–1935), for example, bemoaned the elitism that some of his compatriots considered natural and justified: "There is nothing picturesque in the foreign employé," he lamented. "With his club, and

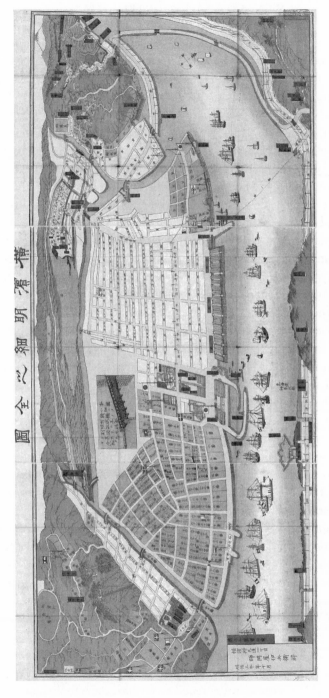

横濱明細之全圖

FIGURE 2.1 *Yokohama meisai no zenzu* (Detailed map of Yokohama), 1873. The Bluff (*far left*) overlooks the harbor and the city's central business and residential districts. International flags mark foreign diplomatic offices.

his tennis-ground, and his brick house, and his wife's piano, and the European entourage which he strives to create around him in order to sometimes forget his exile, he strikes a false note."[10]

Cultural differences could also degrade race relations. The celebrity complexes held by some Westerners were often reinforced by reciprocations from the ever-gracious Japanese, whose modesty could generate unfavorable impressions. Japanese hospitality was easily misconstrued as uncritical admiration. The pilot Art Smith, for instance, who came to Japan in 1916 and over a period of four months held fifty-six aerial shows around the country, described the Japanese, of whom he knew little, as incomparably simple, honest, and kind. Smith seemed to have based this assessment on the warm receptions he received, as well as on the extraordinary number of valuable gifts he accumulated as he traveled through the country.[11] Though neither malicious nor hateful, Smith's view of Japanese graciousness extended pretensions that his hosts would come to resent. The quiet, hesitant, occasionally obsequious tendencies of well-mannered Japanese were altogether unimpressive to Westerners, who to Japanese could come across as condescending, rude, and entitled. But within this cultural disconnect the Japanese fared worse, invariably emerging as more deferential and consequently inferior.[12]

Early race relations thus framed a double-edged partnership beset by suspicion and curiosity, contempt and admiration. Seeking to make sense of their own place within this partnership, some Japanese accepted colonialist presumptions of their own racial subordination. Others, humiliated by such propositions, reversed them by expounding on opposing racial narratives. By the 1890s, nationalists were reinforcing jingoistic assertions of Japanese racial superiority by claiming virtues like filiality and loyalty as innately Japanese.[13] Writes Gluck, "The Westerners themselves had never been the point; what had mattered was the idea of the West that the Japanese had created for purposes of self-definition. The real West was irrelevant; in the imagined West people were incapable of loyalty and filiality, and this was sufficient to define these traits as essentially Japanese."[14] Both sides, then, deployed racial presumptions to advance self-validating agendas.

Revisions to the unequal treaties took effect in 1899 and included small victories for both sides, but ultimately changed little. On one hand they afforded Westerners greater mobility, enabled them to live anywhere, and allowed for mixed residence, an idea that had long been opposed by parties on both sides. On the other, treaty revisions corresponded to a decline in the numbers of Westerners employed for the purpose of catalyzing Japanese modernization. Compensatory inequities continued to foster resentment among Japanese, however, and even occasional bewilderment among Westerners. In 1917, resident Jesse Steiner observed, "Even the foreign missionary lived in a house much larger than the average Japanese could afford and received a salary five times the amount that was granted to the native pastor. . . . Indeed, in almost all the relations between foreigners and Japanese, the fact that one was on a higher level than the other was unavoidably apparent. . . . It was continually forced upon their attention that they [Japanese] were as far as ever from being admitted into the inner circle of western society."[15] Other facets of Japanese-Western relations endured, and for many the new treaty provisions neither overthrew racial pretensions nor challenged the desirability of racial segregation. In this regard, life as a foreigner remained a mixture of privilege and prejudice. The sense of perpetual otherness, the racial irreconcilability that defined the foreigner's experience in Japan, necessitated for both sides the continued insularity of Western residential spaces. Life changed little in the Western settlements, which continued to expand their infrastructural and cultural insularity. Throughout the prewar era, physical and cultural separation affirmed the racial distinctions that continued to transfix both sides. An examination of the Yokohama community in the 1930s will illuminate this paradoxical sense of vaunted otherness.

The Yokohama Community

Life as a foreigner in prewar Japan, writes Lucille Apcar, "did not differ much from life in the United States . . . [or] in any western country."[16] Apcar, born in 1926 in Yokohama to parents of Armenian descent, was indeed raised in a cosmopolitan setting complete with Western amenities. The Apcars were one of the wealthy Western families residing on the Bluff, which overlooked Motomachi, Yokohama's shopping district, business district, and waterfront (figs. 2.2 and 2.3). Lucille's father, Michael,

FIGURE 2.2 The Apcar home on the Bluff, 1923. Courtesy of Mimi Malayan.

ran A. M. Apcar and Company, an import-export and antique business that his own father had founded in the 1890s.[17] Though only steps away, the Bluff distinguished itself from residential areas for Asians. Its facilities and Victorian homes were the city's most modern. Most had indoor plumbing and septic systems, gas, electricity, heating, and telephones; its streets were paved and lined with sidewalks and streetlights. Accordingly, Lucille's mother, Araxe, describes the family's life there as a series of luncheons, dances, banquets, celebrations, and sporting events. Oblivious to the war in China, she and her cohort were also unalarmed by the worsening relations between Japan and the United States. Even when Japan froze American assets on March 20, 1941, and foreign embassies issued warnings urging their citizens to repatriate, the Apcars' lives continued as before. Michael dismissed fears that Japan would enter into a second

FIGURE 2.3 *Back row, from left:* Michael, Araxe, Diana, and Ruth Apcar, 1928. Courtesy of Mimi Malayan.

war, and, Araxe writes, "despite these gloomy forebodings my own life continued pleasantly enough. Through Winter to Summer of 1941 it was our busy time. The St. Maur picnic was held in April, the St. Joseph field day in June. I occupied myself with bridge and mahjong."[18]

Apcar's "busy" life was also exceptionally exclusive. Women formed an array of social circles such as sewing, knitting, and mahjong groups, and routinely entertained friends and neighbors at afternoon tea gatherings. Their women's club held additional events; churches offered regular functions; and the Yokohama Country and Athletic Club organized male and female sports teams. The Bluff also boasted a yacht club, the Boat House, along with the Yokohama Race Club, a horse-racing stable and track with a small golf course inside. Michael stabled horses at the race club and served as the official starter at club races. He was also an officer of the community's exclusive Masonic Order, an affiliation that would trigger his arrest and conviction for espionage during the war (discussed in chapter 4). Additionally, the neighborhood housed the private Foreigners' Cemetery, a Roman Catholic church, the Union Methodist Church, the Christ Episcopal Church, and a synagogue. The Bluff Hotel accommodated both long-term and temporary visitors.

Araxe's world afforded minimal contact with Japanese, and her children's only slightly more. Michael had attended Saint Joseph's International College on the Bluff, and he sent his own sons there. A Catholic boarding school established in 1901 to service Japan's largest Western population, Saint Joseph's boasted a diverse student body of about 120 students of multiple nationalities, including several Japanese. It offered ten years of classes and its degree was recognized in the United States.[19] Though the teachers were mostly French priests, the language of instruction was English and in principle the school refrained from proselytizing to non-Catholic students.[20] Catholic students attended catechism classes, while non-Catholics attended secular ethics classes.[21] Like most girls on the Bluff, Lucille was schooled at Saint Maur's Convent, run by French and Irish Roman Catholic nuns. The school was divided into a section for foreign girls and a larger section called Kōran Kōtō Jogakkō (Kōran Girls Higher School) for wealthy Japanese girls.[22] Lucille's classmates originated from Europe, the Americas, the Middle East, and South Asia. Classes were taught in English, but the girls also studied French; gym class was conducted in Japanese by a Japanese instructor.

Until the end of 1940, the Bluff also housed the Yokohama International School, run by a British minister who offered a British curriculum taught in English. Like Saint Joseph's and Saint Maur's, the international school gathered a diversity of nationalities and ethnicities beyond Americans and Europeans, including Russians, Chinese, Japanese, Middle Easterners, and South East Asians. Though students at all three schools spoke their native tongue at home, they studied and played together in English. As a result, many identified less with their native cultures and more with their school's language and culture. Most of these schools' Japanese students had lived abroad and had trouble reintegrating into the Japanese school system. Their presence helped foreign students learn Japanese on the side. A teenager in 1940, Julie Helm's eldest son, Donald (b. 1926), was friends with "Germans, Armenians, Australians, British, Russians, Americans, and Portuguese, but everybody spoke English and nobody cared what nationality their friends were." Yokohama, Leslie Helm writes, "was a place in which a family like the Helms could have brothers of German, Japanese, and American nationality and nobody found it . . . remarkable."[23]

When the Yokohama International School closed at the end of 1940, most of its students entered Saint Joseph's. Isaac Shapiro (b. 1931 in Tokyo) and his brothers commuted to the American School in Meguro (Tokyo) instead, which accepted foreign pupils of other nationalities. Its classes adhered to an American curriculum, were taught by American teachers, and began the day with the Pledge of Allegiance. Shapiro reports that students did not wear uniforms and that academically the school was less rigorous than the British curriculum at the Yokohama school. The commute from Yokohama proved too onerous, however, and after several months the boys transferred to Saint Joseph's. The sole remaining educational option was a Russian school that Shapiro's father suspected of being anti-Semitic.

The Shapiros' educational options were also limited by the fact that in principle Japanese schools were closed to foreigners. Neither side welcomed the prospect of Western children "going native." When the American engineer William R. Gorham (1888–1949) moved his family from Kyushu to Tokyo in 1926 to assume the position of chief engineer at Doa Denki National Industrial Production Company, for example, he had difficulty finding suitable schooling for his bilingual sons, then aged eleven and nine. Gorham judged their best option to be Seijo Gakuen, a prestigious, progressive school known for employing a more Western curriculum. Seijo's principal denied the boys admission, however. It was not that they were foreigners, he said; it was that they were Westerners. "We do not have confidence that we can educate the children of Europeans and Americans together with Oriental children," the principal explained. "We have not had any experience in this area."[24] In a rare exception to the standing practice of segregation, the school ultimately relented when it learned that the boys had, without recourse, attended Japanese school in Kyushu and become proficient in the spoken and written language. The boys' admission to Seijo compelled them to undergo the multiyear military training (*gunji kyōren*) mandatory for all middle and high school boys.[25]

News of the Tripartite Pact (1940) formalizing Japan's alliance with Germany and Italy reverberated through some sectors of the Yokohama community, but impacted relations between adults more than children. Even as the Nazi Party became more active and some German children joined the Hitler Youth, others showed no compunction about continuing to interact with Jewish schoolmates. After matriculating in Saint Joseph's, Isaac Shapiro and his brothers befriended a German boy who had been living in New York. In 1941, the boy's family was passing through Japan en route to Germany when the war commenced. With the Trans-Siberian Railway unusable and the seas too dangerous for civilian ships, the family was stranded. Though the boy was compelled to join the Hitler Youth organization and wear a swastika-emblazoned uniform, neither he nor his family was concerned about befriending the Shapiros, a family of White Russian Jews. Isaac's mother also taught piano to another member of the Hitler Youth whose family was equally disinclined toward anti-Semitism.[26] Despite their mixed blood, some of Donald Helm's cousins were permitted to join the Hitler Youth, a further indication of occasional racial leniency within children's circles.[27] The fact that the Helm children's parents were not accepted as equals on the Bluff suggests that Bluff society could, in this respect, be less racially tolerant than the local Nazi Party!

Indeed, children's race ambivalence often conflicted with their parents' sensibilities, for while some adults tolerated their children's Japanese playmates, many did not. Not only were the Helms' dark-skinned children subjected to unequal treatment at home, Julie beat Donald whenever he caught him speaking Japanese, or even a mixture of Japanese and English. "How well you spoke English was a critical determinant of class, and Julie was intent on making sure his kids could pass in the best society," Helm explains.[28] Girls were afforded even fewer opportunities to socialize with Japanese children, for although classes at Saint Joseph's were integrated, Saint Maur's segregated its Japanese and white students. Lucille Apcar affirms her parents' strictness on this point: "The Japanese and western population did not mingle freely or socialize," she recalls, "but unlike colonial countries the choice was mutual. As children we rode the streetcars, talked in Japanese and were treated politely wherever we went, but we never played with Japanese children nor did they visit our homes."[29]

Nationals from neutral countries were generally spared the ethnic intrigues triggered by Japan's alliance with Germany. While Germany assailed its expats with Nazi ideology and Allied nations responded with evacuation advisories, the Swiss couple Hans and Ethel Baenninger faced comparatively few ideological pressures. The memoir *In the Eye of the Wind*, written by their sons Ron and Martin and based on Hans's firsthand accounts, Ethel's meticulous diaries, and other primary sources, provides one of the most detailed accounts of Yokohama during the 1930s. Its portrayal of foreigner life during this period—"the sailing, the cocktail parties, the life of colonial ease, and the reassuring sense of superiority still maintained by expatriate foreigners"—corroborates details gleaned from the Apcars and the Helms.[30] Hans and Ethel met at the Yokohama Yacht Club in 1933 and married the following year. Max Pestalozzi, Arvid and Estelle Balk's future son-in-law, served as their best man. Ethel quit her secretarial job at Standard Oil, and the couple moved into a Western house on the Bluff, where they remained until 1942.

> The house on the Bluff sat amidst other similar stucco (or sometimes brick) houses, many half-timbered, with shutters and painted wooden trim. A paved street passed in front. The Erklenzes, who were Nazis, lived on the one side, and the Bjergfelts, a pleasant Danish couple, were neighbours on the other. Lawns with flowerbeds and trees surrounded the houses. Down the street, one could just see the steeple of the United Church. As in Saigon, Shanghai, and other colonial cities in the Far East, except for the calls of local peddlers, the exotic smells, and the beautiful tourist-brochure vistas . . . they might have been ensconced in a suburb of Chicago or London.[31]

Socializing at Western restaurants, bars, clubs, and movie theaters, and vacationing in the mountain resorts of Karuizawa and Hakone, their lifestyle was typical. Hans worked in town as a silk exporter for Charles Rudolph and Company. Ethel, formerly Canadian and a relative newcomer to Japan, joined the International Women's Club. "For Ethel, as for most foreigners," her sons write, "life in Japan was manageable as long as she could cover its strangeness with a cloak of familiarity, a cloak that hid the things she did not understand, or that made her afraid."[32] For her and Hans, social life was firmly rooted in the city's foreign clubs, particularly the yacht club, which regularly held sailing, rowing, swimming, shooting, darts, and card tournaments, along with dining, dancing, and other festivities.

Ethel's "cloak of familiarity" precluded interactions with Japanese, except for her household staff. The Japanese maids, cooks, nannies, and chauffeurs employed in nearly all Western households were expected to acquire a working knowledge of Western practices, skills that bolstered their currency within the community. When a family left Japan, its staff were in high local demand if they had learned to prepare Western cuisine and interact skillfully within a Western household. Despite the measured insularity, accounts consistently describe relationships with Japanese employees as warm and trusting.[33] Hans, whose ability to interact with his office staff without an interpreter distinguished him from other Western businessmen, maintained amicable relations with his Japanese coworkers. Despite the danger of openly socializing with Westerners, even the neutral Swiss, his Japanese colleagues at Charles Rudolph pooled their rations cards to throw him a farewell party when the family left Japan in 1942.

The Bluff was not the city's only Western settlement. As eastern Japan's busiest port city, Yokohama was a broadly multicultural municipality that accommodated several foreign neighborhoods. Honmoku, a coastal community south of the Bluff, was inhabited by Westerners of more modest means but who were nonetheless permitted use of the Bluff's hospital, churches, and schools. Its proximity to the beach attracted foreigners of all classes in the summer. Though the Helms had been Bluff residents from the beginning, Julius purchased property in Honmoku that became known as Helm Hill. From their residence there, a wooden staircase descended to Society Beach, where foreigners congregated in summers to recreate and socialize.[34] The Balk family lived in Honmoku between 1941 and 1944, as did their close friends Hans and Margot Ries and Heinz Lang. Isaac Shapiro, whose parents were poor musicians without the means to flee Japan prior to the war, also lived near the beach in Honmoku with his family, until they were evacuated to Tokyo in January 1944.[35]

Spatially and culturally, Western neighborhoods functioned independently of Yokohama's other prominent international group: its large Chinese community. Most of Yokohama's Chinese residents lived in Chinatown; those who did not resided in Japanese neighborhoods where they became integrated into Japanese *tonarigumi*. Over one-third of resident Chinese had opted to return to China following the outbreak of hostilities in 1937, but those who remained were generally left alone. In important contrast to enemy nationals from Western nations, they were neither deported nor interned during the war, and unlike Koreans and Taiwanese (Japanese colonial subjects, many of whom were voluntarily or forcefully brought to Japan as laborers), they retained their native citizenship.[36] Considered ethnically inferior, the city's Chinese population suffered myriad forms of racial discrimination. The Apcars' Japanese maids called them "evil," and Syd Duer relates how a guard at the Uchiyama internment camp had thought nothing of lopping off the heads of Chinese POWs while deployed on the mainland.[37]

Ornaments in Isolation: The Frank and Balk Families

Hugo and Ludy Frank's father, Louis Hugo Frank, had studied at Berlin University under the Nobel laureate physical chemist Walther Nernst, completing his PhD in chemical engineering with honors in 1909. He married Amy Lucy Fisher in 1912, and the following year accepted a teaching position at Otaru Commercial College (Otaru kōtō shōgyō gakkō) in Otaru, Hokkaido, becoming Japan's first instructor in the fields of commercial materials and commercial material experimentation. (Established in 1909, OCC was one of several commercial schools created by the Japanese government to train students in merchandizing and commerce for the purpose of bolstering Japanese international trade.) In 1913 Louis and Amy landed to a mixture of admiration and resentment. Though he carried impressive credentials and his field of expertise promised important applications for Japanese industrialization, his arrival corresponded to a period of swelling nationalism and disillusionment with the government's hapless efforts to elevate Japan's international standing.

The *Otaru shinbun* (Otaru newspaper) covered the Franks' arrival, presumably extending Louis the highest of compliments when it reported, "His hair is black and his eyes resemble those of Japanese, yet some of his features remind one of Napoleon. . . . His wife is a young beauty."[38] The newspaper's attention to the Franks' physical rather than cultural otherness reflected not only a central source of Japanese curiosity toward Westerners, but the irrepressible fetishization of race that underlay Japanese-Western relations. Cultural and linguistic barriers could be overcome; racial differences could not.

Only a year after the Franks' arrival, resident Germans, who composed about 37 percent of the entire Western workforce at this time, were rendered enemy nationals by the outbreak of World War I. No deportation policy was enacted, and in great contrast to the trauma the Franks would suffer during World War II, Japan's minimal involvement in the fighting prevented their German citizenship from becoming a source of serious concern.[39] For some Japanese, however, the European war exposed rifts and weaknesses in the edifice of Western power, reinforced nationalistic sentiments, and magnified conflicted opinions of Western residents. It also emboldened some who opposed the sorts of privileges being given to invited scholars like Louis Frank. In 1914 the *Otaru shinbun* issued a vitriolic article blasting foreign faculty as nothing more than luxury items, "high-class migrants" who received exorbitant salaries but provided their students with no direct benefit: "Putting it bluntly, they are ornaments, like precious scrolls hanging in the alcove. . . . We could easily buy five or six top Japanese scholars for the same price."[40]

The newspaper's complaint targeted Louis Frank but referred more generally to the long-standing practice of overpaying invited Western instructors. Its claims were not exaggerated. In 1874, ten such foreigners were receiving higher salaries than Prince Sanjō Sanetomi (1837–91), who held the position of grand minister of state (*daijō daijin*). And, when Tokyo Imperial University was founded in 1877, foreign instructor salaries accounted for a full third of its annual expenditures.[41] Otaru Commercial College president Watanabe Ryūsei was only following established practice, therefore, when he employed Louis at a salary higher than his own. Louis's annual salary in 1926, paid by the Ministry of Education, was 6,300 yen, nearly the same as that paid to the governor of Hokkaido.[42]

Despite conflicted public sentiment toward foreigners and the privileges they enjoyed, by all accounts the Franks were comfortable in Otaru. They occupied a newly built, two-story Western house overlook-

FIGURE 2.4 *Left to right:* Louis, Ludy, Amy, and Hugo Frank in Otaru, 1918.

ing Otaru's harbor. Hugo was born in 1915, and Ludwig (Ludy) two years later (fig. 2.4). Foreign friends from Sapporo and Otaru lent comradeship and cultural support, some visiting the Franks at their "summer quarters" in Ranshima, a coastal town west of Otaru. Meanwhile, Louis thrived at Otaru Commercial College. His chemistry and physics lectures, which he delivered in German-accented English, were popular but largely incomprehensible, requiring that other professors attend to serve as interpreters. In addition to creating a laboratory for teaching and conducting research on vapor pressure of liquids and fuel cells, Louis established a soap manufacturing laboratory at the school. When Crown Prince Hirohito (1901–89), the future Showa emperor, visited in 1922, Louis presented him with the school's signature Kōshō soap.[43]

It was the unavailability of Western education in Otaru that eventually compelled Louis and Amy to relocate. In 1924, when Hugo and Ludy were nine and seven, the family moved to the larger city of Sapporo and rented a spacious Western-style house with a large garden (fig 2.5 and fig. 2.6). Louis commuted the twenty miles to Otaru and the boys entered a private school for Japanese girls run by Wenzeslaus Kinold, a German Franciscan priest. Lessons at the school were taught by German

FIGURE 2.5 Louis (*back right*), Amy (*center*), Hugo (*front right*), and Ludy Frank (*front left*) with friends in Sapporo, 1920s.

FIGURE 2.6 Hugo (*left*) and Ludy Frank, Sapporo, 1920s.

nuns, who also gave the boys private lessons. The family soon found even Sapporo's educational offerings to be inadequate, however, and in 1926 decided to relocate closer to a better international school. They settled on Saint Joseph's College (fig. 2.7), where Hugo and Ludy, aged eleven and nine, would board ten months per year until their respective gradu-ations in 1932 and 1934 (fig. 2.8).[44] Once that decision was made, Louis, who over thirteen years at Otaru Commercial College had taught some five hundred students, sought new employment. He accepted a profes-sorship at Yamanashi Higher Industrial College (Yamanashi kōtō kōgyō gakkō) in Kōfu, Yamanashi, about one hundred miles west of Yokohama. There, Louis and Amy again occupied a large, Western two-story house near campus and employed a maid, Aizawa Haru. In summer they would now vacation in Karuizawa, a resort introduced to them by their friend Katō Taiji.[45]

With Louis Frank's arrival, Yamanashi Higher Industrial College established a department of chemical engineering. In addition to Ger-man, Louis taught electrochemistry (physical chemistry) and electrical

FIGURE 2.7 Saint Joseph International College, ca. 1935.

FIGURE 2.8 *Left to right:* Hugo, Louis, Amy, and Ludy Frank in Kamakura, 1934.

FIGURE 2.9 Louis Frank in his laboratory, Kōfu, 1938.

materials, both new fields in Japan (fig. 2.9). In the 1930s, militarism called for expansion of the nation's industrial infrastructure, and although Louis entertained no such intentions, some inevitably found indirect military applications for these fields of study. Soon other universities followed Yamanashi by creating programs based on Louis's work.[46]

Louis carved out a fine career in Kōfu and acquired a degree of local celebrity. He was venerated by his students, who of necessity conducted their studies in German or English.[47] He also published regularly and patented a process for neutralizing the odor of fish oils. In 1936 he received the Fifth Order of the Sacred Treasure Award (*Zuihō-shō*) from the Japanese government for his scientific achievements and service to Japanese education. At this time he was, according to Ministry of Education employee records, the highest-paid foreign instructor in the country.[48] Japanese domestic policy as yet betrayed no trace of anti-Semitic prejudice, but he and Amy took pains to allay undue suspicions. Both contributed articles to national newspapers, a shrewd diplomatic gesture welcomed by the Japanese media. In May 1929, Amy wrote supportive pieces for *Jiji shinpō* (Current events) and *Tokyo asahi shinbun* (Tokyo

Asahi newspaper) comparing the British and Japanese royal families, and the following January Louis wrote an opinion piece for the *Asahi* praising Japan's electoral system.[49] Later, in a newspaper article from November 30, 1938, about the Focke-Wulf Fw 200 Condor, the new German long-range patrol plane that had just arrived in Japan, Louis lauded the technical accomplishments of the two nations and expressed excitement that the plane would shorten flight times between them. The plane, the article predicted, was sure to enhance goodwill and further unite German and Japanese citizens.[50] Celebrity and pro-Japanese gestures of this sort help explain why Japanese authorities allowed Louis to continue teaching until 1943, long after his Jewishness had become a liability for his family and his school.

The Franks were atypical of German expats, for with the exception of missionaries and the language teachers employed at provincial schools, few Germans inhabited the Japanese countryside. Their close relations with Japanese colleagues and students certainly afforded them an altogether different sort of existence from that of their urban-based compatriots. Most Germans resided in the Tokyo-Yokohama or Osaka-Kobe regions, their respective communities united by organizations like the German East Asiatic Society (Doitsu Tōyō bunka kenkyū kyōkai, OAG) and the German Scholarly Exchange Association (Doku-Nichi gakujutsu kōryūkai, DAAD). Both were autonomous civilian organizations independent of the Nazi Party. Germans throughout Asia with an interest in studying Asian cultures did so through membership in the OAG. Many were intellectually inclined, had learned a bit of the native language, and voluntarily helped fund the organization. The DAAD oversaw German exchange students and connected them with the Japanese-German Cultural Society (Nichi-Doku bunka kyōkai) in Tokyo.[51] Japanese-German cultural exchange was also promoted through the German embassy, consulates, and the German Culture Research Institute (Dōitsu bunka kenkyūjo) in Kyoto, which worked to advance understanding and appreciation of German culture among Japanese. These organizations' concerted efforts benefited from a measure of historical favoritism. The Meiji oligarchs had looked favorably on Germany, opting to develop their own constitution, military, and educational system from Germanic models. Japanese had also responded to the fact that, as several sources assert, German residents made greater efforts than other Westerners to learn

Japanese and integrate into Japanese society. Their affinity for Japanese culture, Ueda Kōji and Arai Jun suggest, made Germans more flexible and open to Japanese customs and etiquette than other nationalities.[52] The organizations, and the German community generally, maintained friendly relations with other resident Europeans in the prewar period, though extensive study of their writings suggests less amicable relations with Americans, who are scarcely mentioned.[53]

The German community's solidarity was not immune to the racial strains intensifying in Europe. Despite the cases of leniency toward children already noted, by the late 1930s German Jews in Japan faced greater prejudice from their compatriots than from Japanese.[54] Such was the experience of Estelle and Arvid Balk, who arrived in Japan in 1934 and eight years later would become related to the Franks through marriage. The Balk family's centrality to the latter chapters of this study calls for a bit of backstory here.

Estelle Balk's unpublished manuscript, "An Outsider: The Story of a European Refugee in Japan during World War II" (ca. 1947), is a gripping record of wartime living conditions and provides exceptional insight into the emotional lives and race consciousness of Western civilians. Written in the early years of the occupation from the Balks' house in Gora (Hakone), it provides firsthand testimony of civilian wartime travails and details the Kenpeitai's (military police's) counterespionage campaign against foreign civilians. It also details life as a German Jew within that community. Produced soon after her husband Arvid's release from thirteen months of interrogation, torture, and imprisonment, it remains openly disdainful toward the Japanese police, the German community, and even Hugo Frank, whom she blames for her husband's arrest and persecution. But what the manuscript loses in objectivity is more than redeemed by the clarity with which it illuminates the desperation and racial antipathy that defined the expat experience.

Estelle was born around 1898 in Berlin to the prominent German physicist Dr. Heinrich Rubens, a nonpracticing Jew and friends with such intellectual luminaries as Albert Einstein and Max Planck. Her mother, Marie Hirschfeld Rubens (1875–1941), of whom she writes little, was born in London but raised in Germany, and was instrumental in forging Estelle's aristocratic sensibilities. Class was a conspicuous concern during Estelle's childhood in Berlin, where her parents intently limited her associations to peers from her own socioeconomic and intellectual standing. Estelle's own prejudices derived more from class consciousness than race, an outlook readily apparent from innumerable exhortations like "I can't bear common people, never could get along with them."[55] Within the family's exclusive intellectual circle, ethnicity was less a source of scrutiny than social status. Referring to the absence of anti-Semitism among Germany's "wealthy families of good standing and culture" during her parents' generation, it was unremarkable that her parents married, she writes, for "racial discrimination was unknown in those days."[56] Apparently the racial tolerance espoused by her parents' generation eventually deteriorated, for Estelle, fully Jewish, confesses to anti-Semitism herself. "I wonder if it is clever to say here that no one is more anti-Semitic than the Jew himself," she reflects. "We, the cultured, educated people of this race most certainly keep away from the eastern filth as flooded Western Europe. We have no relation whatsoever with their customs and Jewish learning, their dirt, their bright coloured oriental clothing or their ancient caftans."[57] As a German Jew she elevates herself fundamentally above non-German Jews, an ironic vote of solidarity with Nazi claims to racial superiority. If racial prejudice was to be the normative means of legitimizing Germany's wartime social order, then she too, as a German aristocrat, would deploy it as a means of self-validation.

In 1916, Estelle married Dr. Werner Pischel, son of a university professor and thus "one of us."[58] The marriage yielded two daughters, Marie-Elise (1917?–2008) and Irene (1918–2011), but was an unhappy union. While separated from Werner, in 1928 Estelle met Arvid Balk (fig. 2.10) on a cruise to Norway. Also married, Arvid was a German newspaper reporter born in Estonia; the two immediately developed a close bond. Four years later they finalized their divorces, married, and moved to Breslau, Germany (currently Wroclaw, Poland). Several months later, in January 1933, the world watched as Hitler seized power and commenced his anti-Semitic crusade. Einstein had fled Germany a month before, and by October had taken permanent asylum in the United States. As Europe grew less safe, Jews with the means and foresight to do so followed Einstein's example. Arvid had made life difficult for himself professionally by marrying a Jewish wife, though Estelle had become a Lutheran during her first marriage. Violence against Jewish residents in Breslau forced them back to Berlin, but with anti-Semitic restrictions escalating throughout

FIGURE 2.10 Arvid Balk, 1934.

Germany they saw little recourse other than to flee Europe. A well-known journalist, Arvid hoped to use his reputation and connections as a freelance correspondent in Japan. His curriculum vitae from 1933, submitted as part of his application for travel documents, also exhibits the racial defensiveness and class consciousness of German high society. It describes Arvid's mother as "descended from the oldest and most distinguished patrician family of the Balticum," and his wife, Estelle, as "the daughter of one of the most celebrated physicists [in] Germany."[59] Travel documents in hand, Arvid and Estelle fled Germany, leaving Marie-Elise and Irene with Estelle's parents to finish school. After a stop in London, their Japanese ship carried them through the Mediterranean to Egypt—a land of "ragged brown people"—India, Hong Kong, and Shanghai, landing in Tokyo in March 1934.[60]

The Balks arrived unemployed and without social status, a position to which they were unaccustomed. Arvid himself was no political refugee, however, for although he was not a fan of the Hitler regime, he nonetheless remained loyal to Germany and retained the support of certain German authorities. He and Estelle received Christmas greetings from Crown Prince Wilhelm (1889–1951) in December 1936, to which he responded with a lengthy letter of thanks wherein he emphatically expresses their love and loyalty to Germany. The letter discusses in favorable terms the Japanese-German Anti-Comintern Pact signed a month earlier, and mentions that the German minister for national propaganda and national enlightenment had released Arvid's assets and credit line in Germany, making them available to him in Tokyo.[61]

Arvid set about establishing himself as a freelance journalist selling stories on Japanese culture and politics to European newspapers. His business, the German Asiatic Press Service, was prolific, publishing 231 articles between July 1935 and June 1936. As a foreign journalist he attracted the scrutiny of the Foreign Ministry, which required that he periodically submit lists detailing the dates, titles, and publishers of his articles. In a July 23, 1936, letter to the ministry, Arvid describes his articles as generating "very much interest in my homeland" and helping "to build the bridge of mutual understanding between Germany and Japan."[62] The diplomacy and deference of Arvid's language here echo Louis Frank's newspaper submission in 1938, revealing the delicacy with which both men interacted with state authorities.

By all accounts, the Balks were well treated by the Japanese during the 1930s. Affable correspondence between Arvid and the Foreign Ministry confirms warm relations. The ministry invited Arvid to social events to meet government officials to whom he needed access, and even provided him with theater tickets, the sort of goodwill gesture that Japanese authorities also extended to other members of the foreign press. Arvid's December 1936 letter to the crown prince notes that at a ceremony at the Japanese War Ministry, the ministry had given Estelle a pearl necklace in appreciation for Arvid's efforts to unite and further the two countries' mutual understanding.[63] Japanese congeniality toward Westerners is also evident from Estelle's account of the momentous February 26 Incident, the coup d'état in 1936 wherein 1,400 army officers and soldiers attempted to wrest control of the government. The Balks' house in Ochanomizu, she writes, was next door to army officers' barracks, and on the night of the attack they heard shooting and shouting. She was indifferent to the event itself and relates nothing of it, but does note that officers on guard in the street outside their house that evening knocked "politely" on their door to ask for hot tea and to borrow their coal brazier to warm themselves.[64] The manuscript makes no mention of anti-Semitic or prejudicial treatment by the Japanese whatsoever during the 1930s.

In fact, Japan's alliance with Germany afforded Estelle and Arvid a measure of uncritical prestige. For as Germany assumed the dominant position in this unlikely relationship, it not only spread its own nationalist propaganda within Japan but urged Japanese authorities to follow suit. As Estelle writes, "The pupil had to be educated to see through the eyes of the teacher what was good for him. It was the perfect combination of flattery and hypnotic teaching that the exponents of Germany worked on the Japanese, cleverly using their native nationalistic tendencies and conceited racial complexes to their own German benefits."[65] The ironic outcome was that Japanese were subjected to a relentless diet of rhetoric insisting on the racial superiority of "Aryan" Germans, but also on the racial superiority of Japanese.

The importance of this partnership was communicated emphatically to the Japanese public, and the superficiality with which they embraced rhetoric from both countries mirrored the superficial kindness with which they interacted with Westerners. People asked foreigners if they were German, following the question with expressions of admiration for Germans. Estelle writes,

> The simplest folks . . . asked if you were German. Oh, is that so, we love the Germans. Hitora is a great man. The Japanese like puns and their pronunciation of Hitler [sounds like] Hitora, which means "Fire tiger." There

were only the Germans who counted. It was Germany where Japanese artists, students, officers, politicians went to study, [and Germans] were eating up the sweet pie of national socialistic propaganda [doled] out to them with the silver spoon of flattery in big mouthfuls. . . . Very charming indeed, I admit, and I enjoyed it immensely, especially the polite and courteous way the Japanese officials as well as the simple class people treated the foreigners.[66]

Wartime nationalism required that Japanese recognize Germany as their principal ally and the Western locus of their greatest admiration. Yet, as Estelle, Ludy, and others attest, Japanese amity included no interest in discriminating between Nazi Germans and Jewish Germans. Nationality alone bore importance, as racial subdivisions had little place within "the happy unconcern of the simple folks" for whom the war consisted mainly of bidding farewell to conscripted husbands, brothers, and sons, and contending with shortages.[67] Anti-Semitism, therefore, was fueled more by the German than the Japanese community, and the Balks found their compatriots nearly as racially divided as the Europe they had fled. Arvid competed with other German correspondents and news agencies for news about social and political developments, but as a nonparty member was regularly denied the connections, access to information, and cooperation that the German embassy afforded others. Half-German and Jewish, Estelle was also eschewed by the community, which she describes as divided between Jews and everyone else. Many Germans declined to socialize with or even enter the houses of German Jews, leaving the latter little recourse other than to form their own social enclave. Estelle and Arvid were not fully accepted by either group, however. "We were just nobody, stayed nobody, were outcasts from the day we set foot on this island," Estelle laments. "The German colony had been informed of our coming, had also been informed of my racial disquality, and acted accordingly."[68] To this extent, although relocating to Japan had improved their professional prospects, it had not appreciably broadened their associations with their compatriots.

Being German, however, afforded Estelle the opportunity to work briefly as a secretary for Natori Yōnosuke, a photographer and publisher of the magazine *Nippon* (Japan) who had studied in Germany and taken a German wife. The magazine, Estelle writes, was full of nationalistic propaganda, and "for a white woman it is hard to work under a Japanese boss . . . [and] I had never had a job before and don't seem to have the right mentality for one anyway."[69] Racial pride also soured her relationship with Natori's wife, Erna. To her mind, Erna bowed to the "deplorable and humiliating" practice of ingratiating herself to her in-laws, learning Japanese, and adapting to Japanese customs.[70] Estelle had no such intention. Given her marginalized ethnicity and the stubbornness with which she clung to her own racial pretensions, it is no surprise that after several years Estelle remained highly uncomfortable in Japan. She continued to refer to Japan as alien and its food as foreign, her dislocation from Japanese cementing her dependence on an insular foreign community that rejected her.

In 1936 the Balks moved to the coastal town of Hayama, thirteen miles from Yokohama, but financial hardship soon forced their return to Germany. Estelle was elated to return but also horrified by what Germany had become. Life for her daughters, still living with her mother in Berlin, was becoming more difficult. Marie-Elise was a secretary and Irene still in school, but as half Jews they were legally marginalized, socially excluded, and without prospects. Arvid, in danger of being arrested by the Gestapo, stayed only two months to renew his newspaper contracts before returning to Japan alone. After nine months Estelle and Irene departed from Berlin on the Trans-Siberian Railway, returning to Japan in 1938.

The family rented a house on the ocean in the Yokohama neighborhood of Masaka, where they lived in relative comfort for the next three years. Estelle continued to struggle with insularity while also noting greater opportunities for interactions with Yokohama's Western community. She joined the International Women's Club. Irene took riding lessons at the country and athletic club, the hub of high society, and found work as a personal assistant in an engineering firm. In 1941, Arvid returned briefly to Berlin to renew his contracts and retrieve Marie-Elise, then living with his sister in London. After reuniting in Beijing and returning to Japan, the Balks, now a family of four, moved into a larger house near the beach in Honmoku just below an antiaircraft battery. Finally situated within a cohort of non-German friends, they settled into the sort of social circle that Estelle had long missed. Employing a cook, washerwoman, gardener, and two maids, they were "living in ease and

FIGURE 2.11 Marie-Elise and Max Pestalozzi, ca. 1943.

growing prosperity at last."[71] But circumstances were deteriorating. One by one Estelle's American and British friends all left Japan. War between Germany and Russia commenced on June 23, 1941, severing railway and mail communications with Europe and forcing Arvid to communicate with Germany by telegraph. Intensifying hostility from other Germans lent greater precariousness to Arvid's journalistic activities. Wishing to maximize the family's prospects, Estelle sought husbands for her daughters whose pedigree would help mitigate their Jewishness. Irene had met Ludy Frank at the international club in Yokohama. They had dated and he had proposed. Like her, Ludy was German and half-Jewish, though he had converted to Roman Catholicism while at Saint Joseph's. Estelle initially opposed the marriage to Ludy, which would require that Irene convert to Catholicism but would not save her from anti-Semitism.[72] Ludy was also comparatively poor. Nonetheless, Irene was baptized on April 4, 1942, and the two were married a week later. Marie-Elise married the Swiss Red Cross delegate Max Pestalozzi in January 1943 (fig. 2.11).[73]

Class Insularity at Western Resorts

As sites of class insularity, an examination of Western resorts will help to qualify and contextualize our discussion of the racial insularity experienced by the Yokohama community, the Franks, and the Balks. In the late nineteenth century, Karuizawa, a mountain town 120 miles west of Tokyo, became one of the first such protoresorts, so selected for its accessibility and favorable summer climate. Then a rustic stop on the former Nakasendō Highway, Karuizawa was first documented by a German doctor visiting in 1877 and first touted as a potential summer retreat in 1881 by the British scholar-diplomat Ernest Satow (1843–1929). Satow described the spot as a beautiful plateau lying at a comfortable 3,270 feet, an ideal destination for hiking, plant viewing, and escaping oppressive summer temperatures. It attracted more foreigners thereafter. The completion of a railroad between Tokyo and Karuizawa in 1893 greatly facilitated access, though trains took up to seven hours to cover the distance. The 1899 treaty revisions lifted travel prohibitions, prompting greater numbers of Westerners to explore the countryside. "Summering," the Western aristocratic practice of escaping to the cool breezes and panoramas of select mountain resorts, was thus introduced to Japan. Missionaries in particular sought sites to hold mission conventions, but also sites that were pleasant, private, and conducive to recreation.

Much of the land in central Karuizawa was subsequently purchased by Western missionaries who established the site as a venue for summer mission conferences. Until the 1920s, when wealthy Japanese discovered the pleasures of vacationing there, Karuizawa's center consisted largely of cabins and clubs built by missionaries for use during the hot summer months. The town's popularity among this contingent is evident from the fact that none of the 140,000 casualties from the Great Kantō earthquake (September 1, 1923) were Christian missionaries; all had since vacated the city for Karuizawa.[74]

Landholders generally constructed their villas within the town center, either on the town's main street or on side streets in close proximity. Many of the larger residences were owned by diplomats and wealthy foreign businessmen, but 75–80 percent of the foreign villas in Karuizawa belonged to missionaries and delegates to the Federation of the Christian Missions convention held there annually. In 1913, Westerners also formed the Karuizawa Summer Residents' Association (KSRA), which three years later became a legally incorporated foundation (*zaidan hōjin*). Although not a religious organization, it did conduct activities that supported the various churches and missions.[75] Missionaries exerted considerable administrative control over the township, establishing Christian practices like closing businesses on Sundays. Japanese stores opting not to comply risked losing customers.[76] But beyond missionary activities, summering in Karuizawa afforded other attractions, as Rev. Arthur Lloyd (1852–1911) reported:

> Grocers, butchers, and other tradesmen from Tokyo go up for the summer, and, greatest boon of all, there is generally a dressmaker's establishment in the village. Karuizawa's most numerous summer residents are country missionaries, and missionary ladies from out-of-the-way towns in remote districts, where no other Europeans are to be found, have opportunities of replenishing their wardrobes and re-furbishing their bonnets and gowns, which, being human, they enjoy to the full. Karuizawa is a longed-for oasis in many a lonely life at a missionary outpost, and the two summer months in its fresh, cool air have saved many a man and woman from a mental and spiritual breakdown.[77]

Westerners were thus instrumental in shaping the appearance and feel of the community, fashioning a setting that would serve as a surrogate for their homelands. Interacting with friends and other foreigners and frequenting foreign shops in close proximity became antidotes to isolation. Children, too, formed tight but ethnically diverse friendships. Foreign bookstores, antique shops, barbers, Christian churches, hotels, and car and bicycle rentals dominated the townscape around Main Street (fig. 2.12). Recreational offerings were also oriented toward Western tastes. To natural attractions like flower viewing, hot springs, and hiking, the community added tennis courts, a nine-hole golf course, and skiing and skating facilities. The villas themselves were Western: spacious two-story wooden structures with open verandas and roofless patios. Most had no shutters, no insulation, no fences, and little decoration. Simple, rustic, and shaded by trees, they were constructed expressly for summer occupancy by those wishing to recreate outdoors.[78]

FIGURE 2.12 Downtown Karuizawa, Taishō period.

Karuizawa's Western ambience and administrative influence did not forge a culture of exclusivity, however. In the 1920s, when more Japanese adopted the practice of summering, the town grew. By 1930 the proportion of foreign-owned residences dropped from a majority to about one-third, and the number of Japanese vacationing in Karuizawa exceeded the number of foreigners.[79] Most were wealthy Japanese associated with either Western businesses or Christian churches. Others sought such associations. As more Japanese built on outlying plots, the town was transformed into a Western residential and commercial district surrounded by Japanese neighborhoods.[80] Despite this residential division, the settlement itself made efforts to foster Japanese-Western inclusivity. Careful to define itself as an integrated cosmopolitan community, it developed as a multiracial aristocratic enclave.

KSRA operations guided this assimilation. Though formed by Westerners, the association did not exclude Japanese members, and as the town became more racially balanced and collaborative, the association followed suit. This spirit of kinship was formalized in bylaws and articulated in the association's bilingual handbook (1930). The handbook began by affirming the association as an alliance of Japanese and non-Japanese residents with "the purpose of promoting the welfare and contributing to the pleasure of all persons spending the summer in Karuizawa."[81] The KSRA would oversee public events, public affairs, and function to promote "international friendship among the residents of Karuizawa."[82] It also administered the Karuizawa Foreigners' Cemetery, one facility that remained strictly segregated. Additionally, the association founded the Mutual Protective Association, "an organization of cottage-holders desirous of extending help to one another," created "to help one another financially in case of loss or damage to property or fire."[83] Such initiatives constituted institutional and practical precedents for mutual self-help between foreigners and Japanese, an ideal that distinguished 1930s Karuizawa from the exclusive Western communities in Yokohama and elsewhere.

Through the mid-1930s, between 1,500 and 1,600 foreigners and 8,000 and 9,000 Japanese vacationed in Karuizawa each summer, and despite the economic depression, villa construction continued. In 1937 the number of private villas peaked at 1,454. Of these 1,116 (77 percent) were Japanese-owned, a ratio consistent with the racial demographics of Karuizawa visitors without properties. Summer traffic between Tokyo and Karuizawa was so heavy that additional train and even airplane services were provided. Facilities were also expanded to accommodate this flood of vacationers, and by decade's end the town boasted a developed recreational infrastructure: two golf courses, three Western-style luxury hotels, multiple tennis courts, horse stables, a race track, car and bicycle rentals, parks, and museums, as well as markets, public baths, and a range of commercial establishments. Its summer tennis tournament was advertised nationally in newspapers and magazines, and in 1940 a new rail line was opened between Shin-Karuizawa and the hot springs resort of Kusatsu.[84] One was just as apt to come across colleagues and acquaintances in Karuizawa during the summer as in Tokyo or Yokohama the rest of the year. The American journalist Wilfrid Fleisher's (1897–1976) description of encountering and enjoying conversations with the Soviet ambassador, the Turkish ambassador, and the French secretary, all picnicking with their families at a lake near Karuizawa, was certainly a common occurrence.[85]

Karuizawa was not prewar Japan's only foreign resort. Western missionaries were active in establishing summer communities at other sites they deemed accessible, suited to outdoor activities, and sufficiently elevated to escape the summer heat. Takayama (near Sendai) and Lake Nojiriko (northwest of Karuizawa) met these requirements, and by the 1920s missionaries had begun to purchase land and build villas there.[86]

Japan's summer resorts also attracted guests from overseas. Unzen (near Nagasaki), easily accessible from the Asian mainland, attracted 485 Western vacationers in 1932 alone. Only about 10 percent of these resided in Japan, the remainder being diplomats from Shanghai, Tianjin, Beijing, and Hong Kong. The hot springs resort of Beppu in eastern Kyushu also attracted international tourists. In 1932, about two hundred, including many Russians, visited in hopes of reaping the therapeutic benefits of its mud baths. Such destinations also became popular venues for conventions and meetings. In all cases, resort tourism stimulated and diversified the local economy, and Japanese eagerly developed the facilities and service industries necessary to maintain a robust influx of Western tourists.[87] In striking contrast to the Yokohama community, the exclusiveness of these country club settings lay less in racial bias than in the desire of Japanese and Western elites to create cosmopolitan spheres of privilege.

Beyond such spheres, the seemingly insurmountable separation between Westerners and less privileged Japanese derived largely from a sense of being, at best, misunderstood and unappreciated, and at worst hated. That is, it entailed an assault on national and personal identity. As many have shown, demonstrations of disrespect from the West had angered Japanese for generations.[88] Interestingly, resident Westerners insulated themselves from Japanese society for the same reasons, namely as a means of warding off assaults on their national and personal identities. Within their native societies, individuals tend to self-identify through such traits as occupation, creed, gender, lineage, and personal accomplishments. Race also factors into this list. Irene Frank, Estelle Balk, and several other memoirists note that Japanese identified Westerners only racially. If so, then Japanese generally failed to recognize Westerners' occupations, creeds, and other critical sources of self-identification. Recognition solely as Caucasian failed to acknowledge their identities as individuals, a personal affront that some understood as proof of Japanese ignorance—the latter's inability to understand and appreciate Westerners' complexities as individuals. It was also an affront that reduced cross-cultural relations, and indeed the entire expat experience, to a purely racial affair. Members of Western enclaves tended to share a sense of kinship with others bearing an equivalent socioeconomic status, an affinity that often superseded racial barriers. Doing so protected individual identity. Failure to shield one's ethnic or racial identity from external derision elicited powerful existential consequences. Leslie Helm, part Japanese, and Estelle Balk, Jewish, both write of "being nobody," of the permanent estrangement they experienced as "outcasts" and "outsiders" unaccepted by any racial group. Mutual exclusion was a source of outrage for Estelle, who confesses resentment toward the Japanese for her estrangement. It was the mutuality of racial discrimination, the glimpses of Japanese ethnocentrism paralleling her own, that she found intolerable. The mere possibility of a flipped worldview in which Westerners occupied an inferior power position was an insufferable personal affront and an ongoing source of resentment. Reminders that Japanese tend to place less value on how individuals stand out and more on how they "stand in" were little comfort. Collectively, memoirs from this era convey a clear sense that, within a society so reliant on classifications and distinctions, race was the foreigner's singular means of self-identification. Racial ambiguities—being biracial, for example—placed one in danger of the sort of alienation suffered by the Helms and the Balks. Foreigners thus sought communities wherein they could recover and reassert those existential complexities, where their occupations, origins, families, and accomplishments would retain meaning.

The inclusiveness variously embraced by members of the Yokohama community, the disparate cross-cultural experiences of the Franks and Balks, and the culture of assimilation characterizing the administration of Karuizawa are important case studies that lend complexity to our understanding of race relations in prewar Japan. In many ways this coexistence reaffirmed a colonial power structure. Bluff residents occupied the choice environs in Yokohama, the highlands overlooking the Asian sprawl below, and summered at the best beaches and mountain resorts; they hired Japanese house staff that purchased their food, clothing, and other necessities; they employed Japanese clerical workers in their companies; they were generally wealthy and educated and carried an aristocratic sense of entitlement that they reciprocated with noblesse oblige toward others. From birth to death, families like the Apcars and the Helms were self-sufficient and insulated from Japanese society. They attended the same schools, churches, and clubs; bore children and received medical care in the foreign hospital; and were buried in the foreign cemetery. They read English newspapers and watched foreign films at the downtown cinema. Most never learned to speak Japanese or eat Japanese food, a fact that indicates patent disinterest in the native language and culture. Lucille Apcar describes their insularity from Japanese as mutually generated and mutually desirable: "Snobbery," she writes, "if that is the word to use, existed on both sides of the fence."[89] Indeed, Japanese curiosity about Westerners rarely resulted in extensive knowledge of Western languages or cultures, and in this respect Japanese tended to reflect the racial attitudes that Westerners brought to Japan. Both found racial insularity an implicit necessity, and both accepted it as a natural marker of incontrovertible difference. This generally stable arrangement maintained a mutually accepted racial status quo that for most Japanese rarely elicited antiforeign sentiment or racial hatred. This status quo, however, would soon be destabilized by war in the Pacific.

CHAPTER 3

Handling the Other Within

Approaches to Preemptive Containment (1939–41)

> Considering that Japan was at war, the policy of the Japanese government toward foreigners living in Japan was an anomaly. Even though foreigners were often looked upon as spies, in many cases they were treated better than the Japanese themselves. They were afforded a freedom that would have been unthinkable in any other country in similar circumstances.
>
> —George Sidline[1]

As Japan faced the prospect of war against Western powers, it also confronted questions surrounding the containment of Western residents. Not only did those individuals pose potential risks to national security but, as reminders of the racial invectives cast at Japan over the years, their mere presence was a source of irritation. The Western community's diversity of nationalities and professions precluded the state's ability to adopt any single set of overarching principles or policies by which to formulate a coherent containment program, however. As a result, Westerners incurred radically different forms of treatment. Long-term Japan resident Wilfrid Fleisher, editor of the English-language newspaper *Japan Advertiser* and friend of U.S. ambassador Joseph C. Grew (1880–1965), did not hesitate to describe mid-1941 Japan as a police state. "Freedom of speech has long since disappeared and no one dares express any opinion either publicly or privately," he wrote that year. "Telephone lines are known to be tapped, the contents of wastepaper baskets closely investigated, and no one utters a word without first glancing over his shoulder to see who may be listening or who may be near."[2] Fleisher's colleagues within the foreign press record similar forms of police harassment: officers searched their garbage for incriminating documents, watched their homes, and noted the identities of any houseguests; waiters at the American Club recorded their conversations and even their seating arrangements at meals. Other Westerners noticed little evidence of containment and even extolled life in prewar Japan. Arriving in Kobe in March 1941, Jewish refugee Samuel Iwry (1910–2004) was welcomed with free housing and spending money. Soon thereafter, a group of Japanese bearing food, gifts, and flags of the Star of David appeared at his house to welcome him. "Never, never was anybody mistreated here, or even heard a loud voice, while I was in Japan," he wrote. "I never felt enmity from the Japanese during those days."[3]

The disparate experiences of Fleisher and Iwry are emblematic of Japan's contrived, contextual response to the other within, the result being a succession of preemptive measures devised to enable authorities to address problems as they arose. Containment would include a combination of new regulations, some aimed at foreigners specifically, that empowered government, military, and police forces while curtailing private organizations and individual freedoms. These statutes were then validated by rhetorical attempts to instill public fear and suspicion of non-Axis Caucasians. If race was to factor into containment, however, it would do so as a strategic tool, not as a pretext for hatred.

This chapter begins to outline these strategies through a review of the laws, policies, and propaganda directed at foreigners. Of particular interest will be the extent to which imperial Japan's containment measures subjected resident Westerners to forms of institutional racism, or "a system of advantage based on race."[4] Institutional racism employs an array of structures that assign power positions and create material interests around racial prejudice. The 1942 curfew and subsequent internment of individuals of Japanese ancestry in the western United States, for example, were racist structures in that they targeted a specified race rather than specified enemy nationals. After reviewing forms of direct and indirect containment, we shall examine the extent to which the state's spiritual mobilization initiatives attempted to incite public paranoia and antiforeign sentiment. Many of these were effective in constraining foreigners' ability to work and live comfortably. Others, particularly rhetorical efforts to instill xenophobia, were not entirely convincing and achieved minimal traction. Next we discuss Japan's handling of "the Jewish problem," particularly its treatment of Jewish refugees in 1940–41. The state's pragmatic and variable handling of these refugees will then lend context to discussion of its movement against the Christian Church as a means of suppressing Western influence.

Direct and Indirect Forms of Containment

Japan's various police forces became its first line of direct containment. From the 1920s through 1945, police assumed such a broad array of duties that in many cases it was they rather than politicians that represented political authority for the Japanese public.[5] The Ministry of Justice (Shihishō) afforded three administratively separate forces—civil police, Kenpeitai (military police), and Tokubetsu Kōtō Keisatsu (Special higher police), or Tokkō—with maximal discretion and minimal accountability in interpreting and enforcing laws. Civil police, including prefectural police and their various branches and detachments, were overseen by the Police Bureau of the Interior Ministry (Naimushō keihokyoku) and assumed broad regulatory authority over labor, construction, transportation, media censorship, political activities, and business activities. They also issued the growing number of permits required to hold public activities.[6] Surveillance and arrests of foreigners in Kanagawa Prefecture were carried out by the Foreign Affairs Section (Gaijika) of the Kanagawa Prefectural Police Department (Kanagawa-ken keisatsubu, or Kenkei) and the Kenpeitai.

The Kenpeitai had been established in 1881 and assumed collaborative responsibilities with the Ministry of War (Rikugunshō), the Interior Ministry, and the Ministry of Justice. It was through responsibilities to the last two that it assumed civilian policing functions. In the 1930s, the military's growing power and involvement in Japanese politics led to an expansion of Kenpeitai responsibilities, including surveillance of students, laborers, intellectuals, and others whom they perceived to threaten the public order. General Tōjō Hideki (1884–1948) served as the Kenpeitai commander in Manchuria from 1935 to 1937 prior to serving as prime minister from 1941 to 1944.[7] His continuing allegiances to the military and Kenpeitai helped bring a culture of militarism to Japanese political circles and lent the Kenpeitai a license to operate with near-complete impunity.

In addition to its standard counterintelligence, espionage, and "peace preservation" duties, the Kenpeitai also policed POW camps, issued travel permits, regulated transportation of food and supplies, and organized labor parties. It also administered over the comfort women forced to serve Japanese troops, as well as maintained a broad network of civilian informants, including the maids and servants employed in the households of foreigners. Kenpeitai headquarters (kenpei shireibu) received orders from the Japanese military—and, from April 1941, unofficial orders from Nazi Gestapo chief Josef Meisinger (1899–1947)—relaying those orders to local branches and their respective detachments. (It would be the Hakone detachment, a subsection of the Yokohama Kenpeitai, that arrested Hugo Frank and Arvid Balk in 1944.) Postwar records indicate a wartime force of 10,679 Kenpeitai within Japan and smaller contingents deployed in sixteen locations throughout Asia.[8]

The Tokkō, often referred to by foreigners as the "thought police," was established in 1911 to oversee civilian political activities. It collaborated with the Kenpeitai on surveillance and acted to curtail political activism, political crimes, and espionage. Occasionally these overlapping responsibilities resulted in jurisdictional conflict between the two bodies.[9] Like the Kenpeitai, the Tokkō included a department for foreigner surveillance and a separate section for monitoring the Korean population.[10] Under the Public Security Preservation Law (Chian ijihō) of 1925, which prohibited any sort of public organization or gathering construed as political in nature, the Tokkō assumed greater oversight over daily activities. The law's brevity and ambiguity allowed for broad interpretation and discretion, and through the 1930s became useful as a means of suppressing public meetings and leftist groups. The National Defense Security Law, promulgated on March 6, 1941, granted Tokkō officers considerable autonomy in carrying out surveillance. Later that year the Public Security Preservation Law was revised to allow the Tokkō broader authority to persecute individuals and groups, including religious groups that it felt challenged state interests. Publication and newspaper censorship laws prohibited certain inflammatory content but were also open to wide interpretation by the Tokkō, which the Interior Ministry allowed to assume censorship responsibilities. Tokkō officers took these latitudes even further, adopting illegal operating procedures like entering private residences without permits and arbitrarily issuing warnings to newspaper publishers without ministry approval. Elise Tipton asserts that it regularly used torture to acquire the evidence it needed to prosecute suspects, and that it arrested and held suspects without sufficient evidence to justify such seizures. It also held suspects in custody beyond the legal time limit by releasing and simultaneously rearresting them, or releasing them at a different police station, where they were immediately rearrested. In this way they managed to detain suspects for years without formal indictments.[11] Officers often worked undercover. Given its responsibilities to investigate thought crimes, communist activities, and espionage, the Tokkō was naturally interested in the activities of foreigners. Westerners' accounts often refer to Kenpeitai but rarely to the Tokkō, however, indicating that they knew little of its existence or had difficulty identifying its undercover officers.

The collective strength of the three police forces was necessitated by disorganization and weakness at the top. French correspondent Robert Guillain describes Japan's wartime leadership as politically and procedurally flying by the seat of its pants. Beset by ongoing factionalism among the political parties and the military, the state lacked clear objectives and occasionally even the support it needed to actualize vague objectives. Difficulties establishing broad support for any single principle or party rendered resolutions and promises meaningless and attempts to pilot the war effort chaotic. Propelled by a comedy of errors and misunderstandings, Guillain maintains, the trajectory of Japan's war management became "a shambles" and assumed a life of its own.[12] Weakness at the top ultimately necessitated that those in the middle—commanding officers on battlefields abroad and police officers on the streets at home—assume greater initiative. To a great extent, aggressive policing camouflaged the state's factionalism and disorganization. Guillain himself claims to have been watched by police from five separate offices: a uniformed civil policeman, a plainclothes officer from the "special anti-spy police," "secret political police" (Tokkō) from the Interior Ministry, a police officer assigned specifically to monitor members of the foreign press corps, and Kenpei-tai.[13] "In the final analysis," he writes, "real power was in the hands of the police."[14]

In 1941 the state stepped up retrenchment with several laws directly targeting foreigners. These were largely preemptive measures that afforded authorities greater latitude in case of war. The National Defense Security Law promulgated in March 1941 was designed to function in conjunction with the National General Mobilization Law (*Kokka sōdōin-hō*, 1938, discussed later) to place national security and national mobilization in ideological alignment. Enacted to safeguard the regime's interests and to authorize enforcement of those interests, the law gave the government and police broad powers to guard against espionage and subversive activities, and to prevent leakage of "state secrets": sensitive military, economic, industrial, and diplomatic information. It also prescribed punishments ranging from three years' imprisonment to capital punishment for individuals convicted of espionage.[15]

The law's statutes were generally consistent with those passed by other countries on a war footing. Criminal procedure required the chief public procurator to issue a writ of summons to individuals suspected of violating the National Defense Security Law. Suspects could be arrested only if they did not respond to the summons. It did not authorize police to make discretionary arrests for suspected crimes or arrests without first issuing a summons. Surprise or unauthorized police arrests would not be legally recognized. The law also required that suspects be interrogated within forty-eight hours of arrest and be issued a warrant of detention if detained longer. Suspects could be held longer than two months only in special cases and with the approval of the procurator. Article 23 required that suspects in detention be released immediately once cleared of charges. Article 24 permitted police to "seize, search, or obtain evidence by inspection" prior to trial, vague language that police would later interpret as authorizing torture.[16] Foreigners arrested, charged, and convicted of espionage or on suspicion of knowing state secrets would be permitted to appeal their case. Several statutes transgressed established democratic norms, however. Article 33 disallowed appeals of convictions for violating the Public Security Preservation Law or crimes "committed in concert with foreign countries or with intent to benefit foreign countries."[17] Nor, by article 37, would these trials be adjudicated by a jury.

The following month, April 1941, the state effectively froze assets and monies owned by foreigners and foreign businesses. The Foreign Exchange Control Law (*Gaikoku kawase kanri-hō*), commonly known as the "asset freeze ordinance" (*shisan tōketsu-rei*), denied foreigners access to their assets by authorizing the state to prohibit or restrict withdrawal or liquidation of personal or business monies, properties, investments, and collection of loans by foreign residents.[18] The law originally permitted foreigners to withdraw 500 yen per month for living expenses, though from August 23 the Finance Ministry approved raising this amount to 1,000 yen.[19] The asset freeze was a provocative move that compromised residents' ability to continue residing and operating their businesses indefinitely. It also helped convince many Americans and British to heed their embassies' warnings to evacuate the country. By July, 132 British and 118 Americans had repatriated. Viewing further diplomatic negotiations as useless, on July 25 the United States froze Japanese assets in the United States, with Britain and the Netherlands following suit immediately thereafter. On July 28, Japan responded with the Revised Trade Regulatory Rules for Foreigners (*Kaisei gaikokujin kankei torihiki torishimari kisoku*), which prohibited expats from conducting any further trade with those nations, including the British Commonwealth states of Canada, Australia, India, and South Africa. On August 1 the United States imposed an oil embargo on Japan that halted three-fourths of Japan's international trade and nearly 90 percent of its oil imports. In the wake of resulting business closures, from August through October more foreigners boarded ships for Europe and the Americas.[20]

Media censorship, already pervasive since the outbreak of war in China in 1937, was another legalistic means of curbing foreign activities. In an attempt to manage all news media, particularly stories about the war, the government formed its own agency, the Cabinet Information Bureau (Naikaku jōhōkyoku), and merged two private news services into the Dōmei News Service (Dōmei tsūshinsha), which thereafter served as Japan's semiprivate but official news agency. By 1941, the government had both reduced the volume of media being produced and secured broad control over its content.[21] Articles from all news agencies were censored prior to publication, the censor being staffed by a mix of representatives from the army, navy, and the Interior and Transportation Ministries. Reporter Phyllis Argall (1909–77) wrote that foreign papers were never certain what was permissible to print because "the laws were most indefinite; and with the exception of the issuance of an occasional press ban there were no concrete instructions as to what might, or might not, be published."[22] Even stories that received censor approval were regularly suppressed. News media was also curtailed by reducing the number and size of newspapers and magazines.

This included English media. Censors compelled Western journalists to comply meticulously with regulatory protocols. International telephone and wire dispatches, along with stories to be published domestically, were first submitted to the censor for approval. The dispatch was then returned, revised, and resubmitted. Content was scrupulously investigated. As dictated by the terms of the Tripartite Pact, Japan held a policy of noninvolvement in the European Theater, and its press was expected to observe this status by limiting itself to "neutral" coverage of that region. Anything other than supportive coverage of Adolf Hitler and Nazi activities, however, was deemed to violate the noninvolvement policy.[23] Furthermore, Japanese was the only language permitted for long-distance phone calls, requiring foreign correspondents to communicate with each other through interpreters. International mail was to be posted in unsealed envelopes.[24] By mid-1940, the government had issued so many bans on the press that reportage on anything other than the most benign subjects was nearly impossible, Fleisher reports (fig. 3.1). Fleisher's *Japan Advertiser* could not report on war-related events in Manchuria, trade, shipping arrivals and departures, disagreements within the government, activities of government officials, anything construed as critical of or that might reflect poorly on Japan, or "any item liable to stir the public mind."[25] Vague threats of newspaper closures in the case of noncompliance were issued to all within the foreign press corps except the Germans. Embassies were not permitted to distribute or publicize news that they received on their shortwave radios, though the German embassy did so freely. From the summer of 1940, police intensified pressure on the *Advertiser*, demanding apologies for some of its stories. Reporter James Harris reports that all articles had to be rushed to Fleisher's enormous mansion in Aoyama for approval prior to printing. Harris's colleague Burton Crane

FIGURE 3.1 Wilfrid Fleisher with Foreign Minister Matsuoka Yōsuke. Courtesy of the Wilfrid Fleisher Collection, American Heritage Center, University of Wyoming.

was even arrested for a joke. The newspaper office occupied the third floor of a building behind the Imperial Hotel and overlooking the Tōkaidō train line. Periodically, when the emperor's train passed by, office staff received orders to shut their blinds and refrain from looking out the windows. During one such instance Crane had retorted, "Such a thing is entirely unnecessary. Even if I did have a pistol and aimed at the Emperor's train, what's the chance that I could hit him from here?" Word of this remark reached the ears of the Kenpeitai and the following day Crane was arrested, though soon released.[26] The *Advertiser* was not the only newspaper to attract increasing scrutiny; the *English Daily* (Eibun mainichi) and the *Japan Chronicle* in Kobe were subjected to similar treatment.

In July 1940, Prince Konoe Fumimaro began his second term as prime minister by appointing the hawkish General Tōjō to the post of war minister. Antiforeign initiatives intensified within a week. Sixteen British citizens were arrested, among them the Reuters correspondent James M. Cox. Cox was seized at his home in Chigasaki on July 27 and taken to

Kenpeitai headquarters in Tokyo. After two days of interrogation he allegedly leapt to his death from the facility's third-story window. An autopsy revealed that he had recently received thirty-five injections. Japanese police labeled the incident a suicide and as proof produced a confessionary suicide note of questionable authenticity addressed to Cox's wife. Cox had been targeted by authorities for asking embarrassing questions during public press conferences, but he and the other fifteen were also targeted for being British. Since the outbreak of the war in China, Japan harbored greater hostility toward Britain than it did the United States. Britain had invested about $1.5 billion in China, far more than the United States, and so represented Japan's greatest economic competition in the region. Japan also encountered greater resistance from Britain as it expanded into China and seized control of regional resources. Cox's arrest was not a xenophobic or racially motivated act, Fleisher claims, but rather a warning to the British and the entire foreign press corps.[27]

Authorities were particularly suspicious of Japanese employed by foreign news agencies. A statement from the War Office implicated such individuals as willing pawns and thus coconspirators with foreign spies: "The authorities deeply deplore the fact that Japanese are in the pay of foreign information agencies. The army is determined to take firm action against such unpatriotic behavior."[28] Relentless Kenpeitai surveillance and interference in foreign newspapers' reportage culminated in the arrest of several Japanese employees. One reporter for the *Advertiser* was arrested for researching a story about Japanese historic sites.[29] Rumors then circulated that the entire staff would soon be arrested, leaving Fleisher little doubt of his own imminent incarceration. In the fall of 1940, after seventeen years in business, Fleisher sold the *Advertiser* to the Japanese-owned *Japan Times* and left Japan. This proved a wise decision. *Japan News-Week*, the only remaining foreign-owned paper, was closed and its entire staff arrested on the day of the Pearl Harbor attack.

Police had been intentionally conspicuous in their surveillance, making a show of visiting offices and households to ask questions. This disclosed to both the occupants and any unwitting visitors that they were being monitored. Before Fleisher's departure he was visited by a Tokkō detective who had come to his home previously on numerous occasions. This was a farewell visit. They exchanged pleasantries and Fleisher gave the detective a bottle of French brandy. He asked:

"Now, before I leave Japan . . . I want to ask you just one question. Why is it that when you don't like a foreign newspaperman you don't do as in your allied countries—Germany and Italy—or in Russia, and simply serve notice on him to leave immediately or revoke his permit of residence?"

"We can't do that in Japan," the detective replied. "We must have a case. First the police must arrest the man, then they must investigate the case, and then the procurator must decide on the basis of the evidence whether to bring him to trial, deport him, or free him. No other procedure is possible."[30]

The detective's reply is revealing in its explication of why the Tokkō, despite its occasional disregard for procedure in less conspicuous cases, tended to treat foreigners with extreme deference to legal protocols. As we will learn in our discussion of interned civilians, police remained conscientious about conducting surveillance and gathering evidence to build a case prior to and following an arrest, though late in the war such protocols were disregarded more often.[31] Tipton explains this inconsistency in Tokkō practice by noting that rule of law protects citizens from abuses of power by police, but also affords law enforcement a measure of discretion.[32] Enforcing bodies, in other words, were only minimally constrained by the vague, general nature of existing laws. State authorities also understood that national crisis required liberal interpretations of those laws. But the contradiction apparent in Fleisher's example can also be explained by the pragmatism that the Tokkō exercised when handling foreigners who, in 1940, were still protected by their respective embassies. Fleisher, a public figure and influential newspaperman who would certainly not hesitate to publicize any infraction in protocol perpetrated against him, called for particular delicacy. Scandals caused by unprofessional policing were avoided at all costs. Though antiforeign propaganda encouraged the general public to behave otherwise, therefore, police did not permit themselves to target Westerners simply for being Westerners. Japanese law denied them the luxury of racial profiling.

While censorship and intimidation of the Japanese and English media was real, subjective accounts written by the victims of those measures may be exaggerated. An exhaustive study of articles published between 1930 and 1941 in Japan's two major English newspapers, the *Japan Times* (including the *Japan Advertiser*) and the *Osaka mainichi* (including the

Tokyo nichinichi), concluded that as late as the autumn of 1941 these publications continued to enjoy relative freedom of expression, though less than before. Not only did they continue to determine the topics and the content of their stories, they were even permitted to criticize the government in qualified ways.[33]

Spiritual mobilization served as an additional means of containing resident Westerners. Manufacturing public compliance and fomenting ethnocentric nationalism entailed strengthening state supervision. The National General Mobilization Law enacted in 1938 gave the state sweeping powers over labor and labor unions, strategic commodities, economic resources, information, and industrial facilities, enabling it, in Dōmei Tsūshin-sha's words, to control "human and material resources in order that the nation may be enabled to display its total power most effectively for the realization of national defense purposes in time of war."[34] The law also allowed the state to dictate the rationing of goods and the content of information disseminated to individual households through their neighborhood associations. Meanwhile, a central committee formed under the auspices of the National Spiritual Mobilization Campaign (Kokumin seishin sōdōin undō, 1937) had already assumed oversight over ninety-three civilian organizations with the purpose of stimulating patriotism and support for the war in China. Individuals were encouraged to work hard, sacrifice, practice frugality, purchase war bonds, and keep their savings in postal or bank accounts where they could be tapped by authorities as needed. They were also called on to observe various new national holidays, and to assemble and celebrate in front of the Imperial Palace or at temples and shrines.[35] The mobilization law also established stronger government control over the economy, as well as a system for bringing bureaucracy to the neighborhood level. For although citizens could not be forced to join the copious jingoistic celebrations and rallies, necessity compelled their participation in town councils and *tonarigumi*. Refusal disqualified a household from rations disbursements.

But shortages and rationing were also responsible for the partial breakdown of public solidarity. Food and fuel shortages first hit in 1939, after two years of war with China. Rationing of meat, sugar, and gasoline commenced that fall, accompanied by more insistent calls for frugality. Charcoal, the primary means of cooking and heating, was rationed, as were bread, milk, and cigarettes, but all in insufficient quantities. *Tonari-gumi* distributed rations cards to be exchanged for the specified disbursements, but households were nonetheless compelled to patronize black market distributors to make up the difference. Water shortages in Tokyo triggered by the large volumes being diverted to factories around the city aggravated matters. In the spring and summer of 1940, the water utility company limited public water service to one hour twice daily.[36] Though successive poor harvests had exacerbated rice shortages caused by the ballooning exports required to feed Japanese troops deployed around the empire, initially rice was not rationed in order to prevent undue public anxiety over the state of domestic food supplies. Rationing of rice and staples like soy sauce and miso was finally implemented in six major cities on April 1, 1941, those products being distributed by centralized dispensaries rather than *tonarigumi*. By the outset of the war, rationing had been implemented nationally. Though allotments were based on age, gender, occupation, and other factors, the standard ration for individuals aged eleven to sixty was 330 grams of rice and smaller amounts of vegetables, fish, and other products.[37] Other domestic supplies and necessities were also distributed, along with coupons for clothing. Rations were meticulously calculated and recorded for each individual to ensure against inequities and cheating, but the systems proved burdensome and unreliable, particularly later in the war. By June 1942, families had to keep track of thirty-five different rationing ticket books. Starvation was rare, but hunger grew, becoming universal by 1945, when the standard rice ration was cut to 300 grams.[38] Unavailability and perceptions of inequitable distribution of rationing coupons, Simon Partner avers, "sorely tested any sense of wartime unity."[39]

Other forms of enforced stringency wrought hardships that further tested public morale. Workweeks were lengthened to twelve hours daily, six days per week; luxury and imported goods were scarce or unobtainable. The banking sector and fishing industry were placed under government control. By 1941, gasoline was reserved for high-priority vehicles, and an ordinance was issued against the use of public or motorized transportation for recreational purposes. One could not take a train or streetcar to the theater or drive a private car to the mountains or the golf course. Theoretically, one bicycled or walked, though people circumvented the ordinance without much trouble. Sumptuary legislation prohibited public displays of luxury and extravagance, as well as flashy, colorful, and fashionable attire. People were expected to look and act "dreary and drab in conformity with the spirit of the times," Fleisher reported, "which is one of depression."[40] Regular "black out" air-raid maneuvers also required residents to turn off their gas, cover their windows, and remain indoors. These, Fleisher writes, were "largely child's play, consisting in setting off fire crackers and various colored flares which are extinguished by volunteer brigades . . . with great amusement."[41]

Spiritual mobilization also included direct measures to either eradicate or cast suspicion on Westerners and select forms of Western influence. The alarming discovery of the Richard Sorge (1885–1944) spy ring in October 1941 precipitated the advent of annual antiespionage weeks wherein the media reported stories about spies and instructed the public how to detect them; posters, fliers, and matchbox covers reminded people to be conscious that foreigners in their midst may be listening to their public conversations; and *tonarigumi* were instructed to report on foreigner movements.[42] The state's efforts to eradicate potential sources of sentimentality toward Western enemies also included striking Western words and customs from the media and forms of public entertainment. Western literature, film, music, fashion, and other cultural artifacts were branded subversive and suppressed. Foreign words in common parlance were eliminated from use within the military, as well as from Western pastimes like baseball. Decadent Western customs like kissing were censored or removed from films.[43]

Despite concerted efforts to instill public alarm and align individual interests with state interests, concerns about spies and foreign influences remained too distant to merit the attention of many Japanese. "Country people were relatively unaffected by official propaganda," writes Herbert Bix. "Family and village considerations still took precedence over state considerations."[44] Within cities, as well, the state could not easily shift perceptions of the West as villainous and threatening because the West had been integral to the state's own genesis and until recent memory had been its greatest benefactor. The Japanese populace was not duped by spiritual mobilization, Fleisher concurs, though individuals may have accepted it out of fear or complacency.[45] Havens agrees that "Japan's persistent spiritual campaign . . . brought the war home to every doorstep and won the participation, if not yet the support, of most who lived within."[46]

In many cases the Japanese public indeed responded with ambivalence to antiforeign campaigns, which often contained mixed messages. Though study of English itself was eliminated from school curricula by 1943, some teachers disobeyed the moratorium and gave students the option to continue studying it.[47] Publication of the two-page weekly periodical *ABC Weekly* (later *School Weekly: Junior Edition*) for students of English continued throughout the war, a signal that perhaps English was not "really" banned and that it was not as detrimental to state interests as propaganda suggested. The government itself undermined its vilification of Westerners by continuing to provide them with privileges like special rations. In principle it supplied foreigners with greater quantities of rationed goods than it did its own citizens, and also disbursed to them rare items like eggs, meat, potatoes, butter, and milk. Although such goods were difficult for Japanese to procure after 1940, authorities did instruct stores to reserve them, when available, for foreigners.[48]

Otto Tolischus (1890–1967) chronicled how Japanese popular opinion toward Westerners from early to mid-1941 swayed with fluctuating diplomatic tensions between Japan and the Allied powers. Tolischus had arrived in Tokyo in early February to assume his post as correspondent for the *New York Times*. He had been evicted from Germany in 1940 for his reportage on the Nazi regime, for which he had received the Pulitzer Prize for Journalism. Tolischus's book *Tokyo Record*, published in 1943 only months after his repatriation from Japan, weighs a journalist's impartiality and observational acuity against a deep dislike for the Japanese. (Tolischus's revulsion is understandable, for he had just endured arrest, torture, and six months of internment, discussed in chapter 4.) Given this personal antipathy, it is significant that Tolischus notes being well treated by Japanese civilians. He experienced no evidence of racial hatred either on the Tokyo streets or within journalistic circles. Rather, he detected that public sentiment often paralleled current events, a tendency toward greater public hospitality when diplomatic relations warmed and more "latent hostility" when they deteriorated.[49] This changeable but otherwise innocuous nature of Japanese public opinion suggests that citizens felt little personal interest or stake in political matters, or even paid much attention to them. As he described it, most Japanese were wholly disinterested in the national mission. The "new order" promised by the Greater East Asia Co-prosperity Sphere existed beyond their sphere of responsibility.

"Little could be expected of the Japanese people . . . ," he wrote, "who knew little of what was happening and would not have objected . . . even if they knew."[50]

While citizens were warned about foreign spies and children taught to fear Anglo-Americans, even the government-controlled media was not universally disposed to vilify Caucasians. As will be discussed in chapter 9, propaganda films generally avoided racializing the political antagonisms between Japan and its enemies. Some periodicals did, as well. *ABC Weekly*, published in a mixture of Japanese and English, contained brief stories on current events, most pertaining to the war, but little racialized content. Its coverage of the captured Doolittle Raid aviators, for instance, directed no racial hatred toward Americans.[51] The periodical *Daitōa sensō kiroku gahō* (Greater East Asian war illustrated) was similarly diplomatic in its coverage of the capture and execution of the Doolittle airmen. It called the aviators "ignoble" and their motives for attacking Japan "contemptible," but devoted far more space to justifying their punishment and extolling the Japanese state.[52] The reticence of Japanese films and periodicals to vilify their Caucasian enemies reveals that producers remained responsive to public demand. It would be unrealistic to expect Japanese to revile what they had so long admired, and indeed disingenuous to denounce the very Western cultural forms on which Japan had modeled its own modernization. Partner writes that "the majority of Japanese people, if anything, continued to admire Western culture, which had, after all, played an enormous influence in daily life."[53] The state's handling of Jewish refugees further elucidates its contingent and variously ambivalent efforts to contain Western influences.

Japan's "Jewish Problem" and the Kobe Community

By aligning itself with Nazi Germany, Japan alienated itself from the Asian countries it was trying to court and maligned itself among Jews. Nazi anti-Semitism and the influx of Jewish refugees it created thus presented Japan with a dual racial challenge, a "Jewish problem."[54] Though circumstances seemed to favor following its ally and enacting its own exclusionary, anti-Semitic policies, Japanese leadership remained divided on this question throughout the prewar era. The issue also sparked a wave of interest in Jews among the Japanese public. Between 1936 and 1945, the number of books about Jews in Japan grew nearly 300 percent and published articles jumped nearly 600 percent.

Though some took an innocuous interest in the topic, others aimed to manufacture suspicion and hostility. With the purpose of informing future policies on Jewish-Japanese relations, for example, in 1936 the Foreign Ministry established the International Political and Economic Affairs Study Group (Kokusai seikei gakkai) to study Jews. Headed by the army general Shiōden Nobutaka (1879–1962), an ardent anti-Semite with Nazi Party alliances, the group published a journal that repeatedly advanced the premise of Jews as economic conquerors.[55] Suspicions that Jews were indeed conspiring to secure global economic domination, an influential theory first articulated by the fraudulent text *The Protocols of the Elders of Zion* (1903), validate Ben-Ami Shillony's view that Japanese had long eyed Jews with "a mixture of fear and admiration."[56] Disenfranchised White Russians upheld these suspicions by claiming strong Jewish complicity in the 1917 Bolshevik Revolution, accusations that seemed to be verified by the leverage wielded by Jews within the leadership of the new Soviet Union. For some in Japan, such notions constituted evidence that Jews would next proceed to challenge Japan's economic self-determination in Asia, a threat that called for decisive preemptive measures and anti-Semitic propaganda.

Anti-Semitic rhetoric and isolated cases of Jewish persecution in Japan later in the Pacific War have led some to conclude that Japan was a willing collaborator in Nazi anti-Semitism. Shillony has even argued that Jews represented everything that Japan found threatening about the West, and that for some Japanese the war against Western nations was really a war against Jews.[57] One indeed encounters such sentiments, but over the course of the war one finds more evidence of a pragmatic, evolving approach to the Jewish problem that responded to changing political pressures. Pamela Sakamoto is certainly correct in finding that Japanese rarely exhibited either anti-Semitism or altruism toward Jews, but rather an ambivalence that she describes as "a haphazard response to external conditions."[58] Japan had already become favorably disposed to Jews for several reasons. After Japan failed to secure the loans it needed to finance the

Russo-Japanese War (1904–5), Jacob Schiff (1847–1920), a Jewish banker in New York, raised nearly $200 million in loans that ultimately enabled it to win the war and expel Russia from the Korean Peninsula. Japan was so grateful that it awarded Schiff the Order of the Rising Sun, making him the first foreigner to receive the honor.[59] The community of educated Jewish professionals that subsequently settled in Harbin (roughly thirteen thousand by 1932) had also impressed the Japanese. As successful engineers and businessmen, they had contributed substantially to the region's development. Pro-Jewish Japanese had also advanced the idea that as Middle Easterners, Jews were Asian rather than Western and thus shared with Japan a measure of cultural comradeship, a notion that some refugees used to ingratiate themselves with Japanese authorities. Allegedly, two refugee rabbis summoned to navy headquarters and asked why Nazis hated Jews shrewdly allayed suspicion by answering, "Because [they] know that we Jews are Asians."[60]

Themselves targets of the presumptive racial superiority informing Nazi dogma, many Japanese found much in common with the Jews. This sense of fellowship was enhanced by the fact that Jews, like Japanese, offset their status as ethnic outcasts by collectively claiming impressive intellectual and commercial achievements. Dismissing Nazi apprehension over Jewish economic power, some Japanese ideologues came to view the wandering Jew as a resource too tempting to leave unexploited, and racism as too unsavory to contemplate. While willing to justify Japan's own expansion into Asia in racial terms, they would not accept Nazi anti-Semitism.

Adopting a position of racial neutrality also afforded Japan opportunities to maximally utilize Jews. It was with this in mind that navy captain Inuzuka Koreshige (1880–1965), director of the navy's Advisory Bureau of Jewish Affairs, and fellow colonel Yasue Norihiro (1886–1950) advanced a plan to attract Jews to the Far East. This marked a remarkable reversal for both men, who since the 1920s had been outspoken anti-Semites and occupied leadership positions within the military's anti-Jewish faction ever since. Yasue had even helped translate *The Protocols of the Elders of Zion* into Japanese. Their notoriety as anti-Semites, ironically, qualified them as experts in Jewish affairs and lent authority to their plan. Their scheme, later styled the Fugu (blowfish) Plan (Fugu keikaku)—so named because if poorly executed, the plan's savory benefits could easily turn deadly—entailed attracting an educated, knowledgeable population of Jews that would help Japan develop Manchuria economically. The establishment of semiautonomous zones for them, they maintained, would be necessary for Japan's Pan-Asian mission to succeed at all. Not only would their business contacts with fellow Jews worldwide stimulate foreign investment, Japan's charitable treatment of Jews would help stabilize relations with the United States and Britain.

Some were troubled that the Fugu Plan's economic interests conflicted with state political interests. Few of Japan's leaders were explicitly pro-Jewish or voluntarily sought to provide Jews with protection from Nazi persecution. The government had never publicly opposed Nazi anti-Semitism, and Prime Minister Konoe and Foreign Minister Arita Hachirō (1884–1965) had both stated that in principle the immigration of German and Austrian Jews was prohibited. Such refugees were considered stateless and would be permitted entrance only if legally qualified under current immigration law. Japan, they asserted, would make no special provisions.[61] Advocates of the plan had already made placatory overtures to the Jewish population in China, however. In December 1937, Yasue and General Higuchi Kiichirō (1888–1970) announced at the Conference of Jewish Communities in the Far East that Japan harbored no racial prejudice toward Jews and sought to maintain friendship and close business relations with them. Jewish delegates reciprocated by issuing a proclamation to Jews worldwide declaring that they "enjoy racial equality and racial justice under the national laws, and will cooperate with Japan and Manchukuo in building a new order in Asia."[62] Late in 1938, the prime minister and foreign minister met with Finance Minister Ikeda Seihin (1867–1950), War Minister Nakamura Kotaro (1881–1947), and Navy Minister Yonai Mitsumasa (1880–1948) to discuss the establishment of a Jewish quarter in Shanghai, where no entry visas were required. They quickly approved the plan and issued a statement asserting that for Japan to reject Jews would be "contrary to our spirit" and contradict its declared policy of racial equality.[63] Japan would, moreover, treat Jews residing within its territories and wishing to enter its territories in the future no differently than other foreigners. Debuchi Katsuji (1878–1947), Upper House member and former ambassador to the United States, then echoed this statement, declaring that government policy had always espoused racial tolerance and would continue to do so.[64] The following year Japan sent to the

United States a delegation to convince American Jews that the Japanese empire was a friend to the Jewish people. Meanwhile, to further curry favor with the United States and Britain, Inuzuka delivered a pro-Jewish radio broadcast in which he contrasted Japan's treatment of Jews to Germany's. "In our relations with the Jews," he declared, "we will always deal with them on the principle of equality, so long as the Jews remain loyal to the Japanese authorities."[65] Even after Japan signed the Tripartite Pact in 1940, Foreign Minister Matsuoka informed Berlin directly that he rejected anti-Semitism, that he had never agreed to implement Hitler's policies in Japan, and that the Japanese empire renounced racial discrimination outright. Not only would the state be careful to adhere to strictly nonracial policies toward foreigners, it would disseminate propaganda that denounced the racism being practiced within both Axis and Allied countries.[66] To further avoid racializing the issue, some Foreign Ministry reports referred to the refugees in question as European rather than Jewish.

Japan adhered to this position in its handling of Jews within Japan proper. In July 1937 the Nazi government requested from the Foreign Ministry a list of German citizens employed at Japanese high schools and universities. A list containing seventy-four names was produced, enabling the German embassy to identify and then attempt to eradicate German Jews working as instructors, individuals who held great potential for influencing Japanese public opinion.[67] In September 1939, the Japanese-German Cultural Exchange Cooperation Association (Nichi-Doku bunka renraku kyōgi-kai), a group of community leaders and academics established in 1938 to address the treatment of German instructors by the Japanese government, issued a statement to the education minister noting Germany's "race [Jewish] problem" and stating that it sought Japan's cooperation in addressing it. It went on to state that Jews were not welcome as members of the association, nor were they to be considered representatives of Germany in general.[68] The education minister rejected the statement, however, reserving Japan's independent power to appoint and dismiss foreign instructors at its discretion. He also asserted that the issue was not a race problem but rather a culture problem. "Their qualification as teachers is not a matter of race but of their scholarly accomplishments," the minister retorted, adding that foreign instructors held personal contracts with the presidents of the schools where they were employed and that the ministry had no authority to override presidents' discretionary decisions to renew or terminate contracts.[69] This final point made school presidents the targets of future Nazi pressure. For the time being, at least, Japan had preserved its independence, rejected Nazi racism, and protected Jewish instructors.

The July 1940 investiture of the second Konoe cabinet, coupled with September's tripartite agreement, precipitated a hardening of policy against thousands of Jewish refugees fleeing Germany, Poland, Lithuania, and other European states. Indeed, by eliminating any possibility of salvaging Japanese diplomatic relations with the United States, the pact rendered the so-called Fugu Plan meaningless.[70] In July, amid the glut of refugees passing through Japan en route to the United States, Canada, or elsewhere, Foreign Minister Matsuoka had asserted that Japanese policy prohibited issuance of transit visas to those without entry visas for their destinations. One way of curtailing numbers was to charge exorbitant visa application fees. After Japan imposed a one-hundred-dollar application fee later that year, the flow of applications for transit visas at its embassy in Berlin nearly halted. Japan also sought to limit the number of Jewish refugees permitted to enter Shanghai. Thousands of Jews displaced by Germany's invasion of Poland in September 1939 had already arrived, however, and by mid-1940 the city held about eighteen thousand registered and unregistered Jewish refugees.[71]

This hardening of policy was accompanied by extraordinary acts of humanitarianism, however, for it was at this point that Japan itself came to serve as a transit point. Between July and September 1940, Japanese vice-consul in Kaunas, Lithuania, Sugihara Chiune (1900–86) issued Japanese transit visas to roughly six thousand local Jews. In many of these cases Sugihara knowingly violated standing immigration directives requiring transit travelers to complete immigration applications, show proof of sufficient capital, and be in possession of entry visas for their final destinations. For individuals without entry visas, Sugihara circumvented regulations by citing Curaçao, a Dutch colony in the Caribbean and the only state not requiring entry visas, as the final destination. These were individuals, Sugihara knew, that faced imminent internment and death. Technically Sugihara's visas allowed bearers to remain in Japan "in transit" for fifteen days, but few of the Curaçao refugees could continue on because reaching the island entailed passing through other South

Sugihara

American ports that would not accept them without transit visas. Problems securing berths to their final destinations were aggravated as some passenger shipping companies canceled their stops at Japanese ports or suspended operations in the Pacific altogether, and longer waits for passenger ships meant greater numbers of visa expirations.[72] Refugees had no choice but to remain in Japan until further documentation could be obtained, in many cases two to eight months. In the process of becoming a key relay station for those en route to South America, Palestine, or the Dutch West Indies, Japan became an interim destination itself.

Not only did the state honor Sugihara's and other types of invalid visas, it made special accommodations for those carrying them. Yet it was also careful to retain proper oversight. Under Interior Ministry orders, in late 1940 the Tokkō began conducting investigations of incoming Jewish refugees in several prefectures, noting their origins and final destinations. In April 1941, the ministry issued a report on refugee immigration that stated that 5,580 Jews bearing Japanese transit visas had entered Japan between 1940 and March 1941, and several thousand more had been permitted to enter without proper documentation. Most were still residing in Japan two months later. Only about half of those visas had been issued by Sugihara, meaning that roughly three thousand more had yet to arrive.[73]

Many of the Jewish refugees of the Bolshevik Revolution that had settled in Japan ended up in Kobe, the country's second-largest port. In the 1920s, Kobe's Jewish community numbered about one thousand and claimed a Zionist organization and two synagogues, but numbers fell thereafter and by 1940 only about one hundred remained.[74] Nazi persecution had attracted more Jews to Japan in the 1930s, but most, like the Balks, were migrants from Germany and Austria. They arrived with greater resources, proper immigration documents, and prearranged plans to settle in Japan. Most gravitated to Yokohama's small German Jewish community, with which they shared more cultural ties, rather than to Kobe's community of Russian Jews. Germany's invasions of Poland in 1939 and Western Europe the following year, however, triggered a separate migration to Japan that would last from the summer of 1940 to spring 1941. These later refugees, many carrying Sugihara's visas, arrived with few resources or concrete travel plans and shared more in common culturally with Kobe's Russian Jews. The "split in the European Jewish world" was thus replicated in Yokohama and Kobe Japan.[75]

Most European refugees arriving in Kobe had crossed the continent on the railroad to Vladivostok, where they caught ships to Tsuruga, Fukui Prefecture, and then boarded trains to Kobe. The Japanese government happily placed care for these individuals in the hands of the Kobe Jewish Committee (Jewcom), an association of twenty-five Jewish families that formed in 1940 to help Jewish refugees flee Europe. Jewcom vice president Moise Moiseff (1905–91) described the association's relief efforts for these thousands of migrants as consisting mainly of assistance obtaining transit visa extensions for those wishing to remain, assistance with emigration procedures for those wishing to travel elsewhere, and material assistance during their interim stay in Kobe. Moiseff writes that the committee was "so thoroughly recognized by the Japanese Government that even American Jews have found themselves unable to land until the Kobe Jewish representative has given his consent."[76] Jewcom operated on an annual budget of about $20,000 (93,000 yen), which allowed for a daily per capita expenditure of thirty cents. It procured these considerable funds from local donations, private and organizational donors in the United States, and the Jewish humanitarian organizations HICEM and the Joint Distribution Committee.[77]

Jewcom established a close working relationship with local police and Foreign Ministry officers. This accord was facilitated through bribes (its 1941 New Year's gifts to Kobe officials totaled $923.90), for it understood that authorities were under no obligation to admit entry to refugees or to extend their fifteen-day visas. But the relationship was also based on the mutual understanding that Jewcom and Japanese authorities needed each other to handle the influx of refugees, many of whom were destitute and bore questionable, incomplete, or illegal travel documentation.[78] When a refugee ship arrived at Tsuruga, police, immigration officials, and Jewcom representatives boarded it to carry out inspections of passengers' paperwork. As transit visa holders were required to possess entry visas for their final destinations, they were questioned about their transit plans. Some, Sakamoto relates, gave mistaken answers. Others bore fraudulent visas or no visas at all. For those without proper documentation, "[Jewcom representative] Mr. Treguboff would quickly issue [new visas] while the Japanese officials waited, watched, and stamped the papers with the 'ink still wet.'"[79] Another Jewcom representative during this process affirmed that Japanese immigration officers knew that many of the visas were poor-quality forgeries but pretended not to notice. According to

"Regulations Relative to the Entry, Stay, and Departure of Aliens" (Interior Ministry Ordinance No. 6), immigration statutes could be waived if the individual was "guaranteed by a trustworthy guardian," a role that Jewcom was also permitted to fill.[80] Jewcom representatives paid refugees' train fare from Tsuruga to Kobe, and provided those in need with a daily allowance of 1.5 yen. Once in Kobe, refugees received assistance converting their documentation into something more usable, support that included access to the American embassy in Tokyo and assistance communicating with Jewish agencies overseas.[81] Though Poland had been annexed by Germany in October 1939, the Polish embassy and consulate were kept open until October 1941 to help process visa applications and references.[82]

Many of the clerical burdens of acquiring visa extensions were shouldered by Jewcom representatives, but biblical scholar Dr. Kotsuji Setsuzō (1899–1973) is credited with overcoming the political obstacles. Kotsuji, who had previously served as adviser of Jewish affairs under his friend Foreign Minister Matsuoka, was able to convince Matsuoka to grant the transit visa extensions.[83] Matsuoka, who confessed to Kotsuji that he could not openly defy governmental and military pro-Nazi factions, privately agreed to surreptitiously extend the visas as long as his office was not openly implicated. With this approval from the foreign minister, along with 3,000 yen in bribes, Kotsuji was able to lubricate visa documentation at the local police and prefectural levels.[84]

The hospitality proffered by Kobe residents is remarkable given the steady stream of publicity describing Jews as criminals. Since the late 1930s, the Cabinet Information Bureau had characterized Jews as a criminal race by releasing anti-Semitic propaganda and media stories of smuggling and irregular commercial activities perpetrated by Jews in Japan and China.[85] The propaganda was ineffective for several reasons, however. First, it did not reflect the government's official position. Hostility toward Jews was never formally adopted by the emperor or Japanese officials; nor did Japan ever establish any administrative body to deal with Jews. As Shillony writes, active anti-Semites "were all second-rate figures, many of them retired officers or bureaucrats, or right-wing intellectuals."[86] Moreover, anti-Semitic media coverage never became personally meaningful enough to become widely internalized. The roughly nine hundred permanent Jewish residents in Japan posed little credible threat, even to the propaganda producers themselves.[87] In early 1941, for instance, the Tanpei Photography Club (Tanpei shashin kurabu) held an exhibition titled "Criminal Jews" (*Rubō Yudaya*) featuring photos of Jewish refugees in Kobe, but the photographers later admitted to feeling pity rather than hatred for the refugees.[88] Finally, anti-Semitic publicity was balanced by more sympathetic media coverage. An American consulate report from May 1941, for instance, observed that, "notwithstanding Japan's close political relations with Germany, there have been no cases reported of discrimination against Jewish refugees, and newspaper comment has not been unkind."[89] Japanese newspapers indeed reflected public curiosity and sympathy in their reportage on the Kobe refugees. A *Kobe shinbun* article from February 18, 1941, mentioned how school children returning home would stop to ponder the fates of passing Jews clad in blue hats and overcoats, and how other youths remarked on the migrants without fear or hostility.[90] George Sidline, a boy at the time, recalls that Japanese were disinterested in the anti-Semitic propaganda posted around the city and instead demonstrated generosity and goodwill toward his family. From the Japanese perspective, he maintained, both Nazis and Jews were white, and racism based on religion held little meaning. Nor did most Japanese recognize that the German community was split over allegiance to the Nazi Party. "Jews were not singled out for internment in concentration camps," he writes, "nor were they harassed or kept under surveillance any more than any other Caucasians."[91]

Studies of the Kobe community confirm that local Japanese gave Jews a warm welcome.[92] Japanese individuals, schools, and Christian organizations contributed food and money, while a doctor provided hundreds with free medical treatment. Copious stories recount locals offering refugees their own rations cards, shopkeepers reserving for them the most coveted foodstuffs, and farmers donating their fruit to refugee children. Unlike other foreigners, Jews were not required to stand in line to receive their daily ration of freshly baked bread. Their distributions exceeded in quantity what Japanese were receiving, and the refugees were instructed by police not to publicly flaunt their rationed bread so as not to incite resentment. One Jewcom member relates, "Personally with my conversations with my friends, also in checking with some other Jewish residents and the refugees themselves, I can summarize the attitude of almost all Japanese in one word: *Kawaisoy* [*sic*] (We were sorry for them). Here again

I can say definitely there was no antisemitism to the refugees in Kobe, only compassion and kindness."[93] The fact that of all the exhausted, destitute refugees passing through Kobe only two died while in Japan corroborates testimonies of attentive hospitality.[94]

Though refugees found Kobe to be a relative paradise that afforded them unexpected measures of freedom and comfort, some, impoverished and utterly unprepared for life in Japan, did get into trouble. There were several cases of shoplifting, attempts to use the streetcars without paying, and instances of littering. In such cases, Japanese exercised patience, and police handled complaints quietly through Jewcom intermediaries.[95] Numerous stories attest that police and local officials were uncharacteristically lenient and instructed rations distributors, shopkeepers, and the general public to be charitable as well.[96]

Refugees could not be accommodated indefinitely, however. Anti-Semitic factions within the government permitted transparent breaches of immigration policy, but eventually some grew uneasy. Prefectural authorities in Kobe also began to bemoan the influx of refugees. The migrants were poor and not proving to be the economic stimulus officials had hoped. Police also feared they would become a public nuisance. A reasonable number would not be objectionable, wrote the Hyogo Foreign Affairs manager, "but when there are up to one thousand, first there is the security issue, and when the number rises beyond that, it draws a lot of attention."[97] On May 15, 1941, the Soviet Union tightened its borders to transit immigrants, and, as per Tripartite Pact provisions, Hitler's June 22 declaration of war on Russia made the Soviet Union an enemy of Japan.[98] This combination of events promptly ended the stream of refugee ships from Vladivostok. Concerned that the Kobe Jews would become a security threat, the Interior Ministry ordered that the city's transient refugees be relocated. By October, the 1,098 transients that had not proceeded to their intended destinations were transferred to Shanghai, leaving behind only several hundred of the community's original residents. In the end, 4,608 Jewish refugees had entered Kobe, a full third of whom stayed for over eight months. At one point, the city had accommodated over 1,600.[99] Their lenient treatment had been practical, calculated to improve Japan's relationship with the United States and to demonstrate Japan's own moral authority. In each case and at each step, Japan had acted to maximize self-interests and avoid racial policies. Humanitarian motivations were secondary.[100]

Economic and diplomatic concerns thus factored heavily into Japan's wavering treatment of Jews, and Westerners generally, within the empire. Initially reticent to involve itself in a racial problem of Germany's making, in 1938 it reversed this position by touting racial equality. The outbreak of hostilities in Europe, a renewed alliance with Germany, more insistent Nazi pressure, and its own growing concerns over the size of the Jewish migration later caused Japan to check this position. While its leadership included both anti-Semites and Jewish sympathizers, in each stage of this process decision making was informed less by race and more by pragmatism. Moreover, instances of anti-Semitism suffered by Jews in the prewar years resulted chiefly from pressures applied by other Europeans, not Japanese. As will be discussed later, Japan's strategic persecution of Jews, always under the aegis of Gestapo representatives, occurred mainly in the final year of the Pacific War.

A Repressed, Mobilized Christianity

Religion did not meaningfully factor into Japan's position on Jewish immigration. Realizing the alien faith posed no ideological threat, Japanese authorities considered it irrelevant. They developed an altogether different view of Christian missionaries, however, whose theology and proselytizing represented direct challenges to the emperor's religious authority and legitimacy. Banning Christianity outright, a strategy that had failed three centuries earlier and was now unconstitutional, was never seriously considered. Preferring to fashion a centralized, more nationalistic church, authorities moved to impose greater state oversight over Christian organizations.

After several years of heightened police surveillance, in April 1939 the state legalized greater interference in mission activities. The Religious Bodies Law (*Shūkyō dantai-hō*) stipulated the following: if a practice or doctrine of a religious organization or the conduct of its members "disturbs peace and order or proves contrary to the duty of national subjects," it may be lawfully prohibited or suspended; if a religious organization or its members violates the law or "commits an act prejudicial to public interest," the organization or member may be suspended or prohibited; violation of the above articles is grounds for imprisonment; the government is empowered to demand reports from and otherwise investigate religious bodies; all newly established religious bodies and organizations must report the details of their activities and doctrines, their organization and administration, and the identities of their representatives to the authorities within fourteen days; and all such bodies must report the names and permanent addresses of their missionaries.[101] The law curtailed not only the ability of foreign missionaries to preach and proselytize, but the activities of all religious groups. Buddhist sects were brought into line with *tennōsei* ideology, and newer religions like Tenrikyō and Ōmotokyō whose religious independence challenged state ideology were also targeted.

Concurrent with the hardening toward Westerners marked by the commencement of Prime Minister Konoe's second term (July 1940) and only several days after the Cox incident, police arrested seven members of the Salvation Army. Targeted as a British Christian denomination rather than a charitable organization, the Salvation Army was staffed by only three foreigners—one Australian and two Canadians. The foreigners were repatriated and the organization forced to sever connections with Britain. For authorities, this move represented an easy first step in a broader campaign to convert Christian groups into purely Japanese organizations independent of both foreign members and foreign financial assistance. Parishioners who continued to maintain relations with foreign missionaries invited police attention.[102]

The Salvation Army arrests corresponded to two additional mandates meant to terminate church autonomy and give the state direct oversight over Christian activities. Under the authority of the Religious Bodies Law, the government nationalized and consolidated the various Protestant denominations into a single administrative entity. The new body, called the Nippon Kirisuto Kyōdan, or United Church of Christ in Japan, was to be administered by the Department of Education and represented a strategic attempt to establish a purely Japanese Christianity consistent with and ideologically supportive of the theological principles of State Shinto. The *kyōdan* was not only expected to purge itself of foreign affiliations but also to demonstrate allegiance to the state and its military agenda in Asia. The concomitant elimination of financial support from overseas benefactors proved a major source of adversity and forced the closure of many independent and smaller churches. The *kyōdan*'s inaugural meeting on June 24, 1941, where attendees were required to take an oath of loyalty to the emperor, heralded the unification of thirty-three Protestant organizations. Thereafter, foreigners were required to obtain permission to speak at congregations and all church services were attended by the secret police. Missionary work also ceased.[103]

Second, as part of its purge of foreign missionaries, in August 1940 the Kenpeitai ordered member churches of the Nippon Seikōkai (NSKK, Anglican Church in Japan) to remove foreigners from official positions, prohibiting foreign pastors from running their own congregations. This order was also issued to the Roman Catholic Church, which rejected it. Foreign bishops in the NSKK resigned in October and were replaced with Japanese. A debate then ensued within the NSKK over whether to join the *kyōdan*, which was exclusively Protestant. Having already removed its foreign pastors, a resolute demonstration of acquiescence, the NSKK ultimately decided to follow the lead of the Roman Catholics and remain independent. Unification would constitute an unacceptable theological compromise. This defiant decision, made amid rumors that bishops would be arrested if they opposed the *kyōdan*, threatened the legitimacy of the *kyōdan* altogether and provided other churches with the courage to remain independent.[104] Significantly, Japanese authorities accepted the NSKK's decision, but did proceed to persecute certain Japanese and Western bishops. (The arrest of Rev. Samuel Heaslett, who openly opposed the *kyōdan*, will be detailed in chapter 4.)

Though granted more autonomy than churches, Christian schools were also subject to greater state oversight. Foreigners were permitted to remain as teachers but forced to relinquish positions of authority. Kate Hansen (1879–1968), an American missionary who between 1907 and 1941 served as a teacher, dean, and acting president at Miyagi College in Sendai, wrote in October 1940 of the movement to suppress Christianity: "There is a determined effort to eliminate Christianity, and to smash Christian institutions, but, all under the forms of law, and in as veiled a manner as possible, so as not to provoke opposition at home, nor retaliation abroad."[105] A second letter dated April 25, 1941, however, suggests that her initial assessment was exaggerated. Besides the continuous surveillance, her school experienced little further interference, and she describes the state's persecution of Christianity as "subtle."[106] Hansen retained her position until later that spring when her embassy advised the school's American staff to repatriate.

Christian social welfare organizations confronted similar sorts of domestication. The Kōbōkan (Door of hope), established in 1919 by American missionaries and the Japanese Woman's Christian Temperance Union (WCTU) to combat infant mortality in Tokyo slums, had survived a series of economic setbacks. By the late 1930s, however, operations were hampered by the suspicions and pressures it incurred as a Christian organization. American missionaries at the Kōbōkan realized that the organization would survive only if they removed themselves from leadership. They did so in April 1941, leaving it in the hands of Japanese WCTU members. Freed of its enemy affiliation, thereafter the Kōbōkan acquired independent foundation status and continued its social welfare activities with relative autonomy. The organization transitioned from a daycare and kindergarten to a war victims' shelter that also helped propagate nationalistic propaganda. In 1943 it evacuated to Kutsukake, about two miles west of Karuizawa, where it continued its operations throughout the war.[107]

Japan's concern with Christians can also be gauged by its treatment of German missionaries, who as state allies would otherwise merit no particular suspicion. Scrupulous in observing diplomatic obligations to Germany, in domestic matters Japan did not hesitate to assert its administrative independence. Just as it defied Nazi protests over its treatment of Jewish refugees, it made few special accommodations for German missions. Although missionaries could not be evicted from Japan without due cause, testimonies from three such families reveal that their German citizenship afforded them little protection from surveillance and occupational restrictions.

Germany's Liebenzeller Lutheran Mission deployed several missionaries to Japan. In 1928, Bernhard Buss, Ernst Lang, and Karl Notehelfer arrived for two years of language training and were joined by Otto Mosimann the following year. Buss and Lang had been engaged in Germany to women at the mission, and in 1930 their fiancées, along with Rose Henner, Notehelfer's future wife, joined them in Tokyo. Missionary work required cultural assimilation, and the families set about cultivating trusting relationships with their parishioners. But they also benefited from the insularity and privilege that typified life for expats in Japan. The families, each of which lived in a Western home and had six children, remained close, living, studying, and vacationing alongside others within the foreign community. Their children grew up as playmates and schoolmates at the German school in Ōmori, Tokyo, and they summered in Karuizawa, where the Busses and Notehelfers purchased property and built summer houses. Buss was a leading member of the German community, and the family established and serviced several missions, the latest in Kugahara. The Notehelfers lived in Horinouchi, Tokyo, and in 1934 built a church in Hōnan where the family worked until relocating to the rural agricultural community of Todoroki, Setagaya-ku, in 1938. The Langs built their church in Kikuna.[108]

Throughout the prewar period the families endured few inconveniences or ill effects from the wars in Europe and China, or from the escalating tensions with Allied nations. Yet each of the families relates that from the late 1930s Japanese had to be more selective about their friends and affiliations. Western ways were drawing suspicion, and sympathetic Japanese risked attracting police attention. The source of public wariness, evidently, was police scrutiny itself, for the missionaries continued to receive generally hospitable treatment. The Langs clearly felt no threat to themselves or their children, who commuted alone one hour to school. Even Ehrhardt Lang, aged seven, made this commute beginning in 1941 without incident. Lang recalls that he and the other missionary children were a source of curiosity and amusement for Japanese children.[109]

Being German afforded the missionaries little immunity, however. The Notehelfers first detected police surveillance of their church in 1937. They were ordered to report their scheduled meetings to the police and to begin their church services by singing the Japanese national anthem. Lang reports similar mandates imposed on his family's church. Such oversight constituted a less direct course of action than that taken by the Osaka police department, which forced all Christian leaders in that city to answer questionnaires explaining the Christian Church's view of the emperor, of imperial rescripts and pronouncements, and of the Shinto deities.[110] Priscilla and Reinhard Buss relate that required demonstrations of fealty to State Shinto were not limited to Japanese citizens. Foreign schools were also pressured to take their pupils to Shinto shrines to have them pay homage to the ashes of the war dead, a practice being imposed on Japanese schools. Accustomed to being on the dispensing end of proselytism, the German missionaries did not take this well. They objected, the Busses write, for "we [missionaries] did not wish to compromise our faith by having our children bow to heathen gods."[111]

F. G. and Rose Notehelfer do not recount episodes of open public animosity toward the family as foreigners or missionaries, but do note that by 1941 more passersby regarded them suspiciously. The Buss family, similarly, reports being treated with kindness and respect, but as the threat of war mounted it confronted a growing "feeling of nationalism and anti-foreigner sentiment."[112] Now regularly subjected to antiforeign rhetoric, fewer pedestrians stopped to listen when the family went out to proselytize. And although they report no instances of hate or hostility by Japanese civilian adults, they do note that children perpetrated acts of antiforeign aggression. "The hostile spirit was fanned, especially among the youth," the Busses relate. "Boys now came to our house, throwing stones and smashing windows."[113] Lang also states that the children that had once laughed with him now taunted him and occasionally threw stones.[114]

Propaganda implicating Westerners as spies may have eroded public trust in missionaries to varying degrees, but it was often unable to overturn the long-term relationships that missionaries had nurtured with local parishioners. In some cases, parishioners attempted to protect Western missionaries from persecution. The Anglican Percy Powles, stationed for two decades in Takata, Niigata Prefecture, wrote in 1938 that "despite the fact that I am well known as an Englishman the good people give me the benefit of the doubt around here, and are often amazed when they see me questioned by the police."[115] Though enough people knew him in Takata to prevent incriminating rhetoric from gaining traction, eventually it became unmanageable even for Powles, who, shortly before his 1941 departure, wrote of an "evident malice against us Britishers" and "an evident spurring up of feelings that [war] cannot be avoided."[116] Another missionary neutralized suspicion by relinquishing her Canadian nationality. Margaret Armstrong, with the United Church of Canada, was able to remain in Japan after retiring in 1940 by taking the unusual step of filing for, and receiving, Japanese citizenship. When other missionaries were leaving Japan or, following Pearl Harbor, being arrested, Armstrong was permitted to remain at her home in Toyama. Although she incurred some interest from the police, which came to inspect her kindergarten, her friends in the community shielded her from any substantive suspicion.[117]

The state's prewar suppression of Christianity was part of a broader movement toward the ideological unification and domestication of competing faiths. The fact that officials did not shy away from targeting German missionaries suggests that the state had little interest in using Christianity as an excuse to persecute and expel enemy nationals. The absence of any systematic subjugation of Judaism also controverts the notion that religious suppression was informed by either racial prejudice or xenophobia. Rather, restrictions imposed on Christianity sought to appropriate sources of ideological competition and then deploy them as sources of spiritual mobilization. Foreign missionaries' mere existence in Japan constituted a test of ideological wills, therefore. As they sought, in Lang's words, "a Christianization of Japan," the state sought a Japanization of Christianity.[118]

Japan's prewar retrenchment reveals several clear patterns. First, authorities were scrupulous in issuing and then observing their own laws and procedures—the notable exception being their sympathetic disregard for immigration regulations for Jewish refugees. Police surveillance, immigration, censorship, and international diplomacy were all carried out "under the forms of law," as Hansen wrote, and with due deference to the responsibilities assigned therein. Syd Duer relates that when he and his father, William, were arrested on December 8, 1941, the arresting Tokkō officers "conducted themselves with scrupulous decorum . . . [and] their questions were always presented respectfully and with courtesy." The Duers received receipts for the confiscated items, and everything except their camera and binoculars was returned to them after the war.[119] Equally significant is the fact that Westerners rarely suffered unauthorized or illegal forms of oppression, violence, or harassment from authorities. Until the foreign assets freeze, in fact, containment included minimal evidence of racial profiling against Westerners. Change was often slow and incomplete. English newspapers likely retained more autonomy than has been suggested, and the eradication of Western influences like English and jazz music was not absolute. In stark contrast to the exclusionary immigration policies erected against Japanese overseas, the residency conditions imposed by Japan on Westerners were lenient, requiring merely the permission of the regional governor for residency exceeding thirty days and submission of a notification of extended residence for residency exceeding sixty days.[120] Hans Martin Krämer has argued that the Religious Organizations Law was neither as draconian nor as unwelcome as is commonly proposed. He notes that some of the principles advanced by the legislation preexisted the bill, and that many restrictions imposed on Christian groups were not rescinded after the war, suggesting that they were not viewed by those groups as entirely unwelcome. Though her own mission was affected by the law, Hansen affirms that the elimination of financial support from abroad was not altogether objectionable, writing that the "evolution of financial independence was going on gradually and in a healthy manner, several churches going independent each year."[121] Outright suppression of Christianity was not the objective of Japanese authorities, Krämer concludes. Though pressure was exerted, compliance was not unilaterally required, a point verified by the fact that Roman Catholics and other sects were permitted to remain largely independent.[122]

Second, Japanese containment efforts acquired symbolic importance for their mere existence but were greeted with varying degrees of public ambivalence. Media control, immigration statutes, surveillance, and religious suppression sought to regulate Westerners' activities in prewar Japan, but in many cases inertia prevailed and their effects took shape slowly or not at all. In fact, accounts suggest that neither Japan's citizenry nor its institutions were as receptive as has been assumed. Apathy toward wartime mobilization initiatives can be explained by the Japanese public's verifiable sense of disengagement from the wars in China and Europe. The Busses relate that the lives of Japanese were impacted little by the wars or by growing tensions with the Allied powers. Conscripted soldiers were deployed and their ashes returned, but Japanese stoically went about their affairs as they had before. "The war was not a subject of conversation by the people," the Busses write. "It was left in the hands of trusted military leaders, and the loss of human life was just accepted."[123] In October 1940, Hansen wrote of the country's disinterest in the recently concluded alliance with Germany and of rumors that Prime Minister Konoe himself was against it: "There were absolutely no demonstrations of pleasure, like decorations or parades, when the [pact] was announced. One semi-official newspaper complained in an editorial about the lack of enthusiasm."[124] And, as living conditions deteriorated and the challenges of survival consumed people's attention, the less the war made sense and the more ambivalent and disillusioned citizens became. Not only did many Japanese silently oppose the war, Saburō Ienaga has argued, but their "latent antiwar consciousness gradually became stronger as the consequences of the deteriorating war situation were felt at home."[125] This was confirmed at the end of the war by Police Bureau reports on subversive activities that found growing antiwar sentiment. More civilians, they asserted, were voicing anger toward the government, the military, and even the emperor.[126]

Equally instructive are testimonies of Westerners themselves, which consistently express frustration over police surveillance and indignation over antiespionage rhetoric but in many cases disclose little sense of alarm. Incredulous of any possibility of war with Western powers, many foreigners continued their accustomed lifestyles. Until the attack on Pearl Harbor, Araxe Apcar asserts that social life on the Bluff continued much at before.[127] In Sendai, Hansen attests, "As far as our own living is concerned, we are going on as if nothing had happened. Everywhere we meet with extra courtesy and even kindness, it seems to us, from strangers we meet. . . . And in school, our students are extra nice to us. . . . We know how ashamed they are of the actions of their government, by the way they keep coming around, in private, to apologize. Naturally, in a totalitarian country they don't express any opinions in public. Neither do we. It isn't necessary."[128]

For our purposes, a third and most revealing feature of Japan's handling of resident Westerners was its tendency to practice flexible decision making by assessing issues and problems situationally. By definition this approach fosters disorganization and unpreparedness, descriptors that many have used to characterize Japan's wartime leadership.[129] Tolischus noted that Japanese policy was readily adaptable to the needs at hand and consisted largely of whatever procedures were necessary to achieve desired results.[130] "The new war economy had nothing to do with erecting a 'New Economic Structure' along ideological lines," he writes, "but was strictly practical."[131] And indeed, laws that placed financial institutions, capital, and foreign assets under greater state control reflected pragmatic decision making that prioritized military needs. In a statement published in the Japanese newspaper *Tokyo nichinichi*, Finance Minister Ogura Masatsune (1875–1961) called for more results-oriented policies, reflecting that "economic policies in the past were rather too ideological" in that they did not maximize profits, the fundamental purpose of business.[132]

Japanese situationism, we have seen, is readily apparent in its handling of Jews and Christians, whose respective cases show Japan responding to different types of Westerners with markedly different containment measures. Racial discrimination played no part in its treatment of either group. Nor do we find Japan acting in accordance with any overarching moral mandate. It assessed each case against its own interests and then determined how best to secure those interests. This "haphazard response to external conditions" was discretionary and thus lacked accountability, but it also permitted Japanese leadership needed flexibility.[133]

Mobilization for war with China naturally imposed greater restrictions on foreigners, and Westerners particularly. Tougher immigration and counterespionage initiatives, censorship, and the freeze on foreign assets were all variously successful in strengthening state oversight and curtailing freedoms. They did not, however, impose systemic racism. The spiritual mobilization directed toward the Japanese public, similarly, aimed to erase Western influences and cast suspicion on foreign individuals, but did so without instilling hatred. Though unevenly observed and often unconvincing, it was also variously successful in the sense that it conveyed new rules of civil engagement with Westerners. Control was thus variable, tailored to address practical necessities, accommodate contexts, and secure strategic oversights. Collectively, all were preemptive, preparatory steps designed to facilitate absolute containment in case of a second war, a contingency brought to life by the attack on Pearl Harbor.

PART II

Lives in Limbo: Wartime Containment in the
Wake of Pearl Harbor

Part II Introduction

[handwritten: Containment AFTER 12/7/41]

Military offensives in the Pacific necessitated defensive actions at home. In preparation for a protracted war, Japan sought to defend itself both from the security risks posed by resident Westerners and from the retribution it would suffer should those residents be harmed. Now without possibility of escaping Japan, Westerners in turn sought to defend themselves from police persecution, air raids, food shortages, and the unpredictability of wartime life. Part II examines how the two sides engaged with one another in the face of these self-defensive challenges. It also considers how war shaped the racial dynamics of those interactions.

Chapter 4 investigates Japan's containment of Western civilians in the wake of its Pearl Harbor attack with a view toward identifying any racial dimensions of that containment. It shows how war necessitated the formulation of a nationality-based taxonomy and concomitant handling protocols for each classification of foreign nationals. Examination of the temporary detention, interrogation, and incarceration of suspicious enemy nationals and the house arrest of diplomatic staff reveals draconian penal settings but little evidence of racial prejudice. Chapter 5 considers the new war's impacts on Western residents and their communities. It discusses fissures that eroded the solidarity of those enclaves, including the ideological divisions, material inequities, and geographical particularities that distinguished living conditions in Tokyo, Yokohama, and Kobe. Our discussion of early wartime conditions will consider Japanese public opinion toward the war, as well as toward the antiforeign propaganda being disseminated by the state. Chapter 6 examines the evacuation order issued in late 1943 and the subsequent exodus from Tokyo and Yokohama. It focuses on the two evacuation communities of Gora (Hakone) and Karuizawa. Memoirs and interviews by the Franks, Balks, and other evacuated families detail the living conditions in these communities while illuminating Western and Japanese racial attitudes toward one another in the face of strengthening police interference.

CHAPTER 4

First Responses and Containment Protocols after Pearl Harbor (1941–43)

> December 8th is the Feast of the Immaculate Conception. . . . So we go to church on that day. I had walked to church up on the Bluff, the one in which I was married. I was going to pick up a blanket from an American friend of mine, who was going to leave the country. . . . I was on my way from church to this American's house when I saw motorcycles with side cars on them. The Japanese Military Police. Just going in all directions.
>
> When I came to this American's house here was one of the military motorcycles with the side car. My American friend was being led out of the house with his hands tied with a rope. . . . I thought I better not go in there. . . . Here the Military Police were just going all over picking up all of the remnant Americans and British, including the Irish nuns, and putting them . . . in the Yacht Club.
>
> —Ludy Frank[1]

On the morning (Japan time) of December 8, 1941, authorities acted swiftly to neutralize the 2,138 enemy nationals remaining in Japan.[2] Within hours of the attack on Pearl Harbor they had interned 342 of them within thirty-four facilities around the country, confined or placed under house arrest 258 diplomats, and arrested 109 others for suspicion of espionage. These roughly 700 enemy nationals accounted for about one-third of the total number residing domestically.[3]

A New Taxonomy of Foreigners

With the onset of war, passport-bearing Westerners found that they had formally incurred the status of enemy, neutral, or allied nationals. The Interior Ministry had already formulated containment programs for these categories, and on the morning of December 8 it set those programs in motion. Besides the coordinated roundup of select enemy nationals and the confinement of enemy diplomats, suspicious journalists and missionaries were imprisoned and interrogated, and citizens from nations that Japan considered neutral—Switzerland, Sweden, France, Hungary, Portugal, and the Soviet Union, among others—were monitored and their movements curtailed (table 4.1 and table 4.2). The following day, a law was passed requiring Westerners to apply for permission to travel outside their region of residency and barring them from areas deemed sensitive to national defense.

The Interior Ministry's guidelines dictating procedures for treating and, as necessary, interning resident citizens of Allied nations enabled it to act quickly. Though the designation "enemy national" applied to citizens of all twenty-seven countries that had declared war on Japan, authorities

Table 4.1
Populations of select enemy nationals
in Japan on December 8, 1941

Enemy Nationals	
Americans	1,044
British	690
Canadians	188
Dutch	109
Australians	41
Belgians	38
Norwegians	19
Greeks	9
Total	2,138

SOURCE: Interior Ministry survey, *Gaiji keisatsu gaikyō* (Overview of Foreign Affairs Police), cited in Komiya, *Tekikokujin yokuryū*, 19.

Table 4.2
Populations of select other foreign nationals
in Japan on June 30, 1942

Neutral nationals	
French	465
Soviets	82
White Russians and stateless	1,150
Axis nationals	
Germans	2,482
Italians	246

SOURCE: Interior Ministry, *Tekikokujin yokuryū kankei*, 13.

focused their attention on Americans and British, and to a lesser degree on
Canadians, Dutch, and Australians. The guidelines established three
broad categories of foreign nationals based on their perceived knowledge
and likelihood of leaking information pertaining to Japanese war operations. Those posing the greatest risk—enemy nationals, suspected spies,
and select journalists and missionaries—were to be arrested and investigated. A second category comprising diplomatic staff and more innocuous journalists and missionaries were to be held until they could be repatriated. Others judged to pose minimal risk were to be monitored but
left at large. The diversity of individuals classified as enemy nationals,
however, called for subclassifications, and on November 28, 1941, the
ministry issued a Foreign Affairs Emergency Measures Plan (*Gaiji kankei
hijō sochi ni kan suru ken*) that instructed police to arrest those falling
into any of five categories: individuals enlisted in the military; crew members of ships or airplanes, or those bearing such qualifications; males
between the ages of eighteen and forty-five; individuals with special skills
such as radio operators and munitions factory experts; and suspicious individuals falling outside the above criteria.[4]

In calling for the confinement of enemy males between eighteen and
forty-five, in principle the Emergency Measures Plan left minors and
women immune to the reprisals of enemy status. Children who saw their
elder brothers interned were allowed complete freedom of movement. Joe
Hale (b. 1937), a U.S. citizen, continued living with his Japanese mother,

who resisted Kenpeitai encouragement to change Hale's nationality to Japanese. The Hales remained in Tokyo until the spring of 1945 and then evacuated to Hakone together with Thai embassy staff. When Hale entered Saint Joseph's in 1946, he learned that among the school's students he was the only American to have lived in Japan during the war.[5] (Many of the women allowed to remain at large were eventually interned, which will be discussed in chapter 7.)

In spite of these general guidelines issued prior to Pearl Harbor, the ministry and the military were underprepared for the magnitude of the custodial responsibilities that Japan's military expansion would entail.[6] The process of implementing the basic framework established by the Emergency Measures Plan necessitated further distinctions that would help fine-tune the wartime standing of foreign civilians. In practice, therefore, further unofficial subclassifications of resident aliens were observed, along with concomitant (often discretionary) forms of treatment and handling (table 4.3).

With the exception of Jews and Asians, in principle this was a nationality-based rather than a race-based taxonomy. Unlike race, citizenship was verifiable and unambiguous. An episode related by Ludy Frank illustrates how rigidly Japanese authorities connected rights and treatments with citizenship: "The White Russian always occupied a very hazardous position as far as the Japanese police were concerned. At one time, 10 White Russians went to the Soviet Embassy to request re-instatement into Russian citizenship as Soviet subjects. These ten were immediately arrested and most cruelly treated by the Japanese police and only let out after 10 days of grueling questions upon a protest lodged by the Soviet Embassy. There were no other White Russian applications for citizenship!"[7] Japanese nationality consciousness is further illustrated by the case of Jane Cook-Kobayashi, a Scottish nurse living in Shanghai who befriended and became engaged to a wealthy Japanese widower named Kobayashi. They returned to Japan and lived together in Tokyo as a married couple. The marriage had not been formalized, however, and the day after Pearl Harbor Jane was arrested and imprisoned on suspicion of espionage. Several weeks later she was released, upon which she legalized the marriage, forfeited her British passport, and lived unmolested for the remainder of the war.[8] As a British citizen she was considered a spy but as a Japanese citizen was permitted residency. Retired Canadian mission-

Table 4.3
Unofficial taxonomy of resident Western civilians in wartime Japan

Classification	Example[1]	Treatment
Axis nationals: Non-Jewish[2]	Margot Lenigk	Embassy support
Axis nationals: Missionaries	Busses, Notehelfers, Langs	Embassy support, surveillance
Neutral nationals: Non-Jewish	Robert Guillain (French), Baenningers (Swiss)	Surveillance, occasional arrests
Axis and neutral nationals: Jewish	Franks and Balks (until denaturalized)	Surveillance, harassment, occasional arrests
Italians (after September 1943)	Mario Indelli	Loyal to Mussolini: free Not loyal to Mussolini: interned
Germans (after May 1945)	Erwin Wickert	Surveillance and loose confinement
Jewish refugees in transit (until summer 1941)	Kobe refugees	From officials: cooperation and good treatment From public: sympathy and hospitality
Stateless	Dmitri Abrikossow, Michael Apcar	Surveillance, harassment, occasional arrests
Neutral diplomats	Max Pestalozzi	Immunity
Enemy nationals: Resident men aged 18–45	John Palmer, Robert Crowder	Interned in low-security camps, some repatriated via exchange ship
Enemy nationals: Resident women, children, and elderly	Eleanor Laffin, Alice Kildoyle	Surveillance until December 1943, after which evacuated and interned in low-security camps
Enemy nationals: Diplomats	Joseph Grew, Sir Robert Craigie	House arrest, repatriation via exchange ship
Enemy nationals: Journalists	Otto Tolischus, Phyllis Argall	Variable: in some cases arrest, interrogation, and incarceration; repatriation via exchange ship
Enemy nationals: Clergy and missionaries	Ernest and Edith Bott, Rev. Samuel Heaslett	Variable: in some cases arrest, interrogation, and incarceration; repatriation via exchange ship

(continued)

Table 4.3 (*continued*)

Classification	Example[1]	Treatment
Enemy nationals from noncombatant nations	Greeks	Left alone or interned
Foreigners affiliated with suspicious organizations (Freemasons, Salvation Army)	Michael Apcar	Variable: arrested, incarcerated, released, or repatriated
Foreigners holding Japanese citizenship	William R. Gorham, Margaret Armstrong	Minimal surveillance
Western nationals: Part Japanese/part Caucasian	Laffin siblings; Duers, Joe Hale, Alice Frank	Variable depending on nationality and gender
Japanese nationals: Part Japanese/part Caucasian	James Harris	As Japanese, with some exceptions

[1]These individuals are discussed at various points in the book.
[2]Axis nations included Germany, Italy, Japan, Romania, Hungary, Bulgaria, and Yugoslavia.

ary Margaret Armstrong and American businessman William R. Gorham likewise erased suspicion by taking Japanese citizenship.[9]

In some cases, nationality status fluctuated in parallel with that nation's sovereignty in the European Theater. Benito Mussolini's (1883–1945) Fascist Italian government surrendered on September 8, 1943, but two weeks later Mussolini formed another in Northern Italy, which Germany and Japan recognized as legitimate. The 256 Italian diplomats and civilians residing in Japan at this time were asked to swear loyalty to the Mussolini government. Those who did so, along with individuals who were pro-Japanese, elderly, or infirm, were released. The 42 diplomatic staff, including Ambassador Mario Indelli, who did not pledge loyalty were interned in a new facility in Saint Francis monastery in Den'enchōfu, Tokyo. Nineteen dissident Italian civilians were interned in Nagoya.[10]

Just as Italy's withdrawal from the Axis alliance had necessitated the seizure of resident Italians, France's gradual recovery of qualified independence from Nazi control in 1944 rendered French residents targets of greater police hostility. Though government officials had been careful to honor French neutrality in Japan, in 1944 a number of French citizens, particularly in Yokohama and Kobe, were arrested on espionage charges, arrests that Robert Guillain interpreted as acts of revenge for the Nazi expulsion from France. Japan also took this opportunity to seize the assets of French companies formerly operating in Japan. With France looking increasingly like an enemy nation, Guillain writes, "the authorities were preparing the ground for a reversal of the so-called policy of tolerance that had given most of the French colony its conditional and precarious freedom."[11]

Though nationality was the primary determinant of one's official standing in wartime Japan, some individuals and groups called for discretionary treatment. John Morris (1895–1980) was one such individual. In 1938 the Foreign Ministry invited Morris, a British national, to teach English at Keio University in Tokyo and to advise the ministry on matters of the English language. As such, after the Pearl Harbor attack, Morris was considered a guest of the government and given diplomatic immunity from arrest and internment. Unlike actual diplomats, however, he was not detained and claims to have been the only British national permitted to move freely around Tokyo. Morris reports encountering very little anti-Caucasian sentiment and notes that his Japanese friends continued to interact with him and bring him gifts.[12]

Stateless individuals also called for discretionary treatment. Those who had immigrated as political refugees or had been denaturalized while in Japan lacked the protections afforded by citizenship and were vulnerable to variable forms of handling. Former Russian diplomat Dmitri Abrikossow (1876–1951), stripped of Russian citizenship in 1925 for renouncing the new Soviet government, found his stateless status a mixed blessing.[13] Though ineligible for either evacuation or diplomatic immunity, neither was he beset by the indiscretions of his former government.

Though ethnicity itself bore no legal standing, anyone critical of Adolf Hitler and sympathetic to the Allies was considered an enemy of the state, and this applied to all resident Jews and many of the neutrals.[14] Jews were subjected to variable handling, however, depending on factors like financial status, occupation, family, and political reputation. Some were targeted by the Kenpeitai under orders from the German embassy.[15] In 1942, Estelle Balk's daughter Irene lost her job as a personal assistant for being Jewish, and a year later Louis Frank was stripped of his post and pension at Yamanashi Higher Industrial College. Others were ignored. The Shapiro family, poor Jewish musicians who apparently posed little threat, was treated "kindly and with a show of respect throughout the war," as was most of the Jewish community in Kobe.[16]

Christian missionaries and clergy also received discretionary treatment. While police adhered to prescribed containment protocols for designated nationalities and occupations, their handling of missionaries was inconsistent. Ernest and Edith Bott, Canadian missionaries and English teachers who had worked in Tokyo for twenty years, were free to continue their professional activities until being repatriated via exchange ship.[17] Three other Tokyo-based Canadian missionaries, however, were placed under house arrest and then interned at the Sumire detention center for women in Tamagawa to await repatriation.[18] Some male members of the Kobe diocese were interned at the Canadian Academy, which had been seized and converted to a civilian detention camp, but their female colleagues were placed under house arrest. By September 1942, when police were still in the process of arresting and interning their counterparts elsewhere in the country, nearly all British missionaries from Kobe had been repatriated.[19] The neutralization of Christian sects and missions did not proceed under any unilateral directive, therefore; Japanese authorities focused on the most doctrinally subversive. Groups that espoused more literal interpretations of the Bible or whose theology precluded their acceptance of either imperial or military authority were considered antagonistic to the state's aspirations for a unified church. Some of the Japanese bishops from the Nippon Seikōkai (NSKK), which had refused to join the Nippon Kirisuto Kyōdan, were imprisoned while others were conscripted into the military.[20]

War in the Pacific thus forced the state to assess the security risks posed by subgroups of a highly diverse population of foreign nationals. The Emergency Measures Plan provided containment guidelines for some, but the variable containment measures enacted on others mirrored the multiplicity of the Western community itself.

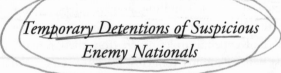

Temporary Detentions of Suspicious Enemy Nationals

The roundup of enemy civilians was completed without fanfare. On December 9, newspapers provided few details about the identities or numbers of those arrested. The *Asahi shinbun* noted merely that authorities had captured enemy nationals plotting against Japan, and that wartime precautions necessitated the detainment of even "good" foreign nationals in order to protect military information.[21] Two days later it reported that 271 British and U.S. civilians had been arrested within the Japanese territories and were being held for the protection of all involved.[22] The whereabouts of the roughly seven hundred enemy nationals arrested in Japan proper was never publicly disclosed.

As enemy aliens were being either interned in low-security camps or monitored in their homes, those engaged in potentially injurious occupations drew special attention. The Sorge spy ring had embarrassed Japan and ignited greater suspicions of foreigners holding certain positions and affiliations. Journalists, missionaries, and diplomats received top priority for repatriation. Their connections to powerful Japanese, access to information about Japan, and means of disseminating that information abroad carried great strategic value to their home countries, behooving Japan to rid itself of these liabilities first. Many such individuals were promptly arrested and imprisoned on December 8. This section examines the detentions of Rev. Samuel Heaslett, Otto Tolischus, Phyllis Argall, and Michael Apcar, all of whom had been pretargeted as possible spies.[23]

At four thirty in the afternoon on December 8, Rev. Samuel Heaslett (1875–1947) was arrested at his home in Tokyo for "suspicion under the provisions of the Safety of the Realm Act."[24] Heaslett had lived and worked in Japan since 1900. A missionary and professor of theology for the first twenty-three years, in 1923 he was consecrated bishop of South Tokyo and then in 1934 bishop of the Anglican Episcopal Church of Japan (NSKK). The Safety of the Realm Act was a near replica of the Defense of the Realm Act issued at the start of World War I by Britain as an expedient means of empowering the state to quickly enact military defense measures, censor media information, and seize and hold without trial individuals suspected of espionage. For Japanese police it served as one of several catchall laws applicable to cases for which they lacked concrete evidence of wrongdoing.

Heaslett was taken to Yokohama police headquarters in Tobe, where he was interned in a cell block containing eight Japanese, including two women, who had been jailed for "dangerous thoughts." His cell was five and a half by nine feet and held three Japanese prisoners, none of whom were incarcerated for war-related crimes. Amenities included a toilet

Prisons

(a covered hole) and futons provided at night. Prisoners received three meals per day and for one yen per meal were permitted to have higher-quality meals prepared by a local restaurant.

Heaslett was held for two weeks without being charged or questioned, a period that allowed authorities time to prepare other long-term facilities. He describes the cell as cramped and the food as inadequate. As large numbers of enemy aliens were arrested and interned at police stations on December 8, it is noteworthy that he mentions seeing no other foreigners and believed himself to be the only one held at the facility. As journalist James Harris (discussed in chapter 7) and others were detained there concurrently, police must have intentionally separated foreigners for their initial two-week detention to prevent them from exchanging information. As prisoners were denied both visitors and hearings with police, they were unable to learn of their own status as suspects or secure outside parties to defend them.

On December 20 Heaslett was taken to Yokohama Prison in Gumyōji (Kamiōoka) and placed in a solitary cell. The prison held well over one thousand prisoners, over forty of whom were foreigners housed in the same ward. Heaslett's cell contained a window, bed, sink, and toilet with running water. He received clothes as well as daily meals delivered from Tokyo by his maid and her daughter, and an additional blanket from a friend. Model prisoners carried the meals to each cell. Medical attention was poor but free; dentistry services were not free. Though prisoners at Gumyōji were confined to individual cells, Heaslett received a Bible and prayer books and against prison regulations delivered sermons from his cell. After a month he was asked to sign a statement giving his consent to remain interned for an additional month, an indication that his captors were taking care to avoid legal violations that might invalidate his detention. Heaslett signed it without asking about the repercussions of refusing.

Interrogations began on January 10, nearly five weeks after his arrest, and continued until late February. Though not physically abused, Heaslett was seated facing a light and was not permitted to hire a lawyer or prepare a defense. His interrogators were civil police, not Kenpeitai, but used the threat of interrogation by Kenpeitai officers to induce confessions. Heaslett describes them as belligerent men who viewed the accused "as a guilty person who must be in some way persuaded to accept the po-

lice estimate of your life, and then sign a statement that the formal indictment is true."[25] The purpose of the interrogation, he relates, was to
prove that the church was a covert organ of the British government and
that it was collecting and supplying political, economic, and military information about Japan. The interrogators mentioned British racism, how
Britain had criminally mistreated native races and how Japan, in comparison, endeavored only to guide weaker Asian nations toward liberation from their servitude to imperialist Western states. They also used
inductive logic to construct charges and prove guilt. With over four decades in Japan, innumerable Japanese friends, and proficiency in the language, Heaslett had acquired considerable knowledge about Japan and its
wartime conditions. These familiarities, and particularly knowledge of
the war's existence, they argued, proved his guilt as a spy. His incidental
glimpses of such daily sights as trains carrying troops and people waiting
in food lines were woven into a case against him. During the course of
questioning, Heaslett stated that he "would have done anything lawful to
avert war between the two countries." This statement appeared in the final
interrogation report, the word "anything" underlined to implicate guilt.[26]
Meanwhile, he learned later, his house was searched, certain property
seized, and certain friends and colleagues questioned.

The viciousness and relentlessness of the questionings began "to raise
doubts in my own head about myself," Heaslett writes, and he became
convinced that confessing to whatever his interrogators wanted was
the only way to conclude those sessions and "bring my weariness to an
end."[27] At the end of February he signed a statement that he had received
knowledge of the contents of the police report against him—not that he
confessed to the content of the report. This, apparently, was sufficient to
mollify his interrogators, one of whom later informed him that they
had no case against him and that his incarceration and interrogation
had been more a matter of "patriotism" than of uncovering criminal activity.[28] He was cleared of all charges in early March but held in custody
for an additional month.

Heaslett was released on April 8 and returned to Tokyo to find that
he had been relieved of his posts as bishop of South Tokyo and bishop of
the Anglican Episcopal Church. He received many visitors and gifts,
and though given relative freedom of movement was required to receive
police permission when planning to venture beyond Tokyo. He was

periodically visited by an officer assigned to him but the visits were a
matter of routine. On no occasion was he publicly insulted or obstructed,
he writes. "The presence and freedom of Germans and Italians and neutrals in Tokyo made my presence here and there not very noticeable."[29]
Previously jailed and released enemy nationals were repatriated at the
earliest opportunity, and the exchange ship that Heaslett boarded on
July 30, 1942, bore many such individuals. Heaslett himself was granted
diplomatic privileges, enabling him to take a portion of his savings, in
cash, and certain personal belongings. Photographs were not permitted.
Those he spoke to on the ship reported experiences similar to his own.

New York Times correspondent Otto Tolischus endured a more
lengthy and brutal inquisition and was ultimately convicted and sentenced. Like most others, he was arrested early on the morning of December 8 by Tokyo metropolitan police. After being taken to the local
police station by taxi, he was charged with violating the National Defense Security Law, specifically with "[sending] political, diplomatic, and
economic information to foreign agents harmful to Japan."[30] Later that
day Tolischus was transferred by taxi to Sugamo Prison, where he occupied a private but unheated cell until May 20. The cell was about six by
eleven feet and contained a cot, toilet, and sink. He had brought a suitcase of clothes; received books and food, including "canned delicacies and
flowers"; and was able to request other items he needed from people outside. Beginning January 7, he was permitted to use his own money to
supplement his meals.

At about the same time, Tolischus was subjected to harsh interrogation that included physical torture. His examiners accused him of espionage and authoring anti-Japanese articles. When he denied the allegations,
he was forced to sit on his knees and heels (seiza) while his examiners
slapped his face, choked him, and kicked and punched his knees and an-
kles. This occurred over several sessions in January and injured his legs
enough to require treatment from the prison doctor.[31] On January 19 torture ceased and his treatment improved.

Tolischus noted that the two types of officers he encountered at the
prison exhibited entirely different attitudes and levels of professionalism.
Facility staff and guards were responsible to the Justice Ministry, but the
interrogating police officers worked for the Interior Ministry. The former
were disinterested in him and his guilt and in any case had no authority

to interfere in interrogations. Some, he relates, displayed levity and kindness. In contrast, his interrogators, whom he nicknamed the Snake, Hyena, Fox, and Wolf, were "two-faced" in that they acted vicious and hateful during the questioning but cordial, even "friendly," afterward. Over the course of his interrogation Tolischus came to understand that his inquisitors expected prisoners to adopt a submissive, penitent countenance. They were enraged by Westerners who exhibited no shame or resignation at being captured or who did not readily apologize. At one point Tolischus apologized for having made a mistake, whereupon one replied, "That's all we want to know, that you're sorry."[32] Tolischus wrote, "I understood by now that the examining policemen had to make a long and detailed protocol to show their own diligence and that if I could furnish them with material for it without incriminating myself, it would be to the advantage of all concerned."[33]

Tolischus also witnessed Japanese and Western prisoners receiving unequal treatment at Sugamo. Japanese were subjected to more thorough searches, and when taken to his trial he saw that Japanese prisoners, unlike himself, were handcuffed and fastened together with rope. He later corroborated these observations while aboard his exchange ship, where he learned that imprisoned Asians and Japanese had received more severe torture than he had. Most of the other Westerners had not suffered much physical abuse. As the exception, Tolischus ventures a guess that police used him as a test case to determine how foreigners would respond.[34]

Tolischus requested but was denied a lawyer for his trial, but the Swiss embassy did find him a lawyer for the sentencing. On May 15 he was sentenced to eighteen months in prison, suspended for three years, for violating the National Defense Act. The sentence was consistent with those handed to other enemy journalists. On May 20 he was transferred to the Sumire internment camp, a holding facility for male enemy nationals— Americans, British, and Dutch, as well as a few Belgians and French Canadian missionaries—awaiting passage on the exchange ships. One of his former interrogators picked him up at Sugamo and took him out for a drink en route to the camp. At Sumire he was taken to the camp supervisor, also a former examiner, who greeted him cordially and expressed his relief that Tolischus had received a suspended sentence. The facility contained a library and kitchens, and internees were allowed to meet with family members and friends from outside and receive gifts from "many friendly Japanese women and loyal missionary pupils."[35] They were also allowed to take furloughs outside the camp to shop or visit family. During the final days prior to their repatriation, Tolischus and other journalists were invited to an elegant luncheon and then asked to write statements attesting to their good treatment. (According to rumor, the Japanese government had learned that its own journalists abroad were receiving good treatment and wanted to atone for its poorer handling of the foreign press.) Having accepted the first invitation, Tolischus and the others were not permitted to decline the latter request.[36]

Canadian Phyllis Argall worked in Japan for over twenty years as a missionary, educator, and journalist. In 1939 she began working as a reporter for *Japan News-Week* under British embassy information chief Vere Redman and her future husband, Bud Wills, eventually rising to the position of managing editor. She also worked for the *London News Chronicle* as the only accredited female correspondent in Japan. Argall was arrested on suspicion of espionage at seven thirty in the morning on December 8 and taken to Kenpeitai headquarters in Tokyo. When slapped by a Kenpeitai officer during her interrogation there, she writes, she recoiled in fury, "fury that an inferior should strike me."[37] Later that day she was transferred to Sugamo Prison, where she languished in a private cell for the next six months. Her ward was staffed largely by women, but otherwise her conditions were identical to those detailed by Tolischus, also at Sugamo.

Interrogation began again several days after her transfer, conducted by officers who had been monitoring her for the past three years. They knew her well and were more affable than the examiners described by Heaslett and Tolischus. Their agenda, she learned, was to uncover evidence that the British embassy and American publisher Bud Wills were operating a spy ring and had manipulated Argall's complicity. (Redman and Wills had been arrested and, unknown to Argall, were also being held at Sugamo.) Argall was not tortured or physically abused, though prison life itself was torturous. She remained in solitary confinement for the duration, suffering mainly from isolation and cold. In winter the unheated facility became so frigid that she developed frostbite on her hands and feet. The ward's daily routine ensued as follows: prisoners rose at 6:00 a.m., dressed and prepared for inspection at 6:20. Inspection, which required prisoners to kneel and bow, was followed by breakfast. Lunch was served at 10:30, and supper at 3:30. A second inspection was conducted at 4:30 and the lights-out bell rung at 7:00. Meals consisted of cold rice-barley porridge, soup, pickles, and tea, and were delivered to the individual cells. As with Heaslett and Tolischus, Argall was allowed to supplement her diet at her own expense, and she arranged to receive bread, milk, and an egg for breakfast. She received one hot bath per week.[38]

At her trial on May 4, Argall was charged with complicity in *Japan News-Week*'s publication of several anti-Nazi editorials, cartoons, and articles. She admitted to the charge. She was provided an attorney but permitted only five minutes to confer with him, and the attorney's defense consisted merely of a plea for leniency. The trial lasted only twenty minutes. Like Tolischus, Argall was sentenced to eighteen months' imprisonment, suspended for three years. She was unaware of the exchange ship negotiations or the fact that she had been designated for repatriation in the coming weeks. When asked by the procurator whether, if given the opportunity, she would leave Japan, she had thought the question purely hypothetical. She discovered that the trial had been a meaningless formality only after being released and learning that her passage on an exchange ship to the United States had been authorized.[39]

Select nonenemy nationals were also targeted. Lucille Apcar's school, Saint Maur's, opened as usual on December 8 but closed early. Lucille had heard that many of the students' families were being arrested that morning, and upon returning home found that plainclothes policemen had detained her own father, Michael. The Apcars were stateless, which precluded suspicions of loyalties to enemy states, but their national origins had generated uncertainties. Michael's wife, Araxe, was an Armenian American who had lost her citizenship in 1922 when Armenia was incorporated into the Soviet Union. His aunt Diana, who had earlier lived in Japan and acquired their house on the Bluff, was British. This was enough to arouse Japanese suspicions. As a precaution, Michael had acquired protectorate papers and passports from the French embassy in Japan, yet following the declaration of war the Vichy government refused to recognize the protectorate documents. As such, the Apcars enjoyed no protection or representation by any foreign diplomatic entity during the war.[40]

Police ransacked the Apcars' house and confiscated financial documents, money, and jewelry. Though Araxe was placed under house arrest, the government claimed a legal right to seize the house, for the property was deeded to Diana, who, though now deceased, had been a British citizen.[41] The police informed Araxe that she and her children would have to vacate. Interestingly, Araxe took a friend's advice and refused to leave, continuing to reside there until the family's evacuation to Karuizawa in the fall of 1943. In this case, either the police considered the eviction order negotiable or they understood a deed held by a deceased enemy national to be insufficient grounds to evict the family, who even as stateless individuals retained certain legal rights.

Michael Apcar was taken to Yokohama police headquarters, where Araxe was instructed to bring him a change of clothes, pajamas, and a razor. As with Heaslett and the others interned at the Yokohama station, Apcar shared a cell with Japanese prisoners, slept on the floor, suffered from cold, and was fed poorly. One week later he was transferred to the Water Police Station on the harbor, and then in January to Gumyōji Prison. At Gumyōji, Apcar endured squalid conditions and questioning, but escaped the brutal privations suffered by those interned later in the war. When his daughter became ill following his arrest, he was allowed to visit her in the hospital, and then to attend her funeral. Araxe was permitted to visit and send him notes with Japanese translations. His family was instructed to bring him food at nine o'clock every morning and clean clothes on Thursdays. Daily food deliveries were inspected, tasted, and then dumped into a receptacle bearing the prisoner's cell number. Apcar reported that he never received the full quantity delivered.[42]

After being transferred to Gumyōji, Apcar was informed that he had been arrested for suspicion of espionage for his activities as a senior officer of the Masonic Order. In fact, immediately after Pearl Harbor, police had seized the Masonic lodges and their property in Yokohama, Kobe, and Nagasaki on the grounds that the group's secrecy and racial exclusivity violated the Peace Preservation Act. This was certainly a retaliatory measure, for in the late nineteenth century the Japanese and American governments had agreed to prohibit Japanese citizens from joining the order. As all other Masonic officers were diplomats and immune from arrest, Apcar was the only member detained. He alone would bear the state's chastisement of the order.[43] Following the war he submitted the following explanation: "No Japanese were made Masons in Japan, and furthermore such Japanese as had received their degrees in foreign countries were not asked to attend our meetings, owing to the understanding with the Japanese Government prohibiting Japanese citizens from participating in Masonic activities."[44] Apcar was released on February 25, 1943, after the Masons were put on trial, found guilty of espionage, and sentenced to three years' probation.

At the time of Apcar's arrest, his business, A. M. Apcar and Company, was closed and its accounts frozen, forcing the family to subsist on rations, handouts from friends, and black market goods. The family was also victimized by the company's office manager, a Japanese man named Aramaki who had been a trusted employee for thirty-five years. Upon learning of Apcar's arrest, Aramaki had emptied the contents of the store's safe and bank accounts, and sold everything of value in the company warehouse. He then transported the office equipment and furnishings to Tokyo, where he opened his own business.[45] For Aramaki, evidently, the boss's incarceration released him from all further professional obligations. Aramaki explained his actions as being the only possible means of ensuring the safekeeping of company assets.[46]

Enemy Diplomatic Staff under House Arrest

The diary of Joseph C. Grew, U.S. ambassador to Japan from 1932 to 1942, and the memoir of Sir Robert Craigie (1883–1959), British ambassador to Japan from 1937 to 1942, lend further testimony to the expediency with which Japanese authorities responded to the onset of war. It took just a few hours for police to lock down the U.S. and British embassies and place their occupants under house arrest. By order of the Japanese government, at eleven o'clock in the morning on December 8 official functions at the embassies and consulates were suspended, staffs were confined to their compounds, and all electronic communications with the outside were severed, although certain unencrypted telegrams were permitted pending review by Japanese liaison officers. Japanese staff employed at the embassies were also confined until their employment was officially terminated. Grew and Craigie were notified that for future interactions with the Japanese government a neutral country would be selected to represent them. The following day Swiss minister Camille Gorgé was informed of his responsibility as mediating representative for all American interests. He would oversee, for example, negotiations over the exchange of diplomats. Argentina became the protecting power for Britain but was replaced by Switzerland in May 1942. As Minister Gorgé was representing the United States, it was recognized that expanding his duties to include Britain would streamline communication.

Craigie relates that he had received an urgent summons by Foreign Minister Tōgō Shigenori (1882–1950) early on December 8. When he called at Tōgō's office he did not receive the declaration of war he was expecting, but rather news that Japan had decided to sever diplomatic relations with Washington. It was not until returning to the embassy that he learned, from his wife, of radio reports about Japanese attacks on Pearl Harbor and Malaya. Embassy staff immediately began destroying documents and summoning staff members living outside the compound. Craigie then traveled to the American embassy to speak with Grew but found the compound surrounded by police. He was permitted to enter and confer with Grew, and learned that Grew had also met with Tōgō that morning and, similarly, had not learned of the attacks until later. It was only at this time that a formal declaration of war arrived for Grew from the Foreign Ministry. Upon returning to his own embassy, Craigie also received a declaration of war. He ascertained that all sensitive records had been destroyed and that embassy staff were accounted for. Telephone lines had been cut and shortwave radios confiscated. A Mr. Simonds, the embassy chaplain, was arrested and held for several days at the Yokohama police station.[47]

U.S. embassy personnel were held within the compound until June 1942, when they were repatriated via exchange ship. Besides the bedding and fuel shortages, the crowding, and the general indignities of confinement, Grew found his captors' audacity particularly annoying. Guards treated embassy staff as criminals and felt entitled to violate "civilized international diplomatic usage."[48] The police were hostile, acted ungraciously, and subjected diplomats to "repeated indignities and humiliations."[49] They also obstructed the smooth acquisition of food, heating oil, and other supplies from outside. A Japanese American with U.S. citizenship named Fujimoto who was employed at the embassy as a translator was secretly taken into police custody. No explanation was given for this arrest, but Fujimoto later sent his family a letter stating his wish to remain in Japan and not be repatriated, a sentiment contrary to what he had expressed to them earlier. Fujimoto was never returned, the official explanation being that a relative had issued a charge against him to prevent him from returning to the United States.[50]

British embassy personnel were held until repatriation in July. Their compound consisted of the embassy building and a number of surrounding structures and residential houses, as well as a squash and tennis court. For the duration, the facility accommodated three times its usual number of occupants, as personnel with homes outside were now living inside. The immediate challenges were the crowding and the bedding and clothing shortages. Daily routines centered on doing laundry, preparing food, and alleviating boredom. Food, fuel, and other supplies were delivered by the Japanese, and the embassy was able to supplement those supplies with its large stock of imported food. Some of the provisions it had ordered from Australia prior to the declaration arrived in January and were confiscated but eventually released.[51]

Personnel were permitted to leave the compound and travel into the city, and were able to hold a dinner party and a concert on the king's birthday. Craigie, with his wife and son, was given permission to escape the summer heat at the mountain resort of Miyanoshita (near Hakone) for two weeks in July. He stayed at the Miyako Hotel, where he encountered numerous other diplomats, including Minister Gorgé.

It is evident from Craigie's memoir that Japanese authorities did not view the diplomatic corps' detention as a punitive measure or intend to inflict hardships on them. Their dual objectives were to contain personnel and decommission embassy operations, the latter being accomplished by severing communications, including contact between other diplomatic corps in Tokyo and even with British consulates in Yokohama, Kobe, and Nagasaki. Craigie echoes Grew's indignation toward lower-ranking police guards who initially exhibited haughty attitudes and entered his staff's residences at will. Higher police and government officials, he writes, showed due respect. He also reports that Emperor Hirohito himself had sent Tokyo's chief of police to the embassy to ask what he could do to make the occupants more comfortable. Craigie's complaints about police intrusions and food shortages were both addressed.[52]

Five British embassy personnel were arrested on suspicion of espionage at various times during the detention, but all were released and repatriated. One was Argall's friend Redman, head of the embassy's Information Department and responsible for compiling daily bulletins on political developments. Redman's editorials had taken care to avoid Japanese politics, but the bulletins had incited the ire of German authorities for taking issue with points of Nazi propaganda. Craigie asserts that the Germans had pressured the Japanese to detain Redman. After several days of requesting that Craigie surrender Redman voluntarily, Japanese police ultimately had to forcefully arrest him at the embassy.

Curiously absent from Craigie's account is information about the outcome of Redman's ordeal in Japanese prison. Craigie mentions his own repeated efforts to secure Redman's release but fails to reveal that in July Redman was tried and acquitted. In fact, Craigie was in Miyanoshita at the time and apparently was unaware that Redman had been released and returned to the embassy in time for repatriation along with the rest of the staff. It was clear that the Japanese had no solid case against Redman, which lends credence to Craigie's theory that the Germans had insisted on his arrest. Only when pressed did Japanese police explain that Redman had not been included on the official roster of embassy staff and therefore did not qualify for diplomatic immunity. In fact, this was a misunderstanding of international law, which stipulated that immunity is extended to an embassy's clerical staff, a point communicated to them by Craigie. Nonetheless, police continued to hold Redman at Sugamo Prison until July. A Foreign Office report from 1943 relates that during this time Redman was stripped naked twice, confined in harsh conditions, and subjected to 840 hours of "severe examination."[53] Other than being denied insulin, he was not tortured.[54] Rather, he was ultimately charged with "conspiring to prevent the execution of Japanese national policy" through the publication of propaganda seeking to destabilize Japanese-German relations.[55] Redman himself later divulged that his darkest moment during the eight months in custody was the day he was interrogated by two Nazi officers. He had established a rapport with his Japanese captors, he related, but found the appearance of Nazi officers much more threatening.[56] As direct Nazi involvement in the Japanese interrogation of a prisoner was extremely rare, it is clear that Nazi officials did take a special interest in exacting revenge on Redman for the anti-German tone of his editorials.

The first news of an agreed diplomatic exchange arrived as early as December 30, but a series of disagreements and misunderstandings over the conditions and logistics of the proposed exchanges, along with intentional or unintentional confusion within the Japanese Foreign Office, delayed the agreement until the following summer. Reciprocity in numbers and "categories" of civilians was a key criterion to be negotiated. It was agreed that nations were to release equal numbers of returnees and ensure that those individuals were of roughly equal occupational standing (government officials, journalists, businessmen, and so on).[57] The notion of assigning graduated values to individuals based on their potential contributions to military matters aligned with Japan's Emergency Measures Plan for enemy aliens, which called for the internment of only adult males. By the same logic, Japanese negotiators judged women and children to be the least desirable among the Japanese slated for repatriation.

A second inclination shared by the combatants was the necessity of defining people by ethnic origin. Of the 120,000 individuals from California, Oregon, and Washington interned in detention camps in the western United States, about 70,000 were born in the United States and carried American citizenship. Both U.S. and Japanese negotiators treated them, along with citizens of Japanese ancestry from other North, Central, and South American nations, as roughly indistinguishable from those immigrants carrying Japanese citizenship. In selecting individuals for exchange, U.S. authorities sought to determine only their country of loyalty and their desire to return to Japan. Both internment and eligibility for "repatriation," therefore, were determined on the basis of race and loyalty rather than citizenship. Japanese authorities, likewise, felt protective of individuals of Japanese ancestry, in many cases not recognizing their Western citizenships. The seizure and coercion of the American translator Fujimoto by Japanese authorities in Tokyo, certainly, was motivated by the same sense of racial inclusiveness.[58]

In the end, four exchanges were carried out, their logistics and arrangements overseen by the Swiss. Diplomats, journalists, missionaries, and educators were given priority for repatriation over other civilians. Foreign passengers aboard the *Tatsutamaru*, an exchange ship that had departed Yokohama for San Francisco five days prior to Pearl Harbor and was recalled following the declarations of war, were also given priority. Tolischus, Argall, Grew, and U.S. embassy staff departed Yokohama on June 25 on the exchange vessels *Asamamaru* and *Conte Verde*. They were permitted to take all their belongings and 1,000 yen. The two ships transported 1,450 North Americans from Japanese and Southeast Asian ports to the neutral port of Lourenço Marques, Mozambique, arriving on July 22, 1942. The Swedish-operated ship *Gripsholm*, carrying 1,468 Japanese from New York and Rio de Janeiro, arrived the same day and the vessels exchanged passengers.[59] The ships also carried food, mail, and medical supplies for delivery to those remaining in enemy custody. The second and final Japanese-American exchange occurred on October 16, 1943, in Mormugao, India. The two exchanges repatriated about 3,000 Japanese from the Americas and 3,000 citizens of North, Central, and South American nations (2,700 from the United States).[60] Heaslett, Craigie and his staff, and diplomatic corps from other European nations departed on July 30, 1942, from Yokohama on the *Tatsutamaru*, which stopped to pick up passengers in Korea and Manchuria. It arrived in Lourenço Marques on August 23 and exchanged its roughly one thousand passengers with the *El Nil* and *Narkunda*, which transported them to Britain. A Japanese-Australian exchange took place in Lourenço Marques on September 6, 1942.[61]

Racialized Others: Jews and Asians

Prior to its attack on Pearl Harbor, Japan had employed racialized containment strategies for Jews and non-Japanese Asians. Nazi anti-Semitism necessitated racial countermeasures even by parties wishing to avoid racial politics, including Japan and Jews themselves. Despite the fact that policies passed to enact the so-called Fugu Plan variously avoided racial language by referring to the refugees as European, the plan was a race-specific strategy for handling migrant Jews. Jewish communities in Asia such as the Far Eastern Jewish Council and Kobe's Jewcom also responded with blanket initiatives to aid Jews specifically.

Following Pearl Harbor, Japan moved immediately against U.S. and British citizens living in the Japanese homeland but saw no urgency to do so in China. It waited a full year before issuing orders to detain the eight thousand British and two thousand American citizens living in Shanghai. Not only would mass detentions of enemy nationals impose a considerable drain on existing resources, they would destabilize the region economically. The Japanese government did acknowledge the need to fundamentally rethink its Jewish policy in Shanghai, however. This had been expected for some time. A year earlier the Tripartite Pact had precluded Japan's continued hospitality toward Jews in East Asia, though this turn took several months to take full effect. The alliance, Japan knew, eliminated any further possibility of Japan befriending American Jews or attracting their investments in China. After enthusiastically participating in the first three Far Eastern Jewish National Conferences (1937–39) in Harbin, Japan recognized Jewish-Japanese amity as a dead end and canceled the fourth, scheduled for December 1941. And while Japan did not fully submit to German pressure to enact harsher measures against Jews, Josef Meisinger's appointment as the German embassy's chief of intelligence in April 1941 made resistance more difficult.[62]

Justification for rethinking its Jewish policy was aided by Germany's announcement that on January 1, 1942, it would revoke the citizenship of former German Jews, an act that would strip those individuals of diplomatic protection and release Japan from legal obligations to treat them as allies. A new policy was laid out by Foreign Minister Tōgō on January 17, 1942, in a directive sent to consulates on the mainland. This "Emergency Measure for Jewish People" stipulated that formerly German, Italian, and Spanish Jews were to be considered stateless. (This policy was unevenly enforced within Japan proper. The German consulate in Kobe rescinded Heinz Altschul's citizenship but not that of his wife, Hanni, who was Protestant, or their half-Jewish son.[63] Elsewhere, German Jews were not denaturalized until years later, as the Franks' story will show.) Second, it called for friendly treatment of "useful" neutral or stateless Jews, including White Russians. Whereas denaturalized and neutral refugees that could be used to Japan's advantage would be treated favorably, the remainder, including those from enemy nations and the poor, would be subject to strict surveillance. This latter mandate was directed primarily at Shanghai, which accommodated Japan's largest community of Jewish refugees. To facilitate surveillance, Japan's Ministry of Greater East Asia (Daitōashō) established the Hongkou detention area, the

"Shanghai ghetto," to accommodate the roughly sixteen thousand refugees that had taken up residence in the city since 1937. During a visit to Shanghai in July 1942, Meisinger tried to persuade Japanese authorities to execute this population of Jews. Though his suggestion was dismissed, Nazi pressure was instrumental in hardening Japanese treatment of that community. This was confirmed after the war by Fritz Wiedemann, the German consul general in Tianjin, who testified that the German government had insisted on the internment of stateless Jewish refugees. "The Japanese themselves were not anti-Semitic," he stated. "There was no doubt in my mind that the internment of the Jews in the Shanghai ghetto had been instigated by German authorities."[64] The Hongkou detention zone became operational in March 1943.

Certain manifestly pro-Jewish Japanese were also targeted. In late 1942, Dr. Kotsuji Setsuzō was arrested, imprisoned, and tortured on charges of complicity in the alleged Jewish plans for world domination. Charges were later dropped at the army's insistence. German pressure was also responsible for the forced retirement of army colonel Yasue Senko (1888–1950), former liaison to the Far Eastern Jewish Council.

Tōgō's policy reveals Japan's pragmatic intention to continue exploiting "useful" Jews but also its continued sensitivity to its international image. Allowing Nazi anti-Semitism to guide its treatment of the Jews it had just been courting, it knew, would only further antagonize its enemies. Instead, Japan adopted a more cautious, contingent position by closing its doors to all Jewish refugees in the homeland and occupied territories, and immobilizing those already in residence. Though officially treating Jews according to the rights afforded them by citizenship, Herman Dicker writes, "in view of their 'racial characteristics' they, their homes and their businesses were to be closely watched and hostile activities were to be eliminated."[65] This was a racialized policy in that it specified particular handling procedures for a specific ethnicity. And, to the extent that it was instituted under Nazi insistence, it also blocked the Foreign Ministry from acting independently or decisively. Throughout the entire evolution of "the Jewish problem," in fact, Japan's racial handling of Jews had been shaped by a combination of military "experts," economic opportunism, government weakness, and Nazi bullying.

This contextual middle course proved exceptionally practical but resulted in a series of mixed messages and uneven treatments. Anti-Semitic propaganda became more prevalent from 1941, even as some officials continued to reject anti-Semitic policy; Kobe's Jewish community was permitted to continue functioning relatively free of police interference, while Jews in other parts of the country faced greater persecution; and Jews holding positions of influence were more likely to be removed from those posts than less conspicuous individuals. The absence of any clear guidelines allowed local police considerable discretionary power and confounded resident Jews, who had difficulty both understanding their own legal standing and anticipating police reprisals.

The fickle, contradictory tenor of Japanese policy toward Jews is evident in anti-Semitic propaganda itself. A caricature from the November 1941 issue of *Manga* magazine (fig. 4.1), for instance, depicts how avaricious Jews had secured financial domination over Britain, the United States, and the Soviet Union. In doing so they had created a "living hell," murderous, self-cannibalizing societies in a state of infernal chaos. Though most such depictions appeared after the Kobe Jews had been transferred to Shanghai, where the Fugu Plan was failing to live up to expectations, it is nonetheless ironic that Japan had attracted and then encouraged Jews to help construct just the sort of capitalist order that the cartoon describes as a living hell. Japanese strategists had adopted the plan precisely because they deemed Jewish refugees more capable of building Manchukuo economically than Japanese. The caricature's bizarre duplicity toward Japan's own capitalist aspirations represents no strong philosophical position vis-à-vis the Jewish race or religion, only a pragmatic reversal of strategy.[66]

The new war also presented the Interior Ministry with the problem of differentiating among the many races it encountered in imperial colonies around Asia. In contrast to the nationality consciousness that framed its treatment of resident Westerners, Japan continued employing a racialized framework for its treatment of other Asians. The racial underpinnings of Japan's Co-prosperity Sphere and its pledge to liberate Asians from Western imperialists entailed forms of racial profiling that rejected Western sovereignty over Asian colonies as politically illegitimate. This included nonrecognition of Asians' Western citizenship. Resolving to recognize colonial residents by their original ethnicities, Japan issued the following policies for categorizing and treating Asian countries and citizens under Western colonization: ethnic residents of Hawaii, an annexed U.S. territory at that time, were considered Americans but Filipinos were

FIGURE 4.1 Kondō Hidezō, "Sei-Jigoku" (Living hell), *Manga* 9, no. 11 (November 1941): 19. Courtesy of The Ohio State University Billy Ireland Cartoon Library & Museum.

not; Canadians and Australians were considered British, but Asian citizens of Britain's Asian colonies were not; White Russians were considered stateless; the Dutch citizenship held by natives of the Dutch East Indies in Indonesia was not recognized, nor was the French citizenship held by natives of Vietnam and Cambodia; and Japanese Americans, as well as those holding dual citizenship, were recognized as Japanese. Nor did the Interior Ministry recognize the American citizenship of Nisei residing in Japan.[67]

If it is true that, as the British colonel Hugh Toye maintained, "most people were racist in 1939–43," it is not surprising that in a complexity of ways the Asia-Pacific War became a "race war."[68] But for Japan it was a race war to the extent that it played out under the auspices of select racist positions that in many cases were controversial among Japan's leadership. In practice, Japanese authorities negotiated wartime challenges with a pragmatism that variously assumed both racial and nonracial positions. Anti-Semitism was explicitly rejected by Japan, but as a racist agenda it also obliged Japan to approach the "Jewish problem" with race-specific policies. While repudiating the racism of Western imperialism, in its desperation to justify military expansion in Asia, Japan advanced identical racial paradigms, first in 1938 in the form of Prime Minister Konoe Fumimaro's New Order in East Asia, and then in 1940 through its Greater East Asia Co-prosperity Sphere. Doing so also elicited exploitative practices against colonial subjects around Asia. Japan's response to certain Western ideologies, therefore, variously drew race into its wartime rhetoric and then into its policies.

Racialized treatment of Jews and Asians foregrounds the nonracial treatment imposed on other foreigners, however. It is clear that Japanese authorities were sensitive to their international image and undertook damage-control measures to win the favor of Westerners they had interned. Persecuted journalists were cajoled with lavish food prior to their repatriation; in the latter months of their respective detentions, Craigie was allowed to vacation in Miyanoshita, and Grew was permitted to play golf (he declined). Leniencies did not prevent instances of illegal prisoner abuse, however. In delaying Heaslett's release for one month following his acquittal, his captors violated the National Defense Security Law's stipulation that detained suspects be immediately liberated once cleared of charges. The use of physical violence, against Tolischus particularly, was a breach of international law. Redman's arrest violated his diplomatic immunity, which Japanese officials had misunderstood, but was also illegitimate given that police possessed no evidence that his controversial editorials had broken the law. The indictment of Argall for complicity in the same offense indicates the undemocratic tendency to judge anything contrary to state interests as illegal. Such abuses were endemic to the circumstantial, discretionary policing routinely employed in wartime Japan. In fact, cases of abuse would soon multiply, for as Japan began to suffer severe shortages, military defeats, and air strikes, officials came to exhibit less leniency toward enemy and nonenemy suspects.

Legal injustices notwithstanding, neither Japanese authorities nor their penal system exhibited evidence of anti-Caucasian prejudice or hatred. After visiting his friends in prison and then learning more details of their imprisonment while aboard his exchange ship, Morris determined that racial discrimination did not factor into Japan's handling of enemy nationals. Treatment in Japanese jails was indeed brutal, he relates, but in the United States and Britain those conditions were being misrepresented as racial and punitive: "The press . . . both in this country [Britain] and in America, has commented indignantly on the barbarous way in which foreigners were treated. It is perfectly true that in many cases they were roughly handled; but not, I think, because they were foreigners. There was not, generally speaking, any discrimination against foreigners as such; they were, as I have said, rather better treated on the whole than Japanese in similar circumstances would have been."[69] Police brutality, poor prisoner treatment, and variously undemocratic judiciary procedures were systemic conditions imposed on all persons regardless of race. Racially motivated brutality against Caucasians—and anti-Caucasian profiling generally—would have been considered untenable in any case due to the uncomfortable fact that both Japan and its Caucasian allies were justifying their respective wars with claims of racial superiority. Indeed, as Tolischus and others observed, Japanese and Asian prisoners were subjected to the same prison conditions but treated more roughly by guards and police than Westerners. (By the same token, the use of torture in Asia, "where the Japanese have been torturing the natives for years," was more prevalent and aggressive than in Japan.)[70] Victims were targeted for the perceived threats they posed to Japan, not for being Caucasian, the select Jews persecuted by Nazi officials being noted exceptions.

Moreover, although the arrests were unquestionably retaliatory and thus unjust, they were also a charade. Police were role-playing. Heaslett's inquisitors were working "as a matter of patriotism," and Tolischus's were transparently "two-faced." The trials were also a pretense, for the suspended sentences were conferred with knowledge that the offenders would be repatriated within weeks and that the sentences would never be served. In many cases, journalists were interned to prevent them from continuing their investigative activities and acquiring sensitive information before they could be expelled from the country.

For foreign victims themselves, naturally, persecution did inflame racial emotions. Already sensitized to the ethnic overtones endemic to life in Japan, many reacted to detainment and persecution as racial insults. Grew, Craigie, Tolischus, Argall, and others all took racial offense. And although some admitted to racial hatred or feelings of racial superiority vis-à-vis Japanese, they also exhibited cognizance of the ugliness of such prejudices. Estelle Balk's manuscript is peppered with racial epithets but also explicitly rejects racial prejudice as immoral. Similarly, Argall recounts that when she was first informed by her prison inquisitors about Japan's victories in the war, "their news was a blow to my pride of race: I hated to think of all those little yellow monkeys in battleships we had taught them to build, capturing our overseas Empire, running amok in the cities we had built."[71] Yet, aboard the *Asamamaru* exchange ship months later, she was repulsed by the elitism of fellow Westerners discussing their Japanese "coolies" and their indignation at now having to carry their own belongings.

In the summer of 1942, Argall, Grew, and their respective cohorts won their freedom in the form of repatriation. Chapters 5 and 6 consider the nonenemy nationals they left behind, who for the next three years would struggle to retain the narrowest of freedoms.

CHAPTER 5

Watched and Unseen

Nonenemy Nationals after Pearl Harbor (1941–43)

In what proved to be exquisitely poor timing, Tokyo staged its first air-raid drill on the morning of April 18, 1942. The drill ended at noon, just as the Doolittle Raiders were flying into view. Recently silenced sirens resumed howling and confusion ensued, for neither Japanese air defenses nor civilians were sure whether the American B-25 bombers were real. People did not flee for their shelters; they ran into the streets and looked up, watching the raid "as though it were a circus act."[1] At home in Yokohama, Irene Frank, who had just returned from her honeymoon at the Fujiya Hotel in Miyanoshita (Hakone), also rushed outside when she heard the enemy planes. She cheered as the B-25s roared so low overhead that she could see the pilots' faces. Ludy ran out and pulled her inside, fearful that her jubilation would incite the ire of the ever-vigilant Kenpeitai.[2] In Tokyo, the Shapiro family was living with twenty-one-year-old Klaus Pringsheim Jr. (1923–2001), son of the eminent German conductor and composer. Klaus Jr. had fled Germany in 1939 and now worked at the Swiss embassy. In November 1944, when enemy bombers were dropping their payloads and everyone else was running for shelter, Pringsheim "liked to climb up on the roof and wave his arms around, screaming. 'Give it to them, Yankees! Give it to them! Come on, keep bombing!' And we'd [the Shapiro siblings] say, 'Klaus, would you come inside? You're going to get us all arrested. Don't keep shouting about your sympathy for the enemy.'"[3] (Isaac Shapiro's warning would prove prophetic, for several months later Pringsheim was arrested on suspicion of espionage and incarcerated for the remainder of the war.) Also in Tokyo, Robert Guillain was likewise enthused by the air raids. "Day or night, I could not help exulting over them," he writes. "They meant the war was no longer a matter of blind and impotent waiting; being in it and under it was already a kind of liberation."[4]

Irene Frank and Pringsheim, both German Jews, cheered not only for Germany's enemies; as refugees, they cheered for the enemies of the country that had provided them sanctuary. Guillain also welcomed Japan's annihilation, finding the bombs falling around him a brilliant portent of the war's ending. These curious reactions to enemy air strikes raise important questions about how resident Westerners viewed the war's combatants. Where did their loyalties lie? Enemy nationals had been swept out of sight expeditiously: adult men, most missionaries, and a handful of suspicious individuals were in custody; women, children, and the elderly were under close surveillance; and diplomats were under house arrest awaiting repatriation. How did those remaining—the nonenemy contingent without hope of repatriation—view the war? Though the loyalties of most foreign Axis nationals are clear, the sympathies of neutral, stateless, and Jewish individuals are more difficult to determine. Most had voluntarily settled in Japan and could claim few personal connections with the Allied nations. On the other hand, as Caucasians living happily excluded from Japanese society, many were swayed by the greater racial kinship they felt with the Anglo-Americans. A large number of nonenemy nationals thus held ambivalent or conflicted views toward all the war's combatants. Relating his own experiences in wartime Kobe, George Sidline affirms that although his family and the rest of the Jewish community there certainly feared the bombers, they felt no hatred or resentment for the Americans piloting them, even after those bombs had destroyed nearly every home and business in the city.

When war started there was an emotional conflict among many of the foreigners as to where their sympathy and loyalty lay. On one hand, they had lived in Japan for a long time and loved the country, its culture, and its people. On the other hand, virtually all of them spoke English better than Japanese. Their children went to schools where English was the primary language and reference in history and geography classes was primarily associated with the United States and Britain.

The result was strong pro-American and pro-British sentiment that existed even before the start of the war. Even when bombs fell on their homes and businesses there was no anger. Just frustration at the duration of the war.[5]

Irene, Pringsheim, Guillain, Sidline, and many other foreigners reflexively aligned themselves with the United States and Great Britain regardless of any prior associations with those countries. They did so largely for practical reasons, for what they desired more than any particular outcome was the war's immediate end. The Americans and British, they felt, were their best hope of achieving this.

This chapter will examine this "emotional conflict" over the war and how it became a source of fracture for the community of nonenemy foreign nationals, particularly the German contingent. Ideological divisions were exacerbated by concomitant factors like Nazi bullying and material inequities. Westerners' conflicting emotions about the war (and about each other) were also magnified by antiforeigner propaganda and threats of police persecution, both of which foreigners viewed as forms of *official* racial profiling. Such conditions—the combination of surveillance, professional disenfranchisement, and privation—left many with little recourse other than to withdraw to invisibility. Japanese also harbored conflicting emotions, both toward the war and toward resident Caucasians, and this chapter will look at their *unofficial* treatment of Westerners. They, like the foreigners, were also watched, disenfranchised, and hungry. The shared horrors of wartime life eroded the power differentials that had divided Westerners and Japanese and contextualized race relations during the war years. Shared living conditions not only defused antiforeigner propaganda; in many cases they elicited Japanese magnanimity toward Caucasians as collateral war victims.

Fracture and Emotional Conflict

Fissures within the foreign community were precipitated by multiple factors, one of which was the community's wildly fluctuating demographics. Between October 1940 and October 1941, the number of American citizens in Japan fell from about 2,500 to 300, the British cohort suffering a roughly equivalent decline.[6] Over roughly the same period, the community of 1,600 Germans ballooned to about 2,500, making it by far the largest contingent of Westerners.

Beyond numbers, community rupture was grounded in two divisive issues: conflicted ideological and emotional support for the war's combatants, and anti-Semitism. One can readily assume that, in principle, non-Nazi Germans and Italians joined Nazi Party members in supporting the Axis coalition, regardless of their feelings for Japan. But Nazis were alone in openly endorsing anti-Semitism. (Nonparty Germans could not explicitly oppose it, making their views on the subject indeterminate.) Nonetheless, these two issues formed the parameters that placed Italians, Nazis, and non-Nazi Germans at odds with a diverse community that was generally unified in its disgust for anti-Semitism. The war thus polarized along national lines a foreign community that had been practicing a qualified "white cosmopolitanism" since Japan's opening some eighty years earlier.

Friendships with associates from opposing camps became strained. "I don't think the average German can fathom the hatred and aversion other people had for them," Estelle Balk wrote of these deteriorating relations.[7] The International Women's Club in Yokohama responded to Nazi antagonisms by barring membership for German women. Estelle's membership was rescinded not for her Jewishness but rather for her husband's nationality. Individuals perceived to be either working for or conciliatory toward the Germans were also condemned. Estelle, whose manuscript is openly contemptuous of Hugo Frank and blames him for Arvid Balk's arrest, asserts that Hugo brought hardship on innocent foreigners by "working for the German community as well as spying for the Japanese police."[8] (Though Hugo would later take a job distributing rations cards for the Germans in Gora, there is no evidence that he, a Jew himself, was working for them while in Yokohama or that he was spying for the police.)

The disintegration of community solidarity had been set in motion years earlier, however. The Anti-Comintern Pact (November 25, 1936) had energized pro-Nazi groups in Japan and prompted three hundred German residents to celebrate by parading through the streets of Tokyo. From this point, German officials exerted direct and growing influence on the

Japanese government. The two countries exchanged police officers, a Nazi adviser was installed in the Interior Ministry, and under Ambassador Eugen Ott (1889–1977) the German embassy issued advice on military matters and pressured Japan to eradicate communism and persecute Jews. Germany also sent a press attaché to Japan to supervise the local media. This attaché attempted to suppress articles printed in English newspapers by filing complaints with the Foreign Office, which in turn relayed those objections to the newspapers. And as Germans protested anti-Axis coverage in the English media, presses protested when forced to apologize for that coverage.[9] German interference in foreign media was accompanied by the arrival of more German correspondents and journalists, who by 1940 had become Japan's largest foreign news corps.[10] And, whereas American and British journalists were prohibited from using shortwave radios and received only restricted access to their own business funds, the German press corps cooperated with Japanese censors on vetting the content of radio broadcasts.

Meanwhile, Japan's loyalty to Germany continued to generate repercussions. The Olympic Games and the World's Fair, both to be hosted by Japan in 1940, were canceled by their respective international governing bodies. War in Europe, combined with Japan's diplomatic isolation, created disruptions in communication, hampering the ability of some embassies to continue providing their expats with services and support. Tensions within the foreign community were aggravated by Japan's signing of the Tripartite Pact, which formalized German entitlement on Japanese soil and threw international commerce into turmoil.

Growing German dominance also upset an established system of national privilege in Japan. While many Japanese saw no reason to distinguish or privilege Westerners by their nationalities, Japan's leadership had done so for centuries. Militaristic overtures by some European nations and rivalries among missionaries had forced Toyotomi Hideyoshi (1537–98) and then the first three Tokugawa shoguns to treat some Western nationals more harshly than others. The government carried out 75 percent of its foreign trade with the British during the final decade of the Edo period (1600–1868), and 50 percent during the Meiji years. This afforded British diplomats what H. J. Jones calls "the deanship of the foreign diplomatic corps in Japan."[11] At the same time, from the late 1870s British and French stubbornness to renegotiate the unequal treaties fostered tensions with those states and desires within Japan's government to strengthen relations with the United States and Germany. The government thereby became accustomed to extending preferential treatment to certain nationalities based on its relations with their respective delegations.[12] The Axis alliance ultimately upended this taxonomy, even as some Western diplomats continued to defend their historical entitlements. On April 29, 1941, British ambassador Robert Craigie refused to participate in a parade to accompany a ceremonial military review, for example, because Japanese organizers had placed him and his entourage behind the Germans and Italians, thereby violating "the British right of diplomatic seniority."[13]

During the war, the Japanese government occasionally continued extending preferential treatment to certain nationalities. The Soviet contingent garnered such privileges. Though neutral toward Japan under the Soviet-Japanese Neutrality Pact (April 13, 1941), the Soviet Union was viewed by both the United States and Japan as integral to victory in the Pacific. In 1941, the Soviet Union had its hands full with Germany to the west, and Japan was busy with its own expansion in China and Southeast Asia. Neither country could afford to be bothered with the other. Japan knew, however, that it lay well within range of Soviet bombers in Vladivostok and that it would be unable to repel or retaliate against Soviet air strikes. Desperate to count the Soviet Union among its military allies, Japan made friendly gestures toward this end by accommodating Soviet interests in Manchuria and in 1944 relocating its embassy to the luxurious Hakone Gora Hotel. Japan also extended Axis and Russian journalists preferential treatment, including use of diplomatic cars.[14] It was unaware that at the Yalta Conference in February 1945, Stalin would promise Franklin D. Roosevelt and Winston Churchill to join the war against Japan.

The French were also afforded modest leniencies, though these were not evident initially. Consistent with their pattern of persecuting a small representative cohort as a means of intimidating a larger constituency, after Pearl Harbor Japanese police arrested six French citizens and held them for over two years. This was widely considered to be a warning to the rest of the three hundred French citizens in Japan, many of whom were missionaries and clergy. Guillain, who worked for the Havas News Agency between 1938 and 1946 as France's only Japan-based correspondent, was placed under surveillance and his journalistic activities curtailed. Papers and photos disappeared from his house and he once found that the lock on a closet containing his documents had been changed.[15] Otherwise, as neutrals he and his French compatriots enjoyed "provisional liberty." The French were afforded this privilege for strategic reasons, Guillain suggests, for "France was the only white nation whose friendship [Japan] thought it could eventually regain" after Japan's imminent defeat.[16] His decision not to evacuate in 1944 when nearly all other foreigners had been instructed to leave the Tokyo-Yokohama area placed him in a unique position to observe the capital during the war's final year. When the Japanese army unseated the French administration in Indochina in March 1945, however, Japanese authorities no longer felt obliged to offer special privileges to French residents. Guillain and his small cohort were relocated to Karuizawa.

Fractures were further aggravated when some Germans sought to capitalize on their privileged status by segregating themselves from other Westerners. They established exclusive churches and schools, tended to socialize among themselves, and instructed each other to avoid interacting with non-Germans. Their comparative freedom of movement facilitated segregation. Gwen Terasaki (1906–91), wife of Terasaki Hidenari (1900–51), who had served as first secretary at the Japanese embassy in Washington, DC, notes that the only foreigners she encountered during her stay at the Imperial Hotel in July 1942 were Germans and Italians.[17] Later, on her frequent visits to the Fujiya Hotel in Miyanoshita, she again encountered only Italian and German guests. During her initial visits there in 1943, she relates, the Italians were friendly, whereas the Germans were generally rude, refusing even to exchange greetings with her. "It was revealing that as the war progressed and the German position in Europe became desperate, the Germans seemed to warm up to my daughter and me and find that we were worth speaking to after all."[18]

Although the alliance rewrote the system of privilege extended to Westerners, it also fractured the German contingent itself. Nazi Party and nonparty Germans isolated themselves from German Jews, but they also defended their respective ideological spaces from each other. Accounts suggest that prior to 1941, members of the large German community continued to interact amicably regardless of affiliation with the Nazi Party, which functioned primarily as a vehicle for channeling and articulating

German nationalism. Members and nonmembers sent their children to the same schools, attended the same athletic and country club events, received treatment at the same hospitals, and vacationed at the same summer resorts. In principle, Germans were free to decide whether to cooperate with the party, and pressure to do so was generally indirect, but conditions varied. Some German businesses in Tokyo forced their employees to join, and resistance was variously punished. In the summer of 1941, for example, a man identified only as Dr. Tzairn was beaten by Nazi "thugs" outside the German Club in Kobe after viewing a Nazi film depicting atrocities committed against Jews. He had been overheard mentioning to an acquaintance that he considered such treatment to be criminal.[19]

In general, Nazi authorities failed to treat their nonparty constituents as allies. Nonparty households were watched and their servants variously used as informants. In many cases pressures to support party events generated disinclinations to cooperate. In 1944 the prospect of imminent evacuation prompted a debate over where to move the German school in Ōmori. Some wanted the older children sent to a school in Hakone run by Japanese-German Youth (Nichi-Doku yūgento), Japan's version of the Hitler Youth, but those opposed to the idea successfully lobbied to move the school to Karuizawa.[20] Propaganda disseminated at the school also generated controversy. The school asked that all boys in the fifth grade and older join summer Japanese-German Youth camps. But parents knew of the difficulties they would face in extricating themselves from such groups. Though initially cooperative, the Buss, Lang, and Notehelfer families eventually saw little recourse other than to avoid the German community and Nazi Party functions altogether. F. G. and Rose Notehelfer attest to being watched, and they mention that the family's mail was inspected and redacted, though they were unsure whether the Nazis or the Japanese were responsible. Such Nazi-Japanese collaborations, they write, disinclined them to cooperate with authorities of either nation. When police showed up to ask for their broken car as a contribution to the war effort (they had not bothered to repair it due to the unavailability of gasoline), the family dismantled the entire car and hid the parts, which they later used to construct a wood-burning stove and other necessities.[21]

Distrust within the German community was exacerbated by despotism at the top. Seeing that German Jews in Japan remained ostensibly unrestricted and fearing that the German community there was also being afforded undue independence, in April 1941 the Gestapo dispatched Colonel Josef Meisinger to police them. As the embassy's head of intelligence, Meisinger collaborated with the Tokkō and Kenpeitai to monitor the German community and variously suppress nonparty holdouts. Embassy radio attaché Erwin Wickert (1915–2008) describes Meisinger as a large, coarse, bald man with a bull neck, cruel and merciless but also cunning and cautious. On no occasion did Wickert hear of Meisinger encouraging lawful treatment of POWs or civilian suspects. Nicknamed the Butcher of Warsaw for atrocities committed in Poland the previous year, Meisinger's arrival instilled fear among German Jews and non-Jews alike. Reportedly, Meisinger kept lists of Japanese and foreign suspects and several weeks before Germany's surrender in May 1945 ordered the Kenpeitai to arrest the list of Germans whom he suspected of being Socialists, untrustworthy, or of low moral character.[22] Though able to enlist only partial compliance from the police, who variously helped themselves to their victims' valuables, many of his targets were subsequently arrested and subjected to interrogation. Even party members were scrutinized. Arrested suspects included the embassy's former wireless operator, whom Meisinger had previously fired for protesting the arrests. Wickert reports that Japanese police repeatedly tortured the operator in order to extract German encryption codes.[23]

Nazi arrogance not only divided the German community, it alienated many within the Japanese leadership. For Japan, the Tripartite Pact protected state interests in Asia but connoted no amity for Germany or Germans. Some authorities resented the superior, contemptuous airs of Adolf Hitler's National Socialist Party representatives, who, since arriving in 1934, had presumed to impose their anti-Semitic, anti-Communist agendas on Japan. The government had retaliated by deploying Kenpeitai to watch Nazi operatives and embassy staff. As Japanese and Germans watched each other, exposure of the Sorge spy ring in 1941 magnified mutual suspicion, each side blaming the other for the embarrassing debacle. The government's distrust of Westerners generally, not enemy nationals exclusively, was then manifested in the "temporary" freeze on all foreigner travel issued the day after the Pearl Harbor attack.[24] (Accounts suggest that Germans either ignored or easily evaded this travel ordinance, which was reissued following the German surrender in May 1945.) Antagonisms between Japanese and Germans were further aggravated by Japan's handling of the Doolittle Raid. News that Japan intended to execute the eight U.S. aviators captured during the raid disgusted the foreign community in Tokyo but especially infuriated the German embassy, which, Guillain observed, saw this action as a "horrendous insult by the 'yellows' to representatives—even if they were enemies—of the Aryan race."[25] Whereas the Japanese saw these crewmen as Americans, the Germans saw them as Caucasians. British ambassador Craigie observed, "A curious consequence of the [Doolittle] raid was that the guards on the Axis and Neutral Diplomatic Missions had to be doubled, so fearful were the police of an outbreak of blind xenophobia. But the diplomatic mission whose guard had to be *tripled* was—the German Embassy!"[26] It is likely, however, that guards at the embassy were tripled not to quash any xenophobic retaliation from the Japanese public, which never occurred, but as a show of strength in response to German outrage. As tensions escalated, German and Japanese children, for whom athletic festivals and other events had been organized as gestures of international amity, were discouraged from playing together.[27]

Lack of ideological solidarity within the German contingent was partially ameliorated by the Nazi Party's assumption of custodianship for all German nationals. Not only were German civilians treated better by Japanese officials and subject to comparatively less scrutiny by Japanese police, they received support and information from the German embassy and retained property and assets that enabled them to buy and barter for necessities. These allowances demonstrated to all that, as Ludy Frank put it, "Germans were a privileged class" among Japan's Western guests.[28] As such, the German settlement benefited from clear material advantages that during the war's early years allowed its constituents to continue subsisting the way they had in Germany. German food stores, bars, restaurants, and other shops in all the major cities continued to supply their constituents with German commodities, which most German families were wealthy enough to afford. Throughout the war, Germans enjoyed greater and higher-quality supplies of food than Japanese and most other Westerners. By their own accounts, they also suffered less hunger than other foreigners, nearly all of whose memoirs focus on hunger as their primary source of wartime adversity.[29]

Conversely, in some cases competition for German provisions would become a further source of community fracture. The nation's German population had swelled considerably since 1940.[30] About seven hundred of the new arrivals were women and children formerly residing in the Dutch East Indies (modern-day Indonesia).[31] When Germany invaded the Netherlands in May 1940, Dutch authorities in the Indies seized resident Germans. Men were imprisoned while women and children were held until they could be repatriated. One year later, amid rumors of an impending Japanese invasion, the women and children were released on ships to China or Japan. The Japanese ship *Asamamaru* transported some to Shanghai, Nagasaki, and then Kobe, but Germany's invasion of Russia in June 1941 prevented these evacuees from continuing on to Vladivostok and boarding the Trans-Siberian Railway back to Europe. They were forced to wait out the war "in transit." A proposal to resettle the refugees in Hokkaido was abandoned. Instead, the German embassy financed their housing and living expenses in the Tokyo, Yokohama, and Kobe regions. Some German residents decried this diversion of resources as inequitable. Margot Lenigk (1911–2011) and her four young sons were among the newly arrived cohort, and their story will help illustrate the resentments that emerged from the embassy's inequitable disbursements.

During repatriation from Sumatra in the summer of 1941, Lenigk and the ninety others aboard her ship were caught in transit and forced to wait out the hostilities in either China or Japan. Opting for Japan, she was given passage on a Japanese ship to Kobe. Kobe's German consulate and German Club, responsible for the well-being of that region's large German population, provided Lenigk and her children a limousine from the Kobe harbor to the luxury Miyako Hotel in Kyoto, where the family occupied two large rooms. She and other German mothers occupying the hotel enjoyed near-complete freedom to explore the city. After three months they were moved to the Nara Hotel, where the German consulate housed them for the following year. Lenigk was also provided a Japanese maid and babysitter, allowing her to take excursions through the countryside. She describes life in Nara as "peaceful" but wholly insular, for she received no news about the war and remained largely unaware of it. When Prime Minister Tōjō Hideki visited the Nara Hotel in 1942, she notes, he was photographed with Lenigk's two boys on his lap.[32] Her account indicates that even Germans of no consequence and without Nazi Party affiliation enjoyed generous material support.

After a year in Nara, Lenigk was moved to a large stone house on the beach in Tarumi, near Kobe, previously inhabited by a German businessman. The family and their maid received moving and startup costs from the German consulate, but Lenigk took a job at the German school to help cover other expenses. The German community also provided monthly rations for its German citizens, which augmented those provided by the Japanese government. After 1942 she experienced difficulties finding food, a universal problem, and had to barter her husband's clothing. When she experienced trouble balancing work with childcare, however, the consulate sent the teenage daughter of a German general to help with domestic chores. Despite the food shortage, Lenigk and her children lived without fear, suspicion, or harassment.

Air raids in 1945 drove many local Germans to Mount Rokkō, a summer resort northeast of Kobe, where they rented villas owned by wealthy Japanese. From there they watched the city burn after a massive air raid on June 15. Lenigk, comparatively safe in her home on the city's outskirts, had delayed evacuating. In July, when bombings grew more frequent, she learned that the German consul's villa on Mount Rokkō was available and so evacuated there with her children. The family was permitted to stay in the barn during the war's final weeks.

Lenigk's account of wartime life in Kobe contrasts markedly with memoirs by neutral, stateless, and Jewish residents, nearly all of whom faced severe hardships—starvation, sickness, cold, and police harassment. Though Lenigk also faced certain shortages, she enjoyed access to good housing, domestic help, compensated work, and rationed food and money. Her monetary allowance must have been especially generous, for despite having brought no money of her own, she was able to order an 800-yen fur coat for herself from a tailor in Tokyo. Anna Vrocina, a fellow East Indies refugee renting a house in Kobe with her sister-in-law, similarly reported that "generally, life wasn't bad at all."[33] These accounts corroborate German resident Fred Flakowski's observation that refugee women like Lenigk and Vrocina received "excellent care."[34]

Among all Germans, Jews faced the greatest threat of persecution. Their experiences varied greatly, however. Some were left alone and experienced few lifestyle changes after the onset of war. Others were denaturalized, fired, harassed, or arrested. Members of Kobe's Jewish community, consisting of about thirty families during the war years, enjoyed considerably better living conditions than their counterparts in Tokyo and Yokohama, where the Nazi Party was larger and more active. The "benevolent attitude" that Japanese in Kobe had shown to Jewish refugees did not abate after those refugees were relocated to China; it continued through the war. The city's unusual cultural sensitivity, Sidline relates, became apparent in April 1944 as the community was making plans to observe Passover, during which it would eat matzo instead of the leavened bread that foreigners were typically rationed. Community representatives asked the city for flour instead of bread so that they could make matzo, adding that they needed the week's supply of flour for the entire community in advance. Their request was readily granted. Sidline reflects, "It is almost inconceivable that anywhere else, except Japan, could such an event take place. Here was a country at war with an official stated policy of anti-Semitism, allied with a virulently anti-Semitic nation, yet agreeing to specific Jewish requests from the Jewish community! Such official acts of kindness from Japanese officials were not uncommon."[35] Anti-Semitic billboard posters depicting Jews with stereotypical features had no appreciable effect on Japanese, Sidline continues, for "the average Japanese had difficulty understanding white against white racism based on religion. . . . Consequently, Japanese anti-Semitism was merely token lip service to appease the Nazi regime."[36] In Tokyo, Shapiro also reports virtually no anti-Semitism during the war years. Japanese authorities never referred to his family as "Jews," he writes. "That was one distinction the Japanese did not make."[37]

Sidline did see evidence of Nazi efforts to manufacture suspicion and hatred of Jews, but notes that they impacted other Westerners more than Japanese.[38] His singular experience of anti-Jewish sentiment originated not from Japanese but from other Caucasian children at his school. Beate Sirota, a Russian Jew attending the German school in Ōmori, likewise relates that in 1935 the schools' teaching staff was replaced with Nazi Party members who required students to profess allegiance to Hitler every morning. Sirota was allowed to continue attending school, but her teachers' overt antipathy eventually compelled her parents to withdraw her.[39] In Kobe, Heinz Altschul (b. 1903) noted that his Western friends started avoiding him. "I could not blame anyone," he related, "because we [Jews] just were outcasts at that time, and [my friends] . . . could not risk any trouble" from the Nazis.[40] Jewish members of the German Club in Kobe all ultimately resigned their memberships and foreign businesses fired their Jewish employees. Altschul's employer, Winckler and Company, resisted and allowed him to continue working. When his continued presence became a liability, however, the company dismissed him, though secretly continued paying him.[41]

Ludy Frank alternately suffered and benefited from being German and Jewish. After graduating from Saint Joseph's in 1934, he worked for six months for a Czech architect, who likely hired him only because he was German. He earned a paltry monthly salary of 200 yen, enough to rent only a small room at the YMCA. He then found employment as a clerk for the Canadian Pacific Steamship Company in Yokohama. Though he does not explain why, Ludy relates being paid on the considerably lower Japanese pay scale and thus being unable to enjoy the sort of extravagant lifestyle typical of Western businessmen. When war broke out in Europe in 1939, Canadian Pacific fired its German employees. A friend then helped Ludy secure employment at the American Express office across the street from Canadian Pacific, but that office closed in late 1941 after its employees returned to the United States. Ludy was then hired to teach English at Yokohama Commercial College and Math at Saint Maur's convent on the Bluff. (Saint Maur's advertised openings for instructors when its Irish sisters were interned as British subjects after Pearl Harbor.[42]) Throughout these years, as a German Jew Ludy struggled to build an appreciable support group and find a comfortable social niche. He taught private English and German conversation lessons to Japanese, but the Kenpeitai drove away his students; he joined the Yokohama Country and Athletic Club, where he enjoyed socializing with other members and playing on sports teams, yet he was never fully accepted there. Excluded both by the Germans for being half-Jewish and by the Americans and British for being German, he found himself the victim of the same sorts of racial profiling mentioned by the half-Japanese Helms and the half-Jewish Balks. Despite being born in Japan and speaking the language, he was also unable to integrate well into Japanese society. Ludy mentions having only one Japanese friend, a former student living in Tokyo who was later conscripted into the army.[43] Anti-Semitism would continue to plague the Franks through the war years. In the summer of 1942, Ludy's wife, Irene, contracted polio, which partially paralyzed the left side of her body. Nazi doctors had assumed administrative control over the Yokohama hospital used by foreigners, however. The doctor admitted Irene, who was four months pregnant, but then refused to treat her. He then billed her. Irene ultimately received treatment at a Japanese hospital in Tokyo.[44]

Jewish disenfranchisement within the Tokyo-Yokohama region also affected travelers caught in transit. Transferring passengers required transit visas obtained in their countries of origin as well as visas guaranteeing admission to their intended destinations. Women wishing to enter the United States, however, were permitted to board U.S.-bound vessels with only a promise of marriage and a transit visa granted on the basis of that promise. Such was Margaret Liebeskind's intention. Liebeskind was German, one-quarter Jewish, and had secured a marriage proposal from an American man she had never met. After acquiring a visa to Panama and departing from Germany in December 1940, she had expected a quick transfer in Yokohama. Japanese immigration officials found irregularities with her visa, however, and removed her from the ship. The German consulate refused to help because she was engaged to an American citizen, and the Jewish committee in Tokyo refused assistance because she did not have a red *J* in her passport identifying her as Jewish.[45] Days later, Hugo Frank encountered Liebeskind, crying, at the U.S. consulate, where both were trying to arrange passage to the United States. Hugo brought Liebeskind back to his house in Yokohama, where she befriended his wife, Alice.[46]

As a German woman trapped in transit, Liebeskind's circumstances matched Lenigk's. As a partial Jew, however, she endured an entirely different wartime experience. Not only was she denied the financial and material assistance being provided to Germans by the embassy, she was not permitted employment within the German community. Like Sidline, Estelle Balk, and Ludy Frank, Liebeskind suffered more discrimination at the hands of other Caucasians than from Japanese. Eventually she found work at the Mexican legation and befriended Marie-Elise Balk, through whom she acquired a circle of foreign friends in Yokohama.[47] Three years later she would be arrested and tortured, and we will return to her story in chapter 8.

Strangely, official action taken against Jews by both German and Japanese officials was hesitant and uneven, indicating either extraordinary disorganization or a disinclination to comply fully with the Nazi government. On December 16, 1941, for example, the German Foreign Ministry directed its embassy in Tokyo to rescind the citizenship of all German Jews in Japan. On December 31 the embassy relayed this directive to the Tokyo-Yokohama Association of Germans. This impacted local Jews at different times and to different degrees, however. Louis Frank and 115 others were denaturalized in late 1942, but the association took no official action against Hugo, Ludy, or the Balks until January 15, 1945, allowing them to continue receiving the benefits of citizenship for most of the war.[48] After Pearl Harbor, Nazis also pressured Japanese authorities to fire German school instructors who were Jewish or anti-Nazi. Louis Frank was dismissed in 1943, whereas Ludy continued teaching until his evacuation to Karuizawa in 1944.

The events that precipitated war in Europe and the Pacific fractured Japan's Western community but did not cleave it cleanly into Axis and Allied camps. Nazi bullying aside, in some cases people's views of the community—of themselves and each other—were changed relatively little by the onset of war. Whereas their respective nations may have aligned with new allies against new enemies, some citizens did not. For long-term residents particularly, "white cosmopolitanism" was too deeply ingrained in professional and social lives to be so easily erased. This was especially true of children. In principle, Saint Joseph's remained free of racial prejudice after the onset of war, and students of all nationalities and religions continued to befriend and play with one another. Social interactions among youths also continued outside school, for no injunctions were issued against consorting with "enemy" nationalities. Shapiro recounts that Italian sailors interacted freely with Jews, Russians, and other nationalities in Yokohama, who in turn congregated at Honmoku Beach to socialize as they did every summer. The war made little difference, he recalls:

[In the summer of 1942], an Italian merchant marine ship, the *Conte Verde*, docked alongside the German ships tied up at Yokohama Harbor. It unloaded, among other things, a large group of Italian sailors, most of them teenagers or young men in their early twenties. They were eager for shore leave and for contacts with foreigners their own age, as none of them spoke Japanese. It didn't take them long to find Honmoku beach. Suddenly, we found ourselves surrounded by young, gregarious Italians, speaking broken English. They played games with us and flirted with the teenage girls among us, bursting into song at every opportunity. They preferred our company to that of their German allies and didn't seem to socialize much with the Japanese or the German sailors from the neighboring ships.[49]

Individuals with the means to do so also resisted wartime austerities, comforting themselves by throwing parties, attending social events, and vacationing. After recuperating from giving birth to her fourth son in March 1943, and amid the shortages afflicting others, Bernhard Buss's wife, Kathe, took a three-week vacation to a ski resort in Shiga.[50] Wealthy Japanese also found ways to pamper themselves. Teenage boys from elite Japanese families were often able to dodge conscription by acquiring certificates from doctors declaring them medically unfit for military service. Though these individuals still had to perform *kinrōhōshi* (several days of voluntary labor in factories), they otherwise remained free of any compulsory wartime service.[51] Meanwhile, for those with surplus time and wealth, cultural and sporting events—concerts, kabuki plays, professional baseball, and sumo tournaments—continued being held into late 1944 or 1945.

Withdrawal and Invisibility

The mutually imposed insularity that characterized foreigner life prior to the war yielded to Japanese-imposed invisibility during the war. Just as much of the Western signage, loanwords, music, and film had disappeared as the prewar foreign community had dwindled, and as enemy aliens were interned or repatriated after Pearl Harbor, so too did nonenemy Westerners fade from sight. Wartime conditions were partly responsible. With international communications severed, most foreign businesses could no longer operate; many industries unrelated to wartime needs were shuttered, their resources diverted as necessary; journalistic activities ceased; and missionaries and Christian churches operated only under Japanese direction. Many Western social clubs were also shut down, some converted to internment facilities. Professionally neutralized, economically disenfranchised, and socially curtailed, most Westerners' spheres of occupational and social activity contracted markedly. Surveillance, and the threat of police harassment generally, also contributed to this withdrawal. All were watched and visited by police as a matter of routine, which deterred Japanese visitors. Japanese employed by foreigners, including domestic help, were expected to inform on their employers lest they bring suspicion on themselves. Information could flow in both directions, however. Arvid Balk's secretary was coerced to inform on him, but also warned him of his imminent arrest.[52]

The fact that the Interior Ministry had devised definitive protocols for treatment of enemy nationals but not for other foreigners made this withdrawal largely circumstantial. Stripped of privacy and unable to work or travel freely, most lived unobtrusively. "I never got into a situation where I had to confront anybody or anything," Ludy Frank recalls. "They would send police once in a while to my house, who would ask questions and look around. . . . I would go to my school to teach and I would have people come to my house [and] take their lessons. . . . They were observing us."[53] Ludy's caution typifies how many other Westerners lived during the war years. The Apcars and others remaining on the Bluff also gradually withdrew. With their business shuttered, the family could no longer afford to host social gatherings or pay their maids and cook. Guillain learned to avoid discussing politics and uttering people's names in public, even in innocuous contexts, lest he implicate them, and to destroy all papers, photos, and notes.[54]

Some, like Dmitri Abrikossow, were attracted to Kobe's comparatively less stringent political environment, including its distance and relative independence from the German embassy. Abrikossow lived in Japan from 1916 to 1946, initially as the secretary of the Russian embassy and then, following the 1917 Bolshevik Revolution, as the new government's chargé d'affaires in Tokyo. Removed from his post when the Soviet Union assumed control of the embassy in 1925, for the next two decades he remained in Japan as a stateless refugee and an unofficial but recognized leader of Japan's White Russian community. In Tokyo, Abrikossow was continuously watched and his servant regularly questioned by police, the harassment finally convincing him to accept a friend's invitation to move to Kobe. The two men lived on the city's outskirts, servantless, from 1942 to 1946. As food became more difficult to obtain, they grew vegetables and waited in line twice a week to receive rations. Though police visits continued, they were not seriously harassed, and Abrikossow found Kobe's living conditions much more agreeable.

In most cases, police surveillance was a formality, not an indicator of genuine suspicion. Abrikossow, Estelle Balk, and Irene Frank all report that officers arrived hungry, drank tea, accepted or took food, and asked inane questions. Abrikossow writes that police came largely because he bribed them with food, and one imagines that they were generally motivated more by the prospect of receiving handouts and making a show of performing their duties than by any expectation of uncovering evidence of subterfuge.[55] Officers sent to investigate foreigners were unable to speak or read foreign languages and so could not conduct thorough, meaningful interrogations in any case. Abrikossow relates that on one occasion his housemate was briefly apprehended when police discovered among his belongings a map on which he had drawn a line connecting Germany and Japan. They had interpreted the map, actually nothing more than a doodle, as some sort of secret plan.[56]

As in other Japanese cities, Kobe residents were forced to participate in formulaic preemptive measures in preparation for enemy air strikes. Abrikossow's bemused observation indicates an apathetic but compliant populace, and looser police enforcement than in Tokyo and Yokohama:

When the alarm sounded early in the morning, nobody paid any attention to it, thinking it was merely another drill. For a year the Japanese had staged ridiculous-looking civil defense exercises in which women, dressed in trousers, seemed to dance a ballet as they passed buckets to each other or climbed ladders. As for the air raid shelters which the police ordered every two households to dig, they would fill with water and dirt whenever it rained, and were of little use. When the police ordered my friend and me to make arrangements for a shelter, he proposed that we use the hole where we kept the manure and the police seemed satisfied. Thus prepared, the Japanese calmly awaited the attack. . . . But while during practice everybody had seemed to understand his task, at the moment of crisis everything was forgotten, and a crowd stood in the open place opposite the station and stared at the sky.[57]

Abrikossow reveals little emotional connection to the war, and little awareness of the hardships and suffering it inflicted on those in his community. Even during the bombings, which arrived regularly in 1945 and by
June had decimated the entire city, he, like Lenigk, remained insulated
from many of the challenges faced by native Japanese. Echoing the fear-
less exhortations of Pringsheim and Guillain in Tokyo, Abrikossow describes the bombings in 1945 as a miraculous act of salvation, seemingly
disinterested in the suffering they caused. He writes that "the approaching planes were a beautiful sight," and "soon the fires began and the whole
sky became red. As I watched I could not help feeling a certain grandeur
at the sight."[58]

Abrikossow's description of his eremitic life in Kobe suggests that his
decision to leave Tokyo, to become invisible, was the right one. Others
suffered for not doing so. The Russian archbishop Sergius (1871–1945) of
the Orthodox mission, for instance, was harassed and eventually left the
mission to live out the war in his private house in Tokyo. Retirement was
not inconspicuous enough, however, and in 1945 he was implicated as a
spy, arrested, charged with economic espionage, and incarcerated for
thirty days. Debilitated from his internment, he died on August 10, shortly
after his release, in a Tokyo suburb.[59]

The general retreat to invisibility was not particular to disenfranchised
Westerners like Abrikossow, the Apcars, and the Franks. It applied to non-
Japanese who continued working and contributing to Japan's war effort,
including naturalized Westerners and Chinese. The American engineer
William R. Gorham, who lived and worked in Japan from 1918 until his
death, responded to the American embassy's December 1940 repatriation
advisory by sending his son Don (1917–2011) to the United States.[60] Gorham and his wife, however, had lived in Japan for twenty-two years, considered it home, and opted to stay despite the country's militarist turn.
After discussing their options with Japanese friends and colleagues, many
of whom were industrial leaders with political ties, they decided to apply
for Japanese citizenship. The application relied heavily on Gorham's im-
peccable reputation. He had served as a pioneering engineer for Jitsuyō
Jidōsha Seizō (later Nissan Motor Company), Toa Denki Kokusan Kogyō
(National Industrial Production Company), and Hitachi Seiki (Hitachi
Corporation). He also occupied a permanent position on the Board of

Directors of Kokusan Seiki (National Precision Machinery Production Company). Gorham was clearly one of the nation's leading mechanical engineers and personally responsible for many of the mechanical advances achieved by Japan's automobile industry in the 1920s and 1930s. His role in the development of Japanese industry and, by extension, his service to the country were beyond doubt. Gorham's application for citizenship was submitted on May 17, 1941, and approved a mere nine days later. For the war's duration, Gorham continued working at Hitachi Seiki, commuting daily by train from Tokyo to a factory construction site in Kawasaki and overseeing the production of machine tools at several other plants. But in other respects his spheres of interaction were restricted. He was unable to correspond with his sons throughout the war, and his Western and Japanese friends, no doubt unsure whether his residence was under surveillance, found it difficult to visit him at home. "Due to wartime restrictions about lights in houses," his biographers relate, "the living room of their house was dimly lit and Mr. and Mrs. Gorham would just sit sadly facing each other."[61]

Though neither interned nor deported, Chinese were also subjected to police surveillance for the war's duration. Some living in Yokohama but outside Chinatown were forced to relocate, presumably to facilitate surveillance and to prevent them from viewing maritime traffic in Yokohama Harbor. Those engaged in atypical endeavors were prone to harassment. A Chinese student attending Saint Joseph's was detained and questioned by the Tokkō. About a dozen outspoken members of the Guomindang, which opposed Japanese aggression in China, were arrested or deported on suspicion of espionage. Chinese who did not publicly express anti-Japanese sentiments were incorporated into neighborhood associations and established mutually reliant relationships with Japanese neighbors. They received rations and were assailed by air raids alongside the Japanese. In exchange they were cajoled by Japanese authorities to openly tout Sino-Japanese amity and voice their support for the war. Though most complied, their relations with Japanese authorities remained tense. In private, many admitted displeasure with propaganda claiming Sino-Japanese goodwill, and Japanese police, suspecting as much, continued to view them with suspicion. Both sides understood rhetoric touting friendly cooperation to be a façade. For Chinese, obeisance would be the price of continued residency.[62]

Japanese Ambivalence and Antiforeign Sentiment

The Japanese government responded to the Doolittle Raid, Guillain attests, with "an extraordinary campaign of racial hatred of a virulence not to be equaled at any other time during the war."[63] Accusing the aviators of targeting schools and hospitals and machine-gunning civilians, it promised death sentences to them and all future enemies caught committing war crimes against Japan. (Three of the eight crewmen captured in China were executed; the others were given life sentences.) Antiforeigner propaganda intensified, attempting to entice all Japanese to spy on the white spies. Japanese newspapers falsely announced that police had uncovered a vast spy ring masterminded by Vere Redman. Citizens were told that Westerners were listening to their conversations and relaying the information to their countries, and were instructed to be vigilant for foreigners acting suspiciously. Antiespionage Week was held and antispy drills were staged "in which actors disguised as foreigners were arrested by real policemen in the streets, in stores, in factories amid terrified and excited crowds who did not know if the scene was real or simulated."[64]

The mere existence of this propaganda and the apparent lack of public opposition to the war have helped propagate two questionable assumptions: that propaganda was effective in generating widespread antiforeign sentiment, and that the Japanese populace broadly supported the war. We will address each of these in turn.

Caucasians occasionally did become targets of public aggression, *Japan Advertiser* reporter Joseph Newman (1913–95) states. In 1941, a French embassy attaché named Count de Tascher was beaten by a group of taxi drivers in Kobe. The wife of an Italian diplomat was slapped on a train by a Japanese "unable to distinguish between white allies and white enemies."[65] (In order to mitigate such misidentification problems, the German embassy arranged for its compatriots to wear badges bearing the national flags of the three Axis nations.[66]) Ronald and Martin Baenninger report that a French woman and her daughter were bullied in a movie theater by some Japanese toughs.[67]

Resident Westerners were alarmed to learn of such incidents, and many drew hasty conclusions from them. Some mistakenly assumed that these isolated events demonstrated public solidarity with xenophobic state rhetoric. The Baenningers assert that "the average man or woman in the street was increasingly influenced by the rabid and unrelenting antiforeign propaganda," but provide little evidence of such.[68] Theirs is a natural assumption given the state of war and the precarious standing of non-Axis Western residents. But the claim is borne out by isolated cases of hostility, not by any evidence of routine, ongoing, or systemic aggression against foreigners. Estelle Balk, Guillain, the Baenningers, and various others could do no better than cite the case of James M. Cox—the British reporter who was arrested and tortured, and ultimately jumped to his death from his prison window, a case of police brutality rather than a crime committed by "the average man or woman in the street"—as evidence of antiforeign sentiment. Their respective memoirs contain much stronger evidence that Japanese people were neither persuaded nor intimidated by state rhetoric. For in fact, public vigilantism was rare.

Unremitting police surveillance and exposure to antiforeigner propaganda created conditions for widespread paranoia among Westerners, including perceptions of hostility from the Japanese collectively. From the late 1930s but particularly following Pearl Harbor, nearly all wartime narratives by foreign residents report feelings of vulnerability, endangerment, and racial aggression. Estelle, who spoke almost no Japanese herself and admits that Japanese had forgotten how to speak foreign languages, was incensed that no Japanese spoke to her in public. She assumed that those around her were whispering maliciously, yet relates no public act of hostility toward her except for children throwing stones.[69] Most of the enmity directed toward her came from other Germans. Westerners able to understand public gossip around them report overhearing a wide variety of comments. On a train, Gwen Terasaki heard a mother threaten to give her sobbing child to the foreigner unless he stopped crying. This unkind statement appears to be exceptional, and in any case was directed at one too young to know any better. Terasaki also overheard one woman say to another, "Don't you think this foreigner is beautiful?"[70] On a separate occasion some students on a streetcar summoned the gumption to ask her nationality. When she told them, one stood up and loudly announced, "Behold this courageous American woman and her daughter! She has braved all danger to stay with her husband. Let us be kind to her and show her that war is between governments, not individuals!"[71]

One would expect wartime hardships to sharpen antiforeign sentiment and to incite desires for vengeance against foreigners. Although the
paucity of trustworthy public testimony from the war era complicates our
ability to assess the real impacts of state propaganda on Japanese attitudes,
resident Westerners indicate that state rhetoric was largely ignored and
that Japanese harbored mixed feelings toward both foreigners and the war.
The Notehelfers, Sidline, Terasaki, and others admit surprise that they
never became the targets of racial vengeance. Instead, many observed a
stoicism and acceptance that precluded the emotional investment required
to either harbor or exhibit racial hostility. Rose Notehelfer notes that she
never heard a Japanese person complain about the war, and never saw a
mother cry when told that her son had been killed or when collecting his
ashes returned to her from overseas.[72] Nor did Notehelfer or other foreign residents detect any public blame being cast on foreigners for Japanese suffering. Frank Gibney avers that "there was relatively little personal
resentment among the Japanese, and even the droppings of the A-bombs
were regarded almost as natural calamities. There was perhaps an almost
unspoken consciousness of the fact that Japan's own army had perpetrated
unspeakable horrors on others to provoke this vengeance."[73]

In fact, very few Westerners report firsthand experience of racial
hostility from the Japanese public, some recognizing that antiforeign
propaganda was ineffective in turning Japanese against them. Robert
Crowder, an American English teacher at Kumamoto University, was
warmly embraced by his entire community. Clearly aware of the growing tensions between their countries, the Japanese around him avoided
talk of politics except to express remorse over their countries' souring relations. When Crowder was arrested on the morning of the Pearl Harbor
attack, students, colleagues, and townspeople bowed respectfully as he
was taken away. "The world had declared us enemies to one another,"
Crowder writes, "but behind the façade of hostility, a warm, binding
friendship existed—one that even war could not destroy."[74] During the
Doolittle Raid, Japanese strangers pulled five-year-old Bill Notehelfer
and the German woman caring for him off the street and into the safety
of their shelter.[75] The American boy Joe Hale emerged from his own
bomb shelter in Yokohama following an air raid that had devastated the
area and relates that as he walked among the rubble and burning houses,
"not one person said anything unkind to me that I can recall even though

I looked foreign."[76] In July 1945, the Sidline family, whose house had been bombed in June, traveled by train from Kobe to Osaka and then on to Karuizawa. As the only Caucasians on train cars filled to capacity with Japanese who had also lost everything in the air raids, they encountered only generosity.[77] Demonization of Anglo-Americans and media hysteria over foreign spies had little immediate effect on how foreigners were regarded by the Japanese public, Shapiro reports. "While a certain degree of hostility developed on the part of the police and other governmental authorities, our Japanese neighbors and friends continued to treat us politely and displayed no change in their attitude toward us as foreigners."[78] Guillain also affirms that "one felt no deep hatred of the United States in the Japanese people."[79]

Even Terasaki, a Caucasian American citizen, was able to consistently form and sustain warm relations with Japanese throughout the war years. Fearing that years of propaganda depicting Americans as Japan's archenemies would turn her neighbors against her, she was surprised to find the opposite. Terasaki regularly used public transportation without incident. (It was only when she wore sunglasses, the spy's signature accessory, that she reports incurring suspicion.) In her Tokyo neighborhood she was able to maintain warm relations with the others in her *tonarigumi* and was "invariably treated with tolerance, at least, and almost always with kindness and generosity."[80] Later, in the coastal town of Manazuru, she hosted a *tonarigumi* meeting in her home. On several occasions Terasaki reports receiving furtive but especially warm treatment when Japanese learned that she was American: a shopkeeper displayed for her his secret stash of foreign goods; a doctor revealed how he missed American music and his displeasure with the war; owners of the local bakery and pharmacy were friendly and generous. At the local beauty parlor other patrons soon accepted her, all taking "the opportunity to feel the softness of my hair."[81] Between 1942 and 1945 she lived in four communities, and in every one received kindhearted support from local Japanese.

Aware that state propaganda had failed to reverse decades of admiration for the West, the Japanese press relentlessly coached citizens in proper public behavior. In December 1942, Akiyama Kunio, who worked for the War Ministry press section, published "*Okawaisō ni*" (The poor things), an article that he hoped would dissuade Japanese from harboring sympathies for the enemy. Recently a former minister and his wife had seen a line of American POWs pass by their house, Akiyama's piece recounted, and the wife had remarked, "The poor things. How sad to treat Americans that way." Reporters on hand overheard the comment and reported that, despite the war, the wife continued to feel respect and affinity for Americans.[82] The article appeared just as the government had incited public controversy by announcing that the captured Doolittle aviators had been found guilty of war crimes and would be executed. Though intending to provide readers with an example of poor public behavior, Akiyama's article created a minor scandal and caused some ideologues to feel that it not only had failed to stir up nationalism but had actually achieved the opposite.[83]

The myth that the Japanese state wielded absolute control over its citizenry extends the misperception that it was also ideologically unified. Historians point to the collapse of the Communist Party in the early 1930s, the relative ease with which police silenced leftist writers and intellectuals, and, as Gibney writes, the public's inability to muster "even a muted expression of concern" as evidence that the Japanese people, if perhaps not overjoyed with the country's militarist turn, were at least content to toe its ideological line.[84] Ienaga Saburō has challenged this view and shown that not all Japanese submitted quickly and quietly. It is true that Japanese did not form secret societies, demonstrate publicly, or protest via other illegal means, which distinguished them from their considerably more active counterparts in Germany, Italy, and Spain. Ienaga contends, however, that in Japan latent resistance was manifested in anonymous letters and graffiti. Some leftists expressed dissent by leaving the country or withdrawing to "domestic exile." Others continued writing and disseminating antiwar invectives through various private magazines, which, though banned, continued to be printed.[85] *Chikaki yori* (From nearby) and *Kashin* (Good news), outlets of intellectual antiwar sentiment, were issued monthly for the duration of the war. Writers criticized the military's rationale for fighting in China, the use of special attack units (*tokubetsu kōgekitai*, or kamikaze), Prime Minister Tōjō, and military brutality generally. Otto Tolischus affirms that some newspapers occasionally printed letters objecting to the government's posturing, and observed that most Japanese had little knowledge of or interest in the state's empire building.[86] Additionally, Ben-Ami Shillony has shown that the government was not a military dictatorship and did not wield absolute control over the population's loyalties or political will. Despite concerted efforts by the government, the military, and the press to install their own candidates into the House of Representatives during the April 1942 elections, for example, enough voters defied state coercion to elect eighty-three unendorsed candidates.[87] Nor did Prime Minister Tōjō wield absolute power, as right-wing opposition ensured that his authority extended only to the limits of the offices he held. Opposing partisan factions, intramilitary power struggles, dissent in the Diet, the continuation of critical voices in the press, and a succession of assassination plots reveal opposition at the top that ultimately compelled Tōjō to resign as prime minister.[88] Dissent was also voiced through legal channels. Despite the collapse of the Communist Party, the Marxist Labor-Farmer faction (Rōnō-ha) remained active and helped fuel labor and tenant disputes throughout the war years. Finally, rising numbers of defections and desertions within the military and the discovery of antiwar sentiments contained in letters and diaries of Japanese soldiers suggest that the military was rather less successful in indoctrinating its ranks than is generally believed.

Widespread skepticism is not surprising given that *tennōsei* ideology attempted to reverse decades of admiration for the West. Nor was it particular to the 1940s. Since the mid-1930s, Herbert Bix argues, "many villagers displayed only the shallowest acceptance of the emperor's authority . . . [and] probably were not devout believers in the emperor."[89] Cynicism from the 1930s gave way to grassroots exhortations against the emperor and his complicity in state militarism, exhortations that grew both in number and intensity during the war. In fact, fears that hidden communist, leftist, and revolutionary energies were swelling and could detonate at any moment became a source of considerable anxiety for the Tokkō and Kenpeitai, former prime minister Konoe Fumimaro, and various government officials.[90]

Given the preponderance of evidence, it is difficult to interpret weak public resistance to the war as strong support for it. After the exuberance surrounding Japan's initial victories in the Pacific, Guillain writes, people became desensitized to the constant celebratory news and gaiety turned to "national indifference."[91] This shift in public morale was also observed by Ambassador Craigie, who notes that Japan's successes overseas received only a tepid response at home. Japanese, he continues, were neither elated by the news nor duped by the propaganda in general. Amid reports of Japanese victories, the public displayed few signs of arrogance and the British embassy's Japanese servants remained wholly apologetic for the hardships suffered by embassy staff. "The popular celebrations seemed to be confined to a few orderly torchlight processions," Craigie continues, "and one noticed an absence of that boastfulness and display which afflicts most peoples in moments of national exaltation."[92] Some secretly rejected the reckless aggression of Japan's military leadership. The missionary Margaret Armstrong in Toyama, for example, reported that at least three Japanese acquaintances separately confessed their abhorrence for the war.[93] Shapiro corroborates these observations, stating that "apart from the military and the government, people generally did not express any great war fervor. Most of our Japanese friends and neighbors, when talking about the international situation, would merely say, 'Isn't war terrible? We wish it were over.'"[94]

One finds multiple explanations for public complacency. First, the war was located beyond public reach. Aside from the relatively ineffectual People's Rights Movement of the 1880s, mainstream Japanese rarely mounted significant protests against existing political structures. Historically citizens resorted to protest only when personally threatened by socioeconomic conditions, and then only after other methods of resistance had been exhausted. Knowing they were being denied accurate information about the war, citizens were unable to become emotionally or intellectually vested in it. Guillain observed that "Japan had been waging [war] and talking about it for ten years without ever seeing it. It was something that happened far away. . . . Official propaganda did nothing to make it more concrete and to bring it home to the people."[95] Because propaganda was so clearly disingenuous, people were denied the emotional content necessary to support it. Moreover, as much of the antiforeign rhetoric did not distinguish between enemy and nonenemy aliens, it failed to explain to Japanese how some Caucasians could be allies and others enemies. This was a critical oversight given that Germans constituted Japan's largest and most visible Western contingent. In these capacities, propaganda backfired.

Second, potential dissidents were handcuffed by the argument that opposition to state militarism was tantamount to disloyalty to the emperor, a position that invalidated any possible ideological counterpoint.

Jōdō Shin and other Buddhist sects may have embraced the Buddhist principle that "war is a crime," for example, but Buddhist unwillingness to defy imperial religious authority left the people without recourse.[96] Third, the fact that citizens were unable to muster much collective opposition was due less to their indoctrination by propaganda and more to authorities' thoroughness in stripping them of any means of resistance. By seizing control over neighborhood associations, labor unions, youth and women's groups, and nearly every other mainstream social organization, authorities left citizens without means of generating collective dissent.[97]

Finally, daily hardships presented people with more pressing matters. While individuals felt compelled to support a war that their sons and husbands had been conscripted to fight, they also found it increasingly difficult to condone a conflict that was causing so much personal suffering. Japan's war in China and alliance with Germany had elicited a U.S. embargo, first on oil and scrap iron and later on all exports to Japan. Wickert, Kate Hansen, and others observed that Japanese people were much less interested in the alliance with Hitler than in the economic repercussions they suffered as a result of that alliance. Nor did Japanese civilians benefit from the economic spoils of Japan's spectacular victories early in the war; rather, living conditions continued to deteriorate. All available resources had been diverted to the war effort, upsetting people's livelihoods; food, fuel, and other necessities for public use were apportioned at minimal levels. Cityscapes became colorless and lifeless and fell into decay; the inaccessibility of gasoline emptied roads; and store shelves were bare. Daily rice rations for civilians were successively cut—in 1945 reduced to a mere three hundred grams—and as citizens' daily caloric intake fell year by year, the incidence of tuberculosis and other diseases rose.[98] Shortages were of greater concern than government propaganda, therefore, and occasionally placed citizens in direct competition with the military. When the 2.4 million troops mobilized to defend the homeland from a land invasion usurped more local supplies, citizens became increasingly angered and emboldened.[99] An Interior Ministry survey found that between 1942 and 1945 the average monthly incidence of "statements, letters, and wall writings" expressing opposition to the war rose from twenty-five to fifty-one, and a police report from March 1945 affirmed that public hostility toward the government was growing bolder and more common.[100]

The authorities themselves recognized as much. Summarizing the psychology and morale of the general populace, a Dōmei News Service report from April 1945 admitted that "the people are wearied [more] by the problem of obtaining food than by foreign enemies."[101]

Irene Frank, Pringsheim, Guillain, and non-Axis Westerners generally viewed American bombers overhead as beacons of the war's end. Seeing Americans as liberators, they saw Japanese as captors. Not only had Japan initiated the war, it had inflicted restrictions and privations and attempted to foment antiforeign sentiment. Foreigners expected no relief from Japanese authorities, nor could they imagine that Japan could be trusted to end the war, through either victory or surrender. Feeling targeted by xenophobic propaganda and hounded by the police, some blamed the Japanese directly for their wartime hardships. And in pinning their hopes on the Allies, they hastened the foreign community's disintegration.

It is true that wartime conditions subordinated and curtailed the freedoms of resident Westerners. To the extent that these factors intensified their antipathy for Japanese, state propaganda succeeded. In turn, some Japanese may have been gratified to find that the war seemed to have placed them atop an inverted colonialist power structure. In their newfound power positions, some police and prison guards exhibited arrogance. This inversion was real within official contexts, such as within police stations and prisons, but was rarely manifested among the mainstream. For while xenophobic propaganda clogged airwaves and covered billboards, in practice wartime life for Westerners and Japanese shared a great deal. Although the former variously considered themselves victims of racial profiling, Japanese were also watched and harassed by civil and military police. Publishers required permissions before printing anything; teachers were investigated and arrested for indiscreet remarks; mail was censored and any mention of the war redacted; and individuals were detained for reckless comments.[102] Westerners and Japanese alike struggled to contend with daily shortages; both coped with restrictions that exacerbated hardship and anxiety; and both lived in fear of air raids. Both also responded pragmatically to this oppressive climate by tending to immediate necessities and retreating to anonymity. Any sense of shared circumstances, however, would end in late 1943 with an evacuation order that sent Westerners fleeing for the hills.

CHAPTER 6

Fleeing for the Hills

Evacuee Communities in Hakone and Karuizawa (1943–45)

Though the Doolittle Raid of April 18, 1942, inflicted little damage on Tokyo and Yokohama, it established those cities as military targets. By 1944, urbanites faced the prospect of much more extensive enemy bombing. They had not forgotten that twenty years earlier a major earthquake had triggered fires that had burned 45 percent of Tokyo and 80 percent of Yokohama to the ground in a matter of hours. Having rebuilt with wood and tatami, as they had for centuries, urban residents now faced the threat of another firestorm. The prospect of these flammable cities being razed by air strikes was too overwhelming for either them or the government to address realistically. When the state issued orders in September 1943 for Tokyo inhabitants to dig bomb shelters, thousands of holes appeared overnight, but these shallow, roofless, muddy trenches burrowed in the dirt offered minimal protection. Air-raid drills were staged regularly and swaths of the city were cleared of construction to serve as firebreaks, but such preemptive measures provided little more than psychological comfort. French journalist Robert Guillain describes the cityscape at this time as a rotting, rusting, colorless dystopia, the bomb shelters making it all the uglier and more morose. Two years of war had reduced the city to an impoverished "swarming anthill" drained of all pleasure and vitality.[1] Its residents, subsisting on scraps of rationed nourishment, seemed similarly brutalized. Estelle Balk portrays Yokohama's wartime scenery in similar terms:

Broken pipes and torn out elevators, heating installation parts and rails were being heaped up everywhere as useful scrap iron. . . . Large water holes and dugouts were being built and [streets were] swarming with soldiers getting everything ready to defend the town against the coming unavoidable air raids. . . .

The trains were still running regularly but had changed their outer and inner bearing. Asiatic dirt, ragged clothes, unwashed bodies—all partly on account of Japan's increasing poverty and because the Japanese does not mind throwing down any trash he wants to get rid of, hygiene unknown to him—filled the compartments now. There was a perpetual traveling, going out into the country from one district to the other to buy food or clothing. The people had bags and bundles, babies and sacks of potatoes, pushing in and out, crowding the trains to capacity. The windows were broken, the glass replaced partly by boards nailed on roughly, the seat coverings slashed and the connecting corridors between the cars oftentimes dangerously damaged. Nevertheless the passengers held on, hanging to the doors like grapes, and the guards did not seem to mind. You saw now no fine clothing, no flowery kimonos or obi buckles anymore. The *kokumin* green drab uniforms and the ugly *monpe*, baggy trousers the women were forced to wear replaced the splendid coloring of prewar times.[2]

In December 1943, authorities recommended the evacuation of children and the elderly from its major cities. The suggestion received a mixed response. (It was only after the massive firebombing of Tokyo on March 9–10, 1945, that they ordered the evacuation of all children.)[3] During the following year dwindling food supplies and the growing frequency of air raids prompted more of Tokyo's seven million inhabitants to relocate, some mounting their houses on wheels and towing them to the countryside. Life in the provinces, evacuees hoped, would afford relief from American bombs as well as greater opportunities to find food. Friends and neighbors helped each other pack, and assisted those who had lost homes in the raids.[4]

Meanwhile, Westerners remained restricted from unauthorized travel outside their home cities and barred from militarily sensitive areas.[5] Now, new coastal military fortifications installed in preparation for an enemy land invasion of coastal cities necessitated the expansion of these restricted zones. Revision of the Air Defense Law (*Bōkū-hō*) in 1943 expanded territories deemed militarily sensitive to much of the Tokyo-Yokohama region, necessitating near-complete evacuation of the noninterned West-erners still residing there.[6] (Foreigners who ventured within restricted zones were seized. When Saveli Lavrov returned to his house on the Bluff because a water pipe had burst and was flooding the residence, he was arrested and held at the Yamate Police Station jail for several days.[7])

The evacuation directive was issued by the Interior Ministry. It stated that for the purposes of protection and counterintelligence, residential ar-eas would be established for non-Japanese nationals living throughout the country. The order excluded Chinese, however. Generally speaking, it stipulated, foreign residents living in or east of the Tokai and Hokuriku regions would be relocated to Karuizawa in Nagano Prefecture, Kawa-guchiko in Yamanashi Prefecture, and the Hakone region in Kanagawa Prefecture. Residents living in or west of the Kinki region would be relo-cated to Takarazuka-chō, Arima-chō, or Takedao in Hyogo Prefecture, or other sites to be determined later. It mandated that empty properties like hotels and summer villas in those locations be used by the evacuees, meaning that Japanese owners of cottages in those areas were obliged to lend those residences to evacuated foreigners. Property owners evacuat-ing there from their primary residences or whose primary residences were destroyed, however, would be given use of their own properties. Reloca-tion expenses would be paid from the National Treasury. Ideally, the order continued, relocation would be completed by the end of July 1944. Also, foreigners' occupations and status would continue to be recognized and individuals would be treated accordingly. That is, evacuees would retain the rights afforded civilians and would not be considered POWs. Fi-nally, the order stipulated that the state would provide Axis and neutral foreigners with food, fuel, and living necessities, and that stateless indi-viduals would be given appropriate compensatory employment to earn their own living.[8]

In practice, the evacuation directive was variously misunderstood, possibly negotiable, unevenly observed, and often delayed. It was an-nounced to foreigners in late 1943, and, because the request contained no sense of urgency, many waited until the following spring or summer to comply. Some diplomats, journalists, and neutral civilians remained in cities as late as spring 1945, when intensifying air raids finally drove them to one of the designated mountain retreats. Language like "in general" and "ideally" contained in the order allowed for considerable flexibility.

For although nearly all but a few dozen families opted to relocate to Hakone or Karuizawa, in principle any unrestricted evacuation site could be requested as long as it was out of harm's way.[9] Gwen Terasaki's family evacuated to Odawara, a town near the coast fifty miles southwest of Tokyo. Isaac Shapiro's family, stateless Russian Jews living in Honmoku, requested evacuation to Roppongi, Tokyo, a diplomatic district outside the city's coastal restricted zone. The government duly financed the move and found them a house in a neighborhood where they encountered a number of other foreign families.[10]

Evacuees themselves give conflicting accounts of the order. The considerable confusion over the evacuation's purpose, timing, and destination suggest that the directive was poorly and inconsistently communicated. Many foreigners report being given the choice of relocating to either Karuizawa or one of the villages in the Hakone region. The Buss family felt the order to be a request and believed that compliance was voluntary. The Haar family, in contrast, mistakenly understood that Germans and Italians were sent to Hakone, that neutrals were sent to Karuizawa, and that families had no choice in the matter.[11] (In fact, most of the Nazi establishment did move to Hakone, but the majority of non-Nazi Germans, numbering about seven hundred, opted for Karuizawa.) Many also felt that the order was a punitive measure leveled against all foreigners. Technically, however, it stipulated evacuation from only those areas designated as militarily sensitive. The American sisters Mary and Mildred Laffin, who were occupying their summer house in Hakone with their mother, Miyo, were not touched. Only their sister Eleanor, who continued to occupy the Laffin house overlooking Yokohama Harbor, was removed and interned in a camp at Nanasawa (discussed in chapter 7).[12] Julie Helm's nephew Walter was not forced to evacuate Yokohama because he was occupying Julie's former home, which was located outside the city's restricted zone. The house was later destroyed in an air raid.[13]

It is also apparent that Japanese authorities, in addition to their mandate to remove foreigners from restricted areas, carried out evacuations to fulfill their legal obligation to protect foreign nationals, which they could not do while those foreigners continued to reside within military targets. This secondary mandate is made evident by the fact that Japanese efforts to evacuate stateless individuals were far less conscientious. In contrast to the charitable assistance provided the stateless Shapiro family, a number of other stateless Westerners remained in Yokohama. When the Notehelfers were urged to leave Todoroki, they were informed that their house would be given to a stateless White Russian engineer who was employed by the Japanese government in a war-related industry.[14] The stateless Lavrovs were removed from their house on the Bluff because it commanded a view of the harbor but were not evacuated from the city. Rather, they moved to the nearby Sagiyama neighborhood, where several other White Russian families were living. The family did not evacuate until after the massive bombing of May 29, 1945, in which they lost their Sagiyama home and their son Constantine.[15] Nonetheless, by May 1944, the great majority of Westerners had evacuated Yokohama while the city's 1,917 Chinese residents remained. Of Kanagawa Prefecture's Westerners, 1,194 (92 percent) had evacuated to Hakone, and of that number, 768 (64 percent) were German.[16]

Hugo Frank was one of these; his brother Ludy was one of the handful who opted for Karuizawa. Now independent husbands and fathers, Ludy's and Hugo's decisions to relocate in opposite directions was informed by both professional and personal factors. On a personal level, Hugo may have welcomed the evacuation order. After graduating from Saint Joseph's in 1932, he had worked as an accountant for Nihon Watson Tokei Kaikei Kikai (Watson Japan), a subsidiary of IBM. His decision to marry Chizuka (Alice) Sumimura (1909–96), a half-Japanese woman, however, disappointed his parents and created consternation within the Frank family. Alice was the daughter of a geisha and Arturo Karlovich Wilm, a Russian diplomat stationed in Nagasaki. Wilm had bought her mother's contract from the geisha house that employed her and installed her in his villa as a mistress.[17] When Wilm was later transferred to Yokohama, diplomatic protocol barred him from marrying a Japanese and so he married a Russian woman and moved the mistress and their daughter Alice to a nearby house in Yokohama. He served as the Russian consul general in Japan, but after the Bolshevik Revolution was exiled by the new Russian government and remained in Japan for the rest of his life.[18] Hugo married Alice in May 1939, but his parents had disapproved of the union and ostracized the couple. Later, Alice would also be treated coldly by her sister-in-law Irene in Karuizawa.[19] A move to Gora (Hakone) distanced Hugo and his family from such tensions.

Estelle Balk also disapproved of Hugo, even when their two families became professionally connected in 1942.[20] After Pearl Harbor, Hugo had lost his job at Watson, an American company, but nearby his brother Ludy's stepfather-in-law Arvid Balk had just fired his Japanese assistant, whom he suspected of spying on him. Arvid agreed to hire Hugo to translate Japanese radio news broadcasts. Meanwhile, as a newspaperman Arvid was receiving clear indications that he had become a person of Kenpeitai interest. German journalists named Serge, Lissner, and Crome had already been arrested, and rumors circulated that Arvid would be next. Arvid sought protection by the German embassy, which informed him that it could not interfere with Japanese police investigations. (The Balks and Franks both learned later that their embassy had been complicit in directing Japanese police to arrest Jews and suspicious non-Nazi Germans.) The Balks resolved to relocate to Gora, giving Hugo both personal and professional reasons to follow suit. Not only did he already own a summerhouse there, but he and Arvid had become professional collaborators in a business that relied heavily on proximity to news contacts in Yokohama and Tokyo.

Ludy had no such ties to Gora. He had lost his job at American Express when the company closed prior to Pearl Harbor, and he had started teaching private lessons. After marrying Estelle's daughter Irene in April 1942, he moved into a Yokohama house that had been abandoned by an American family. The following January, Irene gave birth to Nicholas. The couple had vacationed in Karuizawa in the past, and knew that the Nazi Party had already established a stronghold in Gora. Karuizawa was the obvious choice, and they evacuated there on March 7, 1944.[21]

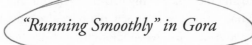

"Running Smoothly" in Gora

The Japanese government, through the Swiss, officially communicated to the Allies that it had designated the Hakone region a foreign evacuation site and a noncombat zone. The number of Western evacuees there totaled about 1,500.[22] Gora, located about sixty miles southwest of Tokyo and a three-hour train ride from Yokohama, was one of Hakone's mountain hot spring resorts. It was accessible via the Hakone Tozan train line, a single-car electric train that ran west, toward Mount Fuji, from Odawara. A favored summer resort for wealthy businessmen and foreign diplomats, Gora consisted largely of hotels and summer villas with baths supplied by natural hot springs. A cable car had serviced the mountainside residences on the outskirts of the village since 1919, but was decommissioned during the war.

Popular among foreigners before the war, Gora was policed accordingly by branches of the Yokohama Kenpeitai and Foreign Ministry. In May 1944, due to the demands of monitoring the new influx of evacuees, the Police Bureau of the Interior Ministry instructed the Odawara station of the Kanagawa Prefectural Police Department to establish a Foreign Affairs Section there. In addition to conducting surveillance and gathering information, this office performed foreigner registrations, issued travel authorizations, and distributed rationed food. It also made arrests.[23] A military hospital and a military police training facility—the Nakano Army School (Rikugun Nakano gakkō), which Honobe Makoto describes as a spy training school—were also located near the cable car line. All of these offices and facilities were installed for the purpose of managing the foreign community.[24]

Gora had also become a German stronghold. It was roughly one mile from the Information Department of the German embassy, which had relocated to the Fujiya Hotel in Miyanoshita, and contained a number of German-owned and Nazi-affiliated establishments. Many of the German women and children from the Southeast Asian and Pacific Islands, who in 1941 had been stranded in Japan while in transit, had evacuated to Gora. Estelle Balk notes that these women were given large shares of rationed food and fuel since many had children and could not work. The neighboring hot spring resort of Sengokubara also contained a German community, and Asanoyū, a second hot spring resort, housed 130 German sailors. These nearby German enclaves were provisioned by the Nazi Party, which established an office in Gora and distributed food, fuel, clothing, and other supplies seized from enemy ships. The Nazi community had its own doctors, nurses, dentist, hospital, church, and school. Estelle claims that Jews and nonparty members were denied access to those rations and facilities, though apparently some such restrictions were overlooked because Hugo's daughter Barbara, technically Jewish, attended the school and Estelle herself mentions acquiring certain European delicacies.

Standing within the evacuee community was determined by one's nationality and proximity to the Nazi Party. Party affiliates dominated the town, followed by nonparty Germans, neutral or stateless nationals, and Jews. Estelle's description of the community reflects a practice of identifying and classifying people by nationality.

> As to the other inhabitants of Gora, there was also an old Swiss acquaintance of Max [Pestalozzi] . . . , a few Swedes we did not know and who kept to themselves, a few half-cast Portuguese, a Hungarian trader with his White Russian wife, both long in Japan and gone more or less native, and Dr. Phil Franz and his family. They were half Jews, German refugees, who after having got stuck in Japan on their way to a new post in America had taken a well paid job in the Japanese industry. This they had lost now too, as the Japanese infected by the everlasting Nazi propaganda had ousted Jews and foreigners alike.[25]

Allied nationals who had repatriated prior to the war either sold or abandoned their villas in Hakone. When the war started, those properties owned by enemy nationals were seized and sold. Japanese property owners in Gora were also ordered by authorities to make their houses available to evacuating foreigners. Foreign families need only go there and select a residence of their choice.[26] Evidently feeling no sense of urgency to evacuate, Arvid and Estelle, along with their cook and maid, waited until April 1944 before settling into a spacious house with a garden and a hot spring bath. The dwelling was the summer villa of a wealthy Japanese "nobleman."[27]

Hans and Margot Ries and Heinz Lang, the Balks' close friends from Yokohama, moved into a villa nearby at about the same time. This threesome, all half-Jewish, had arrived in Japan in 1941. Hans and Margot were married but welcomed Heinz, who also loved Margot, into their union. Hans and Heinz had been interned in the Philippines since 1940 as part of the mass incarceration of German residents of British and Dutch colonies in Southeast Asia. When the three were stranded in Japan while in transit, they moved into a house near the Balks in Honmoku. Like Estelle and Arvid, they had been watched by their German neighbors and their actions reported to Nazi authorities.

Several of the Catholic missionaries from Saint Joseph's College, all in their sixties or older, lived nearby. The school itself had transported thirty truckloads of materials to Gora's Park Hotel after the government had seized their school building on the Bluff and leased it to Ishikawa-jima Heavy Industries. They converted the hotel into a school and Catholic church.

Though Estelle's accounts of her ten years living in Japan are mostly unfavorable, she is uncharacteristically complimentary about her circumstances in Gora and her prospects for weathering the war there. Despite being denied the German disbursements of food and other supplies, the Balks were nonetheless adequately provisioned and secure. They were also able to enjoy social diversions within the community. She writes,

> Everything was running smoothly in Gora. The larder was well stocked, the maid polite and efficient and plenty of fuel to be had, though going up in price as we had no gas and a very low electric current, we made all our food on charcoal braziers and a little wood fire in front of the kitchen door. But that did not bother me. The Japanese maids were used to it at their own home, though Fumi-san grumbled at first missing Yokohama's modern gas range. Well, we had all the safety of the countryside and they knew that too. No bombs would be falling here, where no factories were.
>
> This year we were planning to celebrate our wedding anniversary especially nice. . . . There was no more anguish, no police spying around here and we would all drink to the new security, the happy home, and a safe over bridging for us all until the war was at an end. It did not look so serious anymore.[28]

Estelle's comfort in Gora stands out among the shelves of memoirs describing wartime life as an unrelenting succession of ordeals. It is true that evacuees in Hakone and Karuizawa contended with various degrees of privation and were largely unemployed, but they were also safe, able to benefit from communal support, and generally faced less severe shortages than their Japanese neighbors.[29] Lack of reliable information led to an apathy toward the war that for many fostered impressions that "it did not look so serious anymore." Evacuees re-created in Gora much of the insularity that they enjoyed in Tokyo and Yokohama, though their new lives had the added benefit of being largely supported by the Japanese government. Estelle also observes considerable socializing, and how cliques and cultural disparities coexisted in close quarters. She writes that the Russian women staying at the opulent Hakone Gora Hotel, which the government had requisitioned for use as the Soviet embassy and lodging for Russian diplomatic families, "walked about Gora together in flashy, common outfits with hats and high heeled shoes. . . . These Soviet women, probably quite low class people, looked like overdressed scarecrows compared to the quiet way the German women dressed and the increasing poverty of the Japanese population."[30]

At about the time the Balks relocated, Hugo also moved to Gora. He, Alice, and their daughter Barbara settled into a summer villa on the north side of the cable car line near Naka-Gora station, about half a mile from the Hakone Gora Hotel. Gora residents welcomed the family warmly, Kojima Yutaka claims, and Honobe agrees that Hugo's friendly, gracious personality made him popular among his neighbors.[31] He and Alice were especially close to their neighbors Kurahashi Chikara and his wife, Tefu, whose daughter Akiko played together with Barbara. As the Franks had no bath in their house, they bathed at the Kurahashi residence.[32]

Hugo, Alice, and Barbara were home at eight o'clock in the morning on July 28 when three plain-clothed men entered without bothering to remove their shoes. They ransacked the house, handcuffed Hugo, and dragged him out the door without a word. Alice had never seen the men before, but uniforms and self-identifications were unnecessary. The charge would be suspicion of espionage, so his captors would be military rather than civilian police.

Hugo had attracted police suspicions for a number of reasons. Occupational associations, social associations, and political events in Europe all factored into his arrest and protracted incarceration. Unlike most other foreigners, Hugo could read and write Japanese and after moving to Gora had continued translating and interpreting for Arvid. This connection further endangered Arvid, who as an active nonparty journalist married to a Jew was already a person of police interest. Hugo had also secured a job distributing rations cards, which put him

FIGURE 6.1 At the Fujiya Hotel in Gora, summer 1944. *From left:* Hugo, Alice, and Alice's sister Narikawa Yūka. Hugo and Alice's daughter Barbara, age five, is at front right.

in contact with marginalized nationalities and ethnicities. While Germans generally exercised caution in socializing with neutral citizens, Hugo had often been seen talking to Portuguese and other neutrals. Moreover, he had converted to Catholicism while a student at Saint Joseph's and in Gora had been seen conversing with the Saint Joseph's teachers there. This connection aroused the suspicions of both Japanese and Nazi authorities, neither of whom trusted missionaries. From these various associations it was clear to the Kenpeitai that Hugo was anti-Nazi, and therefore anti-Japanese.[33]

Hugo was indeed anti-Nazi, and other Germans in Gora, fearing the repercussions of noncompliance, had notified Nazi authorities of such. He was thus targeted by both Kenpeitai and Nazi officials soon after his arrival. Years later, his daughter Barbara recalled going to the Fujiya Hotel for a meal and seeing a German man there spying on them (fig. 6.1).

Timing was also a factor in Hugo's arrest. In June and July 1944, Japan and Germany had both suffered significant losses. This, coupled with the failed assassination attempt on Adolf Hitler on July 20, surely steeled the Gestapo's resolve to isolate Nazis from anti-Nazis. Honobe posits that these events also prompted Josef Meisinger to order Japanese police to arrest suspected spies.[34] At five o'clock in the morning on August 1, four days after Hugo's arrest, Arvid Balk and Hans Ries were also taken into custody.[35] The fates of all three men will be detailed in chapter 8.

Karuizawa: A "Strange Miniature Babel"

Karuizawa was a multipurpose evacuation site during the war, serving the dual functions of protecting assets and neutralizing political threats. Many of the wealthier evacuees already owned summer villas there, as did some of Japan's most illustrious writers, including Hori Tatsuo (1904–53), Kawabata Yasunari (1899–1972), Shimazaki Tōson (1872–1943), and Shiga Naoya (1883–1971).[36] Some foreign missionaries who had suffered police harassment had also relocated to Karuizawa before the evacuation order. As the war progressed, hotels and other facilities were opened to accommodate important personnel evacuated from Tokyo. In 1943, the Swiss and Turkish embassies were relocated to the Manpei Hotel. Between 1943 and 1945, over one thousand school children from various coastal cities were evacuated there, entered the local schools, and occupied whatever hotels and dormitories were available. Important documents held at Tokyo Imperial University were also removed to Karuizawa for safekeeping. In 1944, several munitions industries moved there, one taking over the classrooms at the Karuizawa Higher Girls' School.[37] The Foreign Ministry transferred some of its operations to Karuizawa the same year, and Masada Michiko (b. 1934), Japan's current empress, was evacuated there from Tokyo to protect her from air raids. Japanese political and economic leaders, as well as important literary figures like Murō Saisei (1889–1962), Masamune Hakuchō (1879–1962), and Nogami Yaeko (1885–1985) moved there, the stream of evacuated cultural luminaries continuing into 1945.[38] The town became, in Guillain's words, a "strange miniature Babel," an evacuee community consisting of multiple nationalities coexisting in different economic circumstances, all monitored by an army of military and secret police.[39]

Karuizawa also received those miscellaneous foreigners of uncertain status, such as celebrities and cultural figures who needed to be both protected and removed from public view. These included multiracial residents like Jaye and Teruko Kurusu, the daughters of Japanese special envoy Kurusu Saburō (1886–1954) and his American wife Alice. Polish maestro Joseph Rosenstock (1895–1985), conductor of the NHK Orchestra since 1936, was evacuated to Karuizawa in 1944. Victor Starffin (1916–57), a record-breaking pitcher for the Yomiuri Giants, moved there the same year. (Starffin, whose White Russian family had emigrated in 1925, distinguished himself as a pitching phenom but came under suspicion of espionage during the war and was forced to take a Japanese name, Suda Hiroshi, to demonstrate his patriotism.)[40] The town was also a site of exile for Japanese under suspicion of harboring antiwar, proforeign sentiments.[41] Hatoyama Ichirō (1883–1959), Diet member and former education minister, was banished to Karuizawa in 1943 for disagreeing with Prime Minister Tōjō Hideki.[42] The honored and dishonored thus took up residence side by side, their proximity to one another demanding especially close police surveillance.

The eclecticism and diversity of this community became a critical source of self-sufficiency and in many cases made survival possible. Foreign families and their children interacted, played, studied, and found romance. People with various skills and knowledge taught classes, held church services, and provided other public services. The elderly and infirm were given firewood by collectively organized logging operations.[43] Need compelled community members, including Japanese, to allay prejudices and embrace the practical benefits of community solidarity. By 1944, a total of 813 foreigners had evacuated there, along with 2,223 Japanese and over 1,000 school children. These numbers continued to rise, and by 1945 the town accommodated about 1,500 foreigners.[44] Its total summer population peaked at about 12,000, nearly double its population in 1941.

The community was generally unprepared to meet the challenges of this sudden influx, which brought new patrons to businesses but also created shortages and crowding problems. Foreign diplomats, who numbered about three hundred in 1945; International Red Cross officials; Germans; and wealthy Japanese were better supplied with food, subjected to less surveillance, and acquired better accommodations. As in Gora, stateless and neutral families, Jews, and miscellaneous other non-Axis individuals attracted more police scrutiny. Many also possessed neither the knowledge nor the skills to care for themselves and arrived unprepared for residency in uninsulated, flimsy dwellings stocked with inadequate bedding and whose plumbing was unusable in winter. Food and fuel were generally insufficient. Local industries like logging were suspended and their resources redirected toward charcoal and food production. Vegetables were planted in all available spaces, including the Karuizawa Association tennis courts.[45] Foreigners, regardless of nationality and political affiliation, received fixed rations of basic necessities from the Japanese government, the basic daily ration being six hundred grams of bread or rice per person, as well as other items.[46] Though there was no alcohol and little fresh meat, rations occasionally included canned meat, some of which was labeled beef but was actually horse. Shoes were also difficult to procure because Japanese suppliers did not carry foreign sizes. The unavailability of these and other goods quickly devalued cash and gave rise to a localized barter economy. Hungarian evacuee Irene Haar (fig. 6.2 and fig. 6.3) writes of being unable to purchase what she needed. "We could only exchange our belongings for food with farmers at neighboring villages," she writes. "In this manner we got two goats and some rabbits and chickens. The farmer showed me how to feed and take care of the livestock and how to milk the milking goat."[47]

Although most of the Nazi establishment, including the German embassy and diplomatic staff, evacuated to Hakone, Karuizawa also supported a small but active Nazi contingent. From 1938, groups of Hitler Youth had used south Karuizawa as a military training camp, regularly parading the Nazi flag through the streets in their brown uniforms and swastika armbands.[48] When the town was officially designated an evacuation site for Axis nationals at the outset of the war, the German community grew more authoritative. It co-opted for itself the town's two foreign luxury hotels, the Manpei and the Grand. Town meetings were conducted in Japanese and German; street signs were written in both languages; and establishments around town displayed swastika flags. Following the evacuation order, about seven hundred Germans, the

FIGURE 6.2 *Left to right:* Irene, Veronica (b. 1942), Thomas (b. 1941), and Francis Haar with maids in Karuizawa, June 1944. Courtesy of Tom Haar.

majority of the non-Nazi German community and those who already owned houses there, relocated to Karuizawa.[49] While both Hakone and Karuizawa were overwhelmingly German, they thus took on disparate ideological identities.

Karuizawa's German community received financial support through the German embassy as well as extra rations provided by German supply ships arriving in Yokohama. Many of these supplies were held in a central warehouse, but the German community also hid emergency stashes of food with trusted families.[50] (The Buss family buried several barrels of lard in his yard for safekeeping.[51]) Disbursement of supplemental rations

FIGURE 6.3 The Haars at nursery school in Karuizawa, August 1944. Courtesy of Tom Haar.

also reflects the ideological split between Gora and Karuizawa, for whereas Estelle Balk claims to have been denied German rations, German Jews in Karuizawa did receive them. Irene Frank notes that their denaturalization in January 1945 would have been a happy event had it not disqualified them from receiving additional disbursements. Most notably, German Jews lived alongside anti-Nazi German residents of Karuizawa without discord, though some suffered greater police surveillance.

Accounts penned by each of the Liebenzeller mission families—the Notehelfers, Busses, and Langs—corroborate the rather more comfortable conditions enjoyed by the German contingent. The Notehelfers and Busses owned their own cabins, and the Langs occupied a dormitory formerly owned by the Canadian YMCA. The three families give similar accounts of Karuizawa life. Their missionary work was officially stopped, and they did not enjoy many of the comforts received by wealthier members of the German community. All report suffering from cold and certain shortages, but also that the extra rations and the financial support made life there more comfortable and nominally "normal." (The Busses, for example, report that the family was provided with a freight car, "which enabled us to take all of our belongings with us, including the piano."[52]) All three families grew vegetables and kept animals for eggs, milk, and meat. They describe their search for food, both for themselves and their animals, as the singular challenge, but not in such harrowing terms as others do. When the German school in Ōmori moved to Karuizawa, Bernhard Buss took over as principal and also served as pastor at the German Community Church. The Buss children enjoyed music lessons, and Ehrhardt Lang writes of the town as a bucolic paradise whose natural wonders provided him with a continuous source of joy. "Karuizawa," he writes, "became for us children one of our happiest times."[53]

Ludy and Irene Frank relate an altogether different experience. When they arrived at Karuizawa Station on the evening of March 7, 1944, they found snow on the ground and no transportation available from the station. With one-year-old Nick and their belongings, they walked the two miles to the house they had rented on Waterwheel Road. Many of their immediate necessities—food, money, and sundry supplies—were disbursed through the German embassy. They received 400 yen per month, "enough to survive on," but during the winter months few provisions were available for sale in stores.[54] As money lost value, bartering became the most effective means of procuring food. (Karuizawa's black market, in fact, was supplied mainly by local farmers who were supposed to turn over their produce to the government for distribution but were usually willing to barter for clothing or rationed items like cigarettes. Police also benefited from this practice and so generally refrained from suppressing these illegal transactions.) Ludy acquired benches from the Catholic church and ran a private school for foreign children out of his house. He called it Doitsujin Gakuen (A German's Academy). Run by a half-Jewish man and open to Jewish children, the school attracted no German pupils but did draw about ten children of other nationalities.

Meanwhile, Nazi authorities directed Japanese police to watch Jews, and for the next eighteen months the Franks became the targets of police intimidation. Their tenuous position as Jews was impressed on them in dramatic fashion on July 29 when they received word that a day earlier Hugo had been arrested at his home in Gora. On August 3 they were informed that Irene's stepfather Arvid had also been arrested. As the prisoners were not permitted visitors during their interrogations, Ludy and Irene had little news of Hugo and Arvid for the next five months. Ludy's visitation with Hugo occurred only after Hugo had confessed and been transferred to a separate prison (discussed in chapter 8).

News of Hugo's arrest arrived four weeks after Irene had given birth to her second child, Katherine (Kitty). Irene had been due in mid-June, and her mother, Estelle, made the trip from Gora to be on hand for the delivery. "Little Katherine took some time to arrive, so I stayed in Karuizawa longer than I had expected," Estelle wrote.[55] The delayed birth was fortuitous, for despite the town's inflated population of evacuees, its lack of medical personnel, supplies, and power kept its hospital closed until the start of the summer tourist season on July 1. (For this reason, Japanese authorities had instructed Irene not to deliver the child until July!) After midnight on July 1, Irene went into labor, admitted herself, and delivered Kitty. The delay had also given Estelle the opportunity to visit with her daughter Marie-Elise, who in January 1943 had married the Swiss diplomat Max Pestalozzi and then relocated to Karuizawa along with the Swiss embassy. Estelle's manuscript illuminates not only Karuizawa's living conditions and ethnic relations, but also intrafamily strains that the Franks omitted from their own narratives. Her informative account merits extended citation:

The Mampei hotel had a room for me, although crammed full of all kinds of people, especially Russians, who till late at night made a terrible noise by shouting and visiting each other, dancing and singing so that no one could rest. I am sure their beautiful voices sound just as lovely in Russia as they do here, but I wonder if these proud proletarians are allowed to adorn themselves and paint their fingernails [in Russia the way] I saw them running around in Karuizawa and Gora.

Max and Marie-Elise lived quite near to the Mampei hotel. Marie-Elise had now turned into the great lady she had always wanted to be, visiting only people of consequence, asking only men with either a handle to their name or belonging to the rich and smarter set. The Swiss kept to themselves, like all different nationalities [they] were ordered to keep apart from the others, but the diplomats of course met and Marie-Elise having—may I say an inherited flare to find the right crowd—drew a few desirable closer acquaintances around her. She was ever out to bridge parties or to tennis and had hardly ever time for me, whom she now had little use for anyway. Max had an office in Karuizawa too, as well as in Yokohama, so that he was forced at times to make the long journey to town, which took 7 hours ride in a packed train. He is a quiet, very lenient husband towards aggressive and impulsive Marie-Elise, who puts it over him all too easily. It is she who reigns, but he who earns, who gives her the position she is so proud of. I am afraid she had got the values of life a little mixed up as her concentration on outer appearance overweighs her interest toward the inner merit of her neighbors.

While I can describe Marie-Elise's house with servants, furniture, and food as typical for the still reigning smarter set, who felt no privation by the growing scarcity of food or money, when I went to Irene['s], I thought myself in another world. Here was a life apart. She and Ludy were not [part of the] community. . . . No one was in the same boat as they, [who had] no one to turn to and had to survive by their own will power. And I can only say here with appreciation to young Ludy, that he managed it in a grand way, as a proud man and an honest worker against a wall of difficulties. They had a two-story plain log house, as there are many in Karuizawa. The family had the rooms upstairs, dear me, so poorly furnished. . . . Downstairs they had a kitchen and three schoolrooms. Ludy had got benches from the Catholic brothers and he had two helpers in for the many children, who turned up all day long, as he gave private lessons too. It is a wonder to me how he could crowd in all the work he was doing, though getting up at 5 every morning. There were the chickens to feed and the goats to milk, the wood had to be chopped, the vegetable plot had to be dug and weeded. He was building a stable for the goats and a chicken coop and did not forget to go to mass on Sundays. As to the sanitary arrangements, there was the usual Japanese bath tub they heated with firewood, but the toilet quarters, also genuine Japanese style next door, had to be cleaned out every few days, as many children were using it too. Ludy could not afford additional help. So it was he, who at night times emptied out the filthy wooden buckets some place like a common country laborer. . . . The [children] were undernourished and overworked but charming with me and always happy to see me, thankful for the little help I could give them. Marie-Elise, living about ¼ of an hour's walk away, hardly ever showed up in those poor quarters. She had not approved of the marriage, none of us had. We, though, had got over it, seeing Irene happy, honoring Ludy for the diligent, honest and straight character he had, working now for his growing family in steady valor against great odds. Marie-Elise, married in her own class, could not be reconciled to this brother-in-law, thus widening the margin which sisterly love should have over bridged. Ludy and Irene had a crowd of friends and well wishers everywhere. There was constantly someone turning up. . . . The neighbors around, Japanese and foreign residents, Jews evacuated from Kobe with foreign passports, Brazilians, whose children visited Ludy's school, came to the door to ask Irene if Irene's baby had come. Even some Germans furtively gave them a kind word ignoring their order to keep away from the outsiders. I think Ludy and Irene were comparatively happy there in Karuizawa, though Ludy did not like teaching, but there was no other work for him to do and even that had to be fought for as another unmarried man of neutral standing had opened a rival school and was luring away the few foreign pupils there were in Karuizawa. I could watch their life about 3 weeks, then Irene's baby arrived, healthy and sweet, a darling little girl and everybody was happy. I left them all by the middle of July to go back to Gora.[56]

Here Estelle revisits some of her favorite topics: the oddity she feels at witnessing the various nationalities and classes living in close quarters, and her own ambiguous position within this mix as both Jewish and a member of the German intelligentsia. The distinct classes occupied by her two daughters are of intense interest to her, though she indicates a clear disdain for both the "proud proletarians" beneath her and the elitism of Marie-Elise's aristocratic circles. We also see uncharacteristic praise for the resourceful Ludy and Irene amid their political isolation. Her testimony that "no one was in the same boat as they" must be taken as a reference to the marginalization confronted by Karuizawa's Jewish or stateless residents generally. As she notes later, the Franks in fact received critical support from a parade of well-wishers arriving at Ludy and Irene's house to offer aid. The compassion and civility of the disenfranchised individuals of various ethnicities, including Japanese and "even some Germans," is further corroborated by an event that occurred four months later.

On the evening of November 3, 1944, Irene noticed smoke as the family was sitting down to a dinner of rabbit stew on the second floor of their house. A Japanese farmer had given them a rabbit, meat that his own family would not eat but that the Franks considered a rare delicacy. The smoke was curling under the door and already a distinctive crackling was audible. Opening the door, they found smoke billowing from an area under the stairs where they stored canned and dried food, but also saw that fire had already consumed much of the rear of the house. They grabbed the two children and ran out into the rain. Ludy rushed back in to save what he could but found himself trapped and had to jump out the second-floor window. He managed to save his bicycle but nothing else.

Onlookers congregated; the police and lastly the firemen arrived, but "the water pressure was so bad that they could not hose the fire down and they did not try very hard."[57] Irene sought privacy to nurse her baby, but a police officer prevented her from leaving, forcing her to do so in a puddle at his feet. Police then arrested Ludy and Irene on suspicion of arson. Their neighbors, a Belgian couple whose son attended Ludy's school, offered to take the two children for the night and the following day. At the station, the police focused on Irene, whom they interrogated for six hours. Ludy was taken to a different room but largely left alone. Irene's memoir recounts the events:

> The moment we got there, Ludy and I were separated and I had no idea where they were taking him. The policeman pushed me into a smallish room with a low ceiling and a big square hole in the middle that was used for a charcoal fireplace. . . . I walked toward the charcoal pit thinking of warming my hands. "Get back there, you stupid, dirty foreigner, sit on that stool and don't move." . . . The man that snarled at me was short, skinny, with a shaved head that was starting to show stubble and I hated him just on sight. . . . The longer I sat there and watched them, the more my hatred grew and fear had no place left in my heart.[58]

The police drew up a confession in Japanese stating that Irene had committed arson in order to receive insurance money, and also that she was a spy. They demanded that Irene sign, but she could not read it and refused: "'I don't understand your language.' 'If you live in Japan,' he said, 'you better learn to speak it. We do not want to speak English. Don't you like it in Japan and the Japanese people?' I could not believe it. Was he fishing for a compliment? 'I hate Japan, I hate the language and the people and how can you ask me such a stupid thing?' I had nothing to lose anymore."[59] Irene asked to be allowed to feed Katherine, then four months old, whom she knew must be crying for food. She was denied, and also denied use of the bathroom, though permitted later. In the end, Ludy and Irene, separately, refused to sign the confession. "Paradoxically, we were saved by the fact that we were *not* insured," Ludy wrote.[60] The police also wanted the Franks to pay for the house, clearly a futile demand. They were released at about one o'clock in the morning.

Returning to the fire, they saw that their clothing, bedding, food supply, and personal possessions had all been lost. Irene's jewelry, "diamonds and rubies and such" that did not burn, had been retrieved from the ashes and stolen.[61] The silverware and silver dishes had melted; the books and other supplies that Ludy had used for his school were also gone. They had lost not only their belongings and food, but also their ability to barter for anything. The following day, the *Nippon Times* (now *Japan Times*) briefly mentioned the fire, reporting it as accidental; the *Yomiuri shinbun* also reported that the Doitsujin Gakuen run by Mr. Frank had burned to the ground, but noted no other details.[62]

When interviewed in 2006, Irene related that after the fire Max Pestalozzi invited them to stay with him and Marie-Elise, who lived nearby in a large house where Max's diplomatic immunity shielded them from police meddling. Ludy's "Living Conditions in Wartime Japan" and Irene's memoirs both fail to mention this, Irene's making no mention of her sister's existence in Karuizawa at all. Ludy had refused Max's offer. Marie-Elise, like Estelle, had not approved of Irene's choice of husband, thinking Ludy poor and thus below them. Irene accepted the invitation but describes Marie-Elise as "a difficult person," stingy and unkind, refusing to even heat the room where she and Katherine were staying. They left after four days.[63]

Meanwhile, Ludy and Nick were staying at the Catholic church. It was the French community, however, that came forward to offer the Franks use of an unoccupied house with electricity. "Our misfortune had spread around Karuizawa by this time and complete strangers came up to us, offering their help," Irene recalls. "Women would come to me and kiss me and bring food and blankets, clothes and shoes, and even a mattress for Nicky and Kitty to sleep on. Thank God somebody gave me some diapers, as I was having a terrible time without them."[64] No sooner had the Franks moved into the French house than their maid Miyoko arrived with several policemen. She proceeded to insult the Franks and demand some of their donated clothing and blankets. Irene had twice caught Miyoko being suspiciously careless with fire. The first time, Miyoko had put glowing charcoal under the kitchen table. This was both dangerous and wasteful, as they always extinguished charcoal with water after using it to cook. The maid had apologized, but several days later Irene went downstairs to where they kept wood, straw, charcoal, and food and saw that charcoal embers had been placed on the straw, which was just catching fire. She extinguished the blaze, but these episodes left the Franks with little doubt that Miyoko had been responsible for the fire, and that she had been acting under police orders. Miyoko confessed that she had moved her clothing and possessions out in advance and so had lost nothing in the blaze.

Firing Miyoko, Irene states, would be difficult because they knew she was a police informant and feared that doing so would invite reprisals from the Kenpeitai. Under constant surveillance themselves and with Arvid and Hugo already in prison, they were aware of their vulnerability and the danger of giving police any excuse to arrest them. The evening of Miyoko's visit, therefore, they could do nothing but watch their maid walk off with many of the donated items they had just received. The next day the French legation evicted them from the house because a French family had just been bombed out of their Tokyo residence and needed it.[65] Irene recalls the eviction, and the astonishing stroke of fortune that followed:

It was about 5 o'clock in the afternoon and it was starting to snow. We had found this little cart in the yard of the house and put our few blankets and the little bit of food into it. Ludy took Nick by the hand and carried my little baby and we set out to take shelter in the church. You could not see very well where you were going as it was snowing so hard. I felt like the wandering Jew, no home, no country, and no future. This is when the most surprising thing happened. Out of the dimness of the snowstorm a very pretty young oriental woman appeared. She stopped us and asked us where we were going. She had heard about us in the village. Her father was the Chinese Ambassador and her mother was Japanese. When she heard that we did not have a place to go and were on our way to sleep in the Cath[olic] Church she burst into tears.

"No, no, you don't have to do that. My parents have a summer house way out of town. It is a nice house but too cold to occupy in winter. Still it is better than having no place at all. You are welcome to use it. Just walk in, it is not locked. I will come by in a little while and bring you some candles and see to it that you get gas and electricity. . . . You are free to use it free of charge."[66]

This mysterious benefactor attended the same Catholic church as the Franks and, hearing of their need, had asked her parents' permission to lend their summerhouse and its sparse furnishings. Her father, the Chinese chargé d'affaires of Chiang Kai-shek's Nationalist government and no friend of the Japanese, had agreed. Although still German citizens, Ludy and Irene received nothing in terms of compensation for their losses. Once again, however, they became the beneficiaries of an outpouring of charity from other Karuizawa residents. The church contributed a spare altar for them to use as a table, as well as a pocket watch so that Irene could time her baby's feedings.[67] Additionally, Ludy recounts, "the Jews, the Swiss, the Swedes, the Finns, the French and all the rest of the Neutrals got together and supplied us with food, clothing, and money so that we could start over."[68] Estelle also noted how socioeconomic and ethnic barriers gave way to altruism, despite orders against the comingling of the nationalities: "Ludy and Irene were heaped with kindness from people they had hardly known, hospitality, presents and medical support came from everywhere. . . . Bedding and clothes, chinaware, and every possible necessity for a family of four persons all were given to them by Karuizawa friends when they moved into a new house far outside the main village. . . . A new home was built up and they lived like peasants now on what the vegetable garden and the potato plot would produce."[69]

Ludy had earlier returned to the site of the burned house and found the two chickens. The two goats had also escaped during the fire and been caught by neighbors, who returned them. The new house included no stable to keep the goats, and judging that they would freeze if left outdoors, the Franks sheltered them in the bathroom, an unusable room during the winter when the water was turned off. During those months without water, the family would use an outhouse—a hole in the ground with a pot—and would haul water for cooking, drinking, and washing from a tap five hundred yards away.

Louis and Amy Frank, Ludy's parents, had also evacuated to Karuizawa and were having difficulty procuring enough food and fuel for themselves, and so on December 20, 1944, moved in with Ludy and Irene. The couple had never needed to be self-sufficient and was unable to help much. Louis spent his time taking walks, doing thermodynamics calculations at the table, and writing papers. Amy endured without complaining.

Now a family of six, the Franks survived on a combination of meager rations and creative self-reliance. Basic rations had been reduced and were no longer sufficient to sustain the family: one pound (454 grams) of bread per day per person, plus trace amounts (one cup per family per month) of sugar, one egg per family per week, and occasional potatoes. They received one cigarette per person per day, which they saved to trade for food. Supplementary rations received from the German Club amounted to 2.5 pounds of bread per week, milk, and "occasional tinned fish, tinned cream, lard and butter."[70] The house contained a woodstove that enabled them to cook and heat one room. Ludy dug out a vegetable cellar to keep perishable foodstuffs from freezing. He was able to bribe his landlord with cigarettes and money for permission to cut trees on the property for fuel but was unaccustomed to the debilitating ardors of felling, stripping, splitting, and hauling firewood.

On January 18, 1945, the German Club posted a notice stating that Ludy, his father-in-law Arvid, his brother Hugo, and Hans Ries were denaturalized and therefore ineligible for any extra rations or distributions from the German Club. (Arvid, Hugo, and Hans were interned and had already surrendered their passports. The directive mentioned only the family heads but extended to all members of their immediate families. Hugo's wife, Alice, testified after the war that consulate officials arrived to collect her citizenship papers in January 1945.)[71] This order had been issued by Germany in December 1941 but not relayed by the German embassy until October 17, 1944; reasons for the three-year delay are unclear. The Franks' neutral friends "congratulated us on our good fortune at having been denaturalized," Ludy writes, "and the few Germans whom we knew, because they were non-Nazi, envied us."[72]

Now disqualified from special rations, shortages became more critical and food scarcity quickly became the family's primary concern. "Every [waking] hour was concentrated on how to get food and how to make money, how to stay out of trouble," Ludy later recounted. "It consumed our whole mental life, our whole physical life. . . . It was living a night-

Support from Japanese people

mare."[73] They were forced to sell some of their bedding, clothing, and other belongings. Life was so difficult and cold that in February, Ludy writes, their servant refused to work. (He fails to state whether this servant was Miyoko, the woman they suspected of arson, or another.)[74] In the spring Ludy started a garden, which he fertilized with night soil. Their goats and chickens were producing, but neighbors crept in to milk the goats and steal potatoes from their garden.[75] There was little food to buy, and purchasing from the black market was illegal and therefore risky. Black market prices were also prohibitive. Ludy earned 5 yen per hour teaching private math and English lessons to ten Japanese and six foreign children, but the black market charged 35 yen per pound of meat, 200 yen for sugar, and 85 for butter. Nonetheless, he occasionally purchased small amounts for the children.

The Franks' adversity was aggravated by heightened surveillance from police, who visited the house regularly to take food and ask questions about their friends and sources of income. Police also followed them when they went out. Arrest was a daily fear and the harassment a constant source of humiliation. By the summer of 1945, Kenpeitai officers were monitoring the house full time. As noted in Irene's account of her police interrogation following the fire, as well as in accounts penned by Joseph C. Grew, Robert Craigie, and other Westerners, the experience of enforced subordination to Japanese authorities was especially galling. Ludy would later confess, "I wasn't happy with the Japanese [police]. We were there during the colonial days and we didn't look at the Japanese as equals. . . . That's why we suffered that much more when they got us under their thumb."[76]

Relations with local Japanese, in contrast, were generally amicable. Although some Japanese, fearing reprisals, were hesitant to show kindness to foreigners, the Franks did receive considerable assistance from locals. A friendly Japanese lady twice took Ludy into the countryside to introduce him to friends who would sell him food. A Japanese student brought Ludy a bag of charcoal, and a forester took him into the woods and marked which trees he could cut for firewood.[77] Ludy took clothes to surrounding Japanese homes to barter for food. The Franks also found a farmer willing to let them mate their two goats with his billy goat. After a few months it was apparent that only one of the goats was putting on weight, whereas the other was losing weight. Ludy consulted with local farmers about how to handle the birth and care for the litter. Finally, in

May, they were surprised to find that both goats had delivered litters. Irene writes, "The Japanese farmers stood around and watched the crazy foreigner trying to cope with what was for him a difficult situation and they laughed and pointed at him. The big litter impressed them very much, though, and they came and congratulated [Ludy] and everybody was very nice and friendly."[78]

Other Western evacuees in Karuizawa also enjoyed amicable relations with local Japanese. After Michael Apcar's release from prison in February 1943, the Apcar family was informed that its house in Yokohama lay in zone A (with a view of the harbor) and so they would have to vacate. They joined much of the Bluff community in opting for Karuizawa, finally moving into a house of their own choosing in Mikasa, about three miles from central Karuizawa. As their accounts were frozen and their business closed, the government paid their housing and fuel expenses.[79] Cathy Apcar received a full-time job working for a tailor in town, though her mother, Araxe, objected to her working alongside the Chinese tailors also employed there and arranged to have Cathy work separately from them.[80]

The Apcars also endured the same hardships reported by other evacuees. Heating and cooking was done on charcoal or woodstoves. As required under the provisions of the evacuation order, police helped to arrange train transport to and from mountain areas where foreigners could collect branches and treetops left by logging operations, but this proved to be difficult, time-consuming labor.[81] Running water in their house was shut off in October and so through the winter occupants used an outhouse and hauled water from a stream. The four Apcar children were given daily chores—cleaning, tending to the animals, gathering and chopping wood, and helping the maid prepare food—all new experiences that required considerable adjustment.

Although the difficulties procuring sufficient food were a daily concern, the Apcars enjoyed greater access to it than other families. The police in Mikasa were responsible for providing the foreign community with rations and fuel, and Michael was in charge of receiving those disbursements from the police station. Their landlord permitted them to convert a hillside into a vegetable garden; they acquired four goats for milk and meat, chickens for eggs, and a dog; they obtained and illegally butchered two cows for meat; and they built a food storage cellar that protected vegetables and other supplies from freezing. Nonetheless, necessity compelled family members to travel to countryside farms and towns to barter with local Japanese farmers. Japanese exhibited no suspicion or antipathy toward the Apcars, occasionally offering them for free what they did not need themselves.[82] Lucille reports, "Never did [the Japanese people] make us feel unwelcome or show resentment toward us in any way. . . . None of us felt any trepidation venturing into public areas, trains, or other forms of transport."[83]

Araxe's memoir is especially forthcoming in its depiction of Karuizawa life as a rustic version of life on the Bluff. The family's social calendar was surprisingly full. Though she does not reveal whether the money was brought from Karuizawa, received in the form of an allowance from Japanese authorities, or earned in Karuizawa, she discloses that she had some surplus cash, and used it to hold several parties. One daughter took an overnight skiing trip to Sugadaira, and another visited a friend in Hakone. Michael played golf and entered the annual tournament, and others entered tennis tournaments. The family hiked on Mount Asama, invited friends and acquaintances for meals, and, except in winter, always seemed to have a ready supply of good food. Some former Bluff residents organized a choir. Only in the winter of 1944/45, Araxe reports, did life become gloomier as police grew more hostile and aggressive.[84]

The intensification of surveillance noted by Araxe was the result of a larger Kenpeitai presence in town. While the bulk of policing duties in Karuizawa had been performed by civil police, in the spring of 1945 greater numbers of Kenpeitai were deployed, generating jurisdictional disputes between the two forces. This feud was further exacerbated when Kenpeitai allegedly circulated rumors about plans to execute foreigners, gossip that was rejected by civil authorities.[85] Reports indeed spread through the foreign communities in both Gora and Karuizawa that foreigners would be killed because they were consuming food needed by Japanese soldiers. Some rumors, Guillain maintains, consisted merely of discussions among Kenpeitai rather than official decisions issued from above. These consisted of plans to massacre the foreign colony in Karuizawa in the case of either defeat or the food shortages that would accompany a prolonged war. Execution was mentioned and dismissed; marching foreigners deep into the mountains was also mentioned.[86] The Notehelfers heard reports that, should the Russians invade, missionary and Jewish families would be surrendered to them as prisoners.[87] Other rumors, it turned out, had merit, for following the surrender U.S. servicemen found lists of names of foreigners to be killed, lists that included the names of Ludy and Irene Frank.[88]

Germany's unconditional surrender on May 8, 1945, ended its partnership with Japan and immediately soured Japanese-German relations in the evacuated communities. Japanese interpreted the surrender as a German violation of the provisions of the Tripartite Pact, which had proscribed signatories from unilateral surrender. The Busses reported that Germans in Karuizawa were deprived of their freedoms and "indiscriminately considered to be spies," suggesting that due to their sudden change of status, Germans were no longer deserving of their former privileges.[89] A German diplomat named Grimm related, "When Germany ended the war on May 8, Japanese people couldn't understand it. We were in Karuizawa at that time and the Japanese people we met were very perturbed. They declared that Japan would never do such a thing as surrender, a claim that the course of events would soon disprove."[90] Another diplomat wrote that Germans were suddenly regarded as enemies for not honoring the pact: "We were prohibited from having contact with people from neutral countries, an enormous problem for me since I was engaged to a Swede. We were also prohibited from having contact with Japanese."[91] Japanese authorities manifested their resentment by having the Tokkō watch Germans as they did other enemy nationals. A third German related, "Japanese didn't trust Germans. The Tokkō were always watching us, which scared off Japanese afraid of falling under suspicion for interacting with foreigners."[92] Surveillance was aided by the fact that virtually the entire German community in eastern Japan was already concentrated in Hakone and Karuizawa, where they stayed for the remainder of the war. (In western Japan, many Germans had congregated on Mount Rokkō, where Margot Lenigk had fled.[93]) Despite the change in status and the resentment incurred from Japanese, in some cases the lives of German nationals were not significantly disrupted during the war's final months. As one reflected, "The German war was over but for us life didn't change."[94]

Following the German surrender, the Japanese Foreign Ministry placed a moratorium on all further diplomatic activities within the German embassy in Tokyo. Ambassador Heinrich Stahmer (1892–1978) and other Nazi officials summarily dismissed the order and continued activities as before. Meisinger also ignored the order and carried on his collaborations with the Kenpeitai.[95] Air raids soon drove the embassy out of Tokyo, however, largely curtailing its ability to operate. At around ten o'clock at night on May 25, Erwin Wickert writes, the air-raid sirens sounded and radios reported an approaching squadron of U.S. B-29s. The policeman assigned to monitor the foreigners in Wickert's neighborhood near Shibuya appeared and the two stood outside the air-raid shelter watching the incendiary bombs falling. Wickert's house and belongings were destroyed, along with those of other German families in the area.

The next day, Wickert sold his car and packed up whatever necessities he could salvage. Whereas the ambassador and the embassy's Information Section evacuated to the resort town of Miyanoshita, near Gora, Wickert and his family followed other embassy staff to Kawaguchiko, a popular lakeside resort at the northern foot of Mount Fuji thirty miles northwest of Gora. Wickert's neighborhood of Katsuyama and the adjacent area housed about one hundred Germans. Meisinger, others from the embassy, and several German journalists lived in the Fuji View Hotel down the street. Staff turned the hotel cafeteria into the embassy office and continued making efforts to secure food and fuel for German residents and to ensure children's continued access to education.[96] The community was joined by several hundred women and children, Dutch East Indies refugees that had been residing in the Tokyo-Yokohama area.

As elsewhere, Germans in Kawaguchiko received rations of sugar, butter, rice, flour, and other foods. At the meat-processing facility in Fujiyoshida, a few miles distant, they were also able to buy the parts of slaughtered animals that Japanese did not eat. The village being more remote and without train service, residents had to transport foodstuffs from neighboring towns, occasionally by cart. Though German embassy assets were seized after the staff's evacuation, Wickert and the others were temporarily able to continue receiving their salaries from monies that had been deposited in the Bank of Japan. As such, Wickert writes, they lived comfortably and without hunger. Japanese authorities came to inform them that due to food shortages all males would be required to perform farm labor and that families would have to grow their own vegetables. This turned out to be more of a symbolic punitive exercise, a demonstration to these diplomats of the power inversion that had just occurred. Only twice, Wickert reports, did Japanese soldiers take them to dig in the ground.[97] From June through August, he swam in the lake, sat on his veranda, and wrote about his wartime experiences. Though he received little information about the war, frequently he saw U.S. bombers, which, having already razed Japan's major cities, were now targeting its smaller ones.[98]

Contrary to what some foreigners believed, and subsequently wrote, the impetus for the evacuation order was not to institute a form of internment comparable to that imposed on Japanese Americans in the western United States. The comparison is faulty on several counts. Japan had already interned resident enemy nationals; its evacuation of nonenemy civilians from coastal military targets commenced two years later. The order neutralized potential national security threats by removing foreign nationals from militarily sensitive areas while also protecting them from air strikes. Evacuees were given the freedom to decide when, where, and how to move. Some were not relocated, and others chose their own destinations. Once relocated, they were installed in housing, received (insufficient) disbursements of provisions and money, and enjoyed freedom of movement around town and the neighboring countryside. They were also able, with permission, to visit the cities for business or personal reasons. For their further protection, evacuation zone locations were duly disclosed to Allied nations.

Residential restrictions in coastal areas and the ensuing evacuations were informed, in part, by both legal and racial considerations. Both measures targeted Westerners only. The state did not restrict the movements of resident Chinese or other Asian nationals, but neither did it move to protect them through evacuations. As a member of the Axis alliance and an officially declared combatant in the Pacific, Japan was obligated to protect resident enemy and allied expats. It was under no such obligation to protect Chinese, against whose country it had not declared war. Nor did it have any legal obligations to protect stateless individuals. The fact that it relocated all Westerners, regardless of its legal obligations to do so, but not Asians, indicates that the residency restrictions and evacuations were at least partially racially motivated. Despite Japan's rhetorical suspicion of Caucasians, its allocation of resources for their protection reveals its continuing deference to the very racial order it was fighting to overcome.

The evacuee communities of Gora and Karuizawa have proven ideal laboratories for an examination of race relations in wartime Japan. There, Japanese and Westerners representing a diversity of nationalities and ethnicities were subjected to privations that could easily have triggered outbursts of racial hostility. Not only had the racial war in Europe eroded solidarity among Westerners, the war in the Pacific was being sold to the Japanese public as a reason to suspect all non-Axis Caucasians. Gora's and Karuizawa's Japanese residents were also plugged into the same nationalist propaganda and subjected to the same mobilization directives imposed on those in cities: air defense training and drills, *tonarigumi*, vigilante corps, and antiforeigner rhetoric.[99] Despite conditions conducive to racial hostility, however, we find generally amicable race relations between Japanese and Western neighbors. Japanese consistently defied police orders by bartering and even interacting socially with foreigners. Irene and Ludy Frank, the Apcars, the Haars, and Shapiro all relate that locals not only bartered with them but also provided them with assistance in growing crops, harvesting wood, and tending to livestock. Shapiro, whose family had evacuated Tokyo following the incendiary bombing of March 9–10, 1945, recalls he (aged fourteen) and his brothers having considerable independence to travel around the countryside exchanging personal items for food. Farmers even let the boys stay overnight if they had traveled too far to return to town that day.[100] Nor did the Sidlines doubt the safety of sending ten-year-old George and his thirteen-year-old brother unaccompanied into the Japanese countryside for the same reason. The rare demonstrations of overt racial hatred—Irene's interrogation by police and the behavior of her maid Miyoko—all involved police intimidation or individuals under direct police coercion. Contrary to what one would expect, accounts note virtually no instances of racial hatred between Western and Japanese civilians. Rather, they relate that the various races regularly provided each other with critical assistance and support.

Relentless police restrictions on interactions between Japanese and Westerners make Japanese racial ambivalence all the more noteworthy, a point illuminated by an account from Francis Haar. "We received an order from the police saying we would no longer be allowed to communicate with Japanese people," he writes. "Our [Japanese] neighbor used to collect the garbage from her kitchen and bring it over to us to feed our goats. The day after the new restriction was introduced, she left her container on the street in front of our house instead of bringing it to our door. An hour later, the military police were at her house, warning her to stop this kind of contact with foreigners or face imprisonment."[101] Wartime race relations, clearly, were tempered much more by fear of police reprisals than by genuine xenophobia.

We also find some of the oppression, privation, and desolation experienced by Westerners during the war years deriving from parochialism within their own ranks. Occasionally their intolerance for one another compounded their own hardships. Nazi anti-Semitism was particularly, though not solely, responsible for rending the foreign community. As Jews, the Balks and the Franks did suffer from discrimination. They were not legally recognized as equals within the German community, disqualifying them from certain privileges, particularly in Gora, and were disproportionately targeted by Japanese police. In their case, anti-Semitism ultimately culminated in denaturalization. They and other Jews all report maintaining somewhat better relations with Japanese residents than with local Germans, although some Germans in Karuizawa did venture to associate with Jews and neutrals. Estelle, for example, relates feeling comforted by her Japanese maid and receiving occasional visits from Japanese neighbors, though such support from non-Jewish foreigners was minimal.[102] It is also clear, however, that Estelle's alienation in Gora resulted partly from her own prejudices toward foreign families that otherwise might have been disposed to help her. Irene, likewise, never overcame her antagonistic relationship with Marie-Elise, whose high position and diplomatic immunity could have provided her much-needed support in Karuizawa.[103] Instead, the Franks and Balks, as well as Jews and neutrals generally, were able to overcome racial challenges by receiving critical material and emotional support from each other and from local Japanese.

PART III

Lives behind Walls: Japan's Treatment of Enemy Civilians

ENEMY CIVILIANS

Part III Introduction

O n the Chinese front, Japan's military took (or chose not to take) POWs with impunity. Prisoner handling was generally left to the discretion of military commanders. Western agreements like the Geneva Convention were dismissed, the war's unofficial status precluding the necessity of observing such protocols. Lack of centralized oversight resulted in a culture of unaccountability within certain military units on the front lines, with POW treatment ranging from charitable to murderous. Such inconsistencies notwithstanding, Western witnesses naturally assumed that military atrocities were carried out as a matter of policy. In the wake of the Nanjing Massacre (1937–38), an American diplomat stationed in China reported that the Japanese military followed "a definite policy of destruction."[1]

Following Pearl Harbor, Japanese leadership understood that its new war in the Pacific called for different rules of engagement. Implementation would prove variously unsuccessful, however. Japan's abuses of Allied POWs fueled Anglo-American outrage, became a focal point of the Tokyo War Crimes Trials (1946–48), and then was the focus of voluminous retaliatory postwar scholarship. Although maltreatment of POWs in the Pacific is well known, the contexts and conditions surrounding civilian internment camps within Japan proper are consistently overlooked. The tendency to conflate these two distinct types of camps has obscured the critical point that POW camps fell under military administration, whereas domestic civilian camps were overseen by the Interior

Ministry.[2] This oversight has yielded glaring misunderstandings. Raymond Lamont-Brown's study, for example, gives the impression that Japan's inhumane "death camps" in the Philippines typified and indeed functioned under the same set of policies as all others.[3] In fact, military camps around Asia faced conditions and sets of challenges utterly distinct from their civilian counterparts in Japan. How did resident Westerners interned in Japan fare compared to POWs under military administration around Asia? Chapter 7 considers this question by examining the changing policies and conditions within Japan's civilian internment camps. In the process, it lends additional context to the evacuations of nonenemy Westerners discussed in chapter 6. The experiences of these nonsuspects will also contextualize the fates of those resident civilians arrested and interrogated for suspicion of espionage. Though many of the records chronicling the prison lives of espionage suspects were either lost in the air raids or destroyed by police following the surrender, chapter 8 seeks to recover Japan's poorly understood procedures for handling suspected spies by returning to the stories of Hugo Frank and Arvid Balk following their arrests in 1944.

CHAPTER 7

From Humiliation to Hunger

The Internment of Enemy Nationals (1941–45)

The roughly seven hundred civilian enemy nationals (including diplomats and suspected spies) interned or detained in Japan immediately following the Pearl Harbor attack constitute only a small fraction of those held by Japan throughout its empire. It is a fraction, however, that is largely omitted from studies of the subject. This chapter will not discuss Allied POWs held under military jurisdiction in the Pacific, nor will it detail the experiences of the military and civilian prisoners captured abroad and transferred to Japan during the war. Rather, it recovers the stories of enemy residents interned in Japan under the (civilian) Foreign Affairs Section of the Interior Ministry's Criminal Affairs Bureau (Naimushō keihōkyoku gaijika). Explaining the wildly divergent mortality rates, general conditions, and racial dynamics within civilian and military camps shall lend important context to our knowledge of Japan's custodianship of enemy nationals.

Camp Administration

The mortality rate of Anglo-American POWs taken by Japan in the Asia-Pacific Theater reached a staggering 27.1 percent, this compared to a rate of 4 percent among those held by Germany and Italy.[1] Prisoners in different internment contexts tell dramatically different stories, however. Werner Gruhl reports that within Japan's civilian camps around Asia,

Americans and Dutch suffered mortality rates of 11 and 16 percent respectively.[2] Prisoners interned in Japan fared better. About 36,000 Allied POWs were transferred to Japan over the course of the war, and at war's end this number stood at 32,418. About 3,500 had died, for a mortality rate of 9.7 percent.[3] While still unacceptably high, this enormous disparity speaks to the difficulties that camps overseas faced procuring adequate food and medical supplies. It indicates that multiple circumstantial factors, not willful neglect or cruelty exclusively, contributed to high mortality rates in military camps. Civilians interned in Japan, including the roughly 450 captured and transferred from overseas, fared even better. Of the 908 individuals who were neither released nor repatriated, fifty died during captivity, a mortality rate of 5.5 percent. Twenty of those fifty deaths occurred at one particularly impoverished camp in Otaru, Hokkaido. Here we focus on the approximately 740 resident enemy nationals (excluding those transferred from overseas) interned under the Interior Ministry throughout the war. After some were repatriated or released, at the end of the war they numbered 412. Twelve had died, several from natural causes, for a mortality rate of 1.6 percent, or 2.9 percent for those remaining in custody for the war's duration. These figures indicate dramatically different cultures and conditions within military and governmental camps. They refute claims that the Japanese government's handling of enemy aliens adhered to wanton brutality and illegal practices as unofficial modus operandi. They also reveal that while one may justifiably level charges of atrocities against the Japanese military, and specifically against its leadership, one cannot extend such accusations to "Japan" or "the Japanese" generally.

Study of resident civilian camps also reveals glaring disparities in how governmental and military authorities handled racial others. As discussed in chapter 4, nationality was the criterion used to officially define and categorize foreign civilians in Japan. With the exception of certain Jews, Westerners were not arrested, interned, or subjected to race-based treatment as a matter of policy. This was not the case in camps under military control. "Processing Procedures for Prisoners of War" (*Furyo shori yōryō*), released by the Army Ministry on May 2, 1942, applied to both POWs and captured civilians in the occupied territories, categorizing them as "white prisoners" (*hakujin horyo*) and otherwise. The procedures did not provide camps with standard protocols for processing their POWs, however, so most facilities used a combination of nationality, skin color, and general appearance as criteria for making racial determinations. Some camps in Korea cataloged prisoners' heights, weights, body types, nose lengths and widths, ear sizes, face lengths, complexions, and eye and hair colors. Hybrid enemy armies that incorporated colonial soldiers and soldiers of mixed blood or other Asian races thus presented problems for Japanese captors forced to separate white from nonwhite.[4]

Racial categorization was necessitated by the Army Ministry's divergent handling procedures for Caucasian and Asian prisoners.[5] Captured Asian natives, who numbered over 153,000 in 1942 alone, were subjected to much harsher treatment than white POWs. Unprotected by POW status, many were brutalized or killed.[6] Most, however, were required to take oaths of loyalty, released, and then covertly put to work doing laborious tasks like mining and cargo handling. This practice provided Japan a source of slave labor while allowing it to abide by its rhetorical claims of liberating Asian territories from Western imperialism. The policy of transferring "white" POWs captured abroad to prisons in Japan also served practical and propagandistic purposes. Using them as labor in shipbuilding, machinery, and metalworking put their technical skills to practical use.[7] They could also be paraded before the domestic media, a practice that both extolled Japanese martial prowess and reinforced notions of the conflict as a race war waged to liberate Asians from whites.

Naturally, racial segregation policies compelled the military to ensure that POWs' appearance conformed to what Japanese thought Caucasians should look like. Two examples illustrate its meticulousness in separating "whites" from others. On January 23, 1942, the Imperial Army invaded Rabaul on the island of New Britain in Papua New Guinea, then Australian territory. Caucasian military and civilian captives were sent to Japan, but Angela Choy, a civilian nurse of Chinese ancestry and the sole non-Caucasian of the group, was released.[8] On June 8, 1942, the Imperial Navy overtook the small village of Chichagoff Harbor on Attu Island off the Alaskan coast. As no camp would be constructed to hold the island's forty-five Attuan residents, racially related to Inuit, the natives were shipped to a facility in Hokkaido, where twenty would later die of tuberculosis and extreme privation. Their sixty-two-year-old Caucasian English teacher, however, was transferred to the Bund Hotel in Yokohama.[9]

The administrative division of military and civilian prisoners was a matter of historical practice.[10] International protocols established at The Hague Peace Conference in 1899 referred specifically to captured military personnel and made no reference to civilians. Japan followed this example in instruction number 22 of its own army regulations (promulgated in 1904 and later revised), in which the term "prisoner of war" (*horyo*) referred only to enemy combatants.[11] In its various early incarnations, the Geneva Convention was also intended to ensure the protection of military personnel only, though article 81 of the document from 1929 stipulated that "individuals who follow armed forces without directly belonging thereto, such as newspaper correspondents and reporters, sutlers, contractors . . . shall be entitled to be treated as prisoners of war."[12] Japanese authorities thus viewed military and civilian custodianship as fundamentally distinct, and because "POW" essentially referred to military personnel, the military took the leading role in determining POW treatment. Guidelines issued on December 23, 1941, placed the administration of (overseas) POW camps under military jurisdiction. Thereafter, Prime Minister Tōjō Hideki, the War Ministry, and the army and navy exercised considerable influence and often acted independently in formulating POW handling policies.[13]

The military also took an active role in directing discussions over whether Japan would abide by the Geneva Convention. At the war's outset, governmental and military leaders discussed a U.S. request that convention provisions be applied to civilian as well as military POWs. As a result of this meeting, Japan agreed that it would take "measures corresponding with the convention's conditions," abiding by the convention *mutatis mutandis*, or making changes as necessary.[14] Japan's military and its newly formed POW Information Bureau (Horyo jōhōkyoku) interpreted the phrase to mean, in Ikuhiko Hata's words, "we shall apply it with any necessary amendments; not that we shall apply it strictly."[15] Prime Minister and acting minister of war Tōjō and POW Information Bureau director Uemura Mikio (1892–1946) both took a dim view of the convention and ignored its provisions when determining the military's initial POW treatment policies. Rather, they approached POW affairs with the view that Japanese soldiers who allowed themselves to be taken alive forfeited all legal rights and that the same applied to enemy POWs. Subsequently, the military acted independently in interpreting the extent to which it would abide by the convention, as well as in devising amendments to existing legislation concerning POW treatment. "Processing Procedures for Prisoners of War," "Japanese Disciplinary Law for Prisoners of War," and "Japanese Detailed Regulations for the Treatment of Prisoners of War" were amended in 1943 to provide camp administrators with more detailed guidance. Some of the articles contradicted convention provisions, such as those forcing POWs to pledge not to attempt escape and permitting the extended imprisonment or execution of those who broke that pledge.[16]

The government's own approach to prisoner custodianship reflected greater circumspection. On January 30, 1942, the Interior Ministry issued "Handling Guidelines for Interned Enemy Nationals" (*Yokuryū tekikokujin toriatsukai yōkō*), which explained that civilian internment honored and protected the internees while mitigating espionage activities. Though in principle internees would remain cut off from external contact, guidelines allowed them to return home temporarily to manage household affairs. The guidelines also permitted inmates to exercise, read newspapers and magazines, listen to the radio, and freely practice their religion.[17] On March 6, the Foreign Ministry confirmed to the United States and Britain that, given the mutual cooperation of those nations, it would in principle abide by the Geneva Convention in its treatment of enemy noncombatants to the extent that it was able (*atau kagiri*).[18]

In December 1942 the Foreign Ministry established the Office Related to Resident Enemy Nationals (Zaitekikoku kyoryūmin kankei jimushitsu) to centralize and standardize state policies and treatments of internees, which for the first year of the war had been overseen by its various local offices. Then, in February 1943, the Interior Ministry replaced the "Handling Guidelines for Interned Enemy Nationals" issued a year earlier with "Standards for the Treatment and Control of Enemy Detainees" (*Yokuryū tekikokujin shogū torishimari kijun*). These new rules were issued to align camp conditions with what state intelligence revealed about the condition of Japan's own expatriates being interned abroad. The standards prohibited any interaction with outside persons except for bimonthly visitations from immediate family. In principle, inmates were prohibited from leaving camp compounds and could receive supplies only during family visits. Internees were also expected to perform camp maintenance, including cleaning, laundry, and in some cases transportation

of camp supplies. Needy individuals would be given the option of performing compensated indoor labor.[19]

Civilian camps in Japan benefited from a host of advantages over
POW camps holding prisoners captured by military personnel during
military operations. Able to choose from existing facilities, many of which
had been schools, clubs, and churches used by Westerners, the Interior
Ministry had greater access to internment housing than did military units
overseas. It also benefited from existing supply infrastructures. Most critically, its camps held fewer and more compliant inmates. Many of the
enemy nationals interned in the wake of Pearl Harbor were long-term residents with careers, families, and roots in Japan. Seeing a protracted war
as unlikely, some found the prospect of temporary internment preferable
to repatriation. To the extent that they had ignored advisories from their
respective governments and opted not to repatriate, their internment was
a personal choice, and knowledge of this fact helped mitigate hostilities.
Mutual familiarity between foreigners and local police also helped ame-
liorate tensions. Internees generally brought their own belongings from
home and received other forms of external support from the community,
the importance of which is well conveyed by Estelle Balk's description of
the scene outside the yacht club camp in Yokohama: "Many girls met in
front of the guarded [Yacht] Club house every day, calling to their friends
over the high wall in presence of the police, who stood by grinning. [The
girls] brought them cigarettes and foodstuff, but hope and pleasure especially, helping them while away the time waiting, till they would be allowed to go back home."[20] Initially, internees were allowed unsupervised
visitations from family members and permitted to leave the camps for
shopping and other errands. Escape presented no temptation, for not only
were internees known locally, there was no viable place of escape. Their
civilian guards were also more lenient than soldiers, who were more disposed to perpetuate within civilian contexts the harshness endemic to life
within the Japanese military.

Internees were also permitted to make monthly withdrawals from
their savings to supplement the meals and amenities provided. Access to
funds was limited, however, for in many cases assets had been seized. The
state had launched surveys of foreigner assets in May 1941, data that would
later inform the structure of the Enemy Assets Control Law (*Tekisan
kanrihō*) promulgated on December 22. The law empowered the govern-

ment to compensate itself for war damages by seizing the properties and monies of enemy nationals and then selling or using them as necessary to strengthen the wartime economy. It excluded individuals with annual incomes of less than 5,000 yen. Under the law, individuals could withdraw up to 500 yen monthly from their accounts for personal expenses, and up to 1,000 yen monthly for living expenses. This posed no immediate adversity for those with generous savings and those able to replenish their accounts with a source of income. It imposed greater hardships on individuals who had worked for shuttered foreign companies. Needy families were eligible to receive monthly allowances from the state. *Gaiji geppō* (Monthly report on external affairs) reported that in October 1942, 7,159 yen in relief aid was withdrawn from the property management account created by the control law and distributed to forty-nine needy foreigners, including families of interned men.[21] Seized American assets totaled 230 million yen, British assets 197 million yen, and Dutch assets 6 million yen. These accounts, managed by the Ministry of Finance, held over 385 million yen at the end of the war.[22]

Though few records survive (extant Japanese documents consisting mainly of the fairly limited *Gaiji geppō*), International Committee of the Red Cross (ICRC) inspection reports and testimonies by former internees enable us to piece together a sense of camp conditions. The ICRC assumed the central role in providing relief to POWs and enemy civilian detainees. The Japanese branch was established on January 14, 1942, and charged with distributing donated food and money, conducting camp inspections, monitoring prisoner health, and facilitating communication and transparency between the respective parties.[23] Dr. Fritz Paravicini (1874–1944), a physician living in Yokohama, had retired since serving as the Swiss Red Cross delegate in Japan during World War I but was persuaded to resume this post after Pearl Harbor. Paravicini initially took Hans Baenninger, whose silk trade company had ceased operations, as his assistant.[24] When Baenninger left Japan in August 1942, Paravicini replaced him with Max Pestalozzi, Estelle Balk's future son-in-law and Baenninger's friend and best man. Pestalozzi then took over for the ailing Paravicini as head delegate in December 1943. Dr. Paravicini died on January 19, 1944. Between 1943 and 1945, Pestalozzi was deployed by the ICRC to inspect POW camps in Japan, Korea, China, Hong Kong, and Taiwan (fig. 7.1).[25]

FIGURE 7.1 ICRC representatives Fritz Paravicini (in bowtie) and Max Pestalozzi
inspecting an internment camp in Ōmori, Tokyo.

The ICRC faced daunting obstacles and its effectiveness was impeded
by a combination of Japanese disorganization, unpreparedness, and obstructionism. Not only were access to and communication with regional
camps routinely blocked, the ICRC's very legitimacy was compromised
by Japan's refusal to ratify the 1929 Geneva Convention, whose provisions
would have obligated Japan to cooperate with the ICRC and extend humane treatment to all sick and injured enemy nationals. Despite Japan's
1942 pledge to provisionally adhere to the Geneva provisions, it repeatedly denied ICRC delegates the access they needed.[26] Withholding cooperation, the ICRC understood, was Japan's legal prerogative. During a
camp visit in Tokyo, Pestalozzi reportedly told POWs that "because the
Japanese have not ratified the Geneva Red Cross Convention they can
do as they like. All I can do is transmit complaints to [your] respective
countries through Geneva. I must warn you, it could boil down to reprisals [from the Japanese]."[27]

Fractures between Japan's political and military leaderships also hampered the ICRC's ability to respond quickly and resolutely to Allied and

Swiss complaints over POW handling. Between the start of the war and mid-1942, Dr. Paravicini filed seventeen inquiries about internees with the POW Information Bureau but received only four replies, all declining to cooperate. The bureau, which, Keiko Tamura writes, "had a hard time comprehending the concept that a neutral organization [the ICRC] would assist both sides in war in order to provide humanitarian relief," also refused to meet with Paravicini personally.[28] A joint Allied-ICRC proposal to coordinate deliveries of relief supplies to POWs in Asia was filed with the bureau in January 1942, which waited six months before rejecting it. The government then continued to obstruct or delay ICRC attempts to establish humanitarian relief supply lines to POWs in Asia: it acknowledged only three of the ICRC delegates in its Asian territories, and it hampered delegates' ability to carry out camp inspections and distribute the quantity of relief packages initially intended. In the end, the ICRC was able to visit only 42 out of 101 camps in Asia, a number far below what the Swiss and Allied powers expected. Japanese obstructionism also compromised the reliability of the inspections themselves. Not only were Red Cross delegates required to schedule camp visits in advance, they were generally denied unsupervised discussions with camp internees. Inmate testimonies assert that their camps' conditions and rations improved on inspection days. ICRC camp inspection reports were then subjected to Japanese censorship before being submitted to the Interior Ministry and Red Cross headquarters in Geneva.[29] Ironically, Japan's failure to abide by Geneva Convention provisions and its obstinacy in permitting assistance exacerbated its own inability to provide humane conditions for POWs.[30]

The Initial Roundup (1941–42)

Of the 2,138 enemy nationals living in Japan at the time of the Pearl Harbor attack, 342 (excluding diplomats and suspected spies) were seized in the initial wave of arrests. Thirty-four civilian internment camps were prepared for this contingent (table 7.1), but the numbers of camps and internees would fluctuate constantly. The horrors experienced by Otto Tolischus and the other espionage suspects were not characteristic of life in

Table 7.1

Foreigners interned at the start of the war, as reported in the December 1941 issue of the Foreign Ministry's *Gaiji geppō*. Locations are arranged geographically, north to south.

Location	Number by nationality	Total
Muroran City, Hokkaidō, Sapporo, Hokkaidō	1 British, 1 Norwegian	2
Aomori City, Aomori	4 Canadians, 1 Dutch	5
Yokotemachi, Akita	1 American	1
Morioka City, Iwate	6 Belgians, 4 Canadians, 3 Americans	13
Sendai City, Miyagi	40 Canadians, 11 Americans, 2 British	53
Fukushima City, Fukushima	1 Canadian	1
Takaoka City, Tōyama	1 British	1
Kanazawa City, Ishikawa	1 American, 1 British, 1 Canadian	3
Maebashi City, Gunma	3 British, 2 Canadians	5
Utsunomiya City, Tochigi	1 Canadian	1
Mito City, Ibaraki	1 Canadian	1
Urawa City, Saitama	2 Canadians	2
Tamagawa Den'enchōfu, Tokyo	13 Americans, 9 British, 5 Canadians, 5 Dutch, 2 Belgians, 1 Australian, 1 Honduran	36
Negishi racetrack, Yokohama	47 British, 24 Americans, 13 Greeks, 3 Dutch, 3 Norwegians, 2 White Russians, 1 Canadian	59
Yacht Harbor Boat Club, Yokohama		34
Shizuoka City, Shizuoka	3 Americans	3
Tsu City, Mie	1 American	1
Ujiyamada City, Mie	1 American	1
Ōtsū City, Shiga	4 Americans, 1 Dutch	5
Kyoto City, Kyoto	4 Americans, 1 Canadian, 1 Belgian	6
Sanuki Hotel, Osaka City, Osaka	2 Americans, 2 British, 1 Japanese	5
Nara City, Nara	1 American	1
Canadian Academy, Kōbe City, Hyōgo	25 British, 8 Dutch, 6 Americans, 2 Guatemalans, 1 Belgian, 1 Greek, 1 stateless	35
Indian Hotel Eastern Lodge, Kōbe City, Hyōgo		9

(*continued*)

Table 7.1 (*continued*)

Location	Number by nationality	Total
Okuyama City, Okuyama	11 Americans, 1 British	12
Miyoshichō, Hiroshima	6 White Russians, 3 British, 3 Belgians, 1 American, 1 Malaysian	14
Matsue City, Shimane	1 American	1
Catholic Research Center, Fukuoka	4 Canadians, 4 French	4
Catholic Fukuoka Chōkan, Fukuoka		4
Nagasaki City, Nagasaki	6 Canadians, 5 Americans, 4 British, 4 Dutch, 2 Belgians	21
Takahama-mura, Kumamoto	1 British, 1 Dutch, 1 Belgian	1
Kutama-mura, Kumamoto		1
Yashiro City, Kumamoto		1
Total		342

SOURCE: Komiya, *Tekikokujin yokuryū*, 26–28. The table does not include the diplomats held and then repatriated on exchange ships, the 437 civilians captured and transported from overseas, or the more than 100 resident foreigners arrested for suspicion of espionage.

the camps, which were never intended as penal facilities. As the Interior Ministry had not yet standardized administrative protocols, rules and conditions varied by camp. Ambassador Joseph C. Grew's observation that "there seems to be no co-ordination [in the camps], and each official takes such arbitrary decisions as he sees fit" correctly summarizes camp management during the first year.[31] Nonetheless, most accounts indicate that internee treatment was generally satisfactory during this period. Van Waterford's assessment of camp conditions more accurately applies to these initial months than to the years that followed:

> Foreigners were interned in Western-style buildings and compounds. There were sufficient beds and other furniture. Sanitary conditions were generally excellent, with Western-style toilets and hot and cold water.
> The internees had regular contact with the International Red Cross. Visits to the hospital and dentist were allowed, and they could shop regularly

for extra food and other necessities. They could also correspond once a month with relatives overseas and once a week with friends, acquaintances, and family in Japan.

The upkeep of the internment buildings or compounds was quite good. The supply of food stuffs, clothing, soap, medicine, and other necessities was adequate. Japanese cooks prepared the meals, and the Japanese in charge of the camps and the guards acted properly toward the internees.

Religious services and lectures, courses, concerts, and other forms of entertainment were allowed, as well as sporting events. Forced labor did not exist.[32]

Enemy nationals not initially interned or detained—roughly two-thirds of the total population—did not factor significantly into Japan's preliminary counterintelligence efforts. Citizens of noncombatant enemy nations were judged to pose little threat and were usually left untouched.[33] The six Ailion siblings in Kobe, for example, all born in Japan but holding Dutch citizenship, were not interned. This may have been for reasons of age (the male siblings were all in their forties or fifties in 1941) or the Ailion family's local prestige (their father, Isaac [1848–1918], had received the Japanese Order of the Rising Sun for his accomplishments as a businessman). In part, however, it is likely that local police deemed their Dutch citizenship comparatively unthreatening.[34] Women, children, and the elderly were also allowed to remain at large. Jennifer Rainsford, whose brother had been a diplomat at the American consulate in Yokohama and as such was given passage on the first exchange ship, testified as follows: "[In Yokohama prior to evacuation,] my sister and I were permitted to live at home as were most of the other civilians. We remained in our houses and were not allowed to leave except for certain essentials, such as visits to doctors, the procuring of food, etc."[35] Alice Kildoyle, a passenger aboard the *Tatsutamaru*—the vessel bound for the Americas but recalled to Japan after the Pearl Harbor attack—testified that when the rerouted ship had docked at Yokohama, Kildoyle and the other Americans were arrested by the water police. "We were held by them for one week and were well treated," she recounted. Though male passengers were transferred to internment camps, the women were permitted to remain at large in comparative comfort. Kildoyle continues,

I lived in a hotel. The only thing they required of me was to keep a diary of my comings and goings. Once a week a Japanese policeman would call on me, read my diary, and I would not be bothered until the following week.

I had sufficient money to last me some months. After that was gone, the U.S. State Department, through the Swiss Legation, gave me an allowance of about $60.00 per month. Everything came out of this money. The Japanese paid for nothing, nor did they supply any of the necessities of life.[36]

In urban commercial centers like Yokohama, Tokyo, Kobe, and Nagasaki, most of those interned following Pearl Harbor were businessmen. Tokyo's single camp held thirty-six, Nagasaki's twenty-one, and the two in Kobe held forty-four total.[37] In the outlying provinces a larger number of Christian missionaries and nuns were seized and their churches and mission buildings converted to internment facilities. In locations with few foreigners, individuals were simply confined to their homes.[38] In January 1942, Japanese authorities began consolidating internees within fewer, more permanent facilities.

The largest roundup occurred in Yokohama, which accommodated about three hundred U.S and British citizens at the start of the war. Most were businessmen, merchants, and missionaries and their families, and many were long-term residents who had attended Saint Joseph's together as children. They were also known to the Interior Ministry's Bureau of Police Affairs, which had commenced surveillance before the war. Their houses were searched and some belongings confiscated, but in most cases detainment proceeded without charges or interrogations.[39] Two holding facilities were prepared in Yokohama: the Negishi horse-racing track in Naka-ku (Kanagawa camp 1) and the Yacht Harbor Boat Club in Shinyamashita (Kanagawa camp 2), on the Bluff near the foreign schools and the foreigners' cemetery. (The yacht club was relocated to this site in 1940 after the Japanese navy protested that its original location was too close to the naval base in Yokosuka.) In accordance with the Geneva Convention article stipulating that "belligerents shall, so far as possible, avoid assembling in a single camp prisoners of different races or nationalities," Americans were interned at the racetrack and nationals from British Commonwealth states were held at the yacht club. Both camps were administered by Kanagawa Prefecture's civilian police.[40] The December 1941 issue of the *Gaiji geppō* reports that the Negishi racetrack held fifty-nine and the yacht club held thirty-four, for a total of ninety-three. This tally accounted for about one-quarter of the total number arrested nationally.[41]

An ICRC delegate inspected both Kanagawa camps on May 30, 1942, and submitted reports to Geneva that were then relayed to Washington. The reports found satisfactory conditions at both locations, noting that internees were being provided with sufficient food, clothing, bedding, and medical care. At the racetrack camp, internees slept six to a room in the jockeys' quarters but otherwise lodged no complaints. "The internees have picnics several times in the park," the delegate wrote, "with beer and whiskies if they care for it."[42] At the yacht club, "cooking is that of a middle class hotel," and "treatment, morale, and discipline are all good." Internees enjoyed unlimited visitations, the report continued, and missionaries held services whenever they wanted.[43] Keio University professor John Morris visited internment camps on several occasions and found conditions "good, and except for the lack of privacy, better than outside [in terms of food]."[44] Although these reports are generally corroborated, several of their claims are suspect. The delegate's comparison of the meals to that of a middle-class hotel is surely overstated. Moreover, the facility was unheated, contained only a charcoal stove, and internees received only one hot bath per week. The claim of unlimited visitations is also dubious, for it conflicts with several internee accounts. Finally, the reports fail to note that the diversity of a camp's inmates yielded uneven levels of adversity within the same camp. Those being provided with food, clothing, and other provisions by family or friends lived more comfortably than those without sources of external support.[45]

James Harris (or Hirayanagi Hideo, 1916–2004) provides one of the more balanced accounts of camp conditions. Harris was born in Kobe; his father was a British correspondent for the *London Times* and his mother was Japanese. Harris held British citizenship until his father died in 1933 and then received the Japanese citizenship necessary for him to remain in Japan with his mother. Though raised in Japan and fully bilingual, he was educated extensively in international schools and describes his worldview as British; he also describes his appearance as "nearly British."[46] Harris attended Saint Joseph's, graduating with Ludy Frank in 1934. After graduation he took a job with the *Japan Advertiser* and by 1940 had become one of the newspaper's most trusted reporters. He stayed on staff when Wilfrid Fleisher sold the paper to the *Japan Times* in 1941. Harris had heard that foreign reporters were being rounded up but assumed that his Japanese citizenship would protect him from such treatment. The fact that the Kenpeitai had interrogated him several times in the past had also reassured him that they knew his nationality and had satisfied their suspicions. Nonetheless, on the morning of December 8, hours after news of the war was released, Harris was arrested as an enemy alien at the *Times* office behind the Imperial Hotel. The arresting officers took him to the police station in Higashi Kanagawa, Yokohama, where he was processed and placed in a cell with an assortment of Japanese suspects. Harris was not permitted to visit with his mother when she came to the station, but did receive the food and clothing she had brought for him.

After a two-week detention at police headquarters, Harris was transferred to the yacht club. Though inmates' movements were restricted by a wall surrounding the compound, they were not confined to cells and had free run of the facilities. They were neither interrogated nor charged. Detainment, they were told, was an interim measure while authorities arranged repatriation. They were also informed that the camp would be administered in accordance with international law. Upon the occasion of a visitation by ICRC representatives, the camp director addressed the inmates and expressed cognizance of his responsibilities under the Geneva Convention. "When the inspectors come I want them to see the camp as it really is," he added. "I expect that you all have various complaints about your treatment here but we are doing the best we can."[47]

Harris does describe club conditions as comfortable. Its yard was large enough for softball and soccer, and inmates received permission to hold a softball game against the Negishi camp. As the inmates included a number of missionaries and clergy of various denominations, multiple religious services were held on Sundays. Harris started his own newspaper, the *Camp News Daily*, which he issued weekly. As external news was limited, the paper consisted mainly of stories about camp events like softball and soccer games, or of individuals taken to nearby hospitals for medical attention.[48] In contrast to the ICRC report's claim of unlimited visitations, Harris writes that inmates were permitted one visitor per week but were able to receive supplies from outside more often. The president of the Standard

Oil Company, he reports, feasted on meals prepared and delivered daily by his private chef.[49] Greater leniencies were afforded after a few months. Internees were taken to meet their counterparts at the Negishi camp, taken blossom viewing, and from May enjoyed weekly excursions. Each Wednesday those with families could return home between nine o'clock in the morning and four o'clock in the afternoon, and others were taken to the country club for recreation.[50]

In May, internees were informed that exchange ship arrangements were progressing. Harris describes being heartbroken to see his name on the list of passengers given berths on the *Tatsutamaru*, due to leave for Europe in July, for he had no wish to leave his mother. Just as passengers were preparing to depart, however, Kenpeitai officers appeared and announced, "So you're Hirayanagi Hideo. Just today we learned that you're a Japanese citizen. You are free to return home."[51] Despite appearances, we cannot count Harris's internment as a case of mistaken identity; the Kenpeitai were too meticulous to commit such an error. As a journalist with considerable knowledge of Japan and its military capabilities, Harris's freedom posed too great a security risk. The fact that he was half-Japanese did appear to entitle him to half the persecution, however, for whereas peers like Tolischus and Phyllis Argall were interrogated, incarcerated, and indicted, Harris was merely detained until authorities found it prudent to acknowledge his Japanese citizenship. Acknowledgment meant eligibility for military service, however, and Harris was summarily conscripted, sent to China for training, and then deployed to the front. He survived the war and later returned to Japan.

Despite the general leniency, internment fueled hostilities toward Japanese, even among those who had previously harbored no such sentiments. Confinement under guard naturally created an adversarial "us" versus "them" dynamic that hardened the loyalties of otherwise ambivalent civilians. Harris's former classmate from Saint Joseph's initially spoke openly of his loyalty to Japan but eventually reversed his allegiance. As resentment grew, Harris's own Japanese citizenship and Japanese name generated disdain from some inmates.[52]

John Palmer, a British citizen who since 1925 had worked for a British insurance company in Tokyo, paints a grimmer, more hostile portrait of yacht club life. Palmer had sent his family to Canada in 1940 and on December 8 was in the mid-Pacific bound for Los Angeles on the *Tatsu-*

tamaru. After the ship was recalled to Yokohama, Palmer and six other male passengers were interned. His humiliation at this turn of events ignited his contempt for captors he considered beneath him. "Our guards [were], for the most part, a crowd of ill-dressed, evil-spoken, ignorant fellows brought in from out-lying districts for this special duty. Many of them had never had any contact with Europeans and they regarded us with ill-concealed distaste. One of the more unpleasant effects of being stared at contemptuously week after week by these arrogant little men was to provoke in us an almost uncontrollable rage which simply had, somehow, to be mastered. The feeling was one of primitive fury which, if unleashed, would certainly have resulted in bloodshed."[53] As this statement suggests, internment camps forced individuals from diverse backgrounds and power positions to coexist under conditions that fostered cultural and racial discord. Whereas elites accustomed to privilege found themselves corralled, Aiko Utsumi writes, Japanese "who had never eaten chocolate or cheese, or seen Parker pens and Omega watches, found themselves in a position of control."[54] In some respects the indignation harbored by Palmer and others was indeed informed by a mixture of culture shock and genuine adversity. (After arriving, Palmer had to wait three weeks to receive his luggage.) Conditions that inmates perceived as hardships, camp officials viewed as normal. Internees complained that the rooms were small, that they had to sleep on futons on the floor, that they had received no pillows, and that they were responsible for cleaning and laundry. Anger over these indignities was often manifested, as Palmer's is, as racial aspersions. The Swiss consul in Kobe, for example, complained to the interior minister in Tokyo that the lodgings and food provided at the internment camps were "below a white man's minimum standard."[55] Furthermore, assumptions about appropriate behavior within a camp context were interpreted altogether differently by internees and their guards. Accounts indicate that Japanese guards felt it natural to use their authority to reciprocate on internees the forms of intimidation inflicted on them by their own superiors. Harshness that they considered appropriate to their power position, Western internees interpreted as racial abuse. In female camps established later, poor understanding on both sides about normal gendered behavior also became a source of culture shock. Japanese personnel were unprepared for Caucasian women's forward speech, behavior, and demands, which they found offensive and disrespectful.[56]

Food was a particular source of "cognitive differences" over what constituted proper treatment of detainees.[57] Palmer acknowledges receiving three daily meals of fish, vegetables, and bread or rice. But the tea was "without sugar" and the meals "badly cooked." This was surely a hardship for Palmer, who describes himself as "rotund" and admits to having never experienced hunger. And while many of the internees attributed any weight loss or loss of health to the relatively little meat being served, the amount of meat fed to Japanese interned in U.S. camps also became a source of contention. Following the first exchange, the Japanese government filed a complaint with U.S. authorities over their treatment of Japanese returnees, stating that the "inhuman cruelty and insult" they suffered while interned constituted a violation of the Geneva Convention.[58] Returning Japanese internees' principal complaint, Rod Miller notes, was being served excessive meat and insufficient rice and condiments.[59]

Palmer's bitterness is understandable. En route to reunite with his family, he had ended up interned under guard back where he had started. And though he clearly hated his Japanese captors, he also realized the need to distinguish civilians from the military. Palmer, who was among the few yacht club internees repatriated via exchange ship in June 1942, did not find within Japan's civilian population any singular penchant for brutality. Its military's cruelty, however, in his view matched Adolf Hitler's. "In Hitler we see the very incarnation of the system with all its rottenness that we are fighting in this war," Palmer announced in a 1943 speech after returning to Canada. Allied nations, he avers, must "try and think of the Japanese Military as a group in the same concentrated manner as they think of Hitler as an individual."[60]

Conditions were roughly comparable at the Tokyo camp, where thirty-seven men from Saitama, Gunma, Ibaraki, and Tochigi Prefectures were interned at Sumire Women's Academy in Tamagawa Den'enchōfu.[61] These men, mostly teachers, priests, journalists, and businessmen, ranged in age from eighteen to seventy-six. Sleeping quarters were separated roughly by nationality. Meals were provided but an additional kitchen on the second floor also enabled the men to cook for themselves. Though the *Gaiji geppō* indicates that internees followed a rigid schedule—in bed until eight o'clock in the morning, fixed meal times, daily supervised exercise periods, and baths every third day—inmate journals reveal that the facility was run more loosely. Internees were permitted to throw parties on Christmas and New Year's and allowed daily visitors, including nonfamily members. The diary of Paul Rusch (1897–1979), an instructor at Aoyama Gakuin, describes it as a winter campground with high-quality food provided: "In principle interaction with the outside is prohibited, but once we learned that we could receive items from outside, my students supplied me with bread, butter, milk, meat, and other luxurious foodstuffs . . . even pans, an oven, and other cooking implements."[62] A certain "normal" lifestyle ensued, Rusch reports. To help alleviate boredom, he produced and circulated a newspaper called *Sumire Summary*, which noted that the camp had procured a turkey for Christmas dinner (1941). Men passed their idle hours playing poker and holding table tennis tournaments, which the guards also joined.[63]

United Press correspondent Robert Bellaire, also interned at Sumire, delivered to American readers an altogether darker portrait of the Tokyo camp. His article in *Collier's Weekly*, published on September 26, 1942, shortly after his repatriation, claims the camp was known as "the worst in Japan."[64] Like accounts by Palmer, Tolischus, Argall, and other exchange ship passengers, Bellaire's story is especially critical of Japanese camp officials and guards, whom he claims were hostile until he bribed them with shoes, suits, and other gifts. "During the first two months of imprisonment," he writes, "we were on display like circus freaks. High government officials, some bringing wives and children, visited the camp daily to see 'white men behind bars.' This attraction was especially popular with army officers; we were forced to stand while they stared at us. . . . We were left completely at the mercy of low-ranking police officials who by training and nature knew only how to treat criminals."[65] Bellaire also relates that initially missionaries were forbidden from holding religious services in the camps, and that internees were permitted visitors only five times in six months, though most never exercised this opportunity because visitors were browbeaten by police.[66]

Testimonies from repatriated inmates and reports from Swiss inspectors indicate that conditions at the two camps established in Kobe were at least as favorable as those in Kanagawa and Tokyo. The Canadian Academy (camp 1), an international school, was converted to a camp the day after Pearl Harbor but continued holding classes for its students through June 1942.[67] The Swiss delegate's report, based on his visitation on June 15, relates that the camp's thirty-nine internees were receiving all necessary amenities: "Discipline and morale very good. . . . Internees are in good health and are gaining weight. . . . Plenty of exercise, tennis, volleyball, working in gardens, and excursions twice a week, with camp maintenance work. There is a library with own special books, radio, victrola, and piano. Financial situation good, but money is spent according to approval of authorities. There is one without funds, but [money] isn't necessary because everything is furnished."[68]

Kobe's Indian Hotel Eastern Lodge (camp 2) held forty-three internees, including twenty-seven Catholic nuns and five married couples. This hotel was owned by an Indian family and was also well stocked with the necessary amenities.[69] Some of its cooks and staff had also stayed on to care for the internees. The June 15 inspection found the following: "Unrestricted supplementary rations, vegetable garden. . . . Hygiene and health good with medical and dental care when necessary in a hospital in the city. No deaths, daily baths. Billiards, ping pong, cards, checkers, newspapers, books, walks. The financial situation is good except for two who cannot support Japanese wives. . . . Permission is given for visits to or from the outside."[70]

Though accounts vary widely, it is clear that through the summer of 1942 camps operated with the purpose of immobilizing enemy nationals—predominantly males, missionaries, and nuns—not of punishing them. As inmates struggled to suppress their indignation and make difficult adjustments, at no time during this period did they suffer severe privations. In reviewing our various sources on the camps, it is noteworthy that the most unfavorable, hostile, and racial were produced by Palmer and Bellaire soon after their repatriation. The fact that their North American audiences, like Tolischus's and Argall's, were preconditioned to nationalistic, racist rhetoric may have encouraged or even required particularly critical assessments of the enemy.[71]

As males were targeted for internment by the Interior Ministry's initial guidelines, it was largely males who were released from camps for repatriation on the first exchange ships. The *Asamamaru* departed from Yokohama on June 25, 1942, carrying seventy-six former internees: seventy Americans, five Canadians, and one Honduran. On July 30, the *Tatsutamaru* departed, carrying sixty former internees: forty British, fourteen Dutch, four Greeks, one Belgian, and one Norwegian. Twenty-three of the thirty-seven prisoners held in Tokyo, thirty-four held in Yokohama, and forty-six held in Hyogo since December secured passage aboard these two ships. The third exchange ship (and second Japan-U.S. exchange), the *Teiamaru*, departed on September 14, 1943, carrying seventy-three former internees. The number of interned foreigners thus fell dramatically. Many of those who remained opted to do so, either because they had Japanese families or because they were long-term residents who had lost connections to their country of citizenship. The reduction would be short-lived, however, as camps were repopulated following a second wave of arrests.[72]

Stringency and Privation (1942–45)

The exchanges in 1942 coincided with several events that necessitated the development of new guidelines for handling enemy nationals. Japan suffered two major military defeats that summer: at Midway in June and at Guadalcanal in August. Also in June, and as a riposte to the Doolittle Raid, the Justice Department sought to foment nationalistic zeal by publicizing its discovery (eight months earlier) of Richard Sorge's spy ring. These factors, combined with complaints by repatriated Japanese about their treatment in the United States and frustrations over failing negotiations for future prisoner exchanges, convinced authorities of the need for stronger counterintelligence measures. On August 18, the Interior Ministry called on the public to identify all suspicious Westerners and announced that it would detain foreigners, including women and the elderly, who used their positions to influence or otherwise compromise the unity of the Japanese people.[73] The new restrictions limited visitations from family and friends to twice monthly and prohibited temporary leave from camps, effectively confining inmates for the remainder of the war.

These new measures placed educators, missionaries, and nuns squarely within police crosshairs and resulted in the arrest of 152 more foreigners, 126 of whom were women. With this, missionary groups, schools, and clinics were effectively shuttered.[74] The influx of female internees necessitated new gender-specific facilities and precipitated more inmate shuffling.

The Sumire camp in Tokyo, for example, became a facility for women from the Kanto region. (The thirty-seven displaced male internees were subsequently transferred to the former Saint Francis monastery in Urawa, Saitama.) Though holding 90 women when it opened in October 1942, the Sumire camp held 123 by December. The memoir of Olive Hodges (1877–1964) describes its austere conditions: "We were enclosed in our small rooms and allowed outside only when we became ill and had to be allowed out for the sake of our health. The uniformed police everywhere made us realize we were in prison, but then we recalled the large number of police surrounding the Imperial Palace and so we decided to think of ourselves not as prisoners but as members of the Imperial family. . . . One of the women collected toast crumbs and used them to make a pudding for Christmas, another made delicious cookies, and a third made pancakes."[75]

Tokyo camp conditions deteriorated, and in March 1943 eleven women were hospitalized. Red Cross inspection reports of the Sumire and Urawa camps understated the marked decline, however. A report filed after an ICRC inspection on May 29, 1943, is apologetic rather than admonitory: "Japanese authorities are doing everything possible for the civilians in these camps. In general the internees seem to be in good physical condition and are satisfied with the way they are being treated."[76] By August, nine women had been released for health reasons.[77] Fifty-three others from the Tokyo camp, along with ten men from the Urawa camp, were among the seventy-three former inmates given passage aboard the third exchange ship, which departed on September 14, 1943.[78] As the war effort absorbed more resources, however, conditions inside and outside the camps continued to decline. An inmate in Tokyo records that the camp cook was embezzling many of the quality supplies and that the meat served to inmates was often dolphin, shark, or whale. For breakfast they received only a roll, and for lunch a cup of mushy rice.[79] At the Urawa camp, Roland Harker noted that detainees were not mistreated because guards had knowledge of the Geneva Convention, but complained that food scarcity grew critical as early as 1942 and that their Christmas dinner that year consisted only of sandwiches.[80]

Such complaints typified the sentiments of enemy internees around Japan between 1942 and 1945, as they did for the Japanese population generally. Shortages necessitated incremental cuts in rations, and by the end of the war the average caloric intake of Japanese civilians was only 60 percent of that in the 1930s.[81] Some Japanese filed complaints over what they saw as preferential treatment of Caucasian prisoners—specifically, that prisoners were eating meat; that their rice rations were double the 330 (later reduced to 300) grams allotted to Japanese; that prisoners performing labor were eating fish while Japanese soldiers were dying of malnutrition; that prisoners were given four rest days per month, double the number given to Japanese; and that prisoners were wearing fine clothing.[82] A number of these complaints were accurate. Testimony from Takezawa Shōgi, head of the Urawa internment camp, affirmed that from December 1942 rice or bread rations for foreign internees were identical to those provided Japanese soldiers, which was double the ration received by Japanese civilians.[83] Foreign internees were not only supplied with locally produced meat, fish, bread, and vegetables; at some camps they kept pigs and cultivated plots of vegetables. Some were also given the option of performing compensated labor, an allowance consistent with Geneva Convention provisions.[84]

As complaints by Japanese civilians averred, comparably greater rations for interned Caucasians had been established through "Rules on Provisions for POWs" (*Furyo kyūyo kisoku*) issued on February 20, 1942. The rules stipulated that POW officers would be given the same rations as Japanese officers, and that the cost of rations for enlisted POWs would fall within the same range as that for the basic rations provided to Japanese soldiers of equivalent ranks. An August 1944 Red Cross report of the Kobe POW hospital confirmed that "prisoners' diet was reported to correspond to that of the camp guards in quantity and quality . . . [and] caloric value was 3,000."[85] Observance of "Rules on Provisions" policy within civilian camps is generally corroborated by ICRC camp inspection reports from Saitama, Tokyo, Kanagawa, Hyogo, Nagoya, and Nagasaki. Compiled between January and March 1944, the reports cataloged camp populations; recreational, sleeping, bathing, toilet, and heating facilities; general inmate health; visitations; and inmate complaints. Their inventories of food rations at each camp (table 7.2) generally verify compliance with prescribed POW rations, but also reveal inadequate sources of protein. Only the Nagoya camp failed to provision its inmates with the specified quantity of rice, bread, oatmeal, or potatoes.

Table 7.2

Daily rations at seven civilian internment camps, based on International Red Cross inspection reports from early 1944. The sixty-one interned at the Kobe camp include twenty-nine Americans, most of whom were captured in Guam and transferred to Japan.

	Saitama	Kanagawa	Tokyo 1	Tokyo 2	Kobe	Nagasaki	Nagoya
Investigation date	January 28, 1944	January 31, 1944	February 24, 1944	January 26, 1944	March 13, 1944	March 16, 1944	March 19, 1944
Number interned	56	49	42	59	61	15	16
Bread	356 g	300 g	600 g	600 g	400 g	225 g	110 g
Rice	555 g	330 g	0	0	167 g	420 g	220 g
Oatmeal	100 g						
Macaroni			2 days/week				15 g
Udon							30 g
Flour			33.3 g			60 g	40 g
Meat	75 g	0	56 g	56 g	10.8 g	37 g	15 g
Fish	180 g	Occasional	112 g	200 g	15 g	167 g	12 g
Eggs	0	0	1.5	0	16.7 g	For sick	14 g
Milk	0	0	0	0	200 g	0	62 cc
Margarine	Occasional	0		100 g	0		
Butter	0	0	52 g	100 g	30 g	10 g	
Cheese	0	0	Little		0	0	0
Vegetables	750 g incl. potato	612 g incl. sweet potato	375 g	750 g	367 g	75 g	Plentiful
Fruit	180 g	0	Seasonal	Every other day	193 g	Little	Seasonal
Potatoes			Occasional	0	100 g	33.3 g	0
Tea	6 g	3.3 g	10.7 g		26.7 g	10 g	0
Sugar	7.5 g	7.9 g	30.9 g	56 g	8.3 g	15 g	25 g
Sweets	Monthly	0	0		6 g	0	

SOURCE: Komiya, "Taiheiyō sensō shita," 29.
NOTE: A blank cell indicates that the camp inspector's rations survey makes no mention of that food item.

General compliance with food ration guidelines in no way suggests that those quantities were adequate to sustain good health. Both sides recognized as much. In their interviews with ICRC inspectors, inmates confirmed that the quantity and quality of food was inadequate, and in one case that it was less than half of earlier provisions. Inmates were thin, the reports noted. One inmate complained that the energy expenditure of forced firewood collection in the hills outside the camp only made him hungrier. The state acknowledged that the national food shortage precluded its ability to provide internees with sustainable provisions, and in 1944 Tokyo informed Washington of this. By the end of the war, Japan had nearly halted its imports of raw materials for weapons manufacturing in order to supply its citizenry with basic necessities. Supplies to POW camps fell to only one-third to one-half of the quantities needed, and civilian camps fared only slightly better.[86]

Doubts also surround the accuracy of Red Cross camp inspection reports. Those drafted by Pestalozzi and Assistant Delegate H. C. Angst between 1942 and 1945 share a generally conciliatory, neutral, or even affirmative tone. In a typical letter to the minister of foreign affairs, they noted that "the living conditions of the prisoners and internees who were visited may be considered satisfactory on the whole," while also noting a number of aspects "which might still be improved upon in a certain number of these camps, especially the Tokyo Civil Internment Camp No. I and the Kanagawa Prefectural Civil Internment Camp No. I."[87] While inspectors clearly aspired to record actual camp conditions, they were also handcuffed by Japanese censorship and regulations. Visits had to be announced in advance, allowing camp commanders time to prepare. An Italian inmate in the Nagoya facility wrote that he received a much greater quantity of food on the day of the Red Cross inspection, and internees in other camps reported similarly duplicitous tactics. Inmates may have also feared punishment if they reported to the ICRC information that reflected badly on the camps.[88] Inspectors conducted their business cautiously, therefore. Careful to retain impartiality, on no occasion do ICRC reports accuse Japanese authorities of negligence or convey a sense of alarm, even for the most squalid facilities. (Western parties expecting greater advocacy from the Swiss would later charge the Red Cross with corruption.)[89]

Though it is likely that the ICRC's rations inventories were inflated, its reports were not entirely fraudulent. They did expose some camp shortcomings. They found, for example, that heating was inadequate or nonexistent in nearly all the camps. In some facilities residents spent much of the day in bed because of the cold, and in others inmates were making their own rudimentary heaters. The Kanagawa facility lacked sufficient bedding and some were sleeping on tables. At the Nagoya facility, which possessed few beds, inmates were sleeping on tatami. Red Cross delegates also requested better provisions for the neediest camps, and internees at nearly all domestic facilities acknowledged receiving critically needed Red Cross relief packages of food, clothing, and medical supplies.

During the war's later years, the inadequacy of camp provisions was particularly evident in Kanagawa. In June 1943 the two Yokohama camps were evacuated and consolidated at the facility where Robert Crowder had been held since he declined repatriation in June 1942. Officially, the move was explained by the navy's desire to convert the more populated Negishi camp to a facility for printing war materials, but Komiya Mayumi speculates that it was also prompted by the Interior Ministry's desire to protect internees from air raids and minimize their interactions with Japanese civilians. The new location was a Catholic monastery at the foot of Mount Ashigara in Uchiyama, about forty miles west of Yokohama. The new location burdened inmates' families, who now faced a lengthy train ride and then a two-and-a-half-mile walk up a winding mountain road from Yamakita Station. Visitations were common nonetheless.[90] The new camp's remoteness obviated basic security measures. No high fences, barbed wire, or guard towers were erected. Only two guards, and occasionally only one, were posted on duty, and no guards were posted on Sundays.[91] Inmates routinely left the camp to gather wood or food or to do work projects, and Uchiyama internee Syd Duer reports that he was once allowed to return home.[92] While camp security was lax, Angst's inspection on January 31, 1944, found deplorable conditions: "Enclosure is low bamboo fence. Both buildings of this camp are in need of repair. One is an old foreign style dwelling and one a Japanese style dwelling with paper panels, no outside panels of wood. Rooms—one large, one medium, and two small. Enclosed veranda on ground floor. Same style on second floor. All used as dormitories. . . . Space is insufficient and overcrowded. Some sleeping on tables. Light sufficient. No heating."[93]

Though Angst had requested repairs and improvements, Pestalozzi's report from August 1944 indicates that the camp remained dilapidated and overcrowded. The Red Cross had continued to supply aid packages and issue monetary aid to four of the inmates, but these provisions were insufficient to stave off camp-wide hunger. Most troubling, although the facility continued to allow two monthly visitations from friends and family, it had since prohibited inmates from receiving external food. This critical lifeline was severed because the camp commander had grown suspicious that supplies brought by visitors had been purchased on the black market. Pestalozzi's report notes inmates' malnutrition and requests greater rations, but in the ensuing months food shortages worsened and conditions grew direr.[94] Duer reports that inmates received less than standard rations because cooks and guards appropriated supplies for themselves or used them to treat camp guests.[95] Shortages became especially critical following the massive May 29, 1945, bombing of Yokohama. Between the autumn of 1944 and the surrender, five prisoners at the Kanagawa camp died of disease or malnutrition and a sixth died of complications from a hernia operation. After the war, a war crimes tribunal indicted Watanabe Katsunosuke, the camp's security chief, for negligence and sentenced him to twelve years in prison. Two other guards received five-year sentences.[96]

The only other resident civilian camp to suffer inmate fatalities was also populated by Kanagawa residents. The 1943 evacuation order that sent nonenemy nationals packing for Hakone or Karuizawa also called for the relocation of noninterned enemy nationals living within coastal restricted zones. This included any wives, children, and elderly family members of men interned at the Kanagawa camp in Uchiyama. On December 7, 1943, twenty-eight individuals from twenty families were installed in the Fukumoto-kan and Tamagawa-kan inns located in Nanasawa Onsen, Atsugi, about twenty-five miles west of Yokohama. Five more later joined the group, bringing the total to thirty-three. Detainees, predominantly females aged three to ninety-three, were supervised by the inns' owners, and expenses were paid by the prefectural office in Yokohama. They cooked for themselves and enjoyed relative independence, their single police guard allowing them to shop and take group walks at will. (This latter privilege was eventually revoked when one woman defied orders by taking long strolls alone.) Allegedly, locals exhibited no resentment or suspicion toward them. After the war, newspapers reported that one lo-cal farmer had felt sorry for the women and repeatedly supplied them with vegetables, milk, rice balls, and charcoal, traveling at night via a mountain road to avoid police detection.[97] Inmate Rainsford's postwar testimony contains no complaints concerning her treatment at the camp. Her inn was divided into small rooms, and most people occupied pri-vate rooms and did their own cleaning and laundry, she related. They had brought everything they wanted and needed with them, including bedding. The inns were safe from the bombings and their police guard treated them "very fairly."[98] She complains only that the diet, which con-sisted mainly of greens, bread, and rice, was impoverished, though she does note receiving Red Cross relief packages.

A suicide was the singular noteworthy event during the group's eigh-teen months in Nanasawa. In June 1944, Eleanor Laffin (1897–1944), a half-Japanese American, left her inn to visit the dentist and stepped in front of a train at Atsugi Station. Motivations for her suicide are uncer-tain, but may have been prompted by news that her brother William (1902–44) had been killed fighting in Burma a month earlier. Laffin's sisters, Mary Cooke and Mildred, along with their mother, Miyo, had evacuated Yokohama to their villa in Sengokubara, Hakone, and it is un-clear why Eleanor did not accompany them.[99] An obituary claims that since her father's death in 1931, his heirs had been disputing the distribu-tion of his considerable estate. (After the war, the Laffin family, longtime residents and business leaders of Yokohama, petitioned the Japanese gov-ernment for 97.7 million yen in compensation.) It also mentions a sui-cide note instructing that her watch and jewelry be given to a friend at the Nanasawa camp.[100]

Japan's preparations for a U.S. ground invasion in the spring of 1945 included deployments of troops to Atsugi. As soldiers needed to occupy the two inns, on May 30 the Nanasawa group was moved north to the Tateai camp in Omonogawa, near Yokote City in Akita Prefecture. The remote location was selected in part due to its distance from likely air-raid targets. The women occupied the headquarters of a local industrial association, a building with offices on the first floor but whose second floor contained about ten small rooms easily convertible to living quar-ters. Before their arrival, officials met with locals to explain who they were and the reasons for their relocation to Tateai. A fence was erected around the building, and curtains hung inside to prevent locals from peering in. A cook from Yokote City familiar with Western food was hired to prepare meals in a kitchen separated from the main building. No malice was exhibited by the locals, Komiya writes, some of whom stopped by to donate vegetables. After the surrender, internees visited the homes of local farmers to barter canned food and chocolate from their Red Cross packages for produce, and, when returning to Yokohama in September, their guards helped pack and carry their luggage to the station. Although such accounts sound overly idyllic, they are nonetheless consistent with stories from Karuizawa and other rural settings where cooperation and charity from locals were widely reported.

They are also corroborated by statements from five inmates. Alice and Lucy Woodruff testified to the U.S. War Crimes Office that they were treated well and were happy at the Tateai camp. They were given freedom of movement, and, though food was scarce, they were neither starving nor maltreated. Regarding the six deaths, Rainsford testified that the women who died were elderly and more susceptible to the long-term effects of poor nutrition. "Several women died at this camp but from old age," she reported. "They were taken ill suddenly and probably because of their meager diet, were not able to resist their malady and died. They did not suffer much. In every case, they were treated by Japanese doctors. . . . At Akita-ken, an old lady almost 80 years of age died. The reason for death was given as old age."[101] Rainsford and her sister Anna Mayers both related that they had to clean the facility but otherwise experienced no abuse.[102] Kildoyle's description of camp conditions corroborates the others, relating that the diet was poor but that she suffered no particular discomforts. She also mentions receiving a monthly allowance from the U.S. State Department.[103]

In stark contrast to the Kanagawa camp, which had unilaterally barred the procurement of external food, at Kobe's Indian Hotel Eastern Lodge conditions and amenities remained comparatively comfortable. Until March 1943 internees were permitted to shop for food and clothing at will in order to supplement camp provisions. After this date, guards did their shopping upon request. Food was "more than plenty, and better than could be obtained outside," the Swiss delegate reported in May 1943. "[The] Indian owner of hotel (a very kind and good man) was paid so much for the [up]keep of internees and could feed them as he wishes within reason and scope of ration tickets."[104] In addition to their own funds, some Eastern Lodge residents received monthly allowances of thirty to thirty-four yen from the Swiss consul in Kobe, whose representative visited them regularly.[105] Political dynamics also factored into camp conditions. An inmate at the Nagoya facility holding Italian civilians wrote that internees were subjected to harsh treatment from police and guards, who viewed them as former allies who had betrayed Japan. (The camp was created in the wake of Italy's September 1943 surrender.) Prisoners were rationed only enough food to keep them alive, he wrote, and some survived only through provisions received from their families (table 7.2).[106]

Circumstantial factors thus exerted enormous impacts on the spectrum of prisoner experiences. The variable conditions at the Kanagawa, Nanasawa/Tateai, Indian Hotel, and Nagoya camps indicate that facility administrators loosely observed government regulations but also retained considerable discretion in adjusting camp procedures to their liking. Camp demographics also contributed to the variability of internment conditions and experiences. The Eastern Lodge and Nanasawa/Tateai contingents, which enjoyed better amenities than most camps, may have benefited from the fact that they were composed largely of female and elderly inmates whom authorities may have felt merited certain leniencies. Waterford writes that the twenty-six nuns at the Sendai camp "were never considered 'real' internees. . . . Their position as nuns was an uncomfortable one for the Japanese authorities, who were not used to guarding such a group of women."[107] In reference to another unspecified cohort of interned nuns, Waterford continues, "Japanese respect for old age showed itself, for example, in their treatment of a small group of nuns and Protestant missionaries interned in Japan. These internees were allowed to go shopping and for walks under guard. They were treated with kindness by their guards and exchanged language lessons with them."[108]

In terms of food, access to medical care, and protection from air raids, state custodianship of enemy nationals was generally adequate, the Uchiyama and Nagoya camps being notable exceptions. Officials remained cognizant of their custodial responsibilities even during the final months of the war. In preparation for a U.S. ground invasion from the south, during the summer of 1945 police detained several communities of Catholic missionaries in Kyushu, the only remaining foreigners occupying the countryside there. Twenty-six European nuns from various missions around Kyushu were installed in the remote hot spring village of Tochinoki-onsen in Fukuoka and held there until the surrender. In late July, only weeks before the surrender, forty-two European catholic priests and nuns were interned at a monastery at Hikosan, also in Fukuoka. One priest wrote that he was notified of the internment on July 27 and then taken on August 2, arriving the following day. They slept six to a room and were kept under police supervision but were released soon after the surrender less than two weeks later.[109]

In total, 740 resident foreigners were interned in low-security camps during the war. Some of these were repatriated; others were released due to illness or for miscellaneous reasons, including police error.[110] At the end of the war, 412 remained interned in fourteen camps (table 7.3). Twelve had died, a mortality rate of 1.6 percent, or 2.9 percent of those remaining in custody. Though not unilaterally successful, the government's administration of civilian camps resulted in conditions that were far superior to those in military camps. It also achieved this without the racial policies employed by the military.

Some prisoners were aware of their comparatively comfortable circumstances, and it is significant that two credited these to civilian jurisdiction. Palmer equated Japan's military to the Third Reich, but saw no evidence of equivalent attitudes among civilian Japanese or even his own camp guards. When asked about the absence of atrocities committed at the Nanasawa and Tateai camps, Rainsford replied, "First of all, we were not guarded by the Japanese Army but by the National Police. Secondly, because we had all been residents of Japan for many years, we were well known to the Japanese in the communities and were well liked by them. We were not considered prisoners of war, and if we had been we would have been subjected to the same atrocities as the American troops were."[111] Both long-term residents, Palmer and Rainsford understood that anti-Caucasian sentiment was pervasive only within military circles and felt it necessary to disavow claims that racial antipathy for Westerners was at all normative within civilian contexts.

In connection with our examination of racialized treatment of resident Caucasians, Japan's two "hidden camps" for enemy civilians captured and transferred from abroad bear brief mention here. Including

Table 7.3
Resident enemy nationals interned at the end of the war, excluding 437 civilians captured and transferred from overseas, diplomats and the other civilians repatriated on exchange ships, and several interned Germans. Locations are arranged geographically, north to south.

Location	Surviving internees	Notes	Deaths
Towada-chō, Akita	48	Staff and families of Italian embassy	0
Omonogawa-machi, Akita (Tateai camp)	27	Women, children, and elderly relocated from Kanagawa	6
Morioka City, Iwate	8 women	French and German nuns	0
Tatamiya-chō, Sendai City, Miyagi	26 women	Canadian nuns	0
Aizu Wakamatsu City, Fukushima	4 women	Canadian nuns	0
Urawa City, Saitama	56	31 Canadians, 10 British, 7 Greeks, 3 Americans, 3 Belgians, 2 Dutch	0
Ochiai, Tokyo (Seibo)	36 women	Catholic nuns of various nationalities	0
Mejirodai, Tokyo	18	German Jews, others	0
Uchiyama, Kanagawa	44	20 British, 13 Canadians, 6 Americans, 3 Greeks, 2 stateless	6
Ishinomura (Nagoya), Aichi	15	Italian civilians	0
Nagasaki City, Nagasaki[a]	41 (35 women)	Resident nuns and families, mostly British. The camp, located in the suburbs, survived the atomic bombing.	0
Mount Hiko, Fukuoka	28	French and Italian missionaries	0
Kiyomizu, Saga	21	Resident French and Portuguese	0
Chōyōmura, Kumamoto	40	Polish missionaries, others	0
Total	412		12

SOURCE: Based on Komiya, *Tekikokujin yokuryū*, 244; and Komiya, "Taiheiyō sensō shita," 37.

NOTE: Komiya's data is generally corroborated by statistics compiled by the U.S. War Department (Hayashi, *Senji gaikokujin kyōseirenkō kankei*, 1085–86). For different data on thirty-three civilian camps and their occupants, see Waterford, *Prisoners of the Japanese*, 206–11. Waterford's data occasionally conflicts with Komiya's and is unannotated. At least in part, it appears to be based on research by Dotje van Velden, presented in *De Japanse Burgerkampen* (The Japanese civilian camps) (Kampen, Netherlands: Uitgeverij, Wever, Franeker, 1977), whose estimates of interned civilians are considerably lower than Komiya's. My research finds Komiya's data to be more comprehensive and accurate than any other.

[a]Part of the internment camp holding foreigners was destroyed in the atomic bombing of Nagasaki on August 9, 1945. Several inmates sustained minor injuries but all survived (Komiya, "Taiheiyō sensō shita," 36).

those transferred from abroad, the number of enemy civilians interned at war's end totaled 858, excluding 50 who died during internment. Of these 50 deaths, 20 occurred at a camp in Otaru, Hokkaido, holding the forty-five Attuans transferred from the Aleutian Islands off the Alaskan coast. The second hidden camp, located in Izumi-chō, Kanagawa, contained the Attuans' Caucasian English teacher and eighteen Australian nurses. This second camp suffered no deaths. Neither camp's existence was acknowledged by the Interior Ministry, and Swiss requests for information about them were denied. The stunning mortality rate (44 percent) at the Attuans' camp has been attributed to several factors, principally disease and the Attuans' difficulty adjusting to the Japanese diet. Equally instrumental, certainly, was the fact that the Attuans bore Asiatic features, making theirs the only camp in Japan holding non-Caucasian enemy civilians. Both the Attuans and the nurses were given the option of performing compensated labor, a virtual necessity given the inadequate rations, but the former were put to work outdoors in clay mines at lower wages than Japanese laborers received. The Australian nurses, in contrast, worked indoors folding envelopes and knitting cloth bags.[112] Also, in January 1945 Japanese authorities finally allowed the ICRC to inspect the nurses' camp, but permitted no such investigation of the Attuan camp. Racial discrimination thus took a heavy toll on the Attuans, whose living and working experiences more closely resembled those of resident Chinese and Korean laborers than Caucasian prisoners.

A final caveat concerns an eleventh-hour Nazi effort to persecute resident Jews. Japan was not legally bound by any treaty to adhere to German policy, and Japanese authorities had resisted German pressure to persecute resident Jews unilaterally. They saw no ideological reason to do so, Ben-Ami Shillony notes, for "against the background of Shinto and Buddhism, the differences between Judaism and Christianity lost their significance."[113] Rather, authorities chose to apprehend Jews whose alleged activities threatened Japanese interests and to protect others, particularly certain cultural luminaries whose professional activities had benefited Japan. In the winter of 1944/45, however, Josef Meisinger exploited the loyalties of Japanese police by ordering the arrest of certain high-profile Jews who had remained active during the war. Klaus Pringsheim Sr. (1883–1972) had fled Germany for Japan in 1931 and established himself as one among an elite cohort of Jewish musicians collectively instrumental in advancing Western classical music in Japan. Originally a professor at the Ueno Academy of Music, throughout the war he had served as director of the Tokyo Chamber Symphony Orchestra. Pianist Leonid Kreutzer (1884–1953), professor at the Tokyo Music School, also continued working and performing throughout the war. In February 1945, Pringsheim and Kreutzer were among eighteen German Jews interned, together with thirty-six female missionaries and nuns, in a new facility at the Tokyo Theological Seminary (Tokyo shingakkō) in Sekiguchidai (Koishikawa), Bunkyō-ku.[114] The camp caught fire during an air raid on May 26 but guards evacuated the inmates safely. The thirty-six women were then transferred to Seibo Hospital in Ochiai, and the Jewish men were held at Japan Women's University in Meijirodai.[115] This final roundup of Jews punctuated a series of isolated Jewish persecutions, all carried out under the orders of the German embassy. Such occurrences had included the incarceration of Hugo Frank and Arvid Balk, whose travails in captivity will be detailed in the next chapter.

CHAPTER 8

Torture and Testimony

The Incarceration of Suspected Spies (1944–45)

On the morning of July 28, 1944, Kenpeitai officers stomped into Hugo Frank's house in Gora without bothering to remove their shoes. They took Hugo to the Yamate Police Station in Yokohama and subjected him to torture for the next three and a half months. The same day and in the same manner, the French national Andre Bossée was arrested for espionage in Karuizawa. At five o'clock in the morning on August 1, Arvid Balk was arrested by five officers from the Kanagawa police department. Inspectors Kobayashi and Kimoto supervised while the others confiscated whatever papers they found on Arvid's shelves. Upon their departure, Arvid's wife, Estelle, fled to her friend Margot Ries's house, where she found Margot's husband, Hans, in the process of being arrested by more prefectural police.[1] Arvid and Hans were also taken to the Yamate Police Station, where Hans remained; Arvid was transferred to the Kagachō Station, also in Yokohama. At nine o'clock in the morning on August 31, Margaret Liebeskind, who in December 1940 had been stranded in Japan while en route to the United States, was also arrested for espionage.[2] So began a second wave of arrests carried out during the final year of the war. In the months that followed, this small cohort of suspects became the victims of a frantic police force and a hostile German embassy. Hugo endured eleven months of imprisonment but would not survive to witness the war's end. Arvid survived the ordeal but never recovered physically or emotionally.

Japan's first wave of arrests, its handling of suspected spies following Pearl Harbor, was introduced in chapter 4. As discussed, the charges of espionage against Samuel Heaslett, Otto Tolischus, and Phyllis Argall were disingenuous and variously vindictive attempts to camouflage some grudge or ulterior motive. Trials were conducted as a matter of pretense and lacked credibility. At this initial stage, persecution was a way for the Kenpeitai either to assert authority and stay busy as it monitored an acquiescent, innocuous foreign community, or to neutralize journalists and other influential individuals until their repatriation. Officers making arrests tended to exhibit reserve and professionalism. Tolischus's arresting officers had even allowed him to change clothes and pack a suitcase before leaving. Confiscated items like cameras and binoculars were cataloged and, in principle, returned prior to repatriation.[3] The baseless interrogations and pointless trials that followed bespoke a smugness derived from what for Japan had been a most jubilant six months.

As the tenor of Hugo's arrest indicates, by mid-1944 Japan's military prospects had turned grim and authorities had become belligerent. Police and prison officials now carried out their duties with desperation, and the German embassy seized greater control over counterintelligence initiatives. Shifts were also reflected in the demographics of those being arrested. Of the 109 resident foreigners arrested for suspicion of espionage in December 1941, nearly all were enemy nationals. Whether convicted or not, these suspects were released and repatriated.[4] During the last year of the war, in contrast, Nazi officials grew more desperate to punish anti-Nazi Germans and other suspicious foreigners. Police complied by targeting such individuals, arresting about fifty for possession of military secrets. About half were German, and the remainder French, Soviet, and White Russian.[5] In fact, six of the nine Caucasians held at Yokohama's central prison in 1945 were German (see table 8.1, later in this chapter). Hugo and Arvid were among this cohort.

This chapter examines how Japan's police and judicial system handled suspected spies arrested in Kanagawa during the final year of the war. Most records on the incarcerations, interrogations, and trials of foreign espionage suspects were either incinerated in the air raids or destroyed by Japanese officials following the surrender. What remains, however, lends authority to a plethora of reports, statements, and testimonies from individuals on hand. I shall cite from these documents extensively, allowing the victims, perpetrators, and witnesses to speak for themselves whenever possible. Their collective testimonies reveal Kenpeitai interrogation techniques and prison conditions during this period as wantonly cruel. Illegal torture was common. In some cases it included an intention to abuse rather than to extract information, and in others it was prolonged even after suspects had confessed. Espionage suspects thus faced considerably harsher interrogations and reprisals than did the enemy journalists arrested in 1941–42. Their ruthless treatment also conflicts fundamentally with the tenor of Japanese-Western relations as discussed in the preceding chapters, which found innumerable instances of Japanese exhibiting tolerance and pragmatism in their engagement with Westerners. This contrast between military police and public treatment of foreigners illustrates the necessity of correlating jurisdiction and authority to the extreme range of wartime experiences faced by resident Westerners.

Interrogation

All those arrested for espionage in Kanagawa during the final year of the war faced a sequence of prosecution procedures that would take them to three separate facilities. Interrogations were carried out at temporary detention centers (*kōryū*) at police and Kenpeitai stations. Suspects generally shared jail cells with Japanese suspects and were permitted no visitors during this period. Their families were required to deliver lunches daily and clean underwear weekly. Interrogations—which often included torture and were conducted by teams of Kenpeitai officers and interpreters—continued until they yielded signed confessions. Suspects were then transferred to the interim jail (*kōchisho*) at Yokohama Prison in Gumyōji (Kamiōoka) to await trial. As inmates at this facility were issued blue uniforms, locals called it the "blue prison." Family members were expected to continue supplying inmates with food and underwear at the blue prison but were allowed short supervised meetings every ten days. After trials and sentencing, prisoners were transferred to the penitentiary for convicts (*keimusho*), the "red prison," a separate facility within the larger prison complex at Gumyōji. Here convicts, clad in red uniforms, experienced harsher conditions. While red prison convicts were permitted visitations, they were prohibited from receiving food or any other item from outside. Torture, illegal in principle, occurred only within the police detention centers. The blue and red prisons generally permitted no corporal abuse, though food shortages, disease, and cold resulted in universal suffering and high mortality rates.

After Hugo's arrest, his wife, Alice, tried to visit him at the Yamate Station but was turned away. She was instructed, however, about her responsibility for supplying him with food and underwear. Daily thereafter she made the six-hour round trip from Gora. The train was often full and Barbara, then aged five, remembers her mother fighting to board, on one occasion having to hand her daughter through an open window to somebody so that she could squeeze aboard herself. Estelle Balk, Margot Ries, and their maids took turns delivering supplies to Arvid at Kagachō and Hans at Yamate. Alice was not invited to join the rotation. Irene Frank twice traveled from Karuizawa to visit Arvid in prison but was denied both times, the guards threatening to arrest her if she returned. On her first visit, Estelle describes being shocked that a "foreign gentleman" had been caged with "native criminals," but also shocked at the general conditions.

> The [Kagachō] Police station is the usual grey block, filthy and unkempt, as all Japanese official buildings are with paper, cigarette butts, or orange peels, the dust of years coating every corner. Reluctantly we stepped in, picking our way gingerly through the dark corridor to a small bleak room, where one barred window let in a grey light. There was a gate, not a door, and we stood there staring in. An old man in uniform was sitting at a table. He had a long, straggly beard and looked strange and repelling. Facing us, as well as right around him, were barred cages like you see in the zoo with filthy matting on the floors. No chairs, no bed, just the bare floor and a bucket in the corner. . . . The unkempt individuals, half naked squatting behind the bars, the slovenly women in the cage facing us, staring enviously at us free people outside, that prisoner, a tottering half-starved Chinese with handcuffs they were just leading off. Hans Ries was not here, but where in all this Asiatic filth was my beloved husband? They could not possibly have put a foreign gentleman in such a place like this? They must have made a difference between these native criminals and him? Lifting up my voice as much as I dared, as I saw a corridor beyond probably leading to other prison cages, I announced in my faulty Japanese I had brought the food for Mr. Arvid Balk, and fresh underwear as well as soap and a toothbrush. A policeman grabbed my thermos bottle and violently

smashed it on the stone floor. "Soap is forbidden." The other food he would first let Kobayashi inspect. Soap and toothbrush out of the question, cigarettes too, though I offered him some. He would take the underwear, letting me wait till Arvid had changed to pass them back to me. The man was purposely insolent, using the vilest language. He threw Arvid's dirty linen at me and banged the gate in our faces.[6]

On August 21, Arvid was transferred to the Isezakichō Police Station in Yokohama and Estelle was brought in for questioning. It was evident to her that the police had been reading Arvid's diary and papers, for they asked her for explanations of certain documents and to translate his account book. Inspector Yamane Ryūji was in charge of the interrogation and Patrick Tomkinson served as police interpreter. The latter, a half-American, half-Japanese man Estelle had known in Yokohama who now confessed to have been working for the Japanese police all along, would also become complicit in Arvid's torture.[7] Estelle states that she was struck with a book repeatedly during the questioning but was scandalized more by the disrespect shown to Arvid by those she considered her inferiors than by the physical abuse itself. "He is a man of culture," she protested. "How dare you stick him into your filthy cells?"[8]

Estelle also pleaded Arvid's case to the German consulate. The indignity of his imprisonment, the injustice of "a high German" being seized by Japanese, was central to her appeal. Arvid is a German citizen, she argued; all of his newspaper articles are inspected by Japan's Foreign Office and German authorities prior to being dispatched; he is a decorated veteran of World War I; and he is a respected gentleman. The consulate rejected her request for assistance securing Arvid's release, citing its inability to interfere with Japanese policing. Estelle would not learn until later that German authorities had themselves ordered Arvid's arrest. Her appeal having failed, Estelle sought legal representation. The only German lawyer on hand rejected the case, fearful that defending Arvid would cast suspicion on himself. Max Pestalozzi introduced Estelle to his own lawyer. Estelle claimed that she had little choice but to pay off the first lawyer to keep him quiet and then hire the second one, who accepted the case but did nothing.

Back in Gora, Estelle faced more than the terror and uncertainty of her husband's predicament. Police invaded her house regularly to confiscate books, papers, letters, maps, and photos. Though perpetually terrified, racial pride prevented her from showing it: "These common people should not be able to degrade us by their brutal intrusion," as she explained it.[9] Police also stole money, clothing, and food. Though still receiving standard rations, Estelle was ineligible to receive German rations and thus compelled to purchase necessities on the black market. Both of her maids quit, and someone stole her dog. Estelle reports that growing numbers of refugees fleeing the cities had created a housing shortage, and after Arvid's conviction Nazi officials and the civil police tried to evict her from her Gora home, claiming that as the wife of a convicted criminal she had lost the right to live there. She defied them and stayed, but fails to explain how she managed this feat. Then, an announcement dated October 17, 1944, was posted at the German Club declaring that Arvid, Hans, Ludy Frank, and their respective families had been denaturalized. It is unclear when each of these parties received this news. In Karuizawa, Ludy did not learn of it until January 1945. And, though the announcement at the German Club had omitted Hugo's name, Alice testified that the German consulate also rescinded her German citizenship following Hugo's conviction for espionage in January.[10]

Meanwhile, Estelle attempted to use her regular deliveries of food and underwear to smuggle notes to Arvid. Her own messages were discovered several times, and only once did Arvid succeed in passing a note to her. It read, "Enduring daily long hours of trial with intolerable tortures."[11]

Intolerable tortures were indeed central to Kenpeitai officials' studied, systematic approach to interrogation. Methods of torture varied relatively little. Testimonies given by Arvid and Liebeskind, who had endured it; Murase Shinji, a Japanese interpreter who witnessed it; and Estelle and Ludy, who heard of it secondhand, all contain clear congruencies. Examiners began with hostile questioning and threats. If these proved ineffective they employed a mixture of physical torture, insults, emotional manipulation, and sleep deprivation. The abuse continued six days per week until suspects lost hope that it would ever end or that interrogators would ever become convinced of their innocence. Heaslett had observed in 1942 that confession was the singular objective of interrogation, even if it was factually inaccurate or even nonincriminating. Tolischus had noted that his accusers sought mainly to force his submission and to hear him apologize.[12] These early interrogations were comparatively symbolic, therefore. In part, they were intended to establish an understanding of the prisoner's subordination within a wartime power structure. They differed fundamentally from what Hugo, Arvid, and the others experienced. In late 1944, forcing humility, reaching common understandings, and establishing a mutually accepted set of facts were secondary considerations. The singular objective, rather, was to secure a signed confession that courts would then cite as conclusive proof of guilt. One former Kenpeitai officer confessed to Honobe Makoto that if he could not extract a confession from his suspects then he had failed in the eyes of his superiors.[13]

At the police prison in Kagachō, Arvid was held without being charged or provided with an explanation for his arrest. His cell measured about fifteen by fifteen feet, had a wooden floor, no ventilation, little light, and contained between seven and fifteen men. Arvid was interrogated the day following his arrival and asked if he had ever been a spy, which he denied. A week later he was interrogated a second time and asked about his sources of income. He replied that his contracts with sixteen German newspapers yielded an annual income of about 5,600 yen. The police verified this and at the third questioning, now at Isezakichō Police Station, insisted that he had used this large sum to purchase military information. Torture ensued, continuing six days per week thereafter for the next three months. Arvid was first made to kneel on the floor for hours until his feet were swollen and painful. While kneeling, a wooden stick was inserted behind his knees. Officers then stood on the protruding ends of the stick, pressing his knees into the floor, driving the stick into his calves, damaging his veins, and severing circulation to his feet. He was also made to kneel on the sharp edge of a stool until he developed sores that subsequently became infected. His head was dunked in buckets of water, and beatings to the face knocked out several teeth. Inquisitors continued these abuses from August into November in an unheated cell with the windows open. With no way to get dry or warm, Arvid developed an ongoing fever. Interrogators also told Arvid that Estelle had been arrested and that she would be cast into the street homeless and penniless unless he confessed.[14] Arvid's own testimony from November 24, 1945, relates the experience:

A: The questioning continued every night from 7:00 P.M. to 10:00 P.M. . . . In order to increase the pain on my legs, they put a wooden pole on the back of my legs and [Inspector] Kobayashi trampled on my thighs while beating me on the face with his fists and pulling my hair. Simultaneously, two policemen stood one on each end of the pole and applied pressure to the calves of my legs. From the third questioning on, a Mr. Patrick Tomkinson was present. He acted as interpreter. Tomkinson was apparently not allowed to touch me, but after the second or third time that he was present, he started to slap me on the face, and as Kobayashi did not stop him, but encouraged him, he continued more and more in the beating and torture. . . . My face was so sore after the torturing that I could hardly breathe through my nose, [only] through my mouth. My right ear became absolutely deaf through constant beating of it. My eyes were nearly swollen shut. The effect of this kneeling was that after about three weeks my feet and legs were hardly recognizable as human. They were black and blue in color and a mass of swollen lumps and blood clots. I showed my feet and legs to Kobayashi and he became so alarmed that the torturing was discontinued temporarily for about a fortnight. . . . I was handcuffed and my feet were tied and I had only a pair of shorts left on me. They placed me in a kneeling position in front of a large bucket of water and ducked my head in it again and again until I was nearly drowned. . . . Absolutely broken down from moral and physical pain and without hope of being saved, I told them I was prepared to sign anything, even that I murdered my own mother.

Q: After you told them that you would sign anything, did the torturing continue?

A: The torturing continued for about two hours. During these two hours I was placed in a cold room where five policemen were present dressed in heavy clothing and drinking tea, while I was in a pair of shorts and wet from the duckings. I became so cold after the first half hour that I could not even speak. After this, the torturing discontinued.

Q: When did you sign the confession that you had military information?

A: On November 22, 1944.

Q: What did the confession contain?

A: The confession contained that from a man named Hugo Frank I had gotten news [of]:

1. The location of anti-aircraft guns in Yokohama
2. Movement of vessels at the Naval Base at Yokosuka
3. Production figures about the airplane factories in Japan
4. Knowledge of fortifications on the islands of Iwo Jima and Okinawa
5. Losses of the Japanese Fleet in southern waters

After I signed this confession I was transferred to the Detention Center, Gumyōji Prison, Yokohama.[15]

Arvid's confession stated that he had received information about movements of naval ships from Hugo Frank and had relayed that information to Pestalozzi, who in turn passed it on to the Swiss embassy and enemy governments. Police crafted it to match the document signed by Hugo two weeks earlier.[16]

Grounds for Hugo's arrest were constructed more from his observed behavior than from hard evidence of conspiracy against Japan or Germany. Born and raised in Japan and likely without strong German loyalties, Hugo was atypical of German residents. From the perspective of Nazi officials, he did not behave like a patriotic German. Not only was he part Jewish himself, he had insulted his German pedigree by entering into an international marriage. He also deigned to socialize openly with the likes of Arvid and Liebeskind, who had fled Germany and could be safely counted as anti-Nazi, as well as with neutrals and other foreigners known to be anti-Nazi.[17] Most Germans in Gora were careful to avoid such associations. As one Gora resident later recalled, "Whenever foreigners spoke to other foreigners they would be suspected as spies. Therefore, we did not speak to one another."[18] Japanese officials also found Hugo suspicious. Rather than accompany his parents and brother to Karuizawa, Hugo had opted to live in Gora, a community teeming with Nazi officials and thus full of military information attractive to spies. He was openly friendly with Catholic priests, which Japanese police never trusted, and had worked for an American company before the war.[19] All of these factors amounted to more than sufficient cause for German and Japanese authorities to distrust Hugo's working relationship with Arvid, who had long attracted their distrust by continuing to engage in private investigative journalism. It would be this relationship that police interrogators would focus on in their investigations of Hugo, Arvid, and Liebeskind.

Few details of Hugo's interrogation are known, but secondhand accounts indicate that he suffered forms of abuse similar to those inflicted on Arvid. Ludy's description of Kenpeitai torture methods is derived from what he learned of Hugo's ordeal:

> They have wooden stools with four legs on them. They turn the stool over and make the person kneel on the up-turned legs of the stool so one of the legs hits the knee and the other leg hits inside of the ankle. They put a bamboo stick behind the knee and they ask a question. If there is no answer they put pressure on the bamboo rod in the back of the knee. Eventually the [prisoners] break down. It's cold winter. They take their clothes off, make them kneel in front of a barrel of ice-cold water and hold [their] heads under the water until they practically drown, and then they repeat it.[20]

Alice's testimony from November 14, 1945, requested in connection with the U.S. War Crimes Commission's investigation of Hugo's death, relates that Hugo was first taken to the Yamate Police Station in Yokohama, where he also suffered three and a half months of torture. Alice knew nothing of his condition, but when she brought food and changes of underwear she always found blood on the garments she received in return. Hugo later informed fellow prisoner Hans Schweizer that, in addition to the types of torture already described, he had been deprived of food and water for several days. He also noted that Kenpeitai interrogators had shown him what they alleged was Arvid's confession, and his own torture continued until he admitted to the crimes contained in this fraudulent document.[21] On November 13, 1944, after signing a confession, Hugo was transferred to the blue prison at Gumyōji to await trial. He stayed there for another three and a half months and, though he was spared further torture, his physical condition failed to improve. Beginning in December, Hugo was permitted five-minute visitations every ten days. It was at this point that he received a visit from Ludy and regular visits from Alice, both of whom he asked for medicine. Alice described him as thin, pale, and weak, noting that his feet were swollen and that he could barely walk as a combined result of the torture and the cold. She brought him medicine but was not permitted to give it to him.[22] Though Hugo could not discuss his treatment or interrogations with Alice, Tazaki Fumiatsu, Hugo's lawyer, whom Alice had hired for 1,000 yen, told Alice that he had been hit so many times that his entire body was swollen and that the pain prevented him from sleeping. Fellow inmate Bossée later reported hearing Hugo being beaten during his interrogations, and Liebeskind caught a glimpse of Hugo at the jail and related that he was thin, had a long beard, and was crawling, unable to walk.[23]

Testimonies from Liebeskind, arrested on suspicion of spying for the Mexican embassy, and the police interpreter Murase provide further details about Kenpeitai interrogations of suspected spies. Though Liebeskind's friendship with Alice and Hugo was incriminating in itself, her maid had informed police that she had sent information to Germany. Josef Meisinger and his assistant Karl Hamel had considered this information adequate cause to order her arrest.[24] Honobe claims, however, that Liebeskind's telegram to Germany was actually a request to have money from Arvid's accounts wired to the needy Ries family.[25]

Liebeskind's testimony from November 19, 1945, recounts the circumstances of her seizure and torture. It begins by asserting that she had worked as a "ladies companion" for a member of the Mexican consulate from August 1941 until May 25, 1942. On that day she was notified that Mexico had declared war on Japan and that she should sever her affiliations with the consulate. Thereafter she tutored German, French, and piano in Yokohama. On August 31, 1944, she was detained on the street by two police officers, who put her on the floor of their car, delivered her to a Kenpeitai station, and placed her in a wooden cell. Torture commenced the following day.[26]

I was held at the Kenpei-tai Headquarters . . . until December 12, 1944. During this period I was subjected to many cruel and inhuman tortures. When I arrived at Kenpei-tai they took me upstairs and they asked me to sit down. . . . I was under the impression that I was to be questioned about Mr. Balk. I had been informed that Mr. Balk had been arrested.

The interrogator asked me about my name, birth place, and everything. He then asked for my handbag. He took out everything. I had plenty of money with me, because that was money given to me for Mr. Balk. . . . I then told him that the two thousand yen in my handbag did not belong to me but to Mr. Balk. This money was sent from China and I had picked it up from the Post Office. I was taken to a cell and on the second day I was informed that the reason for my detention was because I had money in my possession belonging to Mr. Balk, who was suspected of being a spy. When I consistently refused to sign a confession of something I was not guilty of . . . they started inflicting physical punishment upon me. An officer using a bamboo stick started beating me over the head and shoulders. A chair was placed on its side and I was forced to kneel on the legs of the chair in the traditional Japanese sitting position for many hours. . . . On another occasion my hands [were tied] at the wrist behind my back and I was suspended from the ceiling in that position. . . . On another occasion I was handcuffed, my feet were tied, I was carried to a large barrel of water that was full of refuse and they forced my head down into the water and kept it there until I lost consciousness. This was done several times and continued for several days. During all this interrogation over the entire period, my clothing was removed from my body and all beatings and tortures were committed while I was in the nude. After one month of this continued torturing, sometime in the later part of September, I signed a confession even though it was not true. This confession was taken under duress and was false. The paper that I was forced to sign set forth that I was working in conjunction with a Hungarian national who was the Secretary to the Hungarian Legation. That we furnished information on war plants, factories, air fields, transportation of troops, and anti-aircraft plans. This information that I was securing was supposedly being transmitted to the United States through the Swedish Legation. I remained at Ken-peitai Headquarters for two and one half months after I signed the so-called confession and they continued to beat me. . . . I was transferred to [Gumyōji] Prison in Yokohama . . . and tried on the first day of March 1945. I was sentenced at my first hearing to eight years of imprisonment, but was taken to a supplemental court two weeks later, and was sentenced to six years.[27]

In a 1991 interview, Liebeskind corroborates her testimony from 1945 but also relates being subjected to stranger, more perverse forms of abuse, including waterboarding. Her hands and feet were tied and then water poured into her mouth and nostrils. Her pubic hair was burned with a candle. Burning matches and cigarettes were applied to her arms, knees, and elsewhere on her body; her spine was raked with a bamboo stick; and her fingers were beaten until her thumb broke. She also relates attempting but failing to commit suicide with a small pocketknife that a guard had left in the interrogation room. The blade had been too dull to cut deeply.[28] Liebeskind's postwar medical report does confirm cigarette burns on her arms and legs and a scar on her wrist from an attempted suicide.

Liebeskind was tortured for one month and in late September confessed to espionage, including leaking information though the Swedes.[29] She asserted that the document was written in Japanese and that she had no knowledge of what it contained. Incredibly, her torture continued for another two and a half months as police searched for more crimes that would tie her to Hugo and Arvid, who were still being interrogated and would not confess until November. Liebeskind was moved to the blue prison on December 12. The testimony of her interpreter Murase provides less detail but confirms the use of torture:

> In the Liebeskind case, she was suspected of spying. Questioning took place at Gendarme Headquarters in Yokohama. During that time the investigator in charge . . . questioned Liebeskind's background. She did not tell all; she concealed many details. She was German, one quarter Jewish, worked as one of the first air stewardesses for Lufthansa in 1936 in Germany, affianced to an American, had trouble in trying to get a visa and in the latter respect had fraud played upon her by a Panamanian Consul. [On December 26, 1940, she arrived in Japan and] worked as a governess and taught German. She finally got acquainted with a Mexican Consul . . . and from that time on she did spying for this diplomat. She made acquaintance of Hugo Frank, where she boarded.
>
> Liebeskind was questioned . . . about her alleged spying activity, information about the Jap Army, Air Force factories, gun positions, and German shipping. Whenever she did not answer the questions to the satisfaction of the questioners, they beat her with sticks and kicked her and once they forced her down and poured water over her. I heard that the Gendarmes stripped her naked and forced her to sit Japanese style.[30]

Though Murase does not divulge details of Liebeskind's torture, his testimony suggests that what she and Arvid (and presumably Hugo) endured was considered "normal," and that the French national Bossée received the same sort of treatment. Murase's testimony on November 29, 1945, recounts Bossée's interrogation as follows.

Q: Were you present at the arrest of Andre Bossée?

A: Yes.

Q: Was he told at that time why he was being arrested?

A: He was not.

Q: You were present at all of his interrogations?

A: I was.

Q: How many times was he interrogated?

A: He was questioned every day except Sundays.

Q: How was he treated during these questionings?

A: Very cruelly. Beating and striking. So cruelly in fact that he lost consciousness once.

Q: How long did each questioning last?

A: From about 9 am to noon and then from 1 pm to 4 pm. The noon hour was not used for questioning.

Q: You saw him being beaten?

A: Yes.

Q: You mentioned that he was once knocked unconscious—when was that?

A: About two weeks after his arrest when he was weakened by previous beatings and they used a piece of square wood about 2″×2″ to beat him. They kept beating him with this piece of wood on the shoulders, legs, and buttocks until Bossée became exhausted and fainted.

Q: With what was he usually beaten?

A: Generally with a bamboo pole. The gendarmeries were careful not to beat him on any vital parts, only on places covered with muscle. However, the beatings caused his legs to swell and his shoulders and legs were black and blue.

Q: Did these beatings at any time draw blood?

A: No. They were careful not to mark him.

Q: Was he ever forced to kneel with his hands extended into the air during questioning?

A: Yes.

Q: About how many times?

A: About half the total number of times he was questioned.

Q: What happened if he lowered his hands when tired?

A: They beat him.

Q: Did they ever duck his head into filthy water and hold it under until he almost strangled?

A: Yes. Once. It was done as a joke. . . . Once they snipped the end of his nose and once they burnt his nose with a cigarette—but just for fun.

Q: Did you know his jaw had been broken?

A: No.

Q: Wasn't the kneeling position they made Bossée get into, the position known as *seiza*?

A: Yes.

Q: Weren't the Japanese, and these men in particular, aware of the fact that such a position was torture to a foreigner?

A: They were.

Q: Did they put a chair on his shoulders and force down on it?

A: Yes, once they had a man sit in it . . . but that was only in fun.

Q: What happened to Bossée when that was going on?

A: He could not endure it.

Q: Were all foreign interrogations you saw conducted in the same brutal manner?

A: They were.[31]

Murase's account of Bossée's torture is particularly incriminating for it indicates that interrogators used torture not solely to secure a confession, but occasionally to hurt him "in fun." Bossée's interrogation began on August 29 and continued until his confession on September 7. Only part of the confession was translated into German. He was moved to Gumyōji on October 9. Over a two-week period in November, however, his interrogation resumed. The sessions were performed at night and though he was not beaten as before, he was forced to sit *seiza*, one night for several hours.[32]

Three other Europeans had been convicted of espionage and were held at Gumyōji at this time. Ivar Lissner (1909–67), a German journalist working with Meisinger, was arrested in June 1943 by the Kenpeitai on suspicion of leaking Japanese military information to the Soviets. Lissner, whose cell was two doors from Hugo's, was released in early 1945 due to illness and moved to Hakone.[33] Meisinger had followed his crackdown on German Jews in February 1945 (detailed in chapter 7) by intensifying his vendetta against non-Nazi Germans. In a speech delivered on March 15 at the German Club in Yokohama, he hinted that more anti-Nazis may soon be arrested and that those already in jail may never be released. Meisinger's convictions may have prompted Japanese authorities to seize more Germans in Hakone and Kobe. They certainly impacted businessmen Paul Boedner and Hans Weingartner, who had recently defied Meisinger personally—Boedner had declined to attend a party for Germans hosted by Meisinger, and Weingartner, a Swiss citizen, had failed to pick up from him a certificate of German citizenship. Both were arrested as spies on April 14 by Yokohama Kenpeitai and interrogated until July, when they confessed to charges that Weingartner had relayed information to the Swiss embassy and that Boedner had helped him. They were moved to Gumyōji on July 14. When Weingartner later told his interpreter that his confession was forced and untrue and that he wanted to rescind it, police threatened to send him back for more Kenpeitai interrogation. Boedner also asserted that his confessions were forced and that the charges were fabricated. Their appeals became irrelevant, for the war ended a few weeks later. Boedner's postrelease health exam on August 28, 1945, revealed that during his four months in prison his weight had dropped from 155 to 110 pounds and that he was suffering from multiple ailments, including festering sores on his hands, feet, and back; bloody fingernails; and osteomyelitis (bone infection).[34]

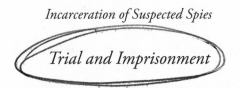

Trial and Imprisonment

Hugo received standard rations and treatment at the blue prison but remained debilitated. Doi Gōsei, one of his guards at Gumyōji, later recalled that the austerities of daily life stalled his recovery. Doi had lost his job as a sculptor of Buddhas and in May 1944 had reluctantly signed on as a jailer. He had tried to help suffering prisoners and even lobbied to have some released. In March 1945 he was instrumental in having Hugo's neighbor, who had also been tortured and was suffering from tuberculosis, released to the Nisseki hospital in Yokohama. Doi's kindness at the prison earned him the nickname the Buddha in Hell (*jigoku ni hotoke*), and Hans Ries later remembered him as the only well-behaved guard of the lot.[35] Doi recalled seeing that Hugo's condition was deteriorating and knew that his brother Ludy in Karuizawa was also close to being arrested by the Kenpeitai. As such, rather than interact with Hugo directly, which might incur repercussions for both Hugo and Ludy, he did so through the prisoner in the neighboring cell. This neighbor was Katsube Hajime (1917–99), a Communist with proficiency in German, and Doi asked him to translate a note and pass it to Hugo. The note asked whether Hugo needed anything and instructed him to reply by means of a note through Katsube.[36] We have only anecdotal evidence of the note, and as Hugo spoke and read Japanese it is strange that Doi asked Katsube to translate it. Yet, in a letter to Hugo's daughter Barbara, Honobe mentions that Doi indeed received a written reply from Hugo, who requested seeds that he could plant on the prison grounds. In a conversation with Honobe in 1987, Doi claimed to remember that seeds were in fact planted on the prison grounds, and Honobe wonders whether Hugo, anticipating his own death in prison, had endeavored to leave a living legacy in the form of planted seeds.[37]

Charges against Hugo included possessing information about the Ogasawara Islands; possessing information about the movements of German ships in Yokohama Harbor and passing it to diplomats of neutral powers; possessing a radio that could receive transmissions from Vladivostok and translating those broadcasts for Arvid; translating Japanese radio broadcasts for Arvid; spying with Liebeskind; collecting data for the Portuguese legation; passing on information about antiaircraft gun stands in Yokohama; asking Japanese people what they thought of General Tōjō Hideki; and receiving from neutral governments money amounting to 4,000 yen in exchange for information.[38] These allegations constituted violations of the National Defense Security Law, enacted to protect secret military and state information.[39]

Hugo was indicted at the Yokohama District Court (Yokohama-chihō saibansho) on November 27 but not tried until February 15, 1945. The trial was attended by Alice and Louis Frank; Hugo's lawyer Tazaki; Tsukahara Bannosuke, Bandō Masao, and Tamane Kenji, the Kenpeitai officers who had interrogated him; an interpreter; and three judges. The confession made the proceedings a formality, and both sides understood that it had been extracted through torture. According to Alice's testimony, Hugo was told to state merely that his mother was half-English and that his father was a German Jew. He was not able to testify, and all the evidence submitted by Tazaki was rejected. His initial plea of not guilty was also ignored.[40] On February 25 he was found guilty on eight of the nine charges, all except receiving money from neutral governments, a crime that would incriminate nations Japan had no wish to antagonize.[41] Sentencing, Tazaki informed him, hinged on the defendant's acceptance of the ruling. Judges were likely to confer harsher sentences on defendants who denied the charges or claimed that their confessions were acquired through torture.[42] Accordingly, when Hugo was sentenced to five years in prison, he neither protested nor filed an appeal. This advice certainly worked against him, and possibly cost him his life.

After sentencing, Hugo was transferred to a solitary cell in the red penitentiary, where family members were permitted monthly visits. His cell measured 5.9×11.8 feet; the floor area was part tatami, part wood; and the door contained a window and a slot below for passing food. The cell contained a sink, a toilet, and a window measuring 15.7×23.6 inches. Inmates were prohibited from contacting each other and were able to minimally interact only during lineup checks each morning and evening. They were permitted only twenty minutes of daily exercise, which took place alone in a separate indoor or outdoor cell.[43] Alice was so horrified by Hugo's appearance during her first visit to the red prison in late March that she suffered an emotional collapse and was unable to leave home to visit him the following month. At her last visitation in June she found him sick and emaciated. Guards stopped him from speaking to her about conditions at the jail, but Alice noted that he once pulled up his shirt to reveal his protruding ribs, saying, "This is what they have done to me."[44]

Hans Ries had confessed on October 12, 1944, and was moved to the blue prison on November 17. Arvid followed him there in December. Like Hugo, both were placed in solitary cells where they would await trial. Ries later reflected that a private cell seemed like paradise after sharing a cell with sixteen other Japanese suspects at the police jail. Inmates' wives could also send in more food, clothing, books, and bedding. Estelle describes her first visitation with Arvid:

> He stood there behind the table long and lean, his white face bearded, his poor head shaven. He stretches his arms across the bare board and I put my face into his hands, kissing them as the only possible way to come nearer to him, to show him my infinite pity and my helpless love. I did not cry. I had made up my mind to show him strength and firm conviction in his innocence, his just case I would fight through for him. His old will power had melted, his cool restraint was broken after the unspeakable mental strain and physical pain he had gone through. What I saw there was the shadow of the man I had known, a poor broken wreck of my once up-right, energetic, and proud husband. He could hardly stand. His poor legs were swollen, sore with terrible infested wounds roughly bound up in rags by himself. Tears streamed down his face as he sobbed helplessly, too happy and thankful to see me once again. And I could not even take him into my arms to console him. . . . I repeatedly assured him of his integrity in all our eyes whatever he might have signed. I told him I would fight for him, we would now see each other often. "Try and keep well, keep alive, eat and sleep! You will be saved. Time will work for us." I could not say more. I could not give him war news. What could I do for my husband? I was shaking like a leaf when they led him out with that basket over his head and the door slammed behind him. Those filthy little Japanese policeman, what had they done to my stately, good-looking husband?[45]

During their several meetings, Estelle was able to slip a word or two past the supervising guard about the progress of the war. It also became clear to her that Arvid was receiving only a fraction of the food she was pre-paring for him. Although prisoners had twice received relief packages from the International Red Cross, malnutrition had given him beriberi; he also suffered from innumerable insect bites.

In preparation for their trials, Arvid and Ries were allowed three-minute meetings with their lawyers. They had prepared written statements explaining that their confessions were untrue and had been extracted through prolonged torture, which they described in detail. Police had nothing to lose by allowing this, and the gesture proved meaningless. Once their confessions had become a matter of official record, the trials would be a formality.

Arvid and Ries were both tried on January 25, 1945. Arvid stated that his confession was given under torture and requested that Pestalozzi be admitted as a witness. Pestalozzi's testimony, Arvid hoped, would refute charges that the two had been relaying illegal information. This request was rejected on February 8, the date of their second trial. On February 22, Arvid was given a four-year sentence for violation of the Military Secrets Protection Law (*Gunkihogo-hō*).[46] The same day, Ries was sentenced to two years for similar offenses. After the war, others testified to receiving similar trials and outcomes. Bossée related that his trial on January 23, 1945, lasted only thirty minutes; one week later he was sentenced to four years for violating the Military Secrets Protection and National Defense Security Laws. Liebeskind was tried on March 1, and on March 12 was sentenced to six years for violation of the National Defense Security Law. She claims to have had no lawyer during the trial.

Arvid, Ries, Liebeskind, and Bossée all immediately appealed their rulings, though more as a means of stalling transfer to the red prison, where conditions were harsher, than from any expectation of having their convictions overturned. In contrast to blue prison inmates, red prison convicts wore only a thin red robe and received no food or supplies from family visitors. Their ploy successfully postponed enforcement of the sentences and allowed all four to remain in the blue prison for the next several months. (Had Hugo also appealed he could have delayed his transfer and possibly survived his ordeal.) The Tokyo Supreme Court finally rejected Arvid's and Ries's appeals on June 12 and both were transferred to the red prison on June 21. At that point Hugo had been moved to the prison infirmary. Ries was placed in Hugo's vacated cell and told that Hugo had died, a statement that preceded his actual death by nine days.

Liebeskind, it appears, remained at the blue prison for the remainder of the war. She reports being made to kneel in her cell from morning to night. Pestalozzi and another friend paid 400 yen to supplement her rations there, an amount meant to cover a five-month period. She received the extra rations for only about six weeks, however, after which her condition worsened and she suffered from dysentery.[47]

Now convicted, Arvid's singular hope of survival lay in a swift end to the war. Estelle, however, found a glimmer of hope in an improbable piece of intrigue. At about the time Arvid was transferred to the red prison, Estelle was approached by a Japanese naval officer, also a Gora resident, who identified himself only as Mr. Go. The officer claimed to represent a military faction conspiring to broker a peace treaty with Japan's enemies prior to the anticipated U.S. land invasion. In order for the plan to succeed, Mr. Go explained, the faction needed a trusted mediator, somebody with the diplomatic skills and political knowledge to help negotiate a truce. If Arvid were willing to assume this role, Mr. Go would arrange for his release from prison and then fly him and Estelle to China, where the peace talks would be held. Her husband facing a four-year prison term, Estelle was in no position to question this officer's dubious plan. As Mr. Go attested, "[Arvid] will not be released, as his high political faculties and knowledge are known to the Japanese authorities and they dare not trust him at large in the increasing crisis the country is in."[48] Estelle breathlessly agreed to cooperate, promising to inform Arvid of the plan and then to await further instructions.

At her visitation several days later, Estelle was shocked by her husband's appearance. Her description of the visit was not entirely negative, however. Their encounter was leisurely, and she was able to tell Arvid about Mr. Go's scheme to have him released. The interrogations and trials behind him, his fate now out of his own hands, Arvid seemed comparatively peaceful:

> This time it would be easier, we could sit together with [the guard] Mr. Ichijo [a Buddhist monk] only around a small table and I would even have up to one hour's time to talk to him. But these "*menkai's*" [visitations] were only allowed once a month and the prisoner was strictly forbidden to accept anything whatsoever from home. A roofed passage, leading from the outer door in the forbidding wall to the little room would be the path from

where I could expect him. I stood there, shivering with anxiety, in anguish of what I should behold: He came out together with Hans, two guards accompanying them. Words cannot describe what I saw, as the mere optical sight vastly differed from the heart wrenching impression I got. He had nothing on, nothing whatsoever but a torn red cotton kimono, much too short and tight for him as a tall foreigner. Though tied by a string around his waist for that special occasion only, he had to hold it together all the time. On his naked feet he wore straw sandals and his head basket he could remove as soon as he was in the room with me.

I don't know if he really noticed my horror in its fullest extent. We were happy at last to be able to touch one another, to kiss, to whisper, to hold hands. Ichijo did not mind. He was a kind man, a real sympathetic human being, the only one we ever met at that jail. Thanks to him, I could tell Arvid whatever I liked, even in German. And he even permitted me to give him the little concentrated nourishment I had carefully concealed in my handbag, though strictly against the rules. So I made him quickly eat some chocolate, my sandwiches, and drink a milk egg shake I had brought along in his own silver hip flask. . . . To my greatest astonishment Arvid told me, he now was never hungry anymore. It was much better in that way in the red prison, as he directly got the food provided for prisoners and that woman outside could not steal it away any more. . . . He could even talk now and then to the other foreign prisoners, to Hans too when airing their blankets up on the roof. They even had mosquito nets, which was a blessing. Since he was working [to make] some straw rope he got a little more food and he did not mind the manual occupation. But there were very many cases of a terrible contagious disease amongst the inmates of the red prison. "*Kaisen*" [scabies] they call it, a spreading sore, which eats festering holes into the skin, slowly covering the whole body. And other bad illnesses too. The medical treatment was insufficient and the patient, in the last minute transported to their so-called hospital, never came back alive. I knew that there were deaths all the time. Many poor foreign helpless men, my poor husband too, now having to live among those sick convicts, slip into the same sandals, the same blanket or kimono was a sickening idea.

An hour is long and Mr. Ichijo patient. So I had plenty of time to tell Arvid all about Go and his mysterious plan. He shook his head. All right, he understood it all and would certainly do as he was told in case it should really work out, but he thought it all too farfetched. He really preferred to wait for the Americans. If they would be in time before the cold of the coming winter set in again, they would still find him alive, after that he hardly thought it likely to survive if practically naked and with beriberi, as he would be in an unheated prison cell.[49]

Though Arvid held out little hope for Mr. Go's plan, the scheme helped tide Estelle through the final weeks of the war. She waited daily for further news from Mr. Go, who finally arrived at her door to report that plans had been delayed because the leader of his faction had been arrested. By the time she summoned the courage to visit his house to inquire further about the plot, which had since collapsed, the war was near an end.

Death and Liberation

Estelle claimed that Hugo was spying for the German community and the Japanese police, and that he had implicated Arvid and Liebeskind as spies.[50] As other testimonies affirm, during the initial days of questioning, police asked Hugo about his sources of income and his professional relationships. Hugo had not been formally charged with any crime at this point and was likely expecting to be released shortly. Arvid and Liebeskind certainly expected the same. It is understandable that Hugo would interpret the interrogation as simply more of the harassment that had come to typify daily life for non-Axis foreigners in Gora. Under this impression, he would have every reason to expect that cooperating with his examiners would hasten his release. Given his work translating Japanese radio and newspaper articles for Arvid, it is certain that Arvid's name was mentioned during these early days of questioning. Even if Hugo had not mentioned Arvid, the two were known to be collaborators and related through Ludy and Irene's marriage. Arvid was a well-known journalist and had been a person of police interest for several years. As his plea for protection at the German embassy indicates, he anticipated arrest at some point. We may even surmise that the Kenpeitai, expecting complaints from the German newspapers to which Arvid contributed, arrested Hugo to help build a case against Arvid. Arvid's incarceration, then, was a predictable, even unavoidable follow-up to Hugo's arrest. Hugo would not have incriminated himself or Arvid during the three days between their respective arrests and then submitted to three months of torture later. These myriad reasons cast considerable doubt on Estelle's allegation that Hugo implicated or was otherwise responsible for Arvid's arrest.

The improbability that Hugo implicated his alleged coconspirators does not exonerate Hugo of "illegal" acts, however. In fact, he may well have engaged in some of the activities for which he was convicted. Fellow inmate Hans Schweizer, who met and developed a friendship with Hugo at the prison infirmary in late February 1945, later wrote to Ludy that Hugo had privately confessed to him:

> Hugo Frank wrote me that he was kept and sentenced in connection with Balk and Ries. He told me that actually he had done a most actively anti-Nazi propaganda, warning his [Japanese] connections not to trust the Nazi or believe the Nazi and not to fall for their propaganda. . . . He actually had listened in to the Russian shortwave radio and had taken down in shorthand the news for Balk. He also admitted that he had a good connection to several neutral diplomats and got from them plenty of information which he could successfully use in his anti-German propaganda.[51]

Here Hugo makes no claim to have leaked information to Pestalozzi for dissemination abroad, but does allege to have been actively brokering sensitive, even secret information to undermine Nazi propaganda within his community. His claim to have illegally used a shortwave radio to intercept transmissions also indicates that at least some of the charges—and some of his confessions—were genuine. Although there is no way to verify the accuracy of Schweizer's statement, the activities it describes do align with Estelle's spiteful description of Hugo as one who "[nosed] into other people's houses to carry gossip about" and who "lived on sensations and uncontrolled political gossip, which he even tried to sell for money."[52] One might also conjecture about the validity of charges that Hugo spied with Liebeskind. The interpreter Murase, who is forthcoming with incriminating details of his colleagues' use of torture on enemy suspects, states that Liebeskind was indeed spying. And, given Liebeskind's close relationship with Hugo and Alice, it is reasonable to assume that if either had engaged in illegal activities these would have been known to the other. (Liebeskind's suspicious claim that the 2,000 yen on her person at the time of her arrest was payment sent from China for Arvid, who had been in police custody for a month already, cannot be verified.)

Unfortunately, one cannot know what evidence, if any, Japanese and Nazi authorities gathered against Hugo or Liebeskind. None was needed, for by all indications the others—Arvid, Ries, Bossée, Boedner, and Weingartner—were arrested without strong proof of wrongdoing. Evidence indicates, rather, that all were victims of Meisinger's vendetta against Jewish and anti-Nazi Germans. Captain Ōtani with the Kanagawa Kenpeitai testified after the war that Meisinger had indeed ordered Kenpeitai headquarters to follow Nazi anti-Semitic policies being implemented in Germany. The orders were then relayed to the various branch stations as far away as Karuizawa, where Bossée was arrested. Under this pressure, Kenpeitai officers and civil police competed to carry out his orders. Yamane, the inspector in charge of Ries's interrogation, affirmed that Ries was arrested as a spy because he was Jewish and thus assumed to be anti-Nazi. Though torture was illegal, Ōtani confessed that officers used it in their earnestness to please Meisinger.[53] Ries claimed that he also uncovered evidence of such while working for Occupation forces after the war.[54] Liebeskind attested that German authorities had ordered Japanese police to arrest her. A friend named Mr. Fürster who had also been arrested as a suspected spy had investigated this following the war and learned that Gestapo representatives in the German embassy had indeed compiled a list of names and given it to the Japanese police. The list contained names of Jews, half Jews, and anti-Nazis.[55] The same information has been confirmed by researcher Arai Jun.[56] This was a collaborative rather than a singularly Nazi initiative, however. As Kenpeitai leadership, including Prime Minister and Army Minister Tōjō, expected its officers to use whatever means necessary, including torture, to achieve desired results, those officers would not have viewed pressure from Meisinger as inappropriate or inconsistent with its modus operandi.

Schweizer's statement also reveals details of Hugo's physical condition at the red prison. The two men's cells were separated by only a single cell, allowing them to exchange letters easily. They did this by writing on toilet paper with a piece of lead broken off a water pipe, putting the notes in a bag attached to a string, and throwing it from their cell's food slot down to the next cell. Schweizer writes that Hugo was extremely thin and covered in sores from infected fleabites. His legs and feet were in particularly severe condition, and pus oozed from between his toes. Both men suffered from impetigo (bacterial skin infection), and as Hugo had no soap to clean the wounds, Schweizer gave him a small piece. Schweizer writes that guards provided Hugo with zinc ointment for the impetigo but hit him when he later asked for more. "Hugo's reaction to being hit was quite passive, he even excused himself for asking for another treatment," he wrote.[57] Hugo's legs and feet worsened and when his toes became infected guards gave him pieces of cotton to cover them. Schweizer had been contending with the same disease for over a year, during which he had been cutting out some of the infected boils with a small piece of glass and wrapping the wounds with pieces of toilet paper or cloth torn from his clothing.

Prisoners were fed according to their productivity, Schweizer explains. Those strong enough to work sewing bags, cleaning, or doing chores received more food; the smallest portions were given to those unable to work. Arvid had told Estelle that he was receiving rations for making rope and was experiencing less hunger at the red prison. Both Hugo and Schweizer were put on the leanest (#5) food rations because their severe impetigo, it was judged, precluded their ability to work. Such prisoners were often too weak to walk. The daily #5 ration consisted of about two hundred cubic centimeters of a mixture of soybeans, barley, and rice, along with two cups of lukewarm water. Daily, both men requested work so that they could receive the larger #3 rations but were refused. Schweizer notes that he had seen Hugo searching the floor for fallen grains of rice. On the emperor's birthday (April 29) they received a Red Cross food parcel, which lasted about two weeks. Schweizer shared his own with Hugo, who recovered somewhat but quickly deteriorated again, and soon became too weak to walk. In early June he was admitted to the prison hospital and held there full-time thereafter.[58]

The friendship between the two men is evident from the fact that shortly after his birthday on April 6, Hugo entrusted Schweizer with a "will." Having been told by his guards that if Japan lost the war all prisoners would be executed, Hugo must have been fairly convinced that his own death was imminent, if not sooner from malnutrition or an air raid, then later by execution. Doi's account of Hugo's request for seeds months earlier in the blue prison suggests that such thoughts had been haunting Hugo for some time. Of the will, Schweizer writes, "[In] this testament which I now can convey only by word because I had to destroy [it] on account of a very thorough room inspection just before the end of the war, he said that: He would forgive all the wrongs which had been done to him by his friends [Arvid, Hans Ries, and Liebeskind] and that he asked them to forgive him in the same way, for the punishment they had to suffer on his account."[59] Hugo's testament demonstrates that torture and internment had not erased his sense of loyalty. He was cognizant of accusations about his complicity in his friends' persecution, and cognizant that they had incriminated each other in their respective confessions. The statement also maintains his innocence of any disproportionately greater guilt for their collective fates. To Schweizer, he had admitted to engaging in certain activities that his captors had interpreted as espionage, and some of these were collaborative "crimes" carried out together with Arvid. To this extent, he and Arvid were complicit in their transgressions. Finally, his will conveys a desire for these four to uphold their friendship and overcome Japanese efforts to divide them.

Schweizer was likely Hugo's sole confidant. Alice knew of his failing physical condition but mentions nothing regarding his personal ruminations. In Karuizawa, Hugo's parents and brother knew nothing of his condition until June 15, when they received word that he was dangerously ill. Louis Frank applied for a travel permit to visit him but was refused. The Franks then sought information about his condition through Pestalozzi with the International Red Cross, receiving word on July 1 that Hugo had died the day before. Ludy was unable to receive a travel permit to claim the body until July 3. That day he traveled to Yokohama, where he, together with Alice, bought a wooden coffin and rented two bicycles, one with a cart hitched to it. (Police in Gora had also informed Alice that she should retrieve Hugo's body.) They arrived at the prison at noon but were forced to wait three hours before being taken to the prison infirmary. Hugo lay on a mattress on the floor of a cell, covered with a sheet. One foot was bandaged and, in Ludy's words, his limbs were as thin as sticks. Flies crawled over his tongue. He had been dead in a hot cell for four days. At his side lay a bundle of papers, his only possessions. "What I uncovered cannot be described—I will not describe it, a sight too horrid," Ludy wrote later.[60] Alice, forced to endure these eleven months

without social or moral support, had already suffered a nervous breakdown after her visitation with Hugo in March. Fearing she would suffer
another, Ludy refused to let her see the body. Ludy loaded Hugo's coffin
into the rented cart and the two bicycled it through the city streets to
Kuboyama crematorium, about three miles from the jail. The city had
been pummeled by high-explosive and incendiary bombs, Hugo's
daughter Barbara recalled, and smelled of death and charred buildings.
Rows of bodies covered with rice mats lined the streets; corpses floated
in the canals; people were starving.[61] At the crematorium Ludy was told
that the facility was short on oil with which to perform cremations but
that in any case he could not have the body cremated without a license,
for which he would have to return to the prison. Ludy returned for the
license, had the cremation performed, and with Alice brought Hugo's
remains to Gora. Estelle recounts his arrival:

> Poor Ludy . . . came all the way up to Gora that same day, carrying Hu-
> go's ashes with him, as he had no place to sleep in Yokohama. Poor child,
> he was so shaken and tired out, hardly able to stand up to the terrible duty he
> was the only one to perform. Hugo's ashes were brought to St. Joseph's
> chapel [near Gora Station] and dear Ludy, later in my room, which had
> witnessed many a sad tale, related the gruesome story of how he had it cre-
> mated. . . . When I opened my door to poor young Ludy, he stumbled
> into the entrance heavily laden and too exhausted to feel hunger or misery.
>   So Hugo Frank after all came back to Gora a last time. His ashes stood
> a short hour in my front entrance, their austere presence turning to me like
> a mute appeal for forgiveness. And I think today, that if the Japanese Kem-
> petai had not used pliant Hugo Frank, they would have found another to
> draw Arvid into their net.[62]

Ludy returned to Karuizawa the following day. A priest at Saint Paul
Church presided over a simple funeral and the urn containing Hugo's remains was interred at the foreigner's cemetery. Hugo's death certificate
lists the cause of death as malnutrition, but also notes that he had been
gravely ill since May 26.[63] Schweizer, who experienced virtually the same
conditions, maintained that Hugo had died of blood poisoning. His feet
had become infected, he contended, "swollen to a tremendous size and . . .

the poisoned blood was breaking through to the upper part of the body and heart."[64]

Back in Gora, the war ended abruptly. Residents could see formations of U.S. bombers passing overhead but neither heard nor saw the destruction they wreaked on Yokohama. Nor did they receive word of the atomic bombings until days afterward. Even then, the brief newspaper articles about how Hiroshima and Nagasaki had been obliterated by new enemy bombs seemed like the usual war news. "It made no special impression on us. . . . Our life went on unchanged," wrote Estelle.[65] For her and Margot Ries it was the emperor's radio address announcing Japan's surrender that changed everything, for it signaled the immediate release of political prisoners.

Arvid, Hans, and Liebeskind would not be granted immediate release, however. Interned enemy nationals and political prisoners assumed "interim" status while their release was arranged through their nations' representatives. Foreigners in the red prison, reserved for convicts serving out their sentences, were moved back to the blue prison to await liberation. Arvid, Hans, and Liebeskind had been denaturalized and left without the diplomatic assistance necessary to process their release. Estelle explains the course of events:

Our "*menkai*," now back in our old meeting room in the blue detention house, was different to those last ones in the red prison. Thank goodness, Arvid was back again in his own clothes. He was very happy, all would be well now. They had heard it from his own cell, not knowing what it meant. Smiles and happy tears had been the answers of the glad news. The very same day they got their clothes back and were taken over to the blue prison, where they now were all waiting their release. The jailers were now treating the political prisoners with consideration and it was nearly like living in a hotel. Everyone could talk as they pleased and one after the other of the foreign prisoners were leaving. They were made to disappear after dark quietly, so as not to excite those who as yet were left behind. First the allied nationals were released, and then even the German prisoners could go. But Arvid and Hans were still there, even when the American Army had landed on Japan proper and you saw them in the streets of Yokohama. They had no consul to claim them and Margot and I could do nothing about it.[66]

Table 8.1

Foreign civilians in custody for suspicion of violating the National Defense Security Law and/or Military Secrets Protection Law as of July 1, 1945. Locations are arranged geographically, north to south. Numbers of female prisoners are in parentheses. Hugo Frank died the day before July 1 and is thus omitted from this data.

Location	Convicted	Suspected or awaiting trial	Total
Sapporo	9	0	9
Akita	1	0	1
Niigata	0	1	1
Yokohama	6 (1)	17	23 (1)
Osaka	4	0	4
Kobe	0	12 (5)	12 (5)
Fukuoka	0	1	1
Total	20 (1)	31 (5)	51(6)

SOURCE: Honobe, *Ruisu Fuugo Furanku Sensei*, 200.

Weeks passed and Arvid, Hans, and Liebeskind remained in custody, seemingly forgotten. Estelle's repeated attempts to have the prison prosecutor release them had failed. Having once fainted riding the overcrowded train between Odawara and Yokohama, she left it to Margot and Heinz Lang to haggle with prison officials. On August 31, Margot and Lang duly threatened to inform the American marshal that Gumyōji Prison continued to hold political prisoners in violation of the conditions of surrender. The threat worked, and Margot and Lang were able to escort Arvid and Hans back to Gora that very day. Liebeskind was liberated on September 3, though only when a friend came to inquire about her and threatened to call General Douglas MacArthur unless guards released her.[67] Prison officials, it seems, were content to let stateless prisoners (and their own crimes) remain hidden there indefinitely.

Records from July 1, 1945, the day following Hugo's death, indicate that Japanese prisons were holding fifty-one foreigners suspected or convicted of espionage (table 8.1). Of these, twenty-four were German and six were women. In the final year of the war, eight were convicted and held in Yokohama's red prison. Lissner had been released and Hugo had perished; the others were Arvid, Hans, Bossée, Schweizer, H. A. Refardt, and

Liebeskind, the sole woman. Boedner and Weingartner awaited sentencing in the blue prison.[68]

Throughout the war, few Westerners convicted of espionage died in Japanese prisons. The Soviet spy Richard Sorge was hanged at Sugamo Prison in 1944 and his accomplice Branko Vukelić (1904–45) died in prison in Hokkaido two months later. Occupation records indicate that Hugo and an unnamed French national were the only two foreigners charged with espionage to die in Kanagawa; one German national convicted of espionage died after being released from prison in Kobe. In comparison, Honobe contends that at Gumyōji an average of two to five Japanese prisoners died each day during the final months of the war.[69] Given the rarity of foreign deaths, Hugo's case was surely a sensitive matter for Japanese authorities, and it is not surprising that his were among the many police and court records destroyed after the war.

The extraordinary mortality rate of Japanese convicts at Gumyōji suggests that police cruelties were not directed unilaterally toward foreigners; they characterized Japanese counterintelligence tactics generally. Like foreigners, Japanese were subjected to close surveillance, arrested, tortured, compelled to sign dubious confessions, and died in prison from neglect and malnutrition.[70] The *tonarigumi* system of neighbor surveillance made privacy a near impossibility for Japanese, and even loyal subjects who let slip a piece of war gossip or whispered doubts about the war effort were summarily dragged into police stations for questioning. Hugo's neighbor Katsube, for example, tells of being forced to kneel on the concrete floor and being beaten by two officers on the thighs with a bamboo rod and hit in the face with a wooden sword until nearly unconscious.[71] The brutalities faced by Hugo, Arvid, and the other foreign suspects did not differ significantly from what Japanese suspects experienced, therefore. Foreign suspects were victims of racial profiling by Kenpeitai, but not of racial abuse in prison.

Japanese and Westerners alike were also subjected to inconsistent or illegal policing and judicial processes. Factionalism and disorganization within Japan's chain of command created a power vacuum that permitted counterintelligence operations to transgress their legal authority. They also allowed Meisinger to partially fill that vacuum. If Hugo, Arvid, and the others were arrested under suspicion of violating the National Defense Security Law, which is unverifiable since they were not charged when arrested but is likely given the charges filed later, then their arrests were illegal. The law required that suspects be issued a summons, prohibited police from making discretionary or unannounced arrests, and stipulated that any such arrests would not be legally recognized.[72] In order to prove guilt, police then performed interrogations that included illegal torture. Moreover, the torture itself was clearly gratuitous and sadistic. Testimonies indicate that inquisitors unnecessarily prolonged their torture of Bossée and Liebeskind as well as used it as a form of perverse amusement. In overlooking these gross procedural lapses, the courts became complicit. Judicial proceedings roughly followed pro forma legal requirements but were fraudulent in the sense that little evidence was admitted or examined other than the signed confessions. The legitimacy of these confessions was immaterial. Prosecution was also aided by the vague wording of the National Defense Security and Military Secrets Protection Laws, both of which permitted police considerable latitude in defining illegal activities.

We have already noted that testimonies given in the months following the war constitute strong evidence that Japanese police possessed no credible case for arresting Hugo or the others and that they had acted to appease the malicious whims of Nazi officials. Forty-four years later any lingering doubts were put to rest. A letter of apology dated October 12, 1989, was sent by Yoshida Nisaku, director of general affairs for the Kenpeitai Kenyūkai (Association of Former Members of the Military Police), to Hugo's daughter Barbara Weldon and Ludy Frank. The letter states that Yoshida had been stationed in China during the war and knew nothing of the events surrounding Hugo's internment, but that in 1987 he had been asked to assist in an investigation of the Yokohama Kenpeitai. Yoshida contacted and met with surviving members of that unit in an attempt to uncover all possible information surrounding the circumstances of Hugo's internment and interrogation. All high-ranking officers connected with the case had passed away, however, and lower officials did not respond to his queries.[73] Yoshida concluded that "there is an extremely strong possibility that [Hugo] was incarcerated as a result of the 'signing under coercion of a groundless confession' at the hands of the Military Police which conducted the investigation and which was under the influence of the Nazi Secret Police in Japan."[74]

Yoshida felt unable to categorically assert Hugo's innocence in his letter, for to do so would have exceeded his authority and his ability to judge innocence based on incomplete knowledge of Hugo's case. Yet he goes as far as he is able as an officer of the Kenyūkai by asserting "an extremely strong possibility" (*kanōsei kiwamete dainari*) of Hugo's innocence. The *Asahi Evening News*, researcher Honobe, and author Kamakura Keizō all interpret the letter's phrasing as tantamount to both an admission of wrongdoing and a declaration of Hugo's innocence.[75] This position was not merely Yoshida's personal opinion, but was the position adopted by the Kenyūkai itself, whose vice president, accompanied by three other Kenyūkai representatives, attended a memorial service held at Hugo's grave in Karuizawa on June 30, 1989, the anniversary of Hugo's death.

CHAPTER 9

Race War?

On Japanese Pragmatism and Racial Ambivalence

The Japanese treated me as if I were Japanese. I don't feel like I'm non-Japanese when I'm with my Japanese friends. . . . It was the Japanese military that was very anti-foreigner, and they were prejudiced and horrible. But the normal Japanese were very kind and helped my mother and me a lot during the war and afterward.

—Barbara Weldon, daughter of Hugo and Alice Frank[1]

The sadistic cruelty and illegal torture inflicted on Hugo Frank, Arvid Balk, Margaret Liebeskind, and the others in Kanagawa police custody contrast markedly with the narratives that have informed the remainder of this study. As such, inclusion of their stories here foregrounds the tolerance and racial ambivalence afforded to Westerners at large in Hakone, Karuizawa, and elsewhere. Tolerance and ambivalence are unexpected findings. If Japan's home front were as unified as slogans suggested and as xenophobic as wartime ideology demanded, authorities and local civilians would have united to thoroughly suppress all resident foreigners. Yet the great majority of Western residents, irrespective of nationality, were neither persecuted nor targeted by either systemic or "on the street" racial profiling. Under such circumstances, it is indeed remarkable that they did not suffer greater maltreatment.

The preceding chapters have illuminated the living conditions of resident Westerners during the war years. In the process they have also exposed dimensions of wartime life that question the extent to which Japanese conceptualized the conflict as a race war. Consideration of two overarching questions will allow us to take stock of our findings. First, why was state propaganda (the depoliticization of the public through a process of misinforming it) relatively unsuccessful in altering the public's racial ambivalence toward Westerners? Second, how are we to distinguish between racism as it is commonly understood and the sorts of race relations and race consciousness exhibited by the Japanese public during the war? In addressing these questions we shall discuss how situationism and virtue ethics set parameters for interpersonal relations, and consider the nature of what has been styled Japanese "soft" or centripetal racism.

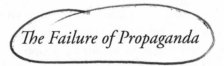

The Failure of Propaganda

The vocabularies, phrases, images, films, and symbols used in wartime rhetoric are the artifacts that form the core of *War without Mercy*, John Dower's seminal study of wartime racism. Though issued by the government-sponsored propaganda industry, in Dower's work these materials too easily come to represent the totality of Japanese public opinion, or, as he titles one section, "The War in Japanese Eyes." Regrettably, the bulk of his analysis of wartime racism omits explicit consideration of popular opinion. (In fairness, it never purports to do so, and in a rigorous investigation of Japanese public sentiment published later, Dower uncovers widespread evidence of popular resistance to the very propaganda that had informed his discussion of Japanese racism in *War without Mercy*.)[2] He makes extensive use of racialized political cartoons from the magazine *Manga*, for instance, which he admits to being an "officially sponsored" publication.[3] Published between 1940 and 1944, the magazine lauded Japan's alliance with Adolf Hitler while depicting Franklin Delano Roosevelt, Winston Churchill, and Joseph Stalin as demonic and wicked. Endorsed by the Propaganda Department of the Imperial Rule Assistance Association and a fund raiser for the military, *Manga* was clearly created and deployed as state propaganda and in no way represents public sentiment. Nonetheless, Dower's use of this sort of material has attracted large numbers of uncritical followers eager to assume that the existence of propaganda alone constitutes evidence of an indoctrinated public. Many of these misperceptions derive not from Dower's fine scholarship but from facile interpretations of it. Nancy Brcak and John Pavia's assertion is representative: "During World War II, propaganda produced by Japanese and American artists reflected and shaped the emotions and attitudes of that era," they write. "Graphic propaganda on both sides revealed an undercurrent of racism that affected how the war was conducted and perceived on both sides."[4] Though such statements are conveniently tidy, they overlook two critical points. Japanese propaganda was less explicitly racist toward Caucasians than is generally assumed. Also, its mere presence is often confused with its effectiveness in swaying public opinion, which has been widely overstated.

Regarding the first point, Japan's partnership with Germany and Italy rendered antiwhite rhetoric problematic, necessitating more qualified, targeted aspersions against Anglo-Americans specifically. Propaganda films released early in the war, for example, resisted launching racial attacks against Japan's Western enemies. Simon Partner notes that such films rarely sought to foster a hatred of Anglo-Americans, an agenda that would have been impractical given the popularity of Western sports, films, and other forms of mass culture. Rather, they endeavored to whip up national solidarity, laud the heroism of Japanese soldiers, and foster a spirit of sacrifice. Filmmakers were permitted a degree of artistic autonomy, he argues, and generally avoided maligning Westerners.[5] Peter High affirms that in contrast to the more vitriolic productions shown to residents of conquered territories in the Pacific, films made for domestic audiences focused more on prognosticating Japanese victory than demonizing Japan's white enemies.[6] When the media did broach the subject of race, it tended to depict Western race hatred of Japanese rather than the reverse. Dower concedes that Japanese wartime propaganda films were softer, less violent, and more subtle than counterpart films produced in the United States. Japan's enemies were often left unidentified, including their color and race.[7] Though early propaganda films did dehumanize Japan's enemies, they were comparatively less racially provocative.

Until the midwar years, therefore, propaganda avoided overt racial attacks on Anglo-Americans. This tendency was overturned by a series of historical dramas that vilified Anglo-Americans by focusing on historical instances of Western imperialism in Asia. These films depicted treacherous whites assailing peace-loving Asians, but High argues that they were generally marginal as entertainment and that their poor quality compromised their effectiveness as propaganda.[8] Although this genre of films did occasionally endeavor to inspire hatred of Anglo-Americans, it did so by showcasing their record of brutality against other races, not by attacking them on racial grounds. Reticence to vilify whiteness aligned with rhetorical efforts to "Caucasianize" the Japanese. Throughout the imperial era, illustrations and other forms of media had consistently portrayed Japanese as paler than the darker Asian peoples they had conquered. This relative whiteness, audiences were to understand, constituted further evidence of Japan's indigenous radiance and purity.[9]

Japanese propaganda also endeavored to underscore the moral and religious failings of its enemies, but, again, tended to avoid doing so in explicitly racial terms. Roosevelt and Churchill were the most ubiquitous targets of wartime political cartoons. Though relentlessly vilified, they were rarely racialized the way Japanese were depicted in America, where cartoonists found humor in lampooning Japanese as a race. When Japanese cartoonists did use their enemies' physical attributes as a means of ridicule, they did so by depicting Roosevelt and Churchill as fiendish creatures (see figs. 9.2 and 9.3 later in this chapter). More often, however, caricatures of these leaders evoked the moral degeneracy of Western racism itself. Such works alluded either to the West's history of predatory colonialism in Asia or to the racism rampant within its societies. Figure 9.1, for example, satirizes the exploitation of African Americans in the United States. President Roosevelt stands alongside the Statue of Liberty, mimicking it in a comic attempt to claim himself as a defender of freedom, justice, and equality. In place of a torch, however, he wields a bullwhip, America's time-honored means of managing its African Americans. His cowboy attire stereotypically American, Roosevelt releases his "black eagles" overseas to fight his wars, while a distressed Statue of Liberty is beset by warplanes.

Japanese ideologues not only showcased their enemies' racism to validate the righteousness of Japan's own wars; they hoped to further inflame that racial turmoil by publicizing it overseas. With the latter agenda in mind, ideologues transmitted shortwave radio broadcasts to the United States that focused on racial injustices in American society. Aiming to foment ire among African American listeners, these broadcasts included testimonies by African American POWs about their poor treatment in the U.S. military.[10]

FIGURE 9.1 Yasumoto Ryōichi, "Amerika no baai: Kari dasareru kurowashi" (In America: Black eagles sent off to hunt), *Manga* 11, no. 11 (November 1943): 13. Courtesy of The Ohio State University Billy Ireland Cartoon Library & Museum.

Ideologues were also careful to avoid sweeping critiques of Western religions. The sudden appearance of anti-Semitic political cartoons in the war's early years led Dower to report "an outburst of anti-Jewish race hate which has no explanation beyond mindless adherence to Nazi doctrine."[11] And in an endeavor to sensationalize Japanese racial hatred, he writes that "mass-oriented graphics . . . offered strains of both anti-Semitic and anti-Christian sentiment that were more vicious than is usually recognized," a statement easily misinterpreted as suggesting widespread public hatred of Judaism and Christianity.[12] Such an interpretation would be misleading. Though police did persecute some Jews to appease German allies, anti-Semitic messages were not meaningfully internalized by many Japanese. Nor did ultranationalists see Judaism as a source of ideological competition, as they did Christianity. During the war years the Japanese public's engagement with Judaism and Jews reveals little racial interest at all. Testimonies indicate that although official attitudes toward Jews shifted following Japan's entrance into the Tripartite Pact, the public displayed no such inclinations. In Kobe, Shapiro writes, "while a certain degree of hostility [toward us as Jews] developed on the part of the police and other government authorities, our Japanese neighbors and friends continued to treat us politely and displayed no change in their attitude toward foreigners."[13] Dower substantiates his statement by supplying the name of a single anti-Semitic cartoonist, but admits in a footnote (in a different chapter) that "most commentators now regard anti-Semitism as a peripheral and aberrant current in the wartime ideology of the Japanese."[14] Dower's allusions to anti-Christian sentiment are then supported with several caricatures of Roosevelt and Churchill in Christian-themed political cartoons. In these cases, however, the two leaders are depicted as evil heretics whose violence and wickedness violate the spirit of their religion. The cartoons do not represent Christianity as a barbaric creed; rather, Roosevelt's and Churchill's barbarism makes them poor Christians. Although some comics do evoke Christianity as awash in violence, others are neutral, even respectful, and free of value judgments. As in figures 9.2 and 9.3, from *Manga*, most cartoons containing Christian themes do not intend to attack Christianity on doctrinal grounds as an evil religion; they excoriate Western leaders for defiling it. Figure 9.2 depicts the British-U.S. bombing of Rome in July 1943, condemning the gargoylesque Churchill and Roosevelt for their mortal crimes against the

FIGURE 9.2 Yasumoto Ryōichi, "Makoto ni kami wo osorezaru mono" (Really, these guys don't scare God), *Manga* 11, no. 9 (September 1943): 13. Courtesy of The Ohio State University Billy Ireland Cartoon Library & Museum.

FIGURE 9.3 Kondō Hidezō, "Kami ikari" (God's wrath), *Manga* 12, no. 4 (April 1944): 11. Courtesy of The Ohio State University Billy Ireland Cartoon Library & Museum.

religion. It levels no such condemnation against their pious Christian victims. In "God's Wrath" (fig. 9.3), Christ crucifies a demonic Roosevelt, retribution for the latter's presumed atrocities. Neither Christianity nor Christ himself is an object of satire. The subject of both works is the hypocrisy of how enemy leaders have used Christianity in the name of militarism. Although Japanese authorities targeted certain Christian figureheads, therefore, they generally avoided rhetorical attacks on the religion itself.

Wartime propaganda did seek to instill generic anti-Anglo-Americanism by crafting its white enemies as fearsome brutes and devils. The inhumanity of Caucasian enemies lay in their very denial of the humanity of other races.[15] Multiple accounts affirm that scare tactics of this sort were effective, particularly among children and rural populations without firsthand experience with Westerners. A schoolgirl watching the arrival of Occupation troops confessed, "We were convinced that the Americans and the British were demons. Not human beings."[16] Another, in Okinawa, related her terror at the sight of Americans landing on the island. Expecting them to rape and kill Japanese civilians, she hid, and even when troops came passing out cigarettes, chocolates, and gum, adults warned her that the chocolates were bombs and the gum was poisoned.[17] Once discovered to be unfounded, however, fears abated quickly.

Not only has the racial content of Japanese propaganda been overstated, the multitude of personal accounts detailed in the preceding chapters reveal it to be a poor barometer of real public sentiment. Nationalistic propaganda was convincing to only the young, writes John Morris. Even college students, "whose preliminary education was completed in comparatively enlightened times, possess for the most part a liberal outlook" that includes a general dislike of the military and an aversion to military service, a sentiment shared by many among the general public.[18] Uchiyama internment camp inmate Syd Duer, who was three-quarters Japanese, relates being sent into the countryside to barter for food and having the following encounter with a farmer:

> He [the farmer] naturally did not know who I was much less of my nationality being British, he thought I was Japanese—perhaps a cop, so he let go his feeling about the war. . . . He also referred to the machine-gunning of innocent civilians from the air, but rather excused the Amer-

icans saying that it's war *shikataganai* [can't be helped]. . . . But he continued, "when they land here & occupy this area they are not going to bully the farmers, they are humans just as we are, they are not going to annihilate us. . . . Such talks that the Americans are going to kill us are absurd."[19]

"There was not the slightest tinge of hatred against the enemy," Duer concludes. "The Japanese propaganda of stirring hatred among the people has not worked well."[20] Late-war rhetoric conveying the expectation that men, women, and children would willingly sacrifice themselves to defend their sacred homeland, therefore, was noteworthy as a rhetorical landmark but cannot be taken as evidence of any actual "kamikazefication" of the Japanese populace.[21] There is little evidence that these pronouncements had much of an impact at all. More likely, they served to further alienate the Japanese citizenry from authorities whose unconditional surrender soon thereafter clearly belied their own belief that a homeland defense force consisting of famished civilians wielding bamboo spears would willingly and successfully repel the U.S. military.

Many informed Japanese adults viewed antiforeign propaganda as contrived and unconvincing, as merely a mantra for subjects to vocalize. Public opinion polls indeed reveal that citizens were aware of being manipulated, and one suspects that this awareness steeled their resistance to it. Actual public sentiment toward military-government hegemony and its wars is more accurately reflected in popular reactions to the surrender, the moment when citizens could finally disgorge publicly their disgust for the entire war agenda. As Dower notes, a "great majority" of Japanese had no difficulty shrugging off state indoctrination.[22] Robert Guillain concurs that Japan's official attempts to incite hatred of and rage against Americans were ineffective. The Japanese public, he claims, never looked at the war in racial or personal terms, and never developed any personal hatred for even those Americans dropping bombs on them from overhead.[23] More immediate concerns—privation and survival—left little room for ideological matters. As they contended with wartime stresses, Japanese civilians found no way to insert race hate sensibly into their daily lives and ultimately resorted to collective ambivalence. This is not to suggest that they were not patriotic or that nationalist rhetoric failed to have any impact, rather that many recognized no contradiction between nationalism and racial tolerance for Westerners. To this extent, ideology backfired and pragmatism prevailed. In erasing any semblance of a civil society, authorities generated near-universal compliance, but also mistrust and apathy. Disparities in official and unofficial treatment are also evident in the wartime experiences of Yokohama's Chinese community. All Chinese residing in Kanagawa Prefecture were relocated to Yokohama's Chinatown. Police viewed the community suspiciously for the remainder of the war and restricted residents' travel; arrests and deportations were common.[24] However, civilian Japanese-Chinese relations normalized during the war, Eric Han writes. The anti-Chinese sentiment that followed the outbreak of Sino-Japanese hostilities in 1937 gave way to recognition of the Chinese community's economic and cultural value to the city. Yokohama's economic and community organizations actively encouraged Chinese not to repatriate. Chinese and Japanese neighbors participated amicably in air-raid drills and rationing, and the local school honored Chinese children's national identity by permitting them to speak Chinese.[25]

Public disgust for the war extended even to open expressions of contempt for the military. During the Doolittle Raid, eyewitness Morris relates, "the general sentiment was one of bewildered interest. . . . Pedestrians just stood around in groups; and then, as a realisation of what was happening gradually dawned upon them, one heard people starting to criticize the army for having misled them."[26] Disillusionment extended to members of the military itself. Following the surrender, soldiers publicly confessed that many among the military's rank and file were privately skeptical or even scornful of both the war and Japan's military leadership. Evidently, intimidation had been as instrumental as indoctrination in maintaining order in the ranks.

Numerous memoirs and testimonies assert that Japanese civilians cautiously retained neutral or amicable relationships with the Westerners with whom they had long coexisted in mutually imposed insularity. Ambassador Joseph Grew noted this fact on February 16, 1942. "In spite of all the war propaganda," he wrote, "there does not seem to exist any fundamental hatred of the United States among the people. We learn, too, from various sources that in spite of Japan's initial successes in the war, people are asking themselves whether, in view of the unlimited resources of America, Japan can ever really win."[27] This view is widely corroborated by other Westerners trapped in Japan. Though many of their writings betray resentment of and even contempt for Japanese, few authors can recount instances of being disrespected, insulted, or abused by members of the Japanese public. Reports of hate crimes against Westerners are exceptionally rare. Feelings of endangerment and imminent persecution derived mainly from police intimidation and surveillance, the disintegration of foreign communities, and the growing influence of the Nazi Party. Others echoing Grew's observation indicate that Japanese displayed a range of attitudes toward the war and resident Westerners but generally remained tolerant. Louis Frank, resoundingly adored by his colleagues and students at Yamanashi Technical College, was only fired due to pressure from the German embassy. Samuel Heaslett had only praise for Japanese civilians during the early war years: his maid and her daughter traveled daily from Tokyo to Yokohama, a four-hour round trip, to deliver his meals to Gumyōji Prison; his Japanese friends remained loyal and supportive during and following his internment; and strangers on the Tokyo streets bore him no ill will. He also describes his Japanese cellmates at the Tobe jail as civil, considerate, and generous. In Karuizawa, the Franks, Apcars, Shapiros, and others enjoyed cooperation and even camaraderie from Japanese neighbors and farmers, and Gwen Terasaki reports similar experiences in other rural locales.[28] The cohort of enemy women and children interned at Nanasawa and then Akita were treated kindly by those communities. Robert Crowder and Joe Hale each write of equally close relations with local Japanese.[29] Some reports indicate that rural Japanese extended greater civility to foreigners evacuating the cities than they did to native evacuees, who experienced considerable difficulties integrating into provincial communities.[30] Even military POWs transferred to Japan, who generally endured harsher camp conditions than civilian internees, noticed clear attitudinal disparities between their guards and the Japanese public. Richard Arvidson, captured in Guam, expected to find a hostile citizenry when transported to Japan but instead found people curious and hospitable. He relates that as he and fellow captives were being marched from their ship to the Zentsūji camp, a restaurant owner treated the entire contingent to tea and bread.[31]

My findings indicate that, except in extraordinary cases, civilian behaviors responded to immediate needs and circumstances. Instances of public complicity in the containment of Westerners—maids spying on their foreign employers, for example—generally occurred under police orders and supervision. The relative absence of gratuitous racial antipathy also challenges assertions that the Japanese populace was unified in support of the war. The scarcity of public resistance, some suggest, indicates that the slogan *ichioku isshin* (one hundred million souls with one mind) was actually achieved, but ubiquitous accounts of civilians extending assistance and friendship to Westerners suggests otherwise. Racial tolerance was a passive form of ideological dissent.

The evidence presented here has also challenged allegations of institutional racism and assertions that state policies systematized racial prejudice and anti-Semitism. Although the military did employ forms of systemic racism in its treatment of Asian and Western POWs, within Japan proper, state containment of Westerners was strategic and politically rather than racially motivated. Laws passed prior to and during the war gave police broader discretionary powers and placed the economy, media, industry, rationing, and many other operations under state oversight. State control over civilian life was universal and indiscriminant. Legislation directed at foreigners avoided racial profiling, however. The Revised Trade Regulatory Rules for Foreigners that froze trade with the United States, Britain, and the Netherlands were passed in retaliation for similar laws promulgated by those enemy nations. Christian denominations brought under Japanese administration were permitted to worship, provided they did not pose any ideological challenge to State Shinto. Stricter immigration regulations generally amounted to greater information gathering and did not significantly deter immigration from the West. Into 1941, regulations were relaxed for Jewish and other political migrants. Kobe's community of Jewish refugees was eventually relocated to China not for anti-Semitic reasons but mainly from concerns that the community had grown unsustainable. As we have seen, instances of Kenpeitai racial profiling did occur later in the war, but always in connection with its collaboration with Gestapo representatives.[32] Police took interest only in groups or individuals deemed suspicious or ideologically threatening. Jews and anti-Nazi Germans collectively posed no such threats per se, but the Kenpeitai's desire to ingratiate itself with Josef Meisinger eventually made it a willing coconspirator with Nazi racism. Moreover, neither the so-called Fugu Plan to attract and utilize Jewish refugees in China nor the eventual decision to contain those refugees within the squalid Shanghai Ghetto indicates any strong philosophical position vis-à-vis the Jewish race or religion. As David Kranzler has shown, Japan's attempt to use the Jews to bolster the local economy in China and, prior to 1940, to align itself with the United States and Britain on the Jewish question reveals only extreme patriotism and pragmatism.[33]

The pragmatic and circumstantial considerations that figured into Japanese engagements with race bear further explanation. East Asian ethical thought draws on multiple philosophical traditions but gravitates strongly toward principles associated with virtue ethics and situationism. The former, a core feature of Confucian thought, calls on the individual (and the state) to pursue virtues, particularly those that specifically support interpersonal relations: filiality, benevolence, humanity, and loyalty, for example. This pursuit is humanistic and intuitive, and considers the process of pursuing virtue to be as pertinent as the result. Internalizing virtue "emphasizes the ethical importance of social roles, emotions, habits, and imaginative extension," Edward Slingerland writes.[34] It is an affective process that calls for individual engagement with immediate circumstances. As such, it privileges contextualized over categorically mandated behavior. Situationism, in which situational considerations become the dominant determinants of behavior, shares much with virtue ethics. It too subscribes to ethical contextualism and allows for individual initiative, flexibility, and role-playing. Both paradigms are highly pragmatic, but in prioritizing the expedient fulfillment of immediate needs they are also tolerant of inconsistency. Accordingly, Japan has historically adhered to shifting, relativistic relations with foreign races. This allowed it, over the course of a few decades in the nineteenth century, to variously embrace racial exclusionism, xenophobia, and insularity, followed by internationalization, imperialism, and cosmopolitanism, while concurrently espousing principles of racial supremacy and emperorism.[35] Policy shifts addressed practical necessity and political rather than racial interests, accommodating immediate needs on a case-by-case basis.[36]

Situationism is manifested in Japan's formulation of different racial narratives and diplomatic strategies for Asian, Western, Russian, and domestic audiences. Propaganda issued within the territories constructed a colonial discourse around the racial equality of Japanese colonial subjects, while many of its policies implemented a caste system that ensured

Japanese privilege.[37] At home, meanwhile, it asserted Japanese superiority based on racial purity and proximity to the emperor. And as the state deployed racist propaganda against other Asians domestically, it generally omitted mention of race from rhetoric intended for international consumption. In its diplomacy with Western nations, Japan selectively rejected the Western practice of connecting race to color and repudiated Nazi Germany's assertions of Aryan supremacy. Instead it affirmed the tripartite alliance as evidence of a "colorless" racial parity with its Axis allies.[38]

Practical concerns also framed Japan's relationship with the Soviet Union. Geopolitically and culturally, Japan had long seen itself as part of Eurasia. The Trans-Siberian Railway connected its holdings in Korea and Manchuria with Moscow and Europe, making those western destinations much more accessible than locations across the Pacific. Not only had Japan shared close diplomatic relations with the Soviet Union, it had found ethnic kinship with Russia as an East Asian neighbor. In Japanese eyes, Russia was somehow less "white," a point that was corroborated by Nazi rhetoric that associated Russians with Asians and Mongols. Although Japan never went so far as to support Soviet communism, it found much to admire in its communistic egalitarianism, particularly its respect for ethnic diversity and rejection of racial discrimination. There was hope and expectation that Stalin and all Russians self-identified as Asians and understood Asia's desire to rid itself of Western interference. These sentiments informed policy in Manchukuo, where Russian residents were allowed to live harmoniously alongside a multitude of other races.[39] Indeed, Russian immigrants brought the Japanese empire a cosmopolitanism that the latter used to distance itself from the assertions of racial supremacy evident in Nazi and American foreign policy.

The situationism framing Japan's racial diplomacy is also evident in the position consciousness of Japanese individuals. We have noted innumerable cases of officials, guards, and interrogators carrying out duties with steadfast professionalism but then turning lenient and even friendly in off-duty moments. Some confessed that they found their duties repugnant and emotionally draining. This "two-faced" quality was evident not only in their treatment of prisoners, but occasionally even in their ideological outlook. Some even revealed skepticism about Japan's handling of the war. During a private moment, the interrogator that Otto Tolischus nicknamed the Fox mentioned to him, "I feel very sorry for all the correspondents, and I am ashamed of my job."[40] Further examples abound. In a farewell speech to passengers being repatriated on the first exchange ship in June 1942, the chief of the Foreigner Section of the Tokyo Police stated, "Do your best for your country. We are going to do the best for Imperial Japan," explaining that actions taken by his police force, and by combatant states, were neither personal nor racial; they were a matter of professional duty.[41] Lucille Apcar notes the ubiquity of this situationist behavior and correctly connects it to occupational role-playing. "Despite their innate politeness," she writes, "[the Japanese] tendency toward kindliness evaporates immediately upon being placed in a position of authority."[42] Even core members of Japan's leadership stridently supported positions that they privately rejected. Navy commander Admiral Yamamoto Isoroku (1884–1943), who had studied at Harvard and worked in Washington, opposed actions that would lead Japan into conflict with the United States and privately doubted the wisdom of war, yet publicly endorsed war when diplomacy failed.[43] As the advisory bureau chief on Jewish affairs, naval captain Inuzuka Koreshige resisted Nazi anti-Semitism by declaring racial equality to be a fundamental principle of Japanese policy. Between 1939 and 1942 he was also instrumental in establishing the autonomous Jewish settlement in Shanghai, for which he earned heroic status among Japan's resident Jewish community. Simultaneously, however, Inuzuka pseudonymously published anti-Semitic books for domestic consumption.

The limited efficacy of state propaganda in molding public race consciousness merits more comprehensive study than can be provided here. Nonetheless, my findings illuminate several explanations for why many Japanese never developed anti-Western sentiments. First, insinuations that resident Westerners were spies and that Caucasians were fearsome demons contradicted what Japanese had learned to be true from generations of personal experience. Although racial discrimination continued to be directed at native minorities such as hereditary outcast groups (Ainu and Burakumin) and colonial subjects (resident Koreans and Taiwanese), the white progenitors of Japanese modernization could not be vilified so easily. It would be inaccurate to suggest that Japanese collectively subscribed to a Eurocentric racial hierarchy, collectively embraced an Orientalist worldview, or collectively possessed an inferiority complex vis-à-vis

Western races. They were, however, rightfully proud of the success they had earned from decades of earnest participation as "honorary whites" within a Eurocentric racial power structure. Their own inequitable position within that structure notwithstanding, they had also benefited tremendously from the experience.

Second, during the war "the West" grew more distant and abstract. Neither daily experience nor the daily news of Japanese triumphs in the Pacific constituted evidence that Anglo-Americans were as villainous as state rhetoric claimed. The number of resident Westerners declined dramatically prior to the war, and after Pearl Harbor enemy nationals were removed from view entirely. Many of those remaining had become professionally disenfranchised, economically insolvent, and socially restricted. As the Caucasian presence receded and its cultural capital declined, in some cases to the point of near invisibility, the prospect of Western threats lost credibility.

Additionally, the omnipresence of state control proved partially self-defeating. The state imposed intramural surveillance; controlled commodities, information, industry, and the private sector generally; and regulated what and how much people ate, where they went, what they bought, and what they knew. Ideological control disallowed public expression of individual thought, opinion, and action, but in denying people venues of sociopolitical participation it also fostered apathy and a collective unresponsiveness. To this extent, state control ultimately weakened people's receptivity to racial issues and rendered them more immune to indoctrination.

Resident Westerners also escaped public vilification because they never conformed to the role of state enemies. Regardless of their status as enemies, neutrals, or allies, most exhibited no concomitant attitudinal shift during the war or any cognizance of such a need. It was assumed that Westerners whose power positions had declined—those interned as enemy nationals and those suffering from professional or economic disenfranchisement—would subordinate themselves by aligning their attitudes and behaviors with those new subject positions. Most resisted any such adjustments, however. As we have seen, tensions in internment camps and embassies were often exacerbated by guards' surprise at the arrogance of Westerners who failed to humble themselves, as well as by

Westerners' disgust at the arrogance of Japanese guards who expected them to do so. Foreigners' defiance on this point, their nonsituationism, conveyed expectations that their lives and relationships with Japanese would continue as before. In many cases they were treated accordingly.

It is clear, moreover, that while wartime adversities intensified competition for resources, they also fostered solidarity between people, regardless of race. Ronald Takaki has shown that for some in the United States the war helped dissolve racial prejudice by bringing rhetorical ideals like racial equality and freedom to the surface of public consciousness. In the United States, war necessitated the mobilization of racial minorities, who either enlisted in the military or worked for the national defense on the home front. In their respective efforts to fight a war about freedom for a country that represented itself as an archetype of freedom, those minorities encountered forms of racial discrimination that prevented them from doing so on an equal footing with whites. In many cases, their resistance against these obstacles proved highly effective and was later rewarded with a succession of antidiscrimination policies that helped prepare the nation for the civil rights movement. "The fierce fight against fascism," Takaki concludes, "helped to teach Americans of an ethnically diverse society how to live together as one people."[44] In Japan, wartime adversities elicited similar unifying effects, though on a much-reduced scale. Amid their fear, hunger, and loss, some Japanese practiced passive resistance by retaining their appreciation for charity and humaneness. Sharing hardships and cultivating good relations with both Japanese and foreign neighbors was an intuitive way of seeing to one's personal interests. Farmers in particular gained material benefits by defying police orders and bartering with foreigners, trading their excess food for clothing and other items that were otherwise unavailable.

The precarity of daily life—the national shortages, disappearance of male labor, and perpetual threat of air raids in urban areas—called for a pragmatism that undermined the effectiveness of state propaganda. For a multitude of reasons, then, elites' inviolable, fixed "truths" about racial purity, proper place, and the emperor's moral authority failed to resonate as hoped. Their attempts to render race a moral issue—a categorical imperative—conflicted with the public's more contextual engagement with that concept.

Continuity and Change Following the Surrender

Japanese accepted the indignity of occupation as a rightful consequence of defeat. From the outset, however, both sides understood the need to eliminate sources of acrimony and disavow wartime racisms. The paradigm of racial inequality that had defined Japanese-U.S. relations for generations had to be reinvented and the racial trappings of diplomacy removed. The massive responsibility of building and piloting a new Japanese state and then establishing a mutually respectful, collaborative relationship compelled Occupation authorities and Japanese elites to reject their own wartime racisms.

Many have noted the expedient neutralization of Japanese-U.S. racial antagonisms during the Occupation. Position-conscious Japanese officials dispensed with racial arrogance and adopted more subordinate roles. And just as Japanese civilians discovered that their former enemies were not the devils they had been led to believe, Americans were surprised at the enthusiasm, even warmth, with which they were greeted by their former enemies.[45] As impoverished Japanese admired and longed for the material comforts enjoyed by well-fed American GIs, Western culture also quickly regained its prewar prestige.[46] Resident Westerners were particularly delighted by this reversal. Estelle Balk relates that train passengers now gave up their seats for her: "They wished to make themselves agreeable, to be polite and helpful. Dear me, what a contrast to the treatment I had to endure twice a week when coming down from Gora on my pilgrimage to Gumyōji. Now it was all smiles and bows, admiration of foreign clothing and their polite curiosity of my whereabouts. . . . The Suzuki family next door had been told by the chief of police in Odawara that they were to be polite to us again, that Japan had lost the war and therefore, the white people were the masters."[47] In Karuizawa, police "accepted the surrender meekly," Ludy Frank wrote.[48] Irene Frank related her enormous gratification at encountering the city's police chief in town, he who had interrogated her so harshly after the fire. Their positions now reversed, the chief had risen and bowed to her.[49]

In important respects this attitudinal shift indicates greater evidence of continuity than change, however. It suggests not, as Estelle's statement avers, that Japanese blindly obeyed authorities' orders to accept foreigners and Occupation forces, but rather that hatred for those enemies had never been fully internalized. It was clear to Guillain, for instance, that many Japanese had never been convinced by the country's war rationale nor been infused with any racial hatred for Anglo-Americans. In this perceptive statement, he voices what he imagined to be the collective sentiments of the defeated Japanese: "We exalted the Axis, praised Mussolini, showered Hitler with flattery, but this was pure courtesy; we did not like such arrogant people, in fact, we detested them. We cursed America because insults are part of our combat arsenal and are prescribed in military regulations. But even during the war our hatred for the American was never more than transient."[50] Postwar amity toward Caucasians, he concludes, was essentially unchanged from prewar years.

And though race relations during the Occupation were generally amicable, for both sides embedded prejudicial structures took generations to overturn. The United States preserved racist policies long after it had paid lip service to racial equality and universal human rights. The United Nations Charter was promulgated in June 1945 with a pledge to promote "human rights and fundamental freedoms for all without distinction as to race, sex, languages, or religion." The United States, however, did not revise its discriminatory immigration and naturalization policies until 1953, and retained racial immigration quotas until 1965.[51] Segregation policies were also retained in parts of the United States, as well as in its armed forces. Some Japanese found racial hostility toward Caucasians easier to eradicate than disdain for other Asians. A December 1945 study by the U.S. Army Investigation Division in Beijing found that many Japanese stationed there were indeed questioning claims of Japanese racial superiority vis-à-vis Caucasians. The war's outcome had not meaningfully altered respondents' prejudicial views of other Asians, however. More than double the percentage (86 percent) of respondents agreed to the statement "The Japanese are superior to people of the other nations of the Far East" than to the statement "The Japanese race is superior to all other races" (41 percent).[52] Racial discrimination against Asian laborers was deeply rooted in Japanese law, as well. The eradication of the Japanese empire, through which the state had become a multiracial, multicultural political entity, returned Japan to a state of ethnic insularity. Resident Koreans had been granted suffrage in 1925 and ballots in Hangul were made available to them. Following defeat, women's suffrage was implemented but resident Koreans were stripped of their Japanese citizenship, voting rights, and rights to financial compensation for their wartime losses.[53] This return to ethnic insularity perpetuated some forms of Japanese exceptionalism and helps explain why postwar Japan has been slower to adopt antidiscrimination practices than nations like Britain, France, and the United States. Despite antidiscrimination laws promulgated during the Occupation to equalize working conditions and guarantee pensions and insurance to foreign workers, therefore, broader forms of discrimination both inside and outside the workplace have remained common.[54]

Ongoing racial prejudices constitute a qualified perpetuation rather than an eradication of race consciousness. For although Japan and the United States set about forging a new protector-protectorate relationship committed to halting the spread of communism in Asia, the war's outcome had seemingly affirmed certain colonial paradigms and racial inequities. Both sides resorted to certain prewar habits that resurrected unequal power positions. Japanese officials subordinated themselves to Occupation authorities, who resided in segregated communities and took Japanese servants and cooks. To the extent that race consciousness at the top was transformed from an instrument of hatred to one that helped both sides reestablish an inequitable power structure, Yukiko Koshiro argues, it even "provided the basis for a new relationship."[55]

Having discussed the diverse dynamics underlying engagements with race in wartime Japan, I must now clarify how those attitudes differ from race hate, or racism as commonly defined. The distinction I will make is roughly analogous to two definitions of the term "discrimination": (1) prejudicial treatment based on negative value judgments connected to difference; and (2) differentiation, or nonjudgmental recognition of difference. I equate the former definition with "racism," or "a personal ideology based on racial prejudice."[56] The latter, a neutral acknowledgment of difference, does not in itself evoke any negative value judgment that subordinates an individual or group. One would consider the eradication of the former to be an ethical imperative. The latter, which still strongly informs interpersonal relations in Japan, maintains that difference is self-evident and deserves acknowledgment, and that its "proper place" be honored. Significantly, both types of discrimination were practiced in imperial Japan, for whereas many Japanese harbored colonial pretensions that subordinated other Asians, they remained ambivalent toward Westerners.

This double standard was not recognized as a moral problem, but neither was it benign. Japanese discrimination (distinction making) engendered a virulent ethnocentrism that posed real barriers to cross-cultural understanding. The presumption that Japanese were a unique, exclusive race and by that virtue were culturally and spiritually connected in ways impenetrable to outsiders was widely interpreted as racial conceit. It was this intrinsic challenge to the paradigm of white supremacy that Western authorities had found so repugnant prior to the war, and why the International Military Tribunal for the Far East later accused Japan of "racial arrogance."[57] Dower too interprets this parochial ethnocentrism as a form of racism whose wartime effects were as hateful and harmful as white supremacism. As he explains it, "In its language and imagery, Japanese prejudice . . . appeared to be more benign than its white counterpart— by comparison, a 'soft' racism—but this was misleading. The insularity of such introversion tended to depersonalize and, in its own peculiar way, dehumanize all non-Japanese 'outsiders.' In practice, such intense fixation on the self contributed to a wartime record of extremely callous and brutal behavior toward non-Japanese."[58]

Whereas Western "hard," centrifugal racism stems from a crystallization of hatred for racial others, it is argued, Japan's "soft," centripetal racism arises from a narcissistic ethnocentrism, a pattern of exclusion or dismissal of racial others. This preoccupation with self explains why Japanese ideology focused far more on exalting the national polity and the Japanese race than on denigrating non-Japanese. It has also erected a seemingly impenetrable cultural wall between Japan and the rest of the world, a consciousness of race so strong that, as Edwin Reischauer wrote, "it is almost as if they regarded themselves as a different species from the rest of humanity."[59] Japanese "fixation on the self" was tantamount to ignoring or excluding an "other," which some proud Western expats took as no less an affront than being hated. To live in Japan was thus to contend with an ongoing insult to one's personal and ethnic identity. This consensus was certainly behind *Herald Tribune* correspondent and longtime resident Joseph Newman's observation that "of all the strange things about Japan, one of the most curious is the fact that many foreign residents who learned to love the country also lived to dislike her with various degrees of bitterness."[60]

Dower finds evidence of "soft" racism mainly in Japan's military aggression, colonial policies, and state propaganda. As noted in chapter 1, many others have extended this discussion to "the Japanese" generally, variously describing this particular form of "soft" racism as oblique, submerged, hidden, tacitly practiced, passive, indirect, and symbolic.[61] Takashi Fujitani has documented Japan's shift away from exclusionary or "vulgar" racism toward a more inclusive or "polite" racism.[62] Regardless of one's modifier of choice, there is consensual acknowledgment that Japan's engagement with race is somehow different. A particularly troubling dimension of Japanese race consciousness is its immutability throughout the modern era. It cannot be written off as a byproduct of war or as endemic to an earlier, less enlightened age. For whereas systemic centrifugal racism has receded (though by no means disappeared) in the West since the war, Japan's more centripetal version survives largely intact. Biculturalism remains a curse in Japan. Writing in 2013, American author Leslie Helm, who was born and raised in Japan, confesses an inability to assimilate into the racial groups he identifies with, stating that "outsider status became a central part of my identity."[63] Indeed, the ubiquity of "*uchimuki* (insular) youth" in contemporary Japan indicates that racial parochialism remains as strong as ever.[64]

Sadly, this enduring culture of insularity continues to invite international scorn and has prevented Japan from moving past its wartime aggressions. Lingering outrage over Japan's military atrocities and human rights violations sustains perceptions of wartime "Japan" and "the Japanese" as fanatics driven by antiwhite hysteria. Racial tensions remain especially prominent in Asia, where wartime antagonisms continue to rend diplomatic relations. The racial nature of Japan's war crimes—and Japan's difficulties acknowledging and apologizing for those crimes—is indeed difficult to accept and forgive. As a great obstacle to regional healing, they continue to undermine attempts to negotiate resolutions to long-standing territorial disputes between Japan, Korea, China, and Russia. And as imperial Japan's racial transgressions continue to foment unremitting anti-Japanese sentiment around Asia, they also remain a source of shame for the Japanese people.

It is clear that wartime Japan was not unified by antiwhite hysteria and that the actions of its military and military police did not represent public sentiment. From Kobe to Karuizawa the experiences of resident Westerners reveal an expansive cognitive gap between the ways that authorities conducted the war and the ways that civilians negotiated their lives. I have explained this gap as an ideological bifurcation between an esoteric cult (military and state ideologues) and an exoteric cult (the masses) that exposes the nonexistence of any singular Japan or Japanese race consciousness. I have also described it as a product of on-duty role-playing, situational ethics, and pragmatism, showing how different structures and racial narratives were applied to different contexts and ethnic groups. Finally, I have distinguished between centrifugal racial hatred and a centripetal race consciousness rooted in self-absorbed ethnocentrism. For many resident Westerners, the Asia-Pacific War amounted to an existential war that threatened personal identities and eroded national loyalties. Many Japanese, likewise, were too deeply traumatized to be bothered with state ideology or with expectations that they distinguish between Caucasian friends and foes. In this sense, although the war was indeed as intensely emotional and visceral as has been alleged, those emotions were expressed contextually and inconsistently.

EPILOGUE

For evacuees in Karuizawa and Hakone, the Occupation brought immediate job prospects. Learning that Occupation personnel had landed on August 28, Ludy Frank traveled to Yokohama, encountered two U.S. Army officers, and was hired as an interpreter and guide on the spot. "That first night I was in Yokohama I went walking downtown," he recalled. "You could hear English being spoken. Man that felt so good."[1] Two days later, Ludy rode in the lead vehicle as a convoy of Occupation troops first entered Tokyo. Isaac Shapiro also left Karuizawa and found immediate employment in the army, and then the navy, in the same capacity. Max Pestalozzi became acting director of the International Red Cross in Japan and recruited Lucille Apcar to work for the organization. Arvid Balk eventually found employment in Yokohama with the Occupation's public relations office, and Estelle Balk found several jobs but did not hold any of them long. Hans Ries was also employed by Occupation officials.[2] Margaret Liebeskind rented a room with Alice Frank in Yokohama. The American Red Cross found her a job as a secretary at a doughnut factory, and found Alice work at the Red Cross Club.[3]

Peace and newfound opportunities began a healing process, but the war's physical and emotional duress wrought long-term aftereffects on many of its survivors. Arvid continued to suffer from the physical and psychological abuse he had endured in prison. The blood vessels in his feet had been permanently damaged by the torture. He had also become skittish and distant, and initially opted to remain in Gora while Estelle moved back to Yokohama. By the time the Balks immigrated to the United States, Arvid was prematurely aged and senile. He died in a sanitarium in Napa, California, in 1955.[4]

Alice also remained emotionally incapacitated for some time after Hugo Frank's death. Unable to work or care for Barbara, she had Ludy take her daughter to live with him in Karuizawa. A register of sixty-seven Jews from twenty-nine families liberated from Karuizawa in September 1945 includes the names Louis and Amy Frank but not Ludy or Irene. (The register also includes the names Shapiro, Sidline, and Moiseff.)[5] Irene's absence from the list suggests that she and the children had followed Ludy to Yokohama within a few weeks, and that Louis and Amy joined the family there shortly afterward. Irene had been struggling to feed her own children at the time, and Barbara's arrival in early July aggravated the burden. Once back in Yokohama, she placed Barbara in an orphanage. Barbara remained at the facility, which she later described as full of babies screaming and dying of starvation, for several months until her aunt's family in Kamakura took her in.[6]

Surviving Westerners faced an uncertain future, the stateless in particular. Occupation authorities administered medical treatment to released prisoners and others in need but could not compensate them for their material losses. The U.S. War Crimes Commission took former prisoners' testimonies to gather evidence for use in the war crimes trials being held in Japan and elsewhere around the world. (Josef Meisinger was tried for war crimes and executed in Warsaw on March 7, 1947.) Several of the Kenpeitai officers who had tortured foreigners were sued by their victims after the war, convicted, and sent to prison. Reports issued by the Occupation's Investigation Division indicate that the abuses inflicted on Arvid, Andre Bossée, and Liebeskind did constitute war crimes, but the Law Division opted not to prosecute those crimes because the plaintiffs were not U.S. nationals. Thinking Hugo's death suspicious, the division also made inquiries about Hugo with the Japanese Foreign Ministry but soon closed its investigation for the same reason.[7]

Meanwhile, Irene and her children moved into a vacant house on the Bluff while Ludy lived and worked at the Correspondent's Club in the Marunouchi area of Tokyo, a residence and dining hall for U.S. press personnel covering the Occupation. Since Ludy spoke Japanese, he was put in charge of hiring and supervising Japanese staff. Three months later he borrowed a Jeep to visit his family in Yokohama and, having never driven before, ran it off the unpaved road into a wall. A month later he developed intense neck pain and was diagnosed with vertebral tuberculosis. He was put in traction and told that he had six months to live. Two months later, on August 30, 1946, their son Patrick was born in Tokyo. After Ludy had spent six months in bed, Irene asked a Japanese naval surgeon for a second opinion. X-rays revealed that the vertebrae fractures had healed and the terminal tuberculosis had been a misdiagnosis.

A few months later Ludy received permission to immigrate to the United States. A lieutenant in the Occupation's public relations section had enlisted Ludy's help finding and purchasing Japanese art objects, which he had bought for pennies, and returned the favor by arranging sponsorship for Ludy's immigration visa. Ludy found work as a seaman on a freighter bound for Seattle. He arrived in January 1947 and caught a train to San Francisco. After six months living in a Kolping Society dorm and working for American Express, and days before Irene and the children arrived, he found better employment with the American President Lines steamship company and rented an apartment. His parents, Amy and Louis, immigrated later, Louis eventually securing a job teaching chemistry at Philander Smith College in Little Rock, Arkansas.[8] Estelle and Arvid Balk, Margaret Liebeskind, Alice and Barbara Frank, the Helms, the Apcars, the Shapiros, and many of the others who had weathered the war years in Japan eventually immigrated to the United States as well.

Notes

Introduction

1. Frank, Ludwig, "Living Conditions in Wartime," 10.

2. Ibid., 12.

3. Kojima, *Hakone to gaikokujin*, 184.

4. Komiya, "Taiheiyō sensō shita," 38. Komiya's numbers are generally corroborated by statistics compiled by the U.S. War Department (Hayashi, *Senji gaikokujin kyōseirenkō kankei*, 1085–86).

5. Twomey, *Australia's Forgotten Prisoners*, 208.

6. Miyabara, *Rizōto Karuizawa no hinkaku*, 104.

7. Thomas, *Trapped with the Enemy*, 260.

8. Ibid., 72.

9. George Lavrov, *Yokohama Gaijin*, 3, 4. The Lavrovs were White Russians who entered Japan through China in the late 1920s. They eventually settled in Yokohama and opened a clothing store. Being stateless, they were trapped in Japan during the Pacific War and endured those years without diplomatic protection. George was four when his family's house was destroyed and his older brother killed in an air raid on May 29, 1945.

10. Dower's seminal study of this topic is *War without Mercy: Race and Power in the Pacific War* (1986).

11. Dower, *Ways of Forgetting*, 30, 31.

12. I refer here to Dower's "Sensational Rumors, Seditious Graffiti, and the Nightmares of the Thought Police," in *Japan in War and Peace*, 101–54.

13. Ford, *The Pacific War*, 120–26.

14. The term "Caucasian" is a flawed racial designation on several counts. As a referent to Western, fair-skinned people, it fails to specify the parameters of those descriptors. In this sense the term is a poor identifier of racial or ethnic origin. It is also historically connected with myriad forms of systemic racism formulated and propagated by the West, as, for example, racial scientific claims of the biological superiority of whites. For

these reasons some favor the term "white," which avoids some of the historical baggage connected with "Caucasian." "White," however, invokes historical biases associated with skin color and is likewise unable to acknowledge the multitude of ethnic origins that it subsumes. Without satisfactory recourse for these concerns, but with due deference to them, this book will use the term "Caucasian," which remains widely accepted and roughly corresponds to the equally vague Japanese term *hakujin* (see note 31).

15. Horne, *Race War!*, vii–viii, 3, 220.

16. Fujitani, *Race for Empire*, 16–17.

17. Ibid., 7, 25.

18. Ibid., 7.

19. Horne, *Race War!*, 4–5, 281. Both the United States and Britain wished to avoid the topic of racial inequalities and resisted issuing clear statements on the subject, but they were not prepared to renounce the international order's standing racial hierarchies (ibid., 229).

20. Fujitani, *Race for Empire*, 8.

21. Ibid., 17.

22. Koshiro, *Imperial Eclipse*, 47.

23. Ibid., 47, 72–74.

24. Ibid., 72.

25. Here Tatum takes her definition from David T. Wellman's *Portraits of White Racism* (Tatum, "Defining Racism," 127).

26. Interior Ministry, *Tekikokujin yokuryū kankei*.

27. Duer, "Diary of Sydengham Duer," 6. Duer was three-quarters Japanese but held British citizenship. Though Duer was interned after the Pearl Harbor attack, his brother Edward, a minor, was permitted to stay at their home near Ofuna with their Japanese mother. Duer had graduated from Saint Joseph's College in 1936 and at the time of his arrest was a student at Jikei-kai Medical University.

28. Tomita, *Dear Miye*, 14–15.

29. Hanasono, "Stranded in Japan," 158–66.

30. Archer, *Internment of Western Civilians*, 32.

31. The racial and intrinsically confrontational consciousness that had defined diplomatic relations with Japan since the mid-nineteenth century gave rise to a dialectic between Caucasians (*hakujin*, or *hakushoku jinshu*) and the "yellow races" (*kōshoku jinshu*). *Hakujin* evoked the civilizational advancements by which Japan sought to augment its own prosperity, military might, and international standing, but also imperialist aggression in Asia.

32. Marc Gallicchio reports that some African Americans were treated well by the Japanese but also notes that on one occasion the Japanese proprietor of a Yokohama hotel denied African Americans entrance due to the objections of a white guest (Gallicchio, *The African American Encounter*, 113). See also Onishi, *Transpacific Antiracism*.

33. Between 1939 and 1945 Japan brought at least 667,000 Koreans into Japan, and between 1943 and 1945 it put 38,935 Chinese to work in hard labor jobs at 135 locations around the country (Kaneko, *Yudayajin nanmin*, 257).

34. For a study of wartime Japan's disavowal of discrimination and its subsequent military conscription of Koreans, see Fujitani, *Race for Empire*.

35. Waterford, *Prisoners of the Japanese*, 209.

36. Duus, *Tokyo Rose*, 55.

Chapter 1. Racism, Race Consciousness, and Imperial Japan

1. Julius later founded Helm Brothers, which became one of Japan's oldest foreign-owned businesses and its largest foreign-owned stevedoring and forwarding company.

2. For a comprehensive study of interracial marriages during this era, see Leupp, *Interracial Intimacy in Japan*.

3. Helm, *Yokohama Yankee*, 62, 103–4, 136–38, 176.

4. Ibid., 41.

5. Ibid., 170.

6. Ibid., 174. What prestige the Helms lost in pedigree they redeemed through their generosity and deep roots in the Yokohama community.

7. Fanon, *Black Skin, White Masks*, 94–108.

8. For various perspectives on this process, see, for example, Kim, *Doctors of Empire*; Majima, "Skin Color Melancholy"; and Morris-Suzuki, "Ethnic Engineering."

9. Dower, *Ways of Forgetting*, 48.

10. Kowner, " 'Lighter than Yellow,' " 105, 125.

11. U.S. citizenship had been denied to Chinese since 1882.

12. Majima, "Skin Color Melancholy," 399.

13. The 1924 act was also abhorrent to minorities in the United States. For some African Americans it became a source of solidarity with Japan, the only imperial power resisting white supremacy. Realizing that they faced a common enemy, Japanese elites reciprocated by taking an interest in patterns of racial oppression in the United States. For more on African American admiration for prewar Japan, see Horne, "Tokyo Bound."

14. Geiger, *Subverting Exclusion*, 139–40.

15. Majima, "Skin Color Melancholy," 402.

16. Fujitani, *Race for Empire*, 79.

17. Lotchin, "Japanese Relocation," 155. Some have advanced alternate views. Roger Lotchin has argued that the primary impetus for the internment was not American racism. Rather, a complexity of factors made it a military necessity. Nor can one suppose that the views of individuals within the military and federal government who devised and lobbied for the internment reflected the opinions of the American public. Even amid their outrage over Pearl Harbor, many Americans recognized the order's intrinsic injustice.

18. Majima, "Skin Color Melancholy," 409.

19. Dower, *War without Mercy*, 265.

20. Quoted in Majima, "Skin Color Melancholy," 399.

21. Dower, *War without Mercy*, 5, 8.

22. Ibid., 243.

23. For a comprehensive discussion, see Olson, *Those Angry Days*.

24. Colonel Hugh Toye cited in Thorne, "Racial Aspects," 330.

25. See Takaki, *Double Victory*.

26. Thorne, "Racial Aspects," 367.

27. Ibid., 332.

28. Gallicchio, *The African American Encounter*, 61.

29. Quoted in Majima, "Skin Color Melancholy," 396.

30. Solt, *Shredding the Tapestry*, 75.

31. Gluck, *Japan's Modern Myths*, 135.

32. Dower, *War without Mercy*, 265.

33. Geiger, *Subverting Exclusion*, 8. The sporadic outbursts of anti-Korean sentiment in Tokyo's "Koreatown" represent a clear exception to this tendency.

34. Koshiro, *Imperial Eclipse*, 1; Cleveland, "Hiding in Plain Sight," 215.

35. Howell, "Ethnicity and Culture," 186.

36. For one such story, see Kiyota, *Beyond Loyalty*.

37. Koshiro, *Imperial Eclipse*, 476.

38. Ibid., 490.

39. Ibid., 489–91.

40. Fujitani, *Race for Empire*, 19, 23–24.

41. For more on Japanese racism in Asia, see Ienaga, *Japan's Last War*, 153–71.

42. Koshiro, *Imperial Eclipse*, 486.

43. Ibid., 278–79, 477, 494–95.

44. Ibid., 476.

45. Althusser, "Contradiction and Overdetermination," 99.

46. Tsurumi, *An Intellectual History*, 24.

47. Ibid., 24–25, 51–52, 120.

48. Partner, "Daily Lives of Civilians," 136; Yamashita, *Leaves from an Autumn*, 15–16.

49. For more, see Earhart, *Certain Victory*, 339–42.

50. Morris-Suzuki, "Debating Racial Science," 359, 365.

51. Ibid., 366.

52. For a comprehensive discussion of race and science, see Kim, *Doctors of Empire*.

53. Quoted in Dower, *War without Mercy*, 280.

54. Shiratori, "Make This Mankind's Last," 5.

55. Ibid., 4.

56. Kushner, *The Thought War*, 19.

57. Ibid., 29.

58. Data on how or whether propaganda influenced public epistemology is scarce and unreliable. Scholarship on racial scientist and pollster Koyama Eizō's work does not find measurable impacts of wartime or postwar propaganda (see Morris-Suzuki, "Ethnic Engineering").

59. Young, *Imperial Japan*, 238.

60. Tsurumi, *An Intellectual History*, 30.

61. Doak, "Concept of Ethnic Nationality," 179.

62. Ibid., 168.

63. Zachmann, "Race and International Law," 472.

64. Ibid., 456–57.

65. Ibid., 461.

66. Matsuura, "Ajia taiheiyō sensō," 99–100.

67. Kushner, *The Thought War*, 188.

68. Dower, *War without Mercy*, 204–5.

69. Passin, *Society and Education*, 254.

70. Ibid., 258.

71. The alliance was secured purely for mutual advantage. Adolf Hitler was openly repulsed by the idea of joining forces with those he viewed as his racial inferiors, and Japan disdained the patently discriminatory nature of Nazi rhetoric about the innate supremacy of the German race.

72. Koshiro, *Imperial Eclipse*, 62–63, 67.

73. Ibid., 51–52.

74. Ibid., 54, 57–59.

75. Ibid., 61.

Chapter 2. Privilege and Prejudice

1. John Dower, "Fear and Prejudice in U.S.-Japan Relations," in *Japan in War*, 316.

2. Ludwig Ernest Frank, "Lou's Life," 17.

3. Ludy Frank's memoirs reveal that the family's few Japanese friends had all lived abroad for extended periods and sought Western associates themselves.

4. Cortazzi, *Victorians in Japan*, xii.

5. Jones, *Live Machines*, 57–58, 108.

6. Williams, *Tales of Foreign Settlements*, 113.

7. Ibid., 61.

8. Horne, *Race War!*, 25.

9. Ibid., 26–27.

10. Quoted in Jones, *Live Machines*, 72.

11. Karaki, *Gaikokujin no mita Nihon*, 314–16.

12. Guillain, *I Saw Tokyo Burning*, 48.

13. Gluck, *Japan's Modern Myths*, 136.

14. Ibid., 137.

15. Steiner, *The Japanese Invasion*, 28.

16. Lucille Apcar, *Shibaraku*, 11.

17. Michael Apcar, a French citizen of Armenian descent but born in Japan, imported shellac and motorcycles and exported silk, toys, and pearls. His wife, Araxe, had been an American resident of Canada but lost her American citizenship when they married in 1922.

18. Araxe Apcar, *Six Survived*, 58.

19. Honobe, *Ruisu Fuugo Furanku Sensei*, C7.1.22–23.

20. Circumstantial proselytization was unavoidable. Ludy's memoirs indicate that, as a boarding student, he was expected to participate in morning prayers and say grace before meals. Under such circumstances he soon developed a desire to become Catholic.

21. Shapiro, *Edokko*, 47–48.

22. Foreign girls in Tokyo attended either the American School or the International School of the Sacred Heart.

23. Helm, *Yokohama Yankee*, 176. Julie Helm was born in 1887 in New York, where his father was temporarily employed, and so possessed American citizenship. He began working at Helm Brothers' Yokohama headquarters at age fourteen after attending Saint Joseph's College and took over the company in 1933. He was friends with the Armenian exporter-importer Michael Apcar, Lucille's father.

24. William R. Gorham Memorial Committee, *Biography of William R. Gorham*, 71.

25. Ibid., 159, 161. From the late 1930s, foreign students were exempted from *gunji kyōren*. Don Gorham went on to attend Tokyo Imperial University from 1938 to 1941, becoming the university's first Western student.

26. Shapiro, *Edokko*, 49.

27. When the family returned to Germany in 1940, their mixed blood disqualified those cousins from joining the Hitler Youth (Helm, *Yokohama Yankee*, 224).

28. Helm, *Yokohama Yankee*, 210. Julie and his family departed for California in September 1941.

29. Lucille Apcar, *Shibaraku*, 20–21.

30. Baenninger and Baenninger, *Eye of the Wind*, ix.

31. Ibid., 51–52.

32. Ibid., 75.

33. Household staff typically worked and lived with their employers, and many evacuated with them during the war.

34. Helm, *Yokohama Yankee*, 170, 209.

35. Isaac was the fourth of five sons. His father, Boris, was a cellist, composer, and conductor, and his mother a pianist. Boris had fled from Russia to Europe during the Bolshevik Revolution and later fled to Japan.

36. Han, "True Sino-Japanese Amity?," 588. As colonial subjects, resident Koreans and Taiwanese were forced to take Japanese citizenship.

37. Lucille Apcar, *Shibaraku*, 72; Duer, "Diary of Sydengham Duer," 70–71.

38. "Gaijin kyōshi," 5a. Unless otherwise noted, all translations are my own.

39. Though most German civilians were left alone, pressure from Britain did prompt Japanese authorities to take preemptive measures against some. In Otaru, the Franks were too distant to bother with, but the Helms' business in Yokohama was temporarily stripped of its German leadership. Julius and his son Jim, German citizens, were removed and the company was left to their brothers Julie, who held U.S. citizenship, and Karl, who took Japanese citizenship in order to circumvent Japanese regulations against foreign-owned operators (Helm, *Yokohama Yankee*, 109).

40. Kurata, "Otaru kōshō no senseitachi," 76.

41. Honobe, "Ruisu Fuugo Furanku-tei," 15, 17.

42. Ibid., 18.

43. Kurata, "Otaru kōshō no senseitachi," 75–76.

44. Possibly wishing to strengthen their independence, the boys' parents never visited them at the school (Patrick Frank and Irene Frank, "Interview," 5).

45. Honobe, "Ruisu Fuugo Furanku-tei," 21.

46. Honobe, *Ruisu Fuugo Furanku Sensei*, C7.1.25.

47. Many of Louis's students went on to become industrial and economic leaders during Japan's postwar recovery.

48. Honobe, *Ruisu Fuugo Furanku Sensei*, C.7.32.

49. Amy Frank, "Sokoku no kōshi denka," 4; Amy Frank, "Warera no kōshi denka," 12; Louis Frank, "Tōzen tadasubeki kōjō," 12.

50. "Kondoruki hirai wo machiwabu."

51. Ueda and Arai, *Senjika Nihon no Doitsujintachi*, 86.

52. Ibid., 73.

53. Ibid., 85.

54. Japan's treatment of Jewish refugees will be discussed in chapter 3.

55. Balk, "An Outsider," 85. Quotations from the Balk manuscript have been minimally edited for misspellings and grammatical errors.

56. Ibid., 10.

57. Ibid., 139.

58. Ibid., 28.

59. *Gaikoku shinbun kisha*, 24.

60. Balk, "An Outsider," 141.

61. "Rough Translation of Letter."

62. *Gaikoku shinbun kisha*, 299, 305.

63. "Rough Translation of Letter."

64. Balk, "An Outsider," 149–50.

65. Ibid., 150.

66. Ibid., 151–52.

67. Ibid., 202.

68. Ibid., 143.

69. Ibid., 152.

70. Ibid., 153–54.

71. Ibid., 189.

72. Ludy's conversion to Catholicism while at Saint Joseph's did not annul his status as a Jew.

73. Irene Frank, "Interview."

74. Ion, *Cross and the Rising Sun*, 105.

75. Hanazato, "Senzenki no Karuizawa," 251–52.

76. Ueda, "Dainijisekaitaisen izen no Nihon," 107–10.

77. Quoted in ibid., 108–9.

78. Karuizawa Chōshi Kankō Iinkai, *Karuizawa chōshi*, 303–4.

79. In 1927, 1,110 foreigners vacationed in Karuizawa but owned just 37 percent of the town's 587 villas.

80. Hanazato, "Senzenki no Karuizawa," 253–54.

81. Komatsu, *Karuizawa to hisho*, 3.

82. Ibid., 37.

83. Ibid., 38.

84. Karuizawa Chōshi Kankō Iinkai, *Karuizawa chōshi*, 297–300.

85. Fleisher, *Volcanic Isle*, 231.

86. Ueda, "Dainijisekaitaisen izen no Nihon," 115. During the war, the government confiscated seventy villas in Karuizawa owned by enemy nationals and sold them as evacuation sites to Japanese.

87. Ueda, "Dainijisekaitaisen izen no Nihon," 116–19.

88. For example, see Majima, "Skin Color Melancholy," 408.

89. Lucille Apcar, *Shibaraku*, 20–21.

Chapter 3. Handling the Other Within

1. Sidline, *Somehow, We'll Survive*, 15.

2. Fleisher, *Volcanic Isle*, 135.

3. Iwry, *To Wear the Dust*, 82.

4. Tatum, "Defining Racism," 127.

5. Tipton, *The Japanese Police State*, 7.

6. Lamont-Brown, *Kempeitai*, 14.

7. For periods concurrent with his tenure as prime minister, Tōjō also served as interior minister, foreign minister, education minister, and minister of commerce and industry.

8. Lamont-Brown, *Kempeitai*, 35, 41–45.

9. Tipton, *The Japanese Police State*, 124.

10. Lamont-Brown, *Kempeitai*, 15.

11. Tipton, *The Japanese Police State*, 30, 66–67.

12. Guillain, *I Saw Tokyo Burning*, 16.

13. Ibid., 161.

14. Ibid., 163.

15. Dōmei Tsūshin-sha, *Wartime Legislation in Japan*, 1–2.

16. Ibid., 16–19.

17. Ibid., 13, 23.

18. Ibid., 106–7.

19. "Hitotsuki sen'en gendo," 2.

20. Komiya, "Taiheiyō sensō to Yokohama," 342–44.

21. Yamashita, *Leaves from an Autumn*, 61–63.

22. Argall, *My Life*, 156.

23. Fleisher, *Volcanic Isle*, 297.

24. Tolischus, *Tokyo Record*, 89.

25. Fleisher, *Volcanic Isle*, 281.

26. Harris, *Boku wa Nihonhei datta*, 51, 55.

27. Fleisher, *Volcanic Isle*, 124, 215, 307–9, 311–12; Tamura, "Being an Enemy Alien," 37.

28. Fleisher, *Volcanic Isle*, 127.

29. Ibid., 302.

30. Ibid., 319.

31. Guillain, *I Saw Tokyo Burning*, 67–68.

32. Tipton, *The Japanese Police State*, 69.

33. Fält, *Fascism, Militarism, or Japanism?*, 144.

34. Dōmei Tsūshin-sha, *Wartime Legislation in Japan*, 30.

35. Fleisher, *Volcanic Isle*, 134.

36. Ibid., 115–16, 133.

37. Havens, *Valley of Darkness*, 130.

38. Ibid., 117, 127.

39. Partner, "Daily Lives of Civilians," 137–38.

40. Fleisher, *Volcanic Isle*, 114.

41. Ibid., 132.

42. Sorge was fond of alcohol, a known womanizer, and a member of the Nazi Party, all of which helped him disguise his Socialist sympathies and espionage activities. As a radio operator in the German embassy, he was privy to reports sent from Berlin and able to relay information to the Russian military. Specifically, Sorge provided Joseph Stalin with the date of Hitler's planned assault on Russia, as well as assurance that the Soviet Union would not be a target of attack by Japanese troops stationed in Manchuria. The latter point was of critical strategic importance for it enabled Stalin to mobilize troops to his western border and stop German advances short of Moscow. Sorge was captured and arrested in October 1941 and executed in November 1944. His arrest sent shockwaves through the German community, and particularly the embassy. It was also partially responsible for the dismissal of Ambassador Eugen Ott (1889–1977), who had worked closely with Sorge.

43. Partner, "Daily Lives of Civilians," 140.

44. Bix, *Hirohito*, 281.

45. Fleisher, *Volcanic Isle*, 136.

46. Havens, *Valley of Darkness*, 32.

47. Nish, *Japanese in War and Peace*, 12.

48. Fleisher, *Volcanic Isle*, 116; Sidline, *Somehow, We'll Survive*, 15.

49. Tolischus, *Tokyo Record*, 9, 59.

50. Ibid., 77.

51. Nish, *Japanese in War and Peace*, 91–121. The Doolittle Raid's sixteen B-25 bombers departed from an aircraft carrier in the Pacific. After successfully dropping their payloads on Tokyo, Yokohama, Nagoya, and Kobe, the planes ran out of fuel before reaching U.S. airbases in China. Three of the planes ditched into the Sea of Japan and the rest crash-landed at various locations in China. Thirteen of the eighty crewmen died.

52. Nish, *Japanese in War and Peace*, 286–87.

53. Partner, "Daily Lives of Civilians," 144.

54. The ubiquitous phrase "the Jewish problem" is taken from Kiyoko Inuzuka's 1939 treatise *Kaigun Inuzuka kikan no kiroku: Yudaya mondai to Nihon no kōsaku* (Japan's activities on the Jewish problem).

55. Shillony, *Jews and the Japanese*, 170, 173.

56. Ibid., 164.

57. Ibid., 171.

58. Sakamoto, *Japanese Diplomats*, 7.

59. Ibid., 17.

60. Tokayer and Swartz, *The Fugu Plan*, 178. Authors report various versions of this anecdote. Warren Kozak relates that this event occurred in Shanghai (Kozak, *The Rabbi of 84th Street*, 176–77).

61. Bandō, *Nihon no Yudayajin seisaku*, 139.

62. Tokayer and Swartz, *The Fugu Plan*, 56.

63. Medzini, *Under the Shadow*, 123.

64. Bandō, *Nihon no Yudayajin seisaku*, 368–69.

65. Inuzuka quoted in Kranzler, *Japanese, Nazis, and Jews*, 327.

66. Shillony, *Jews and the Japanese*, 175, 181, 184.

67. Honobe, *Ruisu Fuugo Furanku Sensei*, C.7.38.

68. Ibid., C.7.35–36.

69. Ibid., C.7.41–45.

70. Gao, *Shanghai Sanctuary*, 121–26.

71. Bandō, *Nihon no Yudayajin seisaku*, 276–79.

72. Ludwig Ernest Frank, "Lou's Life," 15.

73. Bandō, *Nihon no Yudayajin seisaku*, 281, 290. Moise Moiseff reports that Japan accepted 4,664 Jewish refugees between July 1940 and May 1941 and that throughout this period the Japanese government, as a matter of unofficial policy, adopted an open and sympathetic attitude toward them (Moiseff, "Jewish Transients in Japan," 9).

74. Shillony, *Jews and the Japanese*, 167; Tokayer and Swartz, *The Fugu Plan*, 122.

75. Tokayer and Swartz, *The Fugu Plan*, 124.

76. Moiseff, "Jewish Transients in Japan," 9.

77. Kranzler, *Japanese, Nazis, and Jews*, 319. The acronym HICEM is derived from the union of three organizations: the Hebrew Immigrant Aid Society, the Jewish Colonization Association, and the United Jewish Emigration Committee.

78. Sakamoto, *Japanese Diplomats*, 141.

79. Ibid., 142.

80. Iwadō, *Japan's Wartime Legislation*, 112–19.

81. Iwry, *To Wear the Dust*, 76–88.

82. Shatzkes, "Kobe," 267.

83. Matsuoka was one of the architects of the Tripartite Pact and variously defended anti-Semitic positions.

84. Kranzler, *Japanese, Nazis, and Jews*, 323.

85. Kaneko, *Yudayajin nanmin*, 201–3.

86. Shillony, *Politics and Culture*, 158.

87. Medzini, *Under the Shadow*, 128.

88. Kaneko, *Yudayajin nanmin*, 205.

89. Sakamoto, *Japanese Diplomats*, 142.

90. Kaneko, *Yudayajin nanmin*, 217–18.

91. Sidline, *Somehow, We'll Survive*, 98.

92. For such studies, see Gao, *Shanghai Sanctuary*; Kranzler, *Japanese, Nazis, and Jews*; and Shatzkes, "Kobe."

93. Kranzler, *Japanese, Nazis, and Jews*, 317.

94. Ibid., 320.

95. Ibid., 316.

96. For such accounts, see Shatzkes, "Kobe," 266; and Tokayer and Swartz, *The Fugu Plan*, 148–52.

97. Sakamoto, *Japanese Diplomats*, 134.

98. "Soren, gaijin no nyūkoku."

99. Shatzkes, "Kobe," 257, 266.

100. Gao, *Shanghai Sanctuary*, 137.

101. Iwadō, *Japan's Wartime Legislation*, 288–92.

102. Fleisher, *Volcanic Isle*, 125.

103. Buss and Buss, *Trusting God*, 83–84.

104. Ion, *The Cross in the Dark Valley*, 282–84.

105. Bales and Bales, *Kate Hansen*, 257.

106. Ibid., 261.

107. Ogawa, "'Hull House,'" 386.

108. For a full history of these three families and their missionary activities in Japan, see their respective memoirs: Buss and Buss, *Trusting God*; Lang, "A Child in Japan"; and Notehelfer and Notehelfer, *A Remarkable Journey*.

109. Lang, "A Child in Japan," 19, 37.

110. Notehelfer and Notehelfer, *A Remarkable Journey*, 48, 50–51.

111. Buss and Buss, *Trusting God*, 93.

112. Ibid., 76.

113. Ibid., 77.

114. Lang, "A Child in Japan," 39.

115. Quoted in Ion, *The Cross in the Dark Valley*, 200.

116. Ibid., 202.

117. Ibid., 314–15.

118. Lang, "A Child in Japan," 27.

119. Duer, "Diary of Sydengham Duer," 3.

120. Komiya, "Taiheiyō sensō to Yokohama," 342–44.

121. Bales and Bales, *Kate Hansen*, 257.

122. Krämer, "Beyond the Dark Valley," 181–211.

123. Buss and Buss, *Trusting God*, 77.

124. Bales and Bales, *Kate Hansen*, 259.

125. Ienaga, *Japan's Last War*, 219.

126. Ibid., 221.

127. Araxe Apcar, *Six Survived*, 58.

128. Bales and Bales, *Kate Hansen*, 258.

129. See, for example, Hata, "From Consideration to Contempt," 264; and Masahiro Yamamoto, *Nanking*, 91.

130. Tolischus, *Tokyo Record*, 171.

131. Ibid., 151.

132. Ibid., 153.

133. Sakamoto, *Japanese Diplomats*, 7.

Chapter 4. First Responses and Containment Protocols after Pearl Harbor (1941–43)

1. Lou Frank, "Interview," 26–27.

2. Tamura, "Being an Enemy Alien," 38.

3. Kojima, *Hakone to gaikokujin*, 184; Maruyama Keiko, "Ajia taiheiyō sensō," 26. The 342 interned enemy nationals were predominantly males between the ages of eighteen

and forty-five. Not considered a significant security threat, they were placed in low-security camps without interrogation. We shall address their plight in chapter 7.

4. Komiya, "Taiheiyō sensō shita," 1, 4; Komiya, "Taiheiyō sensō to Yokohama," 345.

5. Hale, *Hydrangea Waving.*

6. Utsumi, "Japanese Army Internment Policies," 179.

7. Ludwig Frank, "Living Conditions in Wartime," 2.

8. Balk, "An Outsider," 194–96.

9. Armstrong and Gorham are discussed in other chapters.

10. Maruyama Keiko, "Ajia taiheiyō sensō," 39; Terasaki, *Bridge to the Sun*, 130.

11. Guillain, *I Saw Tokyo Burning*, 161.

12. Morris, *Traveller from Tokyo*, 143, 156.

13. Abrikossow's name is variously spelled Abrikosov.

14. Shapiro, *Edokko*, 104.

15. Kojima, *Hakone to gaikokujin*, 181.

16. Shapiro, *Edokko*, 105.

17. Ion, *The Cross in the Dark Valley*, 312.

18. Ibid., 313.

19. Ibid., 252; Yamashita, *Leaves from an Autumn*, 167.

20. Ion, *The Cross in the Dark Valley*, 254.

21. "Gaijin supai issei kenkyo," 3.

22. "Zairyū tekikokujin wo shūyō," 3.

23. Grew, *Ten Years in Japan*, 500. Max Hill of the Associated Press, Percy Whiting of the International News Service, Ray Cromley of the *Wall Street Journal*, and the rest of the enemy news corps were also arrested on December 8.

24. Heaslett, *From a Japanese Prison*, 9.

25. Ibid., 41.

26. Ibid., 43.

27. Ibid., 60.

28. Ibid., 45.

29. Ibid., 48.

30. Tolischus, *Tokyo Record*, 323.

31. Ibid., 342, 345, 354.

32. Ibid., 360.

33. Ibid.

34. Ibid., 324, 370, 392.

35. Ibid., 379.

36. Ibid., 379, 382–83.

37. Argall, *My Life*, 232.

38. Ibid., 253–59.

39. Ibid., 262–71.

40. Lucille Apcar, *Shibaraku*, 73.

41. Ibid., 79, 89.

42. Araxe Apcar, *Six Survived*, 70, 80–81, 87.

43. Lucille Apcar, *Shibaraku*, 88.

44. Araxe Apcar, *Six Survived*, 88–89.

45. Lucille Apcar, *Shibaraku*, 80.

46. Araxe Apcar, *Six Survived*, 105.

47. Craigie, *Behind the Japanese Mask*, 134–37.

48. Grew, *Ten Years in Japan*, 502.

49. Ibid., 524.

50. Ibid., 520, 522.

51. Craigie, *Behind the Japanese Mask*, 139.

52. Ibid., 140.

53. Cortazzi, *Collected Writings*, 133.

54. Mark Felton writes that Redman was subjected to torture but cites no sources to substantiate the claim (Felton, *Japan's Gestapo*, 58).

55. Cortazzi, *Collected Writings*, 133.

56. Ibid., 141.

57. Elleman, *Japanese-American Civilian Prisoner*, 14.

58. The United States had adhered to a policy of internment that assessed threats against the country on the basis of race rather than nationality. It reversed this policy later in the war. When, in 1943 and 1944, Japan accused the United States of torturing, maltreating, and forcing labor on internees of Japanese ancestry, the United States rebutted that among those in question only Japanese citizens loyal to Japan fell under Japanese jurisdiction. Japan could make no demands concerning American citizens, regardless of their loyalty, or even demands concerning Japanese citizens loyal to the United States (ibid., 114).

59. Komiya, *Tekikokujin yokuryū*, 73–74.

60. Elleman, *Japanese-American Civilian Prisoner*, 6.

61. Komiya, *Tekikokujin yokuryū*, 79–80.

62. Naoki Maruyama, "Facing a Dilemma," 35.

63. Altschul, *As I Record*, 52. During the war Hanni and their son continued receiving their rations at the German Club, which distributed supplies to Kobe's seven hundred to nine hundred German residents, but Heinz was forced to travel to a separate facility for the city's roughly 170 stateless residents. Kobe also had a third food distribution center for neutrals like the Swiss, and a fourth for the roughly two hundred liberated enemy nationals (Tamura, "Being an Enemy Alien," 44).

64. Quoted in Dicker, *Wanderers and Settlers*, 115.

65. Dicker, *Wanderers and Settlers*, 113.

66. Kranzler, *Japanese, Nazis, and Jews*, 327. Meron Medzini suggests that anti-Semitic propaganda during the later war years may have served more to distract Japanese from the country's imminent defeat than to instill hatred of Jews (Medzini, *Under the Shadow*, 127).

67. Utsumi, "Japanese Army Internment Policies, 177–78.

68. Colonel Hugh Toye quoted in Thorne, "Racial Aspects," 330.

69. Morris, *Traveller from Tokyo*, 110.

70. Tolischus, *Tokyo Record*, 393.

71. Argall, *My Life*, 238.

Chapter 5. Watched and Unseen

1. Guillain, *I Saw Tokyo Burning*, 63.

2. Irene's mother, Estelle, who had just been visiting Irene and was on her way back to Honmoku when the bombers appeared, scarcely mentions the event, noting only that people on the street looked up with "astonishment and fright" (Balk, "An Outsider," 207).

3. Shapiro, *Edokko*, 135.

4. Guillain, *I Saw Tokyo Burning*, 178.

5. Sidline, *Somehow, We'll Survive*, 17.

6. Newman, *Goodbye Japan*, 257.

7. Balk, "An Outsider," 171.

8. Ibid., 211.

9. Fleisher, *Volcanic Isle*, 301.

10. Ibid., 173, 191.

11. Jones, *Live Machines*, 109.

12. Ibid., 114, 116.

13. Tolischus, *Tokyo Record*, 112.

14. Ibid., 185.

15. Guillain, *I Saw Tokyo Burning*, 65–68.

16. Ibid., 199.

17. Terasaki, *Bridge to the Sun*, 102. The Terasaki family was repatriated to Japan via exchange ship in July 1942. Though Gwen apparently retained her American citizenship, she was afforded immunity through her husband's position as bureau chief in the Foreign Office.

18. Ibid., 117. The following year, while living in the coastal village of Manazuru and struggling with sickness and food shortages, the Terasakis would befriend and receive critical assistance from a neighboring German family.

19. Araxe Apcar, *Six Survived*, 60.

20. Notehelfer and Notehelfer, *A Remarkable Journey*, 70. The organization was called Japanese-German Youth so that it could accept half-Japanese children.

21. Ibid., 58, 64.

22. Arai, "Shūsenzen tainichi doitsujin," 156.

23. Wickert, *Senjika no Doitsu taishikan*, 152–53.

24. Ueda and Arai, *Senjika Nihon no Doitsujintachi*, 113–14.

25. Guillain, *I Saw Tokyo Burning*, 62.

26. Craigie, *Behind the Japanese Mask*, 147.

27. Ueda and Arai, *Senjika Nihon no Doitsujintachi*, 107–11.

28. Ludwig Frank, "Living Conditions in Wartime," 2.

29. Ueda and Arai, *Senjika Nihon no Doitsujintachi*, 68–69.

30. By war's end, this number stood at about 2,700. Ueda Kōji and Arai Jun estimate the number at about 3,000 (Ueda and Arai, *Senjika Nihon no Doitsujintachi*, 15).

31. Burdick, "The Expulsion of Germans," 157.

32. Lenigk, "My Life," 39.

33. Quoted in Ueda and Arai, *Senjika Nihon no Doitsujintachi*, 56.

34. Flakowski, "Die Ausweisung der Deutschen," 1.

35. Sidline, *Somehow, We'll Survive*, 97.

36. Ibid., 96.

37. Shapiro, *Edokko*, 104.

38. Sidline, *Somehow, We'll Survive*, 98.

39. Sirota Gordon, *The Only Woman*, 66.

40. Quoted in Spang, "Recollections of a Jewish-German," 21.

41. Ibid., 23.

42. Lou Frank, "Interview," 4–5.

43. Ibid., 46.

44. Irene Frank, "Interview."

45. Bendahan, "Interview," 23–29.

46. This testimony from Barbara Weldon, Hugo's daughter, is the only evidence that Hugo was trying to flee Japan in late 1940. Weldon states that the Pearl Harbor attack occurred shortly before he expected to receive the visa (Weldon, interview by author).

47. Balk, "An Outsider," 197–98.

48. Honobe, *Ruisu Fuugo Furanku Sensei*, 58.

49. Shapiro, *Edokko*, 118.

50. Buss and Buss, *Trusting God*, 92.

51. Shapiro, *Edokko*, 130.

52. Balk, "An Outsider," 200, 204.

53. Lou Frank, "Interview," 37.

54. Guillain, *I Saw Tokyo Burning*, 66.

55. Lensen, "White Russians in Wartime," 268–69.

56. Ibid., 275.

57. Ibid., 278.

58. Ibid., 278, 279.

59. Ibid., 272.

60. Gorham's oldest child, Billy (1915–2003), had returned to the United States in 1929 to attend high school and university. Don left for the United States after completing his degree in Japanese literature at Tokyo Imperial University in March 1941.

61. William R. Gorham Memorial Committee, *Biography of William R. Gorham*, 102.

62. Han, "True Sino-Japanese Amity?," 598–99, 601.

63. Guillain, *I Saw Tokyo Burning*, 60–61.

64. Ibid., 64.

65. Newman, *Goodbye Japan*, 252.

66. Lang, "A Child in Japan," 40.

67. Baenninger and Baenninger, *Eye of the Wind*, 114.

68. Ibid., 115.

69. Balk, "An Outsider," 253.

70. Terasaki, *Bridge to the Sun*, 106.

71. Ibid.

72. Notehelfer and Notehelfer, *A Remarkable Journey*, 63, 68.

73. Gibney, *Sensō*, 202.

74. Crowder, "An American's Life," 264.

75. Notehelfer and Notehelfer, *A Remarkable Journey*, 65.

76. Hale, *Hydrangea Waving*, 24.

77. Sidline, *Somehow, We'll Survive*, 159.

78. Shapiro, *Edokko*, 44.

79. Guillain, *I Saw Tokyo Burning*, 64.

80. Terasaki, *Bridge to the Sun*, 126.

81. Ibid., 138.

82. Other witnesses also note public pity for Western prisoners. Kobe resident Heinz Altschul remembers seeing enemy POWs routinely marched through that city on their way to work. "It was a very unpleasant sight," he writes, "but I must say that none of the Japanese civilians . . . made any bad remarks or showed any hatred; in fact, I had the feeling that they kind of felt sorry for these poor prisoners" (Altschul, *As I Record*, 46).

83. Utsumi, *Nihongun no horyo seisaku*, 473; Gibney, *Sensō*, 175.

84. Gibney, *Sensō*, 169. See also Ienaga, *Japan's Last War*.

85. Ienaga, *Japan's Last War*, 215. For an additional perspective on Japanese nonresistance, see Yoshimi, *Grassroots Fascism*.

86. Tolischus, *Tokyo Record*, 77.

87. Shillony, "Wartime Japan," 5.

88. Ibid., 7, 17.

89. Bix, *Hirohito*, 281.

90. John Dower discusses this threat in "Sensational Rumors, Seditious Graffiti, and the Nightmares of the Thought Police," in *Japan in War*, 138–47.

91. Guillain, *I Saw Tokyo Burning*, 57.

92. Craigie, *Behind the Japanese Mask*, 147.

93. Ion, *The Cross in the Dark Valley*, 314.

94. Shapiro, *Edokko*, 104.

95. Guillain, *I Saw Tokyo Burning*, 55–56.

96. Narusawa and Victoria, "'War Is a Crime,'" 4.

97. Havens, *Valley of Darkness*, 71.

98. Ibid., 127.

99. For examples, see Ishigaki-shi shihenshūshitsu, *Shimin no senji*, vol. 4, 6–9.

100. Dower, *Japan in War*, 129–30.

101. U.S. Strategic Bombing Survey, *Effects of Strategic Bombing*, 17.

102. For examples, see Gibney, *Sensō*.

Chapter 6. Fleeing for the Hills

1. Guillain, *I Saw Tokyo Burning*, 118, 122.

2. Balk, "An Outsider," 209, 252.

3. Havens, *Valley of Darkness*, 161–62.

4. Wickert, *Senjika no Doitsu taishikan*, 155.

5. Foreigners had been restricted from strategic sites much earlier. Guillain reports that upon his arrival in Nagasaki in 1938 he had been given a map of the Japanese coastline showing areas off-limits to foreigners (Guillain, *I Saw Tokyo Burning*, 64). The United States also restricted foreigners from sensitive areas.

6. Authorities also made initial preparations to evacuate foreigners from coastal areas in Kobe. Though evacuations from Kobe never occurred, many families decided to leave voluntarily (Altschul, *As I Record*, 82–83).

7. Victor S. Lavrov, *Son*, 47–48.

8. Interior Ministry, "Gaikokujin kyojū chiiki."

9. Interior Ministry, *I-gō sochi kankei gaikokujin*.

10. Shapiro, *Edokko*, 125.

11. Haar and Harr, "A Lifetime of Images," 103. In Karuizawa the Haars were watched "all the time," which may have led them to believe that, as Hungarians, they were considered neutrals. Hungary had joined the Axis coalition in November 1940.

12. Yokohama gaikokujin shakai kenkyūkai and Yokohama kaikō shiryōkan, *Yokohama to gaikokujin shakai*, 173.

13. Helm, *Yokohama Yankee*, 206.

14. Notehelfer and Notehelfer, *A Remarkable Journey*, 69.

15. Victor S. Lavrov, *Son*, 47–48.

16. Komiya, "Taiheiyō sensō shita," 34.

17. The name is also recorded as Arthur Karlovitch von Wilm.

18. Weldon, interview by author.

19. Ibid.

20. Hugo, Alice, and their daughter Barbara (b. 1939) were ostracized by Estelle until the end of the war. Though Estelle knew Alice in Yokohama and then in Gora, her manuscript makes no mention of her.

21. Ludwig Frank, "Living Conditions in Wartime," 1.

22. Komiya, "Taiheiyō sensō shita," 34.

23. Ibid.

24. Honobe, *Ruisu Fuugo Furanku Sensei*, 95–97.

25. Balk, "An Outsider," 219.

26. Ibid., 214.

27. Ibid., 214–15.

28. Ibid., 226.

29. Honobe, *Ruisu Fuugo Furanku Sensei*, 75.

30. Balk, "An Outsider," 221.

31. Kojima, *Hakone to gaikokujin*, 185; Honobe, *Ruisu Fuugo Furanku Sensei*, 83–84.

32. Weldon, interview by author.

33. Ries, personal letter to Honobe, 1.

34. Honobe, *Ruisu Fuugo Furanku Sensei*, 115.

35. Arvid's papers were seized upon his arrest. His letters and other documents are compiled, many with Japanese translations, in *Gaikoku shinbun kisha, tsūshin-in kankei zakken* (Miscellaneous documents relating to foreign news reporters and correspondents), held in the Diplomatic Archives of the Ministry of Foreign Affairs.

36. Komatsu, *Karuizawa to hisho*, 841.

37. Karuizawa Chōshi Kankō Iinkai, *Karuizawa chōshi*, 309, 335.

38. Komatsu, *Karuizawa to hisho*, 841–43.

39. Guillain, *I Saw Tokyo Burning*, 201.

40. Puff, "The Amazing Story," 18.

41. Guillain, *I Saw Tokyo Burning*, 201.

42. Hatoyama served as prime minister from 1954 to 1956 and helped form the Liberal Democratic Party in 1955.

43. Lucille Apcar, *Shibaraku*, 114.

44. Honobe, *Ruisu Fuugo Furanku Sensei*, 81.

45. Karuizawa Chōshi Kankō Iinkai, *Karuizawa chōshi*, 307, 310, 345–47, 354.

46. Ueda and Arai, *Senjika Nihon no Doitsujintachi*, 94–98.

47. Haar and Haar, "A Lifetime of Images," 105.

48. Sidline, *Somehow, We'll Survive*, 161–62.

49. Lang, "A Child in Japan," 50; Fleisher, *Volcanic Isle*, 305.

50. Lang, "A Child in Japan," 41.

51. Buss and Buss, *Trusting God*, 99.

52. Ibid., 94.

53. Lang, "A Child in Japan," 50.

54. Lou Frank, "Interview," 4–5, 7.

55. Balk, "An Outsider," 222.

56. Ibid., 222–25.

57. Irene Frank, unpublished memoir, 3.

58. Ibid., 5–6.

59. Ibid., 8.

60. Ludwig Frank, "Living Conditions in Wartime Japan," 4.

61. Irene Frank, unpublished memoir, 11.

62. "Doitsujin gakuen yaku: Nagano Karuizawa," 2.

63. Irene Frank, "Interview"; Patrick Frank and Irene Frank, "Interview," 9.

64. Irene Frank, unpublished memoir, 14–16.

65. Ibid., 14.

66. Ibid., 17–18.

67. Ludwig Frank and Irene Frank, oral interview.

68. Ludwig Frank, "Living Conditions in Wartime," 6.

69. Balk, "An Outsider," 265.

70. Ludwig Frank, "Living Conditions in Wartime," 8.

71. "Liebeskind; Meuller-Doedner; Frank," 185.

72. Ludwig Frank, "Living Conditions in Wartime," 8.

73. Lou Frank, "Interview," 50.

74. Ludwig Frank, "Living Conditions in Wartime," 13.

75. Ludwig Frank and Irene Frank, oral interview.

76. Lou Frank, "Interview," 49.

77. Ibid., 44–46.

78. Irene Frank, unpublished memoir, 28.

79. Families whose assets were not frozen or who did not otherwise qualify were not provided a housing allowance. Ludy and Irene indicate that they were paying rent at the house that was destroyed by fire in November 1944.

80. Araxe Apcar, *Six Survived*, 181.

81. Ibid., 121.

82. Ibid., 118.

83. Lucille Apcar, *Shibaraku*, 102.

84. Araxe Apcar, *Six Survived*, 199.

85. Lucille Apcar, *Shibaraku*, 123.

86. Guillain, *I Saw Tokyo Burning*, 267–68.

87. Notehelfer and Notehelfer, *A Remarkable Journey*, 81.

88. Irene Frank, "Interview."

89. Buss and Buss, *Trusting God*, 103.

90. Ueda and Arai, *Senjika Nihon no Doitsujintachi*, 192.

91. Ibid., 192.

92. Ibid., 193.

93. Ibid., 87–89.

94. Ibid., 194.

95. Wickert, *Senjika no Doitsu taishikan*, 162.

96. Ueda and Arai, *Senjika Nihon no Doitsujintachi*, 52–58.

97. Wickert, *Senjika no Doitsu taishikan*, 193.

98. Ibid., 188–90.

99. Karuizawa Chōshi Kankō Iinkai, *Karuizawa chōshi*, 325–26.

100. Shapiro, *Edokko*, 143.

101. Haar and Haar, "A Lifetime of Images," 106.

102. Balk, "An Outsider," 267.

103. Patrick Frank relates that Marie-Elise's hostility toward her family originated in Germany years earlier and stemmed from her resentment at being half-Jewish.

Part III Introduction

1. Masahiro Yamamoto, *Nanking*, 165.

2. For our purposes, "POW" will refer to military prisoners only.

3. Lamont-Brown, *Kempeitai*, 118–33.

Chapter 7. From Humiliation to Hunger

1. Kurosawa, "Nihon-gun ni yoru Ōbeijin," 59.

2. Gruhl, *Imperial Japan's World War*, 188.

3. Fukubayashi, "Nihon kokunai no horyoshūyōjo."

4. Utsumi, *Nihongun no horyo seisaku*, 204–5.

5. For the Japanese military's attitudes toward POWs, its poor treatment of Allied POWs, and its racially differentiated POW treatments, see Kowner, "Imperial Japan and Its POWs," 80–110.

6. Utsumi, "Japanese Racism," 134. Chinese prisoners were not considered POWs, as Japan had not declared war on China.

7. Utsumi, *Nihongun no horyo seisaku*, 204–6.

8. Miller, "Lost Women of Rabaul," 16.

9. Golodoff, *Attu Boy*.

10. Despite the historical independence of military and governmental jurisdictions, during the war the Japanese government did share responsibility for supplying

POW camps with food and other resources, a responsibility that it was often unable to fulfill.

11. Waterford, *Prisoners of the Japanese*, 353–54.

12. U.S. War Department, *Rules of Land Warfare*, 17.

13. Utsumi, *Nihongun no horyo seisaku*, 169.

14. Utsumi, "Japanese Army Internment Policies," 180.

15. Hata, "From Consideration to Contempt," 264. The POW Information Bureau was created to function as a liaison office with the Swiss and the ICRC and to oversee the dissemination of information about Japan's military and civilian prisoners.

16. Levie, *Documents on Prisoners*, 236, 239.

17. Komiya, "Taiheiyō sensō shita," 14–15.

18. Ibid., 14.

19. Maruyama Keiko, "Ajia taiheiyō sensō," 38; Komiya, *Tekikokujin yokuryū*, 102.

20. Balk, "An Outsider," 206.

21. The yen was valued at about twenty-three U.S. cents after the Pearl Harbor attack. At that rate, the average disbursement for the forty-nine individuals was about thirty-three dollars each ("Exchange and Interest Rates," 333).

22. Komiya, "Taiheiyō sensō to Yokohama," 347; Maruyama Keiko, "Ajia taiheiyō sensō," 42–44. The term "enemy assets" (*tekisan*) was coined prior to the war and alerted foreigners that their possessions were in danger of seizure. Some, expecting a speedy resolution to the conflict, entrusted their valuables to Japanese friends with the intention of reclaiming them afterward.

23. Tachikawa and Yadohisa, "Seifu oyobi gun," 116.

24. Baenninger and Baenninger, *Eye of the Wind*, 125.

25. Tamura, "Being an Enemy Alien," 51. Roger Mansell claims that Pestalozzi hoarded Red Cross relief boxes in his Osaka residence for personal use and for distribution to "numerous friends in the Japanese military" (Mansell, *Captured*, 124, 167, 236). The claims are unannotated and cannot be verified.

26. Holmes, *Guests of the Emperor*, 68.

27. McLaughlin, *Sparrow*, 372.

28. Tamura, "Being an Enemy Alien," 51.

29. Tachikawa and Yadohisa, "Seifu oyobi gun," 117; Crossland, *Britain*, 93–94. ICRC inspectors endeavored to draft reports that were both accurate and acceptable to Japanese censors (Tamura, "Being an Enemy Alien," 52).

30. Crossland, *Britain*, 88, 90.

31. Grew, *Ten Years in Japan*, 518.

32. Waterford, *Prisoners of the Japanese*, 205–6.

33. Komiya, *Tekikokujin yokuryū*, 9.

34. Altschul, *As I Record*, 80.

35. U.S. War Department, War Crimes Office, "Testimony of Jennifer Mayers Rainsford." I am indebted to Rod Miller for sharing this file.

36. U.S. War Department, War Crimes Office, "Testimony of Miss Alice Kildoyle." I am indebted to Rod Miller for sharing this file.

37. There were four civilian camps in Kobe, the other two containing prisoners captured and transferred from Guam.

38. Komiya, "Taiheiyō sensō shita," 3, 5, 13.

39. Ibid., 4.

40. Duer, "Diary of Sydengham Duer," 5, 23.

41. Komiya, "Taiheiyō sensō to Yokohama," 342–44. Sources offer conflicting data for numbers of internees.

42. "Kanagawa Civilian Internment Camps."

43. Ibid.

44. Morris, *Traveller from Tokyo*, 131.

45. Tamura, "Being an Enemy Alien," 43.

46. Harris, *Boku wa Nihonhei datta*, 20.

47. Ibid., 75.

48. Komiya, "Taiheiyō sensō shita," 15.

49. Harris, *Boku wa Nihonhei datta*, 70.

50. Palmer, "Experiences."

51. Harris, *Boku wa Nihonhei datta*, 83.

52. Ibid., 70–71.

53. Palmer, "Experiences."

54. Utsumi, "Japanese Army Internment Policies," 202.

55. Tamura, "Being an Enemy Alien," 53.

56. Kurosawa, "Nihon-gun ni yoru Ōbeijin," 61.

57. Utsumi, "Japanese Army Internment Policies," 175.

58. Elleman, *Japanese-American Civilian Prisoner*, 79.

59. Miller, "Lost Women of Rabaul," 75.

60. Palmer, "Experiences."

61. One-fourth of the men interned at the Sumire camp were over the age of forty-five, indicating that officials were not following the criteria issued by the Interior Ministry.

62. Quoted in Maruyama Keiko, "Ajia taiheiyō sensō," 30.

63. Komiya, "Taiheiyō sensō shita," 15.

64. Bellaire, "Tokyo Nightmare," 37.

65. Ibid., 49–50.

66. Ibid., 50.

67. Sidline, *Somehow, We'll Survive*, 66.

68. U.S. War Department, cables to Washington, DC.

69. Though technically British citizens, Indians were not interned. Japan and Nazi Germany jointly supported the overthrow of British rule in India, an independent movement led by Subhas Chandra Bose.

70. U.S. War Department, cables to Washington, DC.

71. As will be discussed, the most charitable sources of information on camp conditions are inspection reports from the ICRC, which was hobbled by regulations and struggled to sustain a working relationship with Japanese authorities.

72. Maruyama Keiko, "Ajia taiheiyō sensō," 32; Komiya, "Taiheiyō sensō shita," 17.

73. Maruyama Keiko, "Ajia taiheiyō sensō," 35.

74. Komiya, *Tekikokujin yokuryū*, 86–90. Many of these internees were approved for repatriation on an exchange ship to depart in the fall of 1942. The exchange was

canceled, however, when the U.S. Navy objected that the planned exchange included individuals of Japanese ancestry living in Hawaii. Returning them to Japan, it felt, risked leakage of information crucial to its defense of Hawaii.

75. Author's translation of a quote in Japanese from Maruyama Keiko, "Ajia taiheiyō sensō," 36. Hodges's original memoir is not readily available.

76. "Saitama Civilian Internment Camps."

77. Maruyama Keiko, "Ajia taiheiyō sensō," 38.

78. Komiya, "Taiheiyō sensō shita," 20, 24–25.

79. Maruyama Keiko, "Ajia taiheiyō sensō," 41.

80. Komiya, "Taiheiyō sensō shita," 22.

81. Utsumi, *Nihongun no horyo seisaku*, 265.

82. Ibid., 270–71.

83. This testimony aligns with my finding that rations for foreigners in Karuizawa were initially set at six hundred grams.

84. Komiya, *Tekikokujin yokuryū*, 103–4.

85. Waterford, *Prisoners of the Japanese*, 196.

86. Kita, "Nihongun no kokusaihō ninshiki," 285.

87. Documents Relating to Greater East Asia War, 44.

88. Komiya, "Taiheiyō sensō shita," 28–30.

89. See, for example, Baenninger and Baenninger, *Eye of the Wind*, 125; and Mansell, *Captured*, 82.

90. Komiya, *Tekikokujin yokuryū*, 111.

91. Duer, "Diary of Sydengham Duer," 25.

92. Ibid., 57.

93. Angst, "Kanagawa Prefectural Civil Internment."

94. Pestalozzi, "Kanagawa Prefectural Civil Internment."

95. Duer, "Diary of Sydengham Duer," 136.

96. Komiya, "Taiheiyō sensō shita," 36.

97. Unless otherwise noted, information on the Nanasawa and Tateai camps is from Komiya, "Taiheiyō sensō to Yokohama," 350–61.

98. U.S. War Department, War Crimes Office, "Testimony of Jennifer Mayers Rainsford."

99. Yokohama gaikokujin shakai kenkyūkai and Yokohama kaikō shiryōkan, *Yokohama to gaikokujin shakai*, 173.

100. Find a Grave, "Eleanor Laffin."

101. U.S. War Department, War Crimes Office, "Testimony of Jennifer Mayers Rainsford."

102. U.S. War Department, War Crimes Office, "Testimony of Anna Mayers."

103. U.S. War Department, War Crimes Office, "Testimony of Miss Alice Kildoyle."

104. U.S. War Department, cables to Washington, DC.

105. Ibid.

106. Komiya, "Taiheiyō sensō shita," 27–28. Authorities at the Nagoya camp used loyalty oaths to determine the allegiance of the sixty-six Italian diplomatic staff and 190 resident civilians. Those who were apolitical or pro-Japanese or who pledged loyalty to Mussolini's new government were discharged along with the infirm, elderly, women,

and children. As a result of this inquest, forty-three diplomatic staff and family members were interned at the Saint Francis monastery in Den'enchōfu (Tokyo), and nineteen civilian residents were interned at the new facility in Nagoya (Komiya, *Tekikokujin yokuryū*, 165–67).

107. Waterford, *Prisoners of the Japanese*, 209.

108. Ibid., 46.

109. Komiya, "Taiheiyō sensō shita," 33.

110. The arrest of Jewcom vice president Moise Moiseff may be considered a case of police error. Moiseff and his family had fled their native Belgium for Japan during the Nazi invasion in May 1940. Though Belgium had never joined the Allied coalition (it had announced its neutrality in 1939), Moiseff was imprisoned as an enemy alien, held until April 1942, and then relocated to Karuizawa. As Belgium itself was holding no Japanese prisoners, Sidline calls Moiseff's release "a face-saving move" given that Belgium had been occupied by Germany since 1940 and was no longer a combatant in the war (Sidline, *Somehow, We'll Survive*, 58).

111. U.S. War Department, War Crimes Office, "Testimony of Jennifer Mayers Rainsford."

112. For more on the Otaru camp, see Golodoff, *Attu Boy*; and Stewart, "Aleuts in Japan." For the Australian nurses, see Twomey, "Australian Nurse POWs"; and Miller, "Lost Women of Rabaul."

113. Shillony, *Politics and Culture*, 165.

114. Komiya, "Taiheiyō sensō shita," 32.

115. Yamamoto Takashi, *Nihon wo aishita Yudayajin*, 218.

Chapter 8. Torture and Testimony

1. Suspects themselves were occasionally uncertain about the identity of their captors. Not only were the two police forces difficult to distinguish from one another, their names—Kenpeitai and Kenkei (Kanagawa-ken Keisatsu)—sounded similar. Ries thought that Hugo was arrested by prefectural police, like himself, not by the Kenpeitai (Honobe, *Ruisu Fuugo Furanku Sensei*, 176–78).

2. Ibid., 118.

3. Morris, *Traveller from Tokyo*, 156. In Kobe, Heinz Altschul reports being permitted to have a camera and film, though he repeatedly drew police suspicion when he carried it (Altschul, *As I Record these Memories*, 46).

4. Kojima, *Hakone to gaikokujin*, 184; Komiya, "Taiheiyō sensō to Yokohama," 344.

5. Honobe, *Ruisu Fuugo Furanku Sensei*, 109–10, 200.

6. Balk, "An Outsider," 231–33.

7. Tomkinson was tried and incarcerated by Occupation forces after the war.

8. Ibid., 245.

9. Ibid., 230.

10. Honobe, *Ruisu Fuugo Furanku Sensei*, 785; "Liebeskind; Mueller-Doedner; Frank."

11. Balk, "An Outsider," 250.

12. Heaslett, *From a Japanese Prison*, 45; Tolischus, *Tokyo Record*, 360.

13. Honobe, *Ruisu Fuugo Furanku Sensei*, 125.

14. Balk, "An Outsider," 289–90.

15. "Testimony of Arvid Balk."

16. Honobe, *Ruisu Fuugo Furanku Sensei*, 147.

17. Arvid may have entertained some ambivalent feelings about Nazism, particularly its potential for helping Germany recover from World War I. I am indebted to Patrick Frank for this insight.

18. Honobe, *Ruisu Fuugo Furanku Sensei*, 93.

19. Ibid., 88–93.

20. Lou Frank, "Interview," 9.

21. Schweizer, "Account of Mr. Hugo Frank."

22. "Liebeskind; Mueller-Doedner; Frank."

23. Honobe, *Ruisu Fuugo Furanku Sensei*, 128–29. During air raids guards opened the cell doors and had prisoners stand in the hallway, and it was on one such occasion that Liebeskind saw Hugo (Bendahan, "Interview," 48).

24. Honobe, *Ruisu Fuugo Furanku Sensei*, 152–55.

25. Ibid., 124.

26. "Testimony of Anna Bertha Margaret Liebeskind."

27. Ibid.

28. Bendahan, "Interview," 31–36.

29. Honobe, *Ruisu Fuugo Furanku Sensei*, 162.

30. "Bossée, Andre and Murase, Shinji."

31. Ibid.

32. Honobe, *Ruisu Fuugo Furanku Sensei*, 132, 161.

33. Ibid., 183.

34. Ibid., 137, 140, 164.

35. Honobe, personal letter, December 9, 1986, 8.

36. Honobe, *Ruisu Fuugo Furanku Sensei*, 168–69.

37. Honobe, personal letter, September 16, 1987, 2. Honobe found a photocopy of a note requesting seeds, but the author and intended recipient of the note cannot be verified. The document is included in the Ludwig E. Frank Papers at Stanford University's Hoover Institution Archives.

38. "Liebeskind; Mueller-Doedner; Frank"; Ludwig Frank, "Living Conditions in Wartime," 11.

39. Honobe, *Ruisu Fuugo Furanku Sensei*, 122.

40. "Liebeskind; Mueller-Doedner; Frank."

41. Honobe, *Ruisu Fuugo Furanku Sensei*, 172.

42. Ludwig Frank, "Living Conditions in Wartime," 12.

43. Honobe, *Ruisu Fuugo Furanku Sensei*, 159–60.

44. "Liebeskind; Mueller-Doedner; Frank."

45. Balk, "An Outsider," 258–60.

46. Honobe, *Ruisu Fuugo Furanku Sensei*, 176.

47. Bendahan, "Interview," 34.

48. Balk, "An Outsider," 293.

49. Ibid., 299–302.

50. Ibid., 211, 221, 256, 262.

51. Schweizer, "Account of Mr. Hugo Frank," 2.

52. Balk, "An Outsider," 211, 221.

53. Honobe, *Ruisu Fuugo Furanku Sensei*, 121, 125, 149–51.

54. Ries, personal letter, July 16, 1987, 1.

55. Bendahan, "Interview," 41, 54.

56. Arai, "Shūsenzen tainichi doitsujin," 156.

57. Schweizer, "Account of Mr. Hugo Frank," 1.

58. Ibid., 3.

59. Ibid., 2.

60. Ludwig Frank, "Living Conditions in Wartime," 15.

61. Weldon, interview by author.

62. Balk, "An Outsider," 303–4.

63. Honobe, *Ruisu Fuugo Furanku Sensei*, 789.

64. Schweizer, "Account of Mr. Hugo Frank," 4.

65. Balk, "An Outsider," 307.

66. Ibid., 311.

67. Bendahan, "Interview," 39.

68. Honobe, *Ruisu Fuugo Furanku Sensei*, 111, 113.

69. Ibid., 111, 245.

70. For some examples, see Gibney, *Sensō*, 169–70, 177–79.

71. Katsube was one of about ninety members of a leftist group arrested in connection with what would later be known as the Yokohama Incident. Many endured torture, from which five died and about thirty were severely injured (Katsube, *Yokohama jiken no saishin*, 63–64).

72. Dōmei Tsūshin-sha, *Wartime Legislation in Japan*, 16–19.

73. Tsukahara Bannosuke and Bandō Masao, two Yokohama Kenpeitai officers who had interrogated Hugo, had both died in 1989. The lawyers, prosecutors, and judges involved in Hugo's trial, mentioned in Alice's postwar testimony, had also died (Honobe, personal letter, October 16, 1989, 3).

74. Honobe, *Ruisu Fuugo Furanku Sensei*, C10–18.

75. Honobe, personal letter, October 20, 1991, 3; Kamakura, "Fuugo Kaaru Furanku," 54–57; "German Jew Who Died," 3.

Chapter 9. Race War?

1. Weldon, interview by author.

2. See Dower, "Sensational Rumors, Seditious Graffiti, and the Nightmares of the Thought Police," in Dower, *Japan in War*, 101–54.

3. Dower, *War without Mercy*, 191. *Manga* was issued by the New Japan Cartoonists Association (Shin-Nihon mangaka kyōkai), a government-organized consolidation of existing independent cartoonist organizations founded in August 1940 for the purpose of unifying and mobilizing cartoonists in support of the Konoe cabinet's New Order Movement (Shintaisei undō).

4. Brcak and Pavia, "Racism in Wartime Propaganda," 671.

5. Partner, "Daily Lives of Civilians," 144.

6. High, *The Imperial Screen*, 422.

7. Dower, *Japan in War*, 39–40, 272.

8. High, *The Imperial Screen*, 424–32.

9. Dower, *War without Mercy*, 209–10.

10. Sato and Kushner, "'Negro Propaganda Operations,'" 17–20.

11. Dower, *War without Mercy*, 258.

12. Ibid.

13. Shapiro, *Edokko*, 44.

14. Dower, *War without Mercy*, 358.

15. Ibid., 236.

16. Cook and Cook, *Japan at War*, 468.

17. Ishigaki-shi shihenshūshitsu, *Shimin no senji*, vol. 1, 134–35.

18. Morris, *Traveller from Tokyo*, 137.

19. Duer, "Diary of Sydengham Duer," 142.

20. Ibid., 143.

21. Earhart, "Kamikazefication and Japan's Wartime," 570.

22. Dower, *Embracing Defeat*, 29.

23. Guillain, *I Saw Tokyo Burning*, 64.

24. Han, *Rise of a Japanese Chinatown*, 137, 148.

25. Ibid., 139.

26. Morris, *Traveller from Tokyo*, 127.

27. Grew, *Ten Years in Japan*, 515.

28. Terasaki, *Bridge to the Sun*, 126, 138.

29. Crowder, "An American's Life," 264; Hale, *Hydrangea Waving*, 24.

30. For a full discussion, see Havens, *Valley of Darkness*, 166–73.

31. Arvidson, "A Diary of Internment," 5.

32. Arai, "Shūsenzen tainichi doitsujin," 156.

33. Kranzler, *Japanese, Nazis, and Jews*, 323–25, 327.

34. Slingerland, "The Situationist Critique," 392.

35. Sakaiya, *What Is Japan?*, 123.

36. We should note that case-by-case policy making was not particular to Japan. Wartime decision making about race in the United States, for example, definitions of "white," was also governed by political or economic necessity. For a discussion, see Takaki, *Double Victory*, 129–34.

37. Fujitani, *Race for Empire*, 47.

38. Dower, *War without Mercy*, 267.

39. Koshiro, "East Asia's 'Melting Pot,'" 489–90.

40. Tolischus, *Tokyo Record*, 363.

41. Ibid., 386.

42. Lucille Apcar, *Shibaraku*, 114.

43. Dower, *Cultures of War*, 26.

44. Takaki, *Double Victory*, 233.

45. Horne, *Race War!*, 279–80.

46. Koshiro, *Trans-Pacific Racisms*, 67.

47. Balk, "An Outsider," 332–33.

48. Ludwig Ernest Frank, "Lou's Life," 29.

49. Patrick Frank and Irene Frank, "Interview," 19.

50. Guillain, *I Saw Tokyo Burning*, 276.

51. Koshiro, *Trans-Pacific Racisms*, 7.

52. Yoshimi, *Grassroots Fascism*, 240–41.

53. Tanaka, *Sengo rokujūnen wo kangaeru*, 154–55; Cook and Cook, *Japan at War*, 391.

54. Tanaka, *Sengo rokujūnen wo kangaeru*, 30, 53–55.

55. Koshiro, *Trans-Pacific Racisms*, 1.

56. Tatum, "Defining Racism," 127.

57. Horne, *Race War!*, 3.

58. Dower, *Japan in War*, 272.

59. Quoted in Gioseffi, *On Prejudice*, 182.

60. Newman, *Goodbye Japan*, 240. Joseph Newman was a journalist with the *Japan Advertiser* and then a correspondent for the *Herald Tribune* until his repatriation in October 1941.

61. Geiger, *Subverting Exclusion*, 8; Koshiro, *Imperial Eclipse*, 1; Cleveland, "Hiding in Plain Sight," 215.

62. Fujitani, *Race for Empire*, 7, 25.

63. Helm, *Yokohama Yankee*, 19.

64. For a discussion of parochialism in contemporary Japan, including its racial dimensions, see Dujarric and Takenaka, "Parochialism," 276–87.

Epilogue

1. Lou Frank, "Interview," 53.

2. Balk, "An Outsider," 349, 404.

3. Bendahan, "Interview," 45–46.

4. Irene Frank, "Interview."

5. World Jewish Congress, "Jews Liberated from Karuizawa."

6. Weldon, interview by author.

7. Honobe, *Ruisu Fuugo Furanku Sensei*, 127, 348–50.

8. Louis Frank's appeal for his pension was approved on July 15, 1947. The amount was 1,540 yen, roughly one-fourth of his annual salary of 5,808 yen (Interior Ministry, "Moto-Yamanashi kōtō kōgyō").

Bibliography

For Japanese sources, place of publication is Tokyo unless otherwise indicated.

Published Primary Sources

Altschul, Heinz. *As I Record These Memories . . . : Erinnerungen eines deutschen Kaufmanns in Kobe, 1926–29, 1934–46.* Edited by Nikola Herweg, Thomas Pekar, and Christian W. Spang. Munich: Iudicium, 2014.

Angst, H. C. "Kanagawa Prefectural Civil Internment Camp No. 1." February 25, 1944. In "Kanagawa Civilian Internment Camps." Allied POWs under the Japanese website. http://mansell.com/pow_resources/camplists/fukuoka/fuk_01_fukuoka/fukuoka _01/CIC/KanagawaCIC.html.

Apcar, Araxe. *Six Survived.* Self-published by Michael Apcar, 1987.

Apcar, Lucille. *Shibaraku: Memories of Japan, 1926–1946.* Parker, CO: Outskirts, 2011.

Argall, Phyllis. *My Life with the Enemy.* New York: Macmillan, 1944.

Bellaire, Robert. "Tokyo Nightmare." *Collier's Weekly,* September 26, 1942, 37–50.

Buss, Priscilla, and Reinhard Buss. *Trusting God in a Changing World.* Chino, CA: Christian Printing Service, 1995.

Craigie, Robert. *Behind the Japanese Mask.* London: Hutchinson, 1945.

Crowder, Robert. "An American's Life in Japan before and after Pearl Harbor." *Journal of American-East Asian Relations* 3, no. 2 (Fall 1994): 258–67.

"Doitsujin gakuen yaku: Nagano Karuizawa" (School for Germans burns in Karuizawa, Nagano). *Yomiuri shinbun,* November 4, 1944, 2.

Dōmei Tsūshin-sha, ed. *Wartime Legislation in Japan: A Selection of Important Laws Enacted or Revised in 1941.* Nippon Shōgyō Tsūshin-sha, 1941.

Flakowski, Friedrich. "Die Ausweisung der Deutschen aus Japan, 1947–1948 und die Marine Jumper Reise 1947." *StuDeO*, September 2007.

Fleisher, Wilfrid. *Volcanic Isle*. Garden City, NY: Doubleday, Doran, 1941.

Frank, Amy. "Sokoku no kōshi denka." *Jiji shinpō*, May 12, 1929, 4.

———. "Warera no kōshi denka wo shūhō no kuni ni mukaeru yorokobi." *Tokyo asahi shinbun*, May 12, 1929, 12.

Frank, Louis. "Tōzen tadasubeki kōjō he no nayami." *Tokyo asahi shinbun*, January 29, 1930, 12.

"Gaijin kyōshi." *Otaru shinbun*, 1913, 5a.

"Gaijin supai issei kenkyo: zenryō na gaijin wa hogo." *Asahi shinbun*, December 9, 1941, 3.

"German Jew Who Died in Jail for Suspicion of Espionage Declared Innocent 49 Years Later, Kempeitai Apologizes to Family." *Asahi Evening News*, December 8, 1993, 3.

Golodoff, Nick. *Attu Boy: Attsushima no shōnen*. Anchorage: National Park Service, 2012.

Grew, Joseph C. *Ten Years in Japan: A Contemporary Record Drawn from the Diaries and Private and Official Papers of Joseph C. Grew, United States Ambassador to Japan 1932–1942*. New York: Simon and Schuster, 1944.

Guillain, Robert. *I Saw Tokyo Burning: An Eyewitness Narrative from Pearl Harbor to Hiroshima*. Garden City, NY: Doubleday, 1981.

Haar, Francis, and Irene Haar. "A Lifetime of Images: The War Years in Japan." *Mānoa* 13, no. 1 (2001): 102–8.

Hale, Joe. *Hydrangea Waving*. West Conshohoken, PA: Infinity, 2012.

Harris, James B. *Boku wa Nihonhei datta*. Ōbunsha, 1986.

Heaslett, Samuel. *From a Japanese Prison*. London: Student Christian Movement Press, 1943.

"Hitotsuki sen'en gendo: Shitei gaikokujin no yokin hikidashi kyoka." *Yomiuri shinbun*, August 23, 1941, 2.

Honobe Makoto. *Tekikokujin yokuryū kankei*. Ref. A05020256400, 82nd Collection of Police Reference Works by Mr. Tanemura, Japan Center for Asian Historical Records, Kokuritsu Kōbunshokan (National Archives of Japan). http://www.jacar.go.jp/DAS/meta/listPhoto?REFCODE=A05020256400&IS_STYLE=eng&image_num =37.

Iwadō, Z. Tamotsu, trans. *Japan's Wartime Legislation, 1939*. Japan Times and Mail, 1939.

Iwry, Samuel. *To Wear the Dust of War: From Bialystok to Shanghai to the Promised Land*. New York: Palgrave Macmillan, 2004.

"Kanagawa Civilian Internment Camps." Allied POWs under the Japanese website. Accessed April 4, 2016. http://mansell.com/pow_resources/camplists/fukuoka/fuk_01 _fukuoka/fukuoka_01/CIC/KanagawaCIC.html.

Kondō Hidezō. "Kami ikari." *Manga* 12, no. 4 (April 1944): 11.

———. "Sei-Jigoku." *Manga* 9, no. 11 (November 1941): 19.

"Kondoruki hirai wo machiwabu Furanku-shi: Ryōkoku shinzen, kangeki no renzoku." *Tokyo asahi shinbun*, November 30, 1938.

Lavrov, George. *Yokohama Gaijin: Memoir of a Foreigner Born in Japan*. Bloomington, IN: Author House, 2011.
Lavrov, Victor S. *Son of the Rising Sun: Memoirs of a Russian Lad Born in Japan*. Mustang, OK: Tate, 2015.

Moiseff, Moise. "The Jewish Transients in Japan." *Canadian Jewish Chronicle*, July 25, 1941, 9.
Morris, John. *Traveller from Tokyo*. London: Cresset, 1943.

Newman, Joseph. *Goodbye Japan*. New York: Fischer, 1942.

Palmer, John Wesley. "Experiences in a Japanese Internment Camp." *Empire Club of Canada Addresses*, February 25, 1943, 367–82. http://speeches.empireclub.org/60979/data?n=1.
Pestalozzi, M. "Kanagawa Prefectural Civil Internment Camp No. 1." August 24, 1944. In "Kanagawa Civilian Internment Camps." Allied POWs under the Japanese website. http://mansell.com/pow_resources/camplists/fukuoka/fuk_01_fukuoka/fukuoka_01/CIC/KanagawaCIC.html.

"Rough Translation of Letter to His Imperial and Royal Highness, the Crown Prince from Arvid Balk." December 25, 1936. Doc. 4040, Item 2, Box 12, Folder IPS Documents 4032–4095, Tavenner Papers and International Military Tribunal for the Far East Official Records, University of Virginia Law Library Special Collections. http://lib.law.virginia.edu/imtfe/content/page-1-3239.

"Saitama Civilian Internment Camps." Allied POWs under the Japanese website. Accessed March 3, 2015. http://www.mansell.com/pow_resources/camplists/fukuoka/fuk_01_fukuoka/fukuoka_01/CIC/SaitamaCIC.html.
Shapiro, Isaac. *Edokko: Growing Up a Foreigner in Wartime Japan*. New York: iUniverse Star, 2009.
Sidline, George. *Somehow, We'll Survive: A Memoir: Life in Japan during World War II through the Eyes of a Young Caucasian Boy*. Portland, OR: Vera Vista, 2007.
Sirota Gordon, Beate. *The Only Woman in the Room: A Memoir of Japan, Human Rights, and the Arts*. Chicago: University of Chicago Press, 1997.
"Soren, gaijin no nyūkoku teishi." *Yomiuri shinbun*, April 26, 1941.
Steiner, Jesse Frederick. *The Japanese Invasion: A Study in the Psychology of Inter-racial Contacts*. Chicago: A. C. McClurg, 1917.

Terasaki, Gwen. *Bridge to the Sun*. Chapel Hill: University of North Carolina Press, 1957.
Thomas, James O. *Trapped with the Enemy: Four Years a Civilian P.O.W. in Japan*. Philadelphia: Xlibris, 2002.
Tolischus, Otto. *Tokyo Record*. New York: Reynal and Hitchcock, 1943.

Tomita, Mary Kimoto. *Dear Miye: Letters Home from Japan, 1939–1946*. Stanford, CA: Stanford University Press, 1995.

U.S. Strategic Bombing Survey. *The Effects of Strategic Bombing on Japanese Morale*. Washington, DC: Morale Division, 1947. https://archive.org/stream/effectsofstrate goounit#page/n9/mode/2up.

U.S. War Department. Cables to Washington, DC, July 1942. In "Hyogo Civilian Internment Camps." Allied POWs under the Japanese website. http://mansell.com/pow _resources/camplists/fukuoka/fuk_01_fukuoka/fukuoka_01/CIC/HyogoCIC.html.

———. *Rules of Land Warfare*. Washington, DC: U.S. Government Printing Office, 1940.

Wickert, Erwin. *Senjika no Doitsu taishikan: Aru chūnichi gaikōkan no shōgen*. Translated by Satō Machiko. Chūō kōronsha, 1998.

Yasumoto Ryōichi. "Amerika no baai: Kari dasareru kurowashi." *Manga* 11, no. 11 (November 1943): 13.

———. "Makoto ni kami wo osorezaru mono." *Manga* 11, no. 9 (September 1943): 13.

Young, A. Morgan. *Imperial Japan, 1926–1938*. New York: William Morrow, 1938.

"Zairyū tekikokujin wo shūyō: 271 mei wo sū-kasho ni hogo." *Asahi shinbun*, December 11, 1941, 3.

Unpublished Primary Sources

For the purposes of writing this book, the Frank family entrusted the author with numerous unpublished memoirs, letters, photos, interviews, and other documents pertaining to the Frank and Balk families. This collection of materials will be donated to the Hoover Institution Archives at Stanford University, where it will be added to the existing Ludwig E. Frank Papers.

Arvidson, Richard A. "A Diary of Internment: A History of the Capture on Guam and the Internment in Japan of Richard A. Arvidson during World War II, December 1941–September 1945." Archival material, Hoover Institution Archives, Stanford University.

Balk, Estelle. "An Outsider: The Story of a European Refugee in Japan during World War II." Unpublished manuscript, ca. 1947.

Bendahan, Margaret. "Interview with Margaret Bendahan." Conducted by Emily Silverman, August 28, 1991. Holocaust Oral History Project, Tauber Holocaust Library of the Jewish Family and Children's Services Holocaust Center, San Francisco.

"Bossée, Andre and Murase, Shinji." November 29 and December 1, 1945. Report of Investigation Division, No. 217, Ref. 5.14–1/6–6/6, Legal Section, General Headquarters, Supreme Commander for the Allied Powers.

Documents Relating to Greater East Asia War / Treatment of Nationals of Enemy Countries and Prisoners of War between Belligerent Countries / General and Specific Problems / Report of Inspection Tour of Prisoner Camp in Japanese Empire of Nationals of Enemy Countries, vol. 1 (A-7-0-173). Ref. B02032517400, Diplomatic Record Office of the Ministry of Foreign Affairs, Japan Center for Asian Historical Records.

Duer, Sydengham. "The Diary of Sydengham Yeend Duer: Being a Record of Life in a Japanese Civilian Internment Camp during World War II." Edited by Edward Y. Duer. Unpublished manuscript, 2009.

Frank, Irene. "Interview of Irene Frank." Conducted by Judith Antelman, November 17, 1994. Holocaust Oral History Project, Tauber Holocaust Library of the Jewish Family and Children's Services Holocaust Center, San Francisco. Videotape.

———. Unpublished memoir. Two parts, typed, 29 pp. Postwar but exact year unknown.

Frank, Lou. "Interview of Lou Frank." Conducted by Judith Antelman, November 1, 1994. Holocaust Oral History Project, Tauber Holocaust Library of the Jewish Family and Children's Services Holocaust Center, San Francisco.

Frank, Ludwig. "Living Conditions in Wartime Japan." Unpublished memoir, 1945–46.

Frank, Ludwig Ernest. "Lou's Life." Unpublished memoir, 2006.

Frank, Ludwig, and Irene Frank. Oral interview, June 12, 1995. Videotape.

Frank, Patrick, and Irene Frank. "Interview with Pat Frank, Irene Frank." Conducted by Sam Oliner, February 23, 2006.

Gaikoku shinbun kisha, tsūshin-in kankei zakken / Doitsu kokujin no bu / "Aruvito Baruku" kankei (A-3-5-024) (Gaimushō gaikō shiryōkan). Ref. B02031036900, Japan Center for Asian Historical Records.

Honobe Makoto. Personal letter to Barbara Weldon, September 16, 1987.

———. Personal letter to Barbara Weldon, October 16, 1989.

———. Personal letter to Barbara Weldon, October 20, 1991.

———. Personal letter to Barbara Weldon and Ludy Frank, December 9, 1986.

Interior Ministry. "Gaikokujin kyojū chiiki ni kan suru ken." June 5, 1945. Call no. main building-2A-013-00・類 02923100, microfilm reel no. 071100, start scene 1660, Kokuritsu Komonjokan Dijitaru Aakaibu (National Archives of Japan Digital Library).

——— *I-gō sochi kankei gaikokujin kibō itensaki-hyō.* Ref. A06030109600, Japan Center for Asian Historical Records, Kokuritsu Kōbunshokan (National Archives of Japan).

———. "Moto-Yamanashi kōtō kōgyō gakkō yatoi Doitsu kokujin Ruisu Fūgō Furanku ni shūshin nenkin atae no gi kokkai e teishutsu no kudan." July 15, 1947. Call no. main building-2A-010-01・類 03113100, microfilm reel no. 076200, start scene 0285, Kokuritsu Komonjokan Dijitaru Aakaibu (National Archives of Japan Digital Library).

Lang, Ehrhardt Imanuel. "A Child in Japan during World War II: Memories of a German Missionary's Son." Unpublished manuscript, 2011.

Lenigk, Margot. "My Life: In Germany, Indonesia, Japan and California." 1996. Archival material, Hoover Institution Archives, Stanford University.

"Liebeskind; Mueller-Doedner; Frank: Weingartner; Jonezura; Murase." August 19, 1948. Report of Investigation Division, No. 220, RG-331, Legal Section, General Headquarters, Supreme Commander for the Allied Powers, National Archives and Records Service.

Ries, Hans. Personal letter to Honobe Makoto, July 16, 1987.

Schweizer, Hans Herbert. "Account of Mr. Hugo Frank's Imprisonment at the Yokohama Prison in Kamiōoka." Unpublished statement, 1945.

"Testimony of Anna Bertha Margaret Liebeskind." November 19, 1945. Report of Investigation Division, No. 217, Legal Section, General Headquarters, Supreme Commander for the Allied Powers.

"Testimony of Arvid Balk." November 24, 1945. Report of Investigation Division, Ref. 5.18–2/5–5/5, Legal Section, General Headquarters, Supreme Commander for the Allied Powers.

U.S. War Department, War Crimes Office, Judge Advocate General's Office. "Perpetuation of Testimony of Anna Mayers." June 11, 1946.

———. "Perpetuation of Testimony of Jennifer Mayers Rainsford." June 14, 1946.

———. "Perpetuation of the Testimony of Miss Alice Kildoyle, Civilian." August 16, 1946.

Weldon, Barbara. Interview by author. July 12, 2013.

World Jewish Congress. "Jews Liberated from Karuizawa, Japan as of September 1945." Submitted by the World Jewish Congress, New York. Unpublished document. Courtesy of the U.S. Holocaust Memorial Museum, Washington, DC.

Secondary Sources

Althusser, Louis. "Contradiction and Overdetermination." In *For Marx*, translated by Ben Brewster, 87–128. London: Verso, 1996.

Arai Jun. "Shūsenzen tainichi doitsujin no taiken (2): Shūsenzen tainichi doitsujin memowāru kikitori chōsa." *Bunkaronshū* 16 (March 2000): 137–79.

Archer, Bernice. *The Internment of Western Civilians under the Japanese 1941–1945: A Patchwork of Internment.* London: Routledge Curzon, 2004.

Baenninger, Ronald, and Martin Baenninger. *In the Eye of the Wind: A Travel Memoir of Prewar Japan.* Montreal: McGill-Queen's University Press, 2009.

Bales, Dane G., and Polly Roth Bales. *Kate Hansen: The Grandest Mission on Earth from Kansas to Japan, 1907–1951.* Lawrence: University of Kansas, 2000.

Bandō Hiroshi. *Nihon no Yudayajin seisaku 1931–1945: Gaikōshi shiryōkan bunsho "Yu-daiyajin mondai" kara.* Miraisha, 2002.

Bix, Herbert P. *Hirohito and the Making of Modern Japan.* New York: Perennial, 2000.

Brcak, Nancy, and John R. Pavia. "Racism in Japanese and U.S. Wartime Propaganda." *Historian* 56, no. 4 (June 1994): 671–84.

Burdick, Charles. "The Expulsion of Germans from Japan, 1947–1948." *The Revisionist: Journal for Critical Historical Inquiry* 1, no. 2 (May 2003): 156–65.

Cleveland, Kyle. "Hiding in Plain Sight: Minority Issues in Japan." In *Critical Issues in Contemporary Japan*, edited by Jeff Kingston, 212–22. Oxon, U.K.: Routledge, 2014.

Cook, Haruko Taya, and Theodore F. Cook. *Japan at War: An Oral History.* New York: New Press, 1992.

Cortazzi, Sir Hugh. *Collected Writings of Sir Hugh Cortazzi.* Vol. 2. London: Routledge, 2013.

———. *Victorians in Japan: In and around the Treaty Ports.* London: Athlone, 1987.

Crossland, James. *Britain and the International Committee of the Red Cross, 1939–1945.* Houndsmill, U.K.: Palgrave Macmillan, 2014.

Delgado, Richard, and Jean Stefancic. *Critical Race Theory: An Introduction.* New York: New York University Press, 2012.

Dicker, Herman. *Wanderers and Settlers in the Far East: A Century of Jewish Life in China and Japan.* New York: Twayne, 1962.

Doak, Kevin. "The Concept of Ethnic Nationality and Its Role in Pan-Asianism in Imperial Japan." In *Pan-Asianism in Modern Japanese History: Colonialism, Regionalism and Borders*, edited by Sven Saaler and J. Victor Koschmann, 168–82. London: Routledge, 2007.

Dower, John W. *Cultures of War: Pearl Harbor, Hiroshima, 9–11, Iraq.* New York: W. W. Norton/New Press, 2010.

———. *Embracing Defeat: Japan in the Wake of World War II.* New York: W. W. Norton, 1999.

———. *Japan in War and Peace: Selected Essays.* New York: New Press, 1993.

———. *War without Mercy: Race and Power in the Pacific War.* New York: Pantheon Books, 1986.

———. *Ways of Forgetting, Ways of Remembering: Japan in the Modern World.* New York: New Press, 2012.

Dujarric, Robert, and Ayumi Takenaka. "Parochialism: Japan's Failure to Internationalize." In *Critical Issues in Contemporary Japan*, edited by Jeff Kingston, 276–87. Oxon, U.K.: Routledge, 2014.

Duus, Masayo. *Tokyo Rose, Orphan of the Pacific.* Tokyo: Kodansha International, 1979.

Earhart, David C. *Certain Victory: Images of World War II in the Japanese Media.* Armonk, NY: M. E. Sharpe, 2008.

———. "Kamikazefication and Japan's Wartime Ideology." *Critical Asian Studies* 37, no. 4 (2005): 569–96.

Elleman, Bruce. *Japanese-American Civilian Prisoner Exchanges and Detention Camps, 1941–45.* London: Routledge, 2006.

Fält, Olavi K. *Fascism, Militarism, or Japanism? The Interpretation of the Crisis Years 1930–1941 in the Japanese English-Language Press.* Translated by Malcolm Hicks. Rovaniemi, Finland: Pohjois-Suomen Historiallinen Yhdistys Societas Historica Finlandiae Septentrionalis, 1985.

Fanon, Frantz. *Black Skin, White Masks.* Translated by Charles Lam Markmann. New York: Grove, 1967.

Felton, Mark. *Japan's Gestapo: Murder, Mayhem and Torture in Wartime Japan.* South Yorkshire, U.K.: Pen and Sword Military, 2009.

Find a Grave. "Eleanor Laffin." December 31, 2012. http://www.findagrave.com/cgi-bin/fg.cgi?page=gr&GRid=102887243.

Ford, Douglas. *The Pacific War: Clash of Empires in World War II.* London: Continuum, 2012.

Foreign Affairs Association of Japan. *Japan Year Book, 1938–1939.* Tokyo: Kenkyusha Press, 1939.

Fujitani, Takashi. *Race for Empire: Koreans as Japanese and Japanese as Americans during World War II.* Berkeley: University of California Press, 2011.

Fukubayashi Tōru. "Nihon kokunai no horyoshūyōjo." POW Kenkyūkai. Accessed November 14, 2014. http://www.powresearch.jp/jp/archive/camplist/index.html.

Gallicchio, Marc. *The African American Encounter with Japan and China: Black Internationalism in Asia, 1895–1945.* Chapel Hill: University of North Carolina Press, 2000.

Gao, Bei. *Shanghai Sanctuary: Chinese and Japanese Policy toward European Jewish Refugees during World War II.* New York: Oxford University Press, 2013.

Geiger, Andrea. *Subverting Exclusion: Transpacific Encounters with Race, Caste, and Borders, 1885–1928.* New Haven, CT: Yale University Press, 2011.

Gibney, Frank, ed. *Sensō: The Japanese Remember the Pacific War.* Armonk, NY: M. E. Sharpe, 1995.

Gioseffi, Daniela, ed. *On Prejudice: A Global Perspective.* New York: Doubleday, 1993.

Gluck, Carol. *Japan's Modern Myths: Ideology in the Late Meiji Period.* Princeton, NJ: Princeton University Press, 1985.

Gruhl, Werner. *Imperial Japan's World War Two, 1931–1945.* New Brunswick, NJ: Transaction, 2007.

Han, Eric C. *Rise of a Japanese Chinatown: Yokohama, 1894–1972.* Cambridge, MA: Harvard University Asia Center, 2014.

———. "A True Sino-Japanese Amity? Collaborationism and the Yokohama Chinese (1937–1945)." *Journal of Asian Studies* 72, no. 3 (August 2013): 587–609.

Hanasono, Mark K. "Stranded in Japan and the Civil Liberties Act of 1988: Recognition for an Excluded Group of Japanese Americans." *Asian American Law Journal* 6, no. 151 (1999): 151–86.

Hanazato Toshihiro. "Senzenki no Karuizawa no bessōchi ni okeru gaikokujin no shoyū, taizai to taijinteki kankyō no yōtai." *Nihon kenchiku gakkai keikaku keiron bunshū* 77, no. 672 (February 2012): 247–56.

Hata, Ikuhiko. "From Consideration to Contempt: The Changing Nature of Japanese Military and Popular Perceptions of Prisoner of War through the Ages." In *Prisoners of War and Their Captors in World War II*, edited by Bob Moore and Kent Fedorowich, 253–76. Oxford: Berg, 1996.

Havens, Thomas R. H. *Valley of Darkness: The Japanese People and World War Two*. New York: W. W. Norton, 1978.

Hayashi Eidai. *Senji gaikokujin kyōseirenkō kankei shiryō-shū*. Vol. 3. Akashi shoten, 1991.

Helm, Leslie. *Yokohama Yankee: My Family's Five Generations as Outsiders in Japan*. Seattle: Chin Music, 2013.

High, Peter B. *The Imperial Screen: Japanese Imperial Film Culture in the Fifteen Years' War, 1931–1945*. Madison: University of Wisconsin Press, 2003.

Holmes, Linda Goetz. *Guests of the Emperor: The Secret History of Japan's Mukden POW Camp*. Annapolis, MD: Naval Institute Press, 2010.

Honobe Makoto. *Ruisu Fuugo Furanku Sensei: Seitan hyakunen kinenshi*. Kōfu-shi, Japan: Ruisu Fuugo Furanku sensei tsuitō shaonkai, 1993.

———. "Ruisu Fuugo Furanku-tei to Katō Taiji hakase." *Kaiji* 87 (1997): 15–24.

Horne, Gerald. *Race War! White Supremacy and the Japanese Attack on the British Empire*. New York: New York University Press, 2004.

———. "Tokyo Bound: African Americans and Japan Confront White Supremacy." *Souls* 3, no. 3 (Summer 2001): 16–28.

Howell, David L. "Ethnicity and Culture in Contemporary Japan." *Journal of Contemporary History* 31 (1996): 171–90.

Ienaga, Saburō. *Japan's Last War: World War II and the Japanese, 1931–1945*. Oxford: Basil Blackwell, 1979.

Inuzuka, Kiyoko. *Kaigun Inuzuka kikan no kiroku: Yudaya mondai to Nihon no kōsaku*. Nihon Kōgyō shinbun-sha, 1982.

Ion, A. Hamish. *The Cross and the Rising Sun: The British Protestant Missionary Movement in Japan, Korea, and Taiwan, 1865–1945*. Waterloo, ON: Wilfrid Laurier University Press, 1993.

———. *The Cross in the Dark Valley: The Canadian Protestant Missionary Movement in Japanese Empire, 1931–1945*. Waterloo, ON: Wilfrid Laurier University Press, 1999.

Ishigaki-shi shihenshūshitsu, ed. *Shimin no senji: Sengo taiken kiroku*. Vols. 1–4. Ishigaki, Japan: Ishigaki shiyakusho, 1983–1988.

Jones, H. J. *Live Machines: Hired Foreigners and Meiji Japan*. Vancouver: University of British Columbia Press, 1980.

Kamakura Keizō. "Fuugo Kaaru Furanku no koto." *Midorigaoka* 76 (1993): 54–57.

Kaneko Martin. *Yudayajin nanmin 1940–1941: "Shūsei sareru" senjika Nihon no Yudayajin taisaku*. Kobe: Mizunowa shuppan, 2003.

Karaki Shunzō. *Gaikokujin no mita Nihon: Dai 4*. Chikuma shobō, 1961.

Karuizawa Chōshi Kankō Iinkai. *Karuizawa chōshi: Rekishi-hen (kin, gendai-hen)*. Karuizawa, Japan: Karuizawa Chōshi Kankō Iinkai, 1988.

Katsube Hajime. *Yokohama jiken no saishin kaishi wo: Seiki no jinken saiban*. Kinohanasha, 1999.

Kim, Hoi-eun. *Doctors of Empire: Medical and Cultural Encounters between Imperial Germany and Meiji Japan*. Toronto: University of Toronto Press, 2014.

Kita Yoshito. "Nihongun no kokusaihō ninshiki to horyo no toriatsukai." In *Nichiei kōryūshi*. vol. 3, *Gunji*, edited by Ian Gow, Hirama Yōichi, and Hatano Sumio, 276–301. University of Tokyo Press, 2001.

Kiyota, Minoru. *Beyond Loyalty: The Story of a Kibei*. Translated by Linda Klepinger Keenan. Honolulu: University of Hawaii Press, 1997.

Kojima Yutaka. *Hakone to gaikokujin*. Hakone sōsho 18. Yokohama, Japan: Kanagawa shinbunsha, 1991.

Komatsu Shōko. *Karuizawa to hisho*. Yumani shobō, 2009.

Komiya Mayumi. "Taiheiyō sensō shita no 'tekikokujin' yokuryū: Nihon kokunai ni sonzai shita eibeikei gaikokujin no yokuryū ni tsuite." *Ochanomizu shigaku*, September 1999, 1–48.

———. "Taiheiyō sensō to Yokohama no gaikokujin: Tekisan kanri to tekikokujin yokuryū." In *Kanagawa no rekishi wo yomu*, edited by Kanagawa-ken kōtō gakkō kyōka kenkyūkai, 341–69. Yamakawa shuppansha, 2007.

———. *Tekikokujin yokuryū: Senjika no gaikoku minkanjin*. Yoshikawa kōbunkan, 2009.

Koshiro, Yukiko. "East Asia's 'Melting Pot': Reevaluating Race Relations in Japan's Colonial Empire." In *Race and Racism in Modern East Asia Western and Eastern Constructions*, edited by Rotem Kowner and Walter Demel, 475–98. Leiden, Netherlands: Brill, 2013.

———. *Imperial Eclipse: Japan's Strategic Thinking about Continental Asia before August 1945*. Ithaca, NY: Cornell University Press, 2013.

———. *Trans-Pacific Racisms and the U.S. Occupation of Japan*. New York: Columbia University Press, 1999.

Kowner, Rotem. "Imperial Japan and Its POWs: The Dilemma of Humaneness and National Identity." In *War and Militarism in Modern Japan: Issues of History and Identity*, edited by Guy Podoler, 80–110. Kent, U.K.: Global Oriental, 2009.

———. "'Lighter than Yellow, but Not Enough': Western Discourse on the Japanese 'Race,' 1854–1904." *The Historical Journal* 43, no. 1 (2000): 103–31.

Kozak, Warren. *The Rabbi of 84th Street: The Extraordinary Life of Haskel Besser*. New York: Harper Perennial, 2005.

Krämer, Hans Martin. "Beyond the Dark Valley: Reinterpreting Christian Reactions to the 1939 Religious Organizations Law." *Japanese Journal of Religious Studies* 38, no. 1 (2011): 181–211.

Kranzler, David. *Japanese, Nazis, and Jews: The Jewish Refugee Community of Shanghai*. New York: Yeshiva University Press, 1976.

Kurata Minoru. "Otaru kōshō no senseitachi." *Shōgaku tōkyū* 45, no. 1 (1994): 53–79.

Kurosawa Fumitaka. "Nihon-gun ni yoru Ōbeijin beijin horyo gyakutai no kōzu." In *Sensō to wakai no Nichiei kankeishi*, edited by Kosuge Nobuko and Hugo Dobson, 59–80. Hōsei daigaku shuppan-kyoku, 2011.

Kushner, Barak. *The Thought War: Japanese Imperial Propaganda*. Honolulu: University of Hawaii Press, 2006.

Lamont-Brown, Raymond. *Kempeitai: Japan's Dreaded Military Police*. Stroud, U.K.: Sutton, 1998.

Lensen, George Alexander, ed. "White Russians in Wartime Japan: Leaves from the Diary of Dmitri Abrikossow." *Russian Review* 25 (July 3, 1966): 268–84.

Leupp, Gary P. *Interracial Intimacy in Japan: Western Men and Japanese Women, 1543–1900*. London: Continuum, 2003.

Levie, Howard S., ed. *Documents on Prisoners of War*. Newport, RI: Naval War College Press, 1979.

Lotchin, Roger W. "Japanese Relocation in World War II and the Illusion of Universal Racism." *Journal of the Historical Society* 11, no. 2 (June 2011): 155–81.

Majima, Ayu. "Skin Color Melancholy in Modern Japan: Male Elites' Racial Experiences Abroad, 1880s–1950s." In *Race and Racism in Modern East Asia Western and Eastern Constructions*, edited by Rotem Kowner and Walter Demel, 391–410. Leiden, Netherlands: Brill, 2013.

Mansell, Roger. *Captured: The Forgotten Men of Guam*. Annapolis, MD: Naval Institute Press, 2012.

Maruyama Keiko. "Ajia taiheiyō sensō ni okeru tekikokujin no shogū." *Keisen Akademia* 11 (December 2006): 24–49.

Maruyama, Naoki. "Facing a Dilemma: Japan's Jewish Policy in the Late 1930s." In *War and Militarism in Modern Japan: Issues of History and Identity*, edited by Guy Podoler, 22–38. Kent, U.K.: Global Oriental, 2009.

Matsuura Tsutomu. "Ajia taiheiyō sensō to hisabetsu buraku: Zenkoku suiheisha, Matsumoto Jiichirō no sensō kyōryoku to sono ronri." In *Sabetsu to sensō: Ningen keiseishi no kansei*, 77–114. Akashi shoten, 1999.

McLaughlin, Grant. *Sparrow: A Chronicle of Defiance*. Havelock North, New Zealand: Klaut, 2012.

McWilliams, Carey. *Prejudice: Japanese-Americans: Symbol of Racial Intolerance*. Boston: Little, Brown, 1944.

Medzini, Meron. *Under the Shadow of the Rising Sun: Japan and the Jews during the Holocaust Era*. Brighton, MA: Academic Studies Press, 2016 (forthcoming).

Miller, Rod. "Lost Women of Rabaul." Unpublished manuscript, 2011.

Miyabara Yasuharu. *Rizōto Karuizawa no hinkaku: Karuizawa wa naze kōkyū bessōchi ni natta ka*. Karuizawa shinbun-sha, 2009.

Morris-Suzuki, Tessa. "Debating Racial Science in Wartime Japan." *Osiris* 13 (1998): 354–75.

———. "Ethnic Engineering: Scientific Racism and Public Opinion Surveys in Midcentury Japan." *Positions: East Asia Cultures Critique* 8, no. 2 (Fall 2000): 499–529.

Narusawa Muneo and Brian Daizen Victoria. " 'War Is a Crime': Takenaka Shōgen and Buddhist Resistance in the Asia-Pacific War and Today." *Asia-Pacific Journal* 12, no. 37:4 (September 15, 2014): 1–6.

Nish, Ian. *The Japanese in War and Peace, 1942–48: Selected Documents from a Translator's In-Tray*. Folkestone, U.K.: Global Oriental, 2011.

Notehelfer, F. G., and Rose Notehelfer. *A Remarkable Journey: Rose Notehelfer and the Missionary Experience in Japan*. Norwalk, CT: East Bridge, 2006.

Ogawa, Manako. "'Hull House' in Downtown Tokyo: The Transplantation of a Settlement House from the United States into Japan and the North American Missionary Women, 1919–1945." *Journal of World History* 15, no. 3 (September 2004): 359–87.

Olson, Lynne. *Those Angry Days: Roosevelt, Lindbergh, and America's Fight over World War II, 1939–1941*. New York: Random House, 2013.

Onishi, Yuichiro. *Transpacific Antiracism: Afro-Asian Solidarity in 20th Century Black America, Japan, and Okinawa*. New York: New York University Press, 2013.

Partner, Simon. "Daily Lives of Civilians in Wartime Japan, 1937–1945." In *Daily Lives of Civilians in Wartime Asia: From the Taiping Rebellion to the Vietnam War*, edited by Stewart Lone, 127–58. Westport, CT: Greenwood, 2007.

Passin, Herbert. *Society and Education in Japan*. New York: Teacher's College, Columbia University, 1965.

Puff, Richard. "The Amazing Story of Victor Starffin." *National Pastime* 12 (1992): 17–20.

Sakaiya, Taichi. *What Is Japan? Contradictions and Transformations*. Translated by Steven Karpa. New York: Kodansha International, 1993.

Sakamoto, Pamela. *Japanese Diplomats and Jewish Refugees: A World War II Dilemma*. London: Praeger, 1998.

Sato, Masaharu, and Barak Kushner. "'Negro Propaganda Operations': Japan's Short-Wave Radio Broadcasts for World War II Black Americans." *Historical Journal of Film, Radio and Television* 19, no. 1 (March 1999): 5–26.

Shatzkes, Pamela. "Kobe: A Haven for Jewish Refugees, 1940–1941." *Japan Forum* 3, no. 2 (October 1991): 257–73.

Shillony, Ben-Ami. *The Jews and the Japanese: The Successful Outsiders*. Tokyo: Charles E. Tuttle, 1991.

———. *Politics and Culture in Wartime Japan*. Oxford: Clarendon, 1981.

———. "Wartime Japan: A Military Dictatorship?" In *Showa Japan: Political, Economic and Social History, 1926–1989*, vol. 2, edited by Stephen S. Large, 3–21. London: Routledge, 1998.

Shiratori Toshio. "Make This Mankind's Last War." International Prosecution Section (IPS), SCAP, Number 2427 Issue 3: 0975–0981 (microfilm). July 15, 1946.

Slingerland, Edward. "The Situationist Critique and Early Confucian Virtue Ethics." *Ethics* 121, no. 2 (January 2011): 390–419.

Solt, John. *Shredding the Tapestry of Meaning: The Poetry and Poetics of Kitasono Katue*. Cambridge, MA: Harvard University Asia Center, 1999.

Spang, Christian W. "Recollections of a Jewish-German Businessman in Early Shōwa Japan." *Outside the Box: A Multi-lingual Forum* 7, no. 1 (Spring 2015): 14–30.

Stewart, Henry. "Aleuts in Japan, 1942–1945." In *Alaska at War, 1941–1945: The Forgotten War Remembered*, edited by Fern Chandonnet, 301–4. Fairbanks: University of Alaska Press, 1993.

Tachikawa Kyōichi and Yadohisa Haruhiko. "Seifu oyobi gun to ICRC to no kankei." *Bōei kenkyūjo kiyō* 11, no. 2 (January 2009): 105–50.

Takaki, Ronald. *Double Victory: A Multicultural History of America in World War II*. Boston: Little, Brown, 2000.

Tamura, Keiko. "Being an Enemy Alien in Kobe." *History Australia* 10, no. 2 (2013): 35–55.

Tanaka Hiroshi. *Sengo rokujūnen wo kangaeru: Hoshō saiban, kokuseki sabetsu, rekishi ninshiki*. Sōshi-sha, 2005.

Tatum, Beverly Daniel. "Defining Racism: 'Can We Talk?'" In *Race, Class, and Gender in the United States: An Integrated Study*, edited by Paula S. Rothenberg, 124–31. New York: Worth, 2004.

Thorne, Christopher. "Racial Aspects of the Far Eastern War of 1941–1945." Raleigh Lecture on History. *Proceedings of the British Academy* 66 (1980): 329–77.

Tipton, Elise K. *The Japanese Police State: The Tokkō in Interwar Japan*. Honolulu: University of Hawaii Press, 1990.

Tokayer, Marvin, and Mary Swartz. *The Fugu Plan: The Untold Story of the Japanese and the Jews during World War II*. New York: Paddington, 1979.

Tsurumi Shunsuke. *An Intellectual History of Wartime Japan, 1931–1945*. London: KPI, 1986.

Twomey, Christina. "Australian Nurse POWs: Gender, War, and Captivity." *Australian Historical Studies* 36, no. 124 (October 2004): 255–74.

———. *Australia's Forgotten Prisoners: Civilians Interned by the Japanese in World War Two*. Port Melbourne, Australia: Cambridge University Press, 2007.

Ueda Kōji and Arai Jun. *Senjika Nihon no Doitsujintachi*. Shūeisha shinsho, 2003.

Ueda Takuji. "Dainijisekaitaisen izen no Nihon rizooto (gaijin hishochi) ni tsuite." *Nagoya gaikokugo daigaku, Gendai kokusai gakubu kiyō* 5 (March 2009): 88–127.

Utsumi, Aiko. "Japanese Army Internment Policies for Enemy Civilians during the Asia-Pacific War." In *Multicultural Japan: Paleolithic to Postmodern*, edited by Donald Denoon, Mark Hudson, Gavan McCormack, and Tessa Morris-Suzuki, 174–209. Cambridge: Cambridge University Press, 1996.

———. "Japanese Racism, War, and the POW Experience." In *War and State Terrorism: The United States, Japan, and the Asia-Pacific in the Long Twentieth Century*, edited by Mark Selden and Alvin Y. So, 119–42. Lanham, MD: Rowman and Littlefield, 2004.

———. *Nihongun no horyo seisaku*. Aoki shoten, 2005.

Waterford, Van. *Prisoners of the Japanese in World War II*. Jefferson, NC: McFarland, 1994.

William R. Gorham Memorial Committee. *Biography of William R. Gorham: An American Engineer in Japan*. N.p.: Don Cyril Gorham, 2005.

Williams, Harold S. *Tales of the Foreign Settlements in Japan*. Tokyo: C. E. Tuttle, 1958.

Yamamoto, Masahiro. *Nanking: Anatomy of an Atrocity*. Westport, CT: Praeger, 2000.

Yamamoto Takashi. *Nihon wo aishita Yudayajin pianisuto Reo Shirota*. Mainichi shinbunsha, 2004.

Yamashita, Samuel Hideo. *Leaves from an Autumn of Emergencies: Selections from the Wartime Diaries of Ordinary Japanese*. Honolulu: University of Hawaii Press, 2005.

Yokohama gaikokujin shakai kenkyūkai and Yokohama kaikō shiryōkan, eds. *Yokohama to gaikokujin shakai: Gekidō no nijūseiki wo ikita hitobito*. Nihon keizai hyōronsha, 2015.

Yoshimi, Yoshiaki. *Grassroots Fascism: The War Experience of the Japanese People*. Translated by Ethan Mark. New York: Columbia University Press, 2015.

Zachmann, Urs Mathias. "Race and International Law in Japan's New Order in East Asia, 1938–1945." In *Race and Racism in Modern East Asia Western and Eastern Constructions*, edited by Rotem Kowner and Walter Demel, 453–73. Leiden, Netherlands: Brill, 2013.

Index

Page numbers for figures and tables are in italics

Harvard East Asian Monographs
(most recent titles)

Harvard East Asian Monographs

Harvard East Asian Monographs

Harvard East Asian Monographs

Harvard East Asian Monographs